Keeping Holy Time

Keeping Holy Time

STUDYING THE REVISED COMMON LECTIONARY
Year A

EDITED BY

DOUGLAS E. WINGEIER

ABINGDON PRESS / Nashville

KEEPING HOLY TIME
Studying the Revised Common Lectionary Year A

Copyright © 2001 by Abingdon Press

This book is printed on acid-free paper.

Library of Congress Cataloging-in-Publication Data

Keeping holy time : studying the Revised common lectionary, year A / edited by Douglas E. Wingeier.
    p. cm.
Includes bibliographical references.
ISBN 0-687-09827-0 (alk. paper)
    1. Bible—Study and teaching. 2. Lectionaries. 3. Christian education of adults.
    I. Wingeier, Douglas E.

BV603 .K44 2001
264'.34—dc21

ISBN 978-0-687-09827-9   2001046182

MANUFACTURED IN THE UNITED STATES OF AMERICA.

07 08 09 10—   4 5 6 7 8 9 10

Contents

Introduction

*W*ELCOME to Year A of your Lectionary study books! By opting to follow this study, you are in for a stimulating and growthful experience. You will be studying the Bible—four passages each week—in a way that will require you to dig deep, find correlations, discover relevance, and grow spiritually in ways that you may not have experienced before. And you will be doing this, not alone, but in a group of fellow seekers and disciples with whom you can explore Scripture, exchange ideas, and develop supportive community.

We have all done Bible study. Usually, this takes one of several forms—studying a book of the Bible, exploring the major themes of the Bible in an extensive, disciplined way through a program like DISCIPLE BIBLE STUDY, studying selected passages through use of a quarterly following the international lesson series, or reading and discussing a book about the Bible. Each has its merits and drawbacks. The lectionary approach, which KEEPING HOLY TIME follows, has these advantages:

1. In churches where pastors follow the discipline of preaching from the lectionary, a group studying the same passages each week correlates its work with that of the pastor, thereby gaining valuable background and insight for response and dialogue with the sermons.
2. The Scriptures studied are selected by a responsible group of Bible scholars and theologians who take care to provide broad and balanced coverage of all major biblical writings and themes over the course of the three-year cycle. This guards against bias and blind spots and introduces readers to both beloved and troublesome passages.
3. The four weekly passages from Old and New Testaments are usually correlated around central biblical themes, thereby demonstrating the coherence of the Bible as a whole and providing a check against distorted opinions and interpretations.

4. As the lectionary is organized around the Christian Year, participants gain a sense of the rhythm and flow of the life of faith in the Christian community, both historically and in the present day.

KEEPING HOLY TIME is designed for use in one of several settings: in an adult Sunday school class to correlate serious study with weekly worship themes; in leadership training to deepen Bible understanding among teachers and leaders; in worship planning sessions where laity and clergy explore the Scriptures together in preparation for an informed corporate worship experience; or in midweek Bible study in which pastor and people engage together in group exegesis and cooperative sermon preparation.

This study aims to link the Bible passages with each other and with the life experience of participants. An effort is made in the weekly commentary to raise questions that stimulate thinking about the relevance of Scripture to everyday life and suggest steps participants might take to put Scripture into practice.

Study suggestions for the weekly studies seek to provide teaching-learning experiences for persons with different learning styles. Following the typology developed by Barbara Bruce in *Seven Ways of Teaching the Bible to Adults* (Abingdon Press, 2000), suggestions are made to accommodate the needs of the verbal learner (the person favoring verbal/linguistic intelligence), the logical learner (logical/mathematical intelligence), the visual learner (visual/spatial intelligence), the physical learner (body/kinesthetic intelligence), the musical learner (musical/rhythmic intelligence), the social learner (interpersonal intelligence), and the independent learner (intrapersonal intelligence).

Here are some concrete suggestions for making your study sessions stimulating and effective:

1. As you prepare, pray for God's guidance in meeting the needs of participants.
2. Read through all four lections, the commentary in this volume, and other commentaries and resources (see starter list below), to steep yourself in the meanings of the selected Scriptures.
3. Identify key and common themes in the four passages.
4. Formulate the central message of each lection in one succinct statement.
5. Think of your own experiences related to these themes and ways of sharing these in the course of the session.
6. Consider the needs and experiences of group members to which these themes might speak, and plan ways of letting the Scripture address these.
7. Make your own session plan, drawing on the suggestions here, but tailoring it to the particular needs and learning styles of your group. The study suggestions offer more than can be used within the time limitations of most groups, so adapt them to your setting.

8. Have the group sit in a circle facing one another, to encourage open sharing and dialogue rather than dependence on an authority figure for interpretation of the texts. Think of this as a process of "group exegesis."

9. Have several different translations and versions of the Bible available. Read from as many as possible to gain fresh perspectives on the text from a variety of translations. Have the passages read aloud whenever possible.

10. Create a study climate that encourages open expression of doubt and disagreement, honest searching as well as affirmation of faith. As leader, do not be the "answer person," but rather facilitate questioning and the free exchange of views. Do not be afraid to let a session end with issues still unresolved. This will encourage members to continue pondering throughout the week, and keep them eager to come back for more.

Here are a few resources to supplement the guidance this book provides:

Harper's Bible Commentary. James L. Mays, general editor. Harper and Row, 1988.

Harper's Bible Dictionary. Paul J. Achtemeier, general editor. Harper and Row, 1985.

The Interpreter's Dictionary of the Bible, Volumes I-IV. George A. Buttrick, general editor. Abingdon Press, 1962. Supplementary Volume, edited by Keith Crim. Abingdon Press, 1976.

The Interpreter's One-Volume Commentary on the Bible. Charles M. Laymon, editor. Abingdon Press, 1971.

The New Interpreter's Bible, Volumes I–XII. Leander E. Keck, convener and senior New Testament editor. Abingdon Press, 1994–2002.

Pastors and other theologically trained persons will have additional suggestions.

May God's Spirit guide, enrich, and challenge you, your study group, and your congregation as you together engage in the ongoing process of linking Scripture to life through exploration of the lectionary.

Douglas E. Wingeier, editor

ADVENT

Lections for First Sunday of Advent

Old Testament: Isaiah 2:1-5

*I*SAIAH'S messianic prophecies are central to the Christian's theological understanding of a divine deliverer coming with great power and righteousness to redeem the world. The writings here are excitingly faith-based and visionary. Eighth-century B.C. Jews and twenty-first-century Christians have a common affinity with the hope offered in the new realm of God.

The Messianic Hope

The messianic age is marked by great vitality, diversity, and promise. Spiritual qualities and just relationships are enhanced in this new age. Brothers and sisters of all nations measure their attitudes and behavior closely with God's will and commandments. Peace and justice within family, city, and nation are standard ways of life.

The establishment of God's house is figuratively placed on the highest of mountains. This mountain imagery tapped into the belief among the Canaanite religions whose gods lived and were worshiped in high places. The God of Israel is the supreme God who dwells in the highest of mountains to which *all* persons and nations will be drawn for guidance and judgment. God lifts us to new heights with gifts of mercy and grace. Hope and justice are realized on the mountain of God. The coming savior will reign in righteousness and peace. Through this Messiah, God fulfills the holy purpose for both Judah and all the world.

Living Together in Harmony

The house of the Lord is a place where the divine will is revealed and put into practice. Nationalism cannot corrupt us. Social, political, and cultural conflicts are void of power, unable to restrict our fight against evil and oppression. We are focused on a God who cares for each individual and all creation. Distractions of daily life that obstruct faithful thought and action are no help in overcoming adverse circumstances. The Messiah turns our hearts to peace and justice and to the Source of our life. We are ushered into the new age with compassion, direction, and a revived hope for the world.

Our Steps Are Ordered

Creation *ex nihilo* (out of nothing) progressed from chaos to order as God fashioned the world. In this new day, Isaiah prophesies, God will once again bring order to the New Jerusalem and all creation, to "teach us his ways" so we "may walk in his paths" (2:3). Life is structured and harmonious on the mountain of God. People can live in peace with justice because they know that, by following God's guidance and living according to God's plan, shalom will reign and all will be good.

> ***Think About It:*** In this new era, weapons will be refashioned for use in peaceful ways. What "weapons" do you want God to refashion to bring peace to you and to our world? What will be eliminated and what will be implemented when this vision is realized? What can we do to work with God to help bring this to pass?

The Undisputed Sovereign

The Lord will also resolve disputes between nations. The "Mighty One of Israel" (1:24) is both majestic and compassionate among the people. Isaiah's vision of hope and emphasis on God's holiness offer great promise to a people experiencing severe tribulation and despair. YHWH (the four consonants only are used, rather than "Yahweh," because Jewish people believe God's name should not be pronounced) does not disappoint the faithful. All weapons are laid down at his feet and turned into farming implements; peace is proclaimed: "They shall beat their swords into plowshares, / and their spears into pruning hooks; / nation shall not lift up sword against nation, / neither shall they learn war any more" (2:4). The new age will be one in which all people and nations will have a will to live in justice and harmony with one another.

Psalter: Psalm 122

The annual pilgrimage to Jerusalem was a highlight, a time for remembrance, celebration, and worship. The people of God used this experience to recall the glory days of the past, discuss the current times, and prophesy about the future. Songs of praise rang out in the Temple and in the streets, for a God who never abandoned the people. This hymn was sung as a testimony to the security of God's city, Jerusalem, and to God as their redeemer and the ruler of the universe.

Epistle: Romans 13:11-14

Love is the true expression of faith. What Paul teaches here parallels the consistent urging of Jesus that we love one another. Now is the time for us to wake up and begin to engage in actions of kindness toward our brothers and sisters. The Day of Judgment is approaching, but will come without warning. Therefore, we must fulfill the love commandment through kind thoughts and good deeds.

The New Life in Christ

This passage is part of a longer discourse, beginning in Chapter 12, on the characteristics of the new life in Christ, which centers in radical love for God and neighbor; humility and hospitality within the body of Christ; and compassionate, forgiving treatment, even of enemies.

Paul uses a powerful cluster of images: waking and sleeping, night and day, darkness and light, and "putting on." Each implies radical change from submission to the power of evil to embodiment of the power of good. Waking is a summons to moral action. Night/darkness versus day/light sets up the contrast between evil from which one must awake and depart and good that one must affirm and express. "Putting on the armor of light" and "putting on Jesus Christ" both depict the transformation from sinful to righteous living.

The fulfillment of our salvation happens when we put on Christ; our life becomes dressed in peace, joy, and benevolence. "To put on the Lord Jesus Christ" is total submission and communion with him. All things are possible through Christ who redeems and strengthens us.

The Urgent Appeal

Now Paul shares his sense of urgency for taking on these characteristics, not just as a behavior shift, but as a profound change in personal identity. Roman society had a moral code quite different from the expectations of Christianity; Paul urges his hearers to put off those old ways and become new persons in Christ—now!

The Dawning Day

One of the most spectacular scenes of a day is the radiant emergence of the light of dawn. Love possesses this same radiance, awakening the desire to live in justice and harmony. Jesus spoke of the treasured loves on earth, the love of money, and the danger of selfish behavior. What we love directly affects our physical, social, and spiritual development. The goal of the Christian life is to live according to God's word for the enhancement of the reign of God on earth and as preparation for life eternal.

The Coming Age Is Here

Debate over when Christ will return continues even today. Soothsayers and false prophets claim to be able to name the exact time of his second coming. They seem to know more than Jesus knew. Paul deals with this by using indefinite terms. Final salvation is "nearer to us now than when we became believers." As each day moves us closer to the final consummation, so must our lives become more faithful in living according to God's ways. We continue expectant and hopeful. Christ both supports our efforts at faithful discipleship and reassures us that our waiting is not in vain.

Gospel: Matthew 24:36-44

The unknown is always frightening. We learn we do not have long to live, that downsizing is coming, or that a long-cherished relationship is crumbling. Likewise, Jesus' urging us to be ready for his return without giving the day or the hour is unsettling.

The Days Before the Flood

No one was prepared for the rains except God's faithful servant Noah. The experience of Noah is a paradigm for what the coming of the Son of Man will be like—both calamitous and redemptive. The parallel exists not only in Noah's embrace of God's will, but in the social context as well. In Noah's days, God was angry with a sinful people for violating the moral law. God called Noah and his family, the only righteous folks left, to go against the grain. Though ridiculed by his neighbors, Noah obeyed God and built the ark that would save them from the Flood.

The Time Is Now

Jesus uses Noah's faithfulness as an example of what God expects of us. The covenant between God and Noah is a collaborative effort to bring about a new creation. Our faith in God must be patterned after that of Noah. Otherwise, the same thing will happen to humankind as happened in the Flood. When the rains came, those living without regard to God's desires were "blotted out" (Genesis 6:5-8).

In the coming age, the righteous will be taken up with Jesus, and the faithless will be left behind (Matthew 24:39-41). No one but God knows when this will take place, but we must be watchful and prepared. If we live righteous lives day by day, it will not matter when the end comes, for we will be found faithful.

Are You Sleeping?

Today's parables depict a certainty of judgment. Like Noah, the two workers in the field, the two women at the mill, and the householder, we too must keep an eye on what is going on. The "thief" is a metaphor for the coming of the Son of Man who does not announce his visit. The warning is to stay alert, live justly, and trust God.

> **Think About It:** On this first Sunday in Advent we begin anew to anticipate the coming of Christ. Would he find you sleeping or awake? What do you look forward to this Advent season?

Are we seeking to help people and to transform situations of poverty and injustice? Are we making visible efforts to carry out Christ's mission, and not just attending Sunday worship? Who stands up for the poor, the lost, and the downtrodden? Are we awake or sleeping?

The Day of the Lord

The day of the Lord represents the time when we will stand before the divine judge. Ancient prophets speculated as to a particular time for this expected coming, but the wisest would not venture to guess. The Day of Judgment will come, and we must endure these trying days in anticipation of the redemption of the world. To try to read the signs and wonders is useless. Instead, we must abide in readiness and live in faithfulness. "Therefore you also must be ready" (24:44).

We prepare by keeping God first in our lives. If we lose ourselves for his sake, he will save us for all eternity. What would Jesus like to see us doing upon his return? How would he want our lives, homes, and churches to look? If we devote our time to readying ourselves for him, we can find purpose in the daily routine and enjoy the service of glorifying him. The faithful have no cares about when Christ comes; they simply know he *will* come in saving glory to usher in the new age.

Study Suggestions

A. Rejoice, a Savior Is Coming

Celebrate the beginning of Advent with morning prayers from your book of worship. Sing "Morning Has Broken" or "Come, Thou Long Expected Jesus." Read Psalm 122 responsively. Pray together in gratitude about what the coming Savior does new every morning in your life.

B. Introduce the Messianic Age

Read Isaiah 2:1-5 aloud. The New Jerusalem is a figure for the messianic age. Have two teams review the passage and identify the images of this new era. Compare lists. Then compare this portrait with the signs of our own times. How is our world alike or different from this vision of a New Jerusalem? What would have to change for our world to resemble the coming reign of God?

C. Take Up the Urgent Appeal

Read aloud Romans 13:11-14, and review the commentary on pages 14–15. Have the group paraphrase it; then compare the paraphrase to the biblical text. Ask: What insights from the text and your paraphrase come to you? In what ways is Paul's context like or unlike our social and ethical situation today?

Ever-increasing evils in society keep us polarized, fragmented, and fearful. How would we today describe what Paul called a battle between night and day, darkness and light? Identify the most salvageable areas in our society, the areas that offer some promise, and the areas where you feel there is no hope. Discuss: What would have to change in order to save what can be saved? What makes some situations seem hopeless? Are they really hopeless?

D. Connect Noah and Us

Read Matthew 24:36-44 aloud, and study the background information. Review Genesis 6–7, the Flood story (and the discussion of it in the lessons for the Sunday between May 29 and June 4, pages 214–15). Ask: How does Jesus use the story of Noah to explain the need for preparedness? How does this ancient story speak to us today? What modern imagery might we substitute to make the same point?

E. Stay Awake

Both Matthew and Romans use the image of wakefulness and sleep to talk about being ready for the coming of Christ. Discuss ways that we sleep (are unaware) and ways we remain awake (are alert). Ask: How will Christ find you? your church? What are you doing to be ready?

F. Creating and Recreating

Creation, Resurrection, and the Second Coming of Christ: Look these up in a Bible dictionary. Each theme in its own way demonstrates the considerable power of God to make things new. Discuss: What makes these events important in the Christian life? Do today's readings help you better understand the thread of salvation God weaves into the fabric of daily life?

G. Look Forward

Summarize the important themes for today: Advent as a time of patient, faithful waiting for Christ's coming; God's power to make everything new (including us); the promise of a new era of righteousness; the need to make ourselves ready for God's revelation in Christ. Ask: How do these themes enrich and deepen our faith and commitment to discipleship? What do they call us to do or to be? What challenges do they present to us?

H. Prepare a Reception

On this first Sunday in Advent, prepare a table of reception for the coming Christ. Ask the group what they want on the table. Discuss the purpose for preparing and keeping a table for Christ in our hearts and lives.

Lections for Second Sunday
of Advent

Old Testament: Isaiah 11:1-10

*I*SAIAH, like almost every prophet, had much to say about rulers, or politicians as we would call them. Often the prophets' words were harsh judgments on the failures of these leaders to obey God and to lead the people in God's ways. The prophets realized that the nation needed godly leadership and longed for those rulers who would not let power corrupt them. In this passage, which many scholars believe is a continuation of Isaiah 9:2-7, Isaiah portrays the ideal king. Many see these characteristics as in fact the standard expected (or at least hoped for) in each new ruler. Indeed, these oracles may have been written and used at the coronation of one of the kings (some suggest Hezekiah—715–687 B.C.). Many others interpret these passages as messianic, that is, as describing the perfect king (messiah) who would one day come. Christians see Jesus as the fulfillment of these passages. Thus they are often used in Advent, a season of preparation for the coming of the Jesus, the King of kings.

Here Comes the King

These verses describe the appearance and anointing of the king. Verse 1 speaks of a "shoot" or "branch" of Jesse, father of David, Israel's greatest king. It was expected that the Messiah would be a biological descendant of David who would equal or exceed David's greatness. Twice in the New Testament this verse is taken to refer to Jesus (Romans 15:12; Revelation 5:5). Isaiah 11:2-3a describes the anointing and gifts of this king. He will be filled with the "spirit of the Lord." (Some see a parallel between this and the baptism of Jesus in which the Spirit came upon him.) He will be empowered with six gifts necessary to rule: wisdom (maturity plus insight), understanding (depth plus empathy), counsel (sound advice and decisions), might (power used justly), knowledge (scholarship plus enlightenment), and especially fear (reverence and humility) before God.

What the King Will Do

With such gifts, this ideal leader will not rule based just on what he hears or sees on the surface. He will be able to look into the hearts of persons and judge based on the truth (11:3b). The poor and oppressed will find a champion in him. This ruler will stand for justice (11:4a) and will impose decisive punishment on evildoers (11:4b).

> *Think About It:* The ideal leader possesses six gifts, including reverence for God. How do our church and secular leaders compare? What criteria do we look for in choosing our leaders? Which of these gifts do you possess? What other gifts and graces might be important for leadership? What can we do to develop and exercise these gifts?

He will not be clothed in royal purple or golden belts; his garments will be righteousness and faithfulness (11:5).

State of the World Address

As a result of his reign, this splendid ruler will be able to stand before all the nations and give the greatest state of the world address ever. Peace and harmony will pervade the human kingdom and reign among even the animals (11:6-7). Animals and human beings will be at peace with one another, so that a child can play near a venomous snake with no fear (11:8). What we see here is a restoration of paradise, that is, a return to Eden. The results of the Fall are reversed (11:9). The enmity between the woman and her offspring and the snake, for example, will be overturned. But more important, the separation between God and human beings will be overcome as this ruler fills the nations with the awareness of God, restoring the divine-human relationship.

Psalter: Psalm 72:1-7, 18-19

Psalm 72 is one of the "royal psalms," composed in honor of the king. These were used at coronations and even at the wedding of a king. This particular psalm is a prayer or song asking for God's blessings on the king. John Calvin, the sixteenth-century Protestant reformer, believed it was written for the coronation of Solomon.

This psalm heavily echoes the theme we saw in Isaiah concerning the role of the king in making sure the poor and needy received justice. The poor were often without a voice. They had no one to defend them. The clear record of the Bible shows that God always champions the poor. Likewise, so should the king (and the leader today) who, after all, must be accountable and answer to God and serve God's purposes.

The psalmist prays in essence, "Long live the king!" (72:5-7), and asks that every blessing may come upon him and the people through his leadership. The health and well-being of the nation are tied to the faithfulness and righteousness of their leaders.

The Epistle Lection: Romans 15:4-13

Disunity was a problem in every church to which Paul wrote, including that in Rome. So in Chapters 14 and 15 he takes up this theme. The differences in faith and practice between Jewish and Gentile Christians are causing problems. Paul pleads with them to love one another, to respect one another's scruples, to do nothing to destroy the peace of the community, and to build up one another in love within the community of faith. Much is at stake in maintaining the unity of the church. If the good news of Jesus Christ is not powerful enough to help them overcome their differences and truly affirm and love one another, then what can they, the church, possibly offer this broken and alienated world?

Harmony

Gentile Christians must honor and learn from their religious heritage—which includes the writings of the Hebrew Scriptures. Though Jewish, these were regarded by Paul as instructional for Gentiles as well as Jews. The Scripture teaches that both Jew and Gentile are included in God's saving work. Jesus is the catalyst who brings them together, so they may live in harmony and with "one voice glorify" God. Their mutual experience of Christ makes them one. This relates to the peace and harmony that Isaiah said the coming messiah would bring.

So Welcome One Another

Drawing upon various verses in the Hebrew Scriptures, Paul stresses that all Christians should welcome and accept one another, for this is exactly what Christ has done for them all. True, Christ first came as a Jew to the Jewish people (the circumcised, 15:8), but this was in order to fulfill the promises made to the patriarchs (see Isaiah 11:1-10).

Christ came and died for both Jew and Gentile—and for all people. Together they (we) are one body, one church, one people. This is not just something Paul made up. This was God's plan all along. Paul quotes or paraphrases four verses from the Hebrew Scriptures to show this inclusive love of God: Psalm 18:49; Deuteronomy 32:43;

> **Think About It:** How can they fail to welcome those whom God has already welcomed? Do we do better than these Romans in showing hospitality to all God's people? Whom do we tend to exclude and for what reasons? How can we make them welcome?

Psalm 117:1; and Isaiah 11:10. He encourages the congregation at Rome (and us) to welcome one another genuinely, as Christ had welcomed them. How could they not accept and honor those whom Christ had already redeemed and called to follow him?

Gospel: Matthew 3:1-12

All the Gospel writers connect Jesus with the ministry of John the Baptist. Matthew, Mark, and John connect them as grown men. Luke goes back and lifts up their kinship at birth (see Luke 1). All the Gospels see John, Jesus' kinsman and forerunner, as the one whose preaching and teaching would help the people prepare for the coming of the Messiah.

Road Work

In most households when someone says, "Company's coming!" everyone works. The house is cleaned. The yard is tidied and mowed. In the days of John, when people heard company was coming to their village, they would go out and prepare the road on which this personage would enter. Potholes would be filled; sticks and stones would be removed. Nothing should hinder the coming of that special visitor. Quoting Isaiah 40:3, Matthew has John proclaim, "Messiah is coming! But do not go out and clean up your roads. Instead, mend your hearts! Clear your lives of any obstacle that would hinder his coming."

Road work requires tools. The tools John has in mind are repentance and baptism. Repentance comes from the Greek word *metanoia* (decisive turning, change of mind, to change one's life completely). Repentance is like driving down the wrong road, then turning around and going in the opposite direction. Baptism is the symbol that one has repented and been cleansed of sin. This was so central to John's ministry that he became known as John the Baptizer.

The Eccentric Baptizer

Many listened to John and were baptized (Matthew 3:5-6). The description of John ties him to the Old Testament prophet Elijah (see 2 Kings 1:8). This was important because it was believed that Elijah himself would return as forerunner of the Messiah (see Malachi 4:5-6). John is a pivotal character in Matthew, the first prophet Israel had seen in four hundred years; and he brings a powerful message. John ate wild honey and locusts, which Leviticus 11:22 identifies as clean food, part of the diet of the desert poor even today. Everything about John—his dress, diet, and presence in the wilderness—tells the reader that Elijah has come; the Messiah cannot be far behind.

21

Flames, Snakes, Roots, Fruits

John, having lived in the wilderness, had no doubt seen many brush fires, causing the snakes to scatter for safety, some unsuccessfully. John, like a prophet of old, saw the religious leaders arriving and compared them to snakes who would not be able to avoid the Messiah's judgment. Then the image changes from vipers to that of a vinedresser who prunes and burns the vines that do not produce fruit.

What the Messiah would look for is not who their ancestor was (Abraham), but who they are. What would matter is not their roots but their fruits. The next image is that of a farmer who threshes out the heads of grain, casts away the chaff and burns it. John's bold criticism of those in power would later be his undoing. His prophecy was understood as both immediate and eschatological (future-looking). He was calling his present hearers to repentance but at the same time pointing to God's ultimate judgment.

> **Think About It:** John called for *metanoia*, decisive change. Most of us resist change. What would John push you to change? Why? Do you think you could change? What factors in your life resist change? What would make you more open to the changes God is calling you to make?

To make clear that he himself was not the Messiah, John stated that he was not even worthy to take off the shoes of the Messiah. Indeed, he only baptized with water. The Messiah would immerse them in the very Spirit of God. This recalls the promise in Isaiah 11:9 that the land will be filled with the knowledge of God.

Study Suggestions

A. Opening

Sing or read a hymn such as "Lead On, O King Eternal" or "Rejoice, the Lord Is King." Read aloud Psalm 72:1-7, 18-19. Pray for acceptance of God's rule in our lives, a welcoming attitude toward others, and openness to repentance and change.

B. Defining an Ideal Leader

On a chalkboard or sheet of paper write: "Characteristics of an Ideal Leader." Ask group members to name such traits. List their responses. Then ask them to name leaders of the past and present who they would say come close to this ideal. Next read in unison Isaiah 11:1-10, which describes the ideal king. Review the commentary on pages 18–19, and define each of the six qualities of a leader. Ask: What made the Israelites yearn for such a king? Do we have the same yearning? Why do many leaders disappoint us by failing to live up to this hope? How can we cultivate these qualities in ourselves and our leaders?

C. Questions

Isaiah links the ideal king with Eden, the primal paradise. Paul sees Christ uniting even Jew and Gentile. Have someone read Romans 15:4-13. Review the commentary about it. Discuss: Is a "return to Eden" a realistic hope? Can there ever be such peace and harmony throughout the world? in the church? Why or why not? What role can leaders play in this? How could and does Christ help bring such harmony? What is our role in working toward this ideal?

Imagine that Jesus is a candidate for the US presidency. Discuss how Jesus meets with participants' ideas of an ideal leader. Describe the characteristics of his campaign: slogans, issues, ads, and how the campaign might differ from the usual ones. Would America really want him as a leader? What are the reasons why people would or would not vote for him? If we really followed his leadership, what changes might we begin to see in ourselves and in our national and international policies?

D. Company's Coming!

Ask how group members prepare for an important guest at home or work. Read Matthew 3:1-12 aloud, then relate their preparation to the ministry of John the Baptist. Ask: What is the content and intent of his message? Why does he seem so harsh to some persons? What are the consequences of failing to make ready? How do your plans compare with his advice?

Invite group members to tell about their Christmas preparations so far and what is left to be done. Then ask how John the Baptist might advise them to get ready for the coming of the Christ at Christmas. How do your priorities compare with John's? What changes do you need to make in your life to be really ready for Christ's coming?

E. Summarize

Isaiah prophesies the ideal leader; Romans describes the welcoming characteristics of persons and communities who follow Christ; John the Baptist declares how to ready ourselves for the Christ and the consequences of not following or believing. Ask: How ready are you to follow this ideal? to change your beliefs or behaviors in accord with his teaching? to take risks for the sake of the gospel? Explain. How do these passages inform or inspire your own sense of discipleship? What do they call you to do or to be?

F. Creative Activity

Form small groups. Have each group read Psalm 72:1-7, 18-19 (a song or prayer for the king) and then compose a song (perhaps to the tune of a familiar hymn), write a prayer for our leaders today, or make a picture or poster welcoming all into the Christian community. Invite each group to present its creation in a closing worship time.

Lections for Third Sunday of Advent

Old Testament: Isaiah 35:1-10

*F*ROM about 597 to 587 B.C. most of the inhabitants and wealth of Jerusalem and the kingdom of Judah were taken into exile by the Babylonians. Prophets like Isaiah, Jeremiah, and Ezekiel had warned the people about this. The final blow was struck in 587 when the city was completely ravaged, the Temple torn down, and even the walls around the city toppled. The land and the people were desolate; it seemed that God had abandoned them.

Imagine what it would be like to be taken from your home and made a virtual slave in another country. Read Psalm 137:1-6 to get a sense of how the people back then felt. They had collapsed into deep despair. But then there came to them this song of joy and hope. (Many songs in Isaiah 40–66 have this same theme, so scholars believe this one should be included in that section.) God was coming back! They would be brought home.

God Returns (35:1-6a)

This passage may best be appreciated by first reading Isaiah 34, which describes the terrible end that would come to the enemies that had overtaken Judah. The despair over the Exile and the havoc in store for their captors is contrasted in Isaiah 35 with the hope for restoration.

In highly poetic language, the prophet describes first how nature itself responds to the return of God (35:1-2a). This area is the wilderness, that is, the Syrian desert (today's Golan Heights) over which the exiles had been taken to Babylon and over which they would soon pass when YHWH would bring them back. The image is that of God's presence moving through this barren wasteland and transforming it. It would become like the famed lush mountain ranges of Lebanon and Carmel and the fertile plain of Sharon (35:2). The wilderness would be turned into a paradise. It would be restored. And this is but a preview of what God would do for the people in times to come.

24

The people are to draw hope once again from this message. Such joy should bring new strength to weak hands and knees, as would be the case with persons exhausted by slavery and oppression (35:3). This message would help them take heart and would give renewed courage, for God was coming to deliver them and to pass judgment on their enemies (35:4). Even the most helpless among them—the blind, lame, and deaf—would not be left out. They also would be renewed and healed by the saving power of God (35:5-6a).

The People Return

In last week's Gospel lesson we saw how the people were encouraged to go out and prepare roads or paths for the coming of the Messiah. Here we see that God is doing the road work! Not only is the desert coming to new life, being turned into a luxuriant paradise (35:6b-7), but God is building a highway through it to provide a path from exile back home (35:8). Highways in those days were dangerous, largely because of wild animals and thieves. But this holy way would have none of those dangers (35:8-9), for YHWH was building and patrolling it. Just as long ago when they crossed over the road God made through the sea out of bondage in Egypt, singing and dancing, so they would sing with joy again on this new highway created by God (35:10a). With each new step on it, their pain and sighing would fade away (35:10b), replaced with unspeakable joy. God promises his presence and guidance, and opportunity for rejoicing, when we trust fully and serve faithfully.

A New Testament Psalm: Luke 1:47-55

In place of a psalm, today's song is the Magnificat (or Mary's Song). It is called the *Magnificat* because this is the first word in the Latin translation, meaning to "magnify" or "make large or great").

The sight and sound of a young mother-to-be singing is a common and a touching one. Mary, visiting her relative Elizabeth (pregnant with John the Baptist), breaks forth in song (as do many of the characters in Luke 1–2). Her song, much like that of Hannah (see 1 Samuel 2), is a joyous prayer of thanksgiving to a God who knows the circumstances of the poor and lowly, reaches down to lift them up, and brings judgment on their persecutors. Mary perhaps senses that in her child God would be doing just this and more.

Epistle: James 5:7-10

Children (as well as many adults in today's fast-paced, instant-gratification world) do not like to hear the words, "Be patient! Just wait! Good things come to those who wait. Patience is a virtue." The persons to whom James was writing were not happy about waiting either. They were being persecuted by the enemies of Christ and abused by the wealthy (see 2:6-7; 5:1-6), and were impatient for Christ to come and give them justice.

A Farmer's Almanac of Faith

A farmer must have an abundance of two things: faith and patience. Thus James can draw on this image to give hope and

> **Think About It:** Faith and patience are hallmarks of the Christian. In our hurry-up, results-oriented world, most of us are very impatient. How do you distinguish between impatience and concern for effectiveness? Are you patient in matters of faith? Does impatience undermine your faith? If so, what might you do about it?

guidance to his fellow Christians. No farmer sows one day and expects to see fully grown crops the next. He must wait for God to give the early rains at planting time, the late rains while the crops are maturing, and plenty of sunshine in between. Likewise, says James, the seeds of faith, love, and discipleship will bear fruit one day soon when Christ appears. Until then Christians must stay focused, go diligently about their work as farmers do, strive to produce a good crop of witness and service, and await the time of harvest.

The Greek word for the "coming of the Lord" is *parousia*. Literally it means the "appearance" of Christ. The early church lived in an intense expectation of the coming of Christ. Similarly, the message of Isaiah 35 was to a suffering people, telling them to have hope and to wait, for God was coming to deliver them.

The Prophets Model Patience

In verse 10, James moves from a farmer to the prophets, including Job as one of them (5:11). They are held up as examples of patience and faithful endurance in tough times. Perhaps James also had Isaiah and the exiles in mind, who, as we see in the Old Testament reading, had to have patience. The point is to draw strength from the example of others who have had to suffer and await God's deliverance.

They needed more than just patient waiting for God, though. They had to have patience with one another (5:9). If they could not strike back at the ones causing their suffering, they would sometimes lash out at each other (see also 4:1-3). The congregation evidently had some serious challenges, both from within and from outside. James reminds them that the ultimate test of their discipleship is near; they must see to their own fitting behavior. Such internal conflict would distract them and cause them to be judged when the Judge comes.

The Gospel Lection: Matthew 11:2-11

The close connection between John the Baptist and Jesus continues this week as we see the prisoner John sending messengers to Jesus. It is

26

interesting that what happens to John—arrest, trial, execution—also awaits Jesus. Indeed, after this point, we see a growing opposition to Jesus.

John's Question

Matthew does not tell the story of John's imprisonment until 14:1-12. John had been arrested by Herod Antipas and imprisoned in his fortress near the Dead Sea. Even there, John heard what Jesus was doing, and what he heard disturbed him. At the Jordan, John had had no doubt that Jesus was the Messiah; but now Jesus is not meeting his expectations. John's message had emphasized judgment, fire, the axe falling; but Jesus was not doing any of this. Perhaps John expected Jesus to set him free from prison; after all, he was the Messiah's forerunner. So this doubt caused him to ask, "Are you the one . . . , or are we to wait for another?"

Jesus Answers

Jesus, in his typical manner, did not answer the question outright, but simply told the messengers to observe what they saw and heard Jesus doing and then go back and report to John. What they saw were the healings and exorcisms reported in Chapters 8–9.

"Come and see" was a common response from Jesus. Words can only go so far. This invitation to follow and observe allows one to invest oneself fully in the discovery of who Jesus is and what he can do by the power of God. In highly poetic language, drawn from Isaiah (29:18-19; 35:5-6; 61:1), Jesus shares with John the kind of messiah he sees himself to be—a suffering servant who seeks to bring healing and wholeness into people's lives.

> **Think About It:** Jesus does not try to prove who he is. He just is, for all to see. What did you come out to see? How do you see Jesus? Who is he to you? Are you convinced by seeing and then believing? How does this lead you to respond?

The Gospels frequently reveal a misunderstanding by many of who Jesus was and what kind of messiah he would be. Even his own disciples did not understand. Jesus did not try to prove who he was, for this was something John had to come to himself. Faith must grow within him. Those who come to this faith, who are able to see and accept Jesus for who he is, are most blessed.

Jesus Praises John

It would seem from his last words (Matthew 11:6) that Jesus was criticizing John. Perhaps some of John's enemies were in the crowd. So Jesus took up a spirited defense of John. He told the crowd that they had come out to hear John, not a weak and uncertain fellow influenced by popular opinion or every wind of doctrine, nor even one swayed by pressure from the authorities. They had come to hear a powerful man—an oak, not a reed—who stood tall for his faith and message. And in humorous, taunting words, Jesus compared the expensive, silky clothes worn by persons in Herod's court to the animal hair worn by a true prophet.

They had come to hear a prophet, and a prophet they heard. He bore witness to someone greater than himself. So if they believed in him (John) and accepted his message, then they should also hear and accept what was happening in Jesus. John was more than an ordinary prophet; he was the forerunner of the Messiah. Yet, John, imprisoned and soon to die, would still not experience in his earthly life the kind of blessings even the lowliest disciples of Jesus would receive as Jesus ushered in God's reign (11:11).

Study Suggestions

A. Prayer

Have members identify situations in their own lives or in the world for which they would like the group to pray. (These may be either spoken or silent requests.) List the concerns on a sheet of paper, and display it from now until Christmas. Update the concerns each week. The texts today deal with patience, so lead participants in patiently praying for these matters. Be sure to celebrate when prayers are answered.

B. Bloom in the Desert

Introduce Isaiah 35 by reviewing the situation described in Isaiah 34. Then turn to the central message of Isaiah 35. Read the passage aloud. If possible, get a video from your local library that shows plants blooming as if in a few seconds to illustrate how God brings new life to the wilderness and to the lives of those in exile.

After contrasting the judgment in Isaiah 34 with the hope in Isaiah 35, ask: What is meant by strengthening weak hands and knees? by the words to the blind, lame, and vulnerable? What does this passage say to us? At what times in our lives would it be especially meaningful? Share an example from your life of when God brought new hope and new life to you, then invite others to tell theirs. Affirm that God has a way of bringing life out of seemingly hopeless situations.

C. Down on the Farm

Have someone read James 5:7-10. James compares Christians to farmers. Ask members to identify some characteristics of farmers that Christians should also have. (Examples might be: hard work, patience, faith, endurance, caring for the earth, anticipation of the harvest.) If you have members with farm experience, ask them what it takes to be a good farmer. Then relate this to the Christian life.

D. Do Not Grumble

Consult a Bible commentary or examine other chapters of James to find out what the congregation might have been grumbling about. Ask: What does James counsel the congregation to do about their complaining? Is there griping in your congregation? Is it about something that Jesus would find important enough to debate? How should contemporary Christians deal with congregational bickering? What would you add to James's advice?

E. The Question

Read Matthew 11:2-11. Examine the context of the passage and why John may have been asking questions concerning Jesus. Discuss: What questions do you have (or have you had) about Jesus? Why is belief in Jesus something one must come to oneself? What has convinced you to believe and follow Jesus?

Have the participants imagine that a friend comes up to them and asks, "How can you be sure that Jesus is the one? Why is he so special?" What answers would they give? What have they seen and felt Jesus doing in their lives? Have a volunteer ready to testify about what Jesus means to him or her.

F. Summarize

Form small groups. Review some of the recurring themes in today's passages: hope, patience, trust in God's promises, concern for the poor and oppressed, anticipation of the restoration and reconciliation possible through God and Christ. Ask each group to create bumper stickers that summarize the message in today's passages. Then have them read or show and explain them.

G. Songs of Hope

Read Luke 1:47-55, a song of trust and hope in God during difficult times. Note how singing has been used during times of adversity, such as striking workers or slaves laboring in cotton fields. Distribute hymnals, and invite members to select hymns they have found comforting and strengthening, then tell why they have special meaning for them. Close by singing or reading some of these hymns together.

Lections for Fourth Sunday of Advent

Old Testament: Isaiah 7:10-16

*R*ULERS have always had advisers. In the days of Isaiah, prophets often advised the king. A faithful king would consult these messengers from God to ascertain God's will. A king who "did evil in the sight of the LORD" might instead just seek support for plans he had already made. Here we see Isaiah advising King Ahaz, ruler of the Kingdom of Judah from 735 to 715 B.C.

Background

The little nation of Judah was between a rock and a hard place (see 2 Kings 16:1-20). The powerful Assyrian Empire was growing and threatening the region. To combat it, Rezin, king of Syria, and Pekah, king of Israel, formed an alliance with neighboring nations; but Judah did not join. As a result, Judah was under siege. Rezin and Pekah threatened to replace Ahaz with "the son of Tabeel."

The political quandary was bad enough, but this attack raised a religious problem as well. Ahaz, as the Davidic king and holder of the promises of God for the nation, had a mandate to heed the word of God and to model faith, even in the midst of calamity, which the people certainly were facing. Isaiah told Ahaz to "take heed, be quiet, do not fear," for the two enemies threatening him would soon vanish.

> **Think About It:** "If you do not stand firm in faith, you shall not stand at all" (7:9). Do you believe this? How do you account for persons and forces that seem to be standing very strong, yet are obviously immoral and unjust? What keeps them standing? How long will they last? Does your faith keep you standing in the face of such opposition?

The Offer and Response

Ahaz was reluctant to accept Isaiah's counsel. So the prophet invited the king to ask for a sign from God, a proof of God's reliability and presence. Ahaz refused, claiming he did not wish to put YHWH to the test. Though this may sound pious, Ahaz may just have been rejecting the divine promise, avoiding Isaiah's advice in favor of a plan he already had in mind—to appeal to the Assyrians, a much larger nation and former enemy, for help.

The Sign of Immanuel

Exasperated that Ahaz would refuse what most would covet, Isaiah insisted that Ahaz would receive a sign anyway. Isaiah prophesied that a child would soon be born to a young woman and that child would be named "Immanuel" (God with us). Furthermore, before that child would even be capable of making his own decisions or choosing between right and wrong, the threat from Syria and Israel would be gone.

Who was this child? Some have suggested it was the son of Ahaz (Hezekiah); others that it was one of Isaiah's own sons. Christians traditionally have seen this as a messianic prophecy referring to the coming of Jesus, which is why we read this passage during Advent. The message was that Ahaz needed to trust in God who was with him and the nation, not in the military might of Assyria. Ahaz finally rejected Isaiah's advice, with dire consequences for him, and for Judah.

The Coming Messiah?

Many Christians see in Isaiah 7:14 a prophecy of the virgin birth of Jesus. (The most accurate translation of the Hebrew is "young woman," one who might or might not be a virgin.) Matthew 1:23 also quotes it in such support. Isaiah was speaking a word for his day to a particular king facing a particular crisis. His emphasis then was not on the woman, but on the child she would bear as a sign to the king that God was with them.

Psalter: Psalm 80:1-7, 17-19

This is a song or prayer asking for God's help and deliverance for the nation. We do not know the reason for the crisis. The psalm was probably sung as the people gathered for worship, chanting the refrain in verses 3, 7, and 19. As a song of confidence in God's presence and power, it goes well with today's Isaiah passage. Two images of God appear. First is the shepherd, the one who is with them, constantly tending and taking care of them. The other is the powerful leader enthroned in might. Right now they very much need a sign that their Shepherd and Ruler is still on duty. The term "son of man" (verse 17, NIV) can be taken as a messianic reference, again a reason for using this psalm during Advent. The Gospels always use the title "Son of Man" to refer to Jesus.

Epistle: Romans 1:1-7

If one were looking for light reading, it would not be Paul's Letter to the Romans. This is Paul's weightiest treatise on the Christian faith. Indeed, one could spend a lifetime studying just the verses in today's passage. Paul had never met the Roman Christians and was planning to visit them in the near future. In introducing his letter, he follows the basic pattern of many ancient epistles—first the writer's name, then the name of the recipient, and lastly a brief greeting—but he expands on it, Christianizing it.

The Writer

He identifies himself by his Roman name *Paul,* which in itself showed he was one of them. Then he moves on to identify himself as a "servant" (Greek, *doulos,* "slave") of Jesus Christ. Thus, Paul describes himself as one who completely belongs to Christ and his cause. He is an apostle, sent on a mission to proclaim the good news of what God has done in Jesus Christ. This was all promised by God through the prophets and has now been fulfilled.

This Jesus was both Son of David and Son of God, whose coming we fervently await during Advent. Though he died in the flesh, his true status was made known in his resurrection. And it was through this risen Lord that Paul and the Roman Christians had received the grace of God and the call to give their lives for the gospel. Paul centers his affirmation in the grace and peace offered by God through Christ.

The Recipients

Paul writes to "all in Rome who are loved by God and called to be saints" (1:7, NIV). Rome was the capital of the most powerful nation in Paul's world. It is understandable that Christians would want to take the gospel there, for "all roads lead to Rome." A thriving Christian community had been established there and was spreading throughout Italy.

Think About It: Saints are not just revered (and dead) Christians but committed, witnessing members of the household of faith. Do you consider yourself a saint in this sense? Why or why not? How can you live out your own sainthood? What gifts are you called to share?

Planning to take the gospel to Spain, Paul writes to the Roman congregation to introduce himself and perhaps also to get their support for this venture. He addresses them as "saints," a common term used of Christians. Today it usually refers to extraordinary (or dead) Christians. But for Paul, each living, active Christian was a saint, a member of the body of Christ called to use his or her gifts to share the good news.

Greeting

As usual in his greetings, Paul chooses two words that are at the heart of the Christian faith—grace and peace. Grace is God's unmerited favor and acceptance, given in Christ, that brings inner peace and harmony between human beings and throughout the world.

Gospel: Matthew 1:18-25

In this passage we have Matthew's account of the birth and infancy of Jesus. It seems to be told from the perspective of Joseph, whereas Luke's version tells the story from Mary's point of view.

Joseph Takes a Wife

In those days there were three steps to marriage. First came the engagement, often transacted by the fathers of the bride and groom. This may have taken place while the couple were still children. Parents believed marriage was too important a matter to leave to fickle romantic attraction. It appears that Joseph was older. Since he is seldom mentioned after the childhood stories, he may have died before Jesus began his ministry.

The second stage was the betrothal. This took place when the children were older and was a kind of ratification of the engagement. At this point the girl could refuse to marry the man. But once they were betrothed, they were considered legally married and the relationship could be ended only by divorce. The betrothal lasted for one year. It is thought that the couple did not have sexual relations during this time.

The final stage was the marriage itself, often a festive time when the groom made his way through the village and took the bride to his home. Mary and Joseph were in stage two at this time. Mary was pregnant. Joseph knew he was not the father.

A Word From Tradition

The noncanonical *Protevangélion* (an account, attributed to the apostle James, of the "perpetual Virgin Mary" and the birth of Jesus) quotes Joseph as saying he is "an old man" who has raised a family and that their age difference is great enough that he might "appear ridiculous in Israel." Mary is twelve and engaged in service to the Temple when the priests seek a widower for her husband; she is pregnant at fourteen. Joseph knew precisely what he had been chosen to do. In Matthew, Joseph discovers the pregnancy during their betrothal.

Joseph's Options

Now, what to do? Joseph's first option was to make a public spectacle of it. Expose Mary and have her charged with adultery. That could have meant death by stoning. Option two was to divorce Mary quietly. He could do this with two witnesses, giving her a paper of divorce without making formal charges.

As highly as Mary stands in Christian thought, Joseph stands tall in these stories as well. He chose option two. He is described as a "just" man, that is, a godly man who observed the laws and traditions of his faith. His action here also showed his love and concern for Mary. He must have felt greatly hurt by her apparent betrayal, but could not bring himself to strike out at her. Most of all, this account shows that Joseph possessed great faith, which he would surely need for what was about to happen to his new family.

Joseph Had a Dream

Like his ancient namesake, Joseph had a dream (as he did again in Matthew 2:13). An angel appeared to tell him that Mary was carrying the very child of God, a son, whom Joseph was to name *Jesus*. (The father often named the child.) *Jesus* is the same name as *Joshua* and means "God saves." It was a fitting name, for this Holy Child would save people from their sins.

Matthew then offers one of his favorite phrases, "All this took place to fulfill what had been spoken . . . ," referring to Isaiah 7:14. More than any other Gospel, Matthew seeks to show that Jesus is the fulfillment of the promises in Scripture. No promise was greater than this one—that in Jesus, God became one of us, came to be with us: Emmanuel! Joseph, ever faithful, obeyed the angel and took Mary as his wife.

Study Suggestions

A. Music

As members arrive, play, "For Unto Us a Child Is Born," the part of Handel's *Messiah* that uses verses from Isaiah 7. Then read responsively Psalm 80:1-7, 17-19, with the group saying the refrain (verses 3, 7, 19), and one person reading the rest. Close with "O Come, O Come, Emmanuel."

B. What's in a Name?

Obtain a copy of a book of baby names that gives the meanings. Look up members' names and meanings. Do the names fit their personality or character? In biblical times a name had special power and meaning and could influence or reflect who and what a person would be. For example, the names of Isaiah's children had a special meaning for Ahaz and for Judah (see Isaiah 7:3 and 8:1). What did *Shear-jashub* ("a remnant shall return") and *Maher-shalal-hash-baz* ("the spoils speeds; the prey hastens") mean for Judah in the midst of their siege crisis?

Now write "Immanuel" and "Jesus" on the chalkboard or a sheet of paper, defining each. Ask: How did Jesus live up to these names? How have you experienced Jesus as "God with us" and as "God's saving power"?

C. In Whom Do We Trust?

The Isaiah passage is about where we put our trust—in human beings and military might, or in God? Discuss: Why did Ahaz place his trust in Assyria rather than God? Where does our nation place its trust? Take out a coin or bill. Note that it reads, "In God We Trust." Ask: Why is this statement on our money? Is it true? In what or whom do you place your trust? Isaiah 7:9 says that if we do not stand firm in faith, we do not stand at all. What does this mean in your life? What prevents your standing firm in faith? What help do you need? Discuss how members can be helpful to one another as they strive to be faithful.

D. Letters

In Romans Paul sets forth what he believes about Jesus. Read aloud Romans 1:1-7, and review the comments about it. Together compose the beginning of a letter that would share what you believe about Jesus. How would participants describe themselves? To whom would they most like to send the letter?

E. Drama

Have someone read Matthew 1:18-25, then summarize the commentary on pages 33–34, especially "A Word From Tradition." Ask: Does this extra-biblical account change your impression of the story? of the role and importance of Joseph? Review Joseph's dilemma and options. (Invite a volunteer to assume his role and tell his story, drawing on information provided in this lesson.) How does Joseph aid the cause of God? What "Josephs" do you know? What moral dilemmas do we face where we are uncertain what to do? Where do we seek guidance? How do we decide?

F. Summarize

Review a key theme of the lections: God's participation in the world to nurture and to save. Ask: What evidence do we see of this saving nurture today? Does God still work in such concrete ways to save? What does this promise from God call us to do or be? How does it nurture our sense of discipleship? How does this time of Advent waiting deepen our faith and commitment?

G. God With Us

Close by inviting members to share how they have felt God to be with them. Explore some things you might do during Christmas and next year to become better aware of the God who comes to be with us at Christmas and every day. Encourage them to take time to pray and keep a journal about this during the coming week of Christmas bustle.

CHRISTMAS

Lections for Christmas Day

Old Testament: Isaiah 52:7-10

A MIDWESTERN farm family had lost their land. They had taken a loan to buy new farm machinery when property values and interest rates were high. Then they were caught in the squeeze between high seed and fertilizer costs and dropping milk prices. When the bank foreclosed, the family was left with nothing but the house and barn. They had nowhere to turn—except to God.

> **Think About It:** "Nowhere to turn—except to God." When have you had the rug pulled out from under you? When have you faced misfortune and despair? When have you felt you had nowhere to turn? What did you do? What kept you going? How was God made known to you? Where did God lead?

They must have felt much like Judah of old. Their fertile land had been overrun by the Babylonians. Their city, Jerusalem, had been besieged and conquered, their Temple destroyed, their homes sacked, their loved ones killed; and they had been driven into exile. Everything beloved and familiar had been swept away. No wonder they felt that their God YHWH, who had delivered them from slavery in Egypt, now seemed to have left them in the lurch. They had become strangers in a foreign land (see Psalm 137:1-6). They had nowhere to turn—except to God.

A Comforting Vision

But Isaiah was there to comfort his people with a vision of the salvation of God. He told them to look up and listen to the welcome sound of the feet of a herald, bringing good news (Isaiah 52:7). Then, in the prophet's vision, behind the messenger came their redeemer, YHWH himself! The watchmen saw him and shouted in ecstasy (verse 8). The God they thought was dead was coming at last to save them (verse 9). As he strode into their midst, he raised his arm in a gesture of greeting and authority, so all the nations could see that YHWH had the power and the will to restore their former glory (verse 10).

The young farm couple heard a similar message from their God. Their farm was gone; but they had their home, their family, their love, their health, and their sense of purpose to live for others and for God. Church members offered their support. He found a job in the city; they could grow much of their food in their garden plot; they continued to worship and work in the church. The God they thought had deserted them they found to be closer than ever, sustaining and guiding them through their crisis. They had heard good news (verse 7). God had comforted his people in the midst of misfortune (verse 8-9). God had bared his holy arm of guidance and strength (verse 10) and had transformed a calamity into a new chapter in their lives.

Such is the good news of Christmas Day—one of the shortest days of the year—news of glad tidings of great joy to all people. When we awake in the morning it is still dark. But then we see the lighted tree, with a star or angel on top, a messenger signaling good news. Below it are many gifts, suggesting the wondrous gift of God given on this day—the Christ Child, born to set his people free. The family is gathered. Expectancy reigns. Gladness is in the air. We sing, "Joy to the world, the Lord is come!" We shout in ecstasy! The promise has been fulfilled. God is with us! Emmanuel! The time of waiting is over. A new chapter in our lives is about to begin.

The Lection From the Psalter: Psalm 98

"Rejoice, for the Lord is coming!" this psalm proclaims. "Joy to the world, the Lord is come" we sing on Christmas morn. The psalm is sung in anticipation; the carol in gratitude that it has happened at last. The long wait of Advent is over; the reign of God has begun. The God of steadfast love and faithfulness (verse 3) will both liberate and judge his people (verse 9). Humanity (verse 4-6) and nature (verses 7-8) both sing with joy because God is coming to right all wrongs. The polluted waters, the poisoned earth, the denuded hillsides are all excited because a God who cares is coming to rescue them. The poor, sick, and oppressed are summoned to "sing to the LORD a new song, for he has done marvelous things" (verse 1). In full view of all the powers, God has made known his redemption (verse 2). No wonder the shepherds were awed, the angels sang, and the wise men knelt! No wonder we "make a joyful noise" on Christmas Day. Something awesome and world-shaking has taken place.

Epistle: Hebrews 1:1-4

The Letter to the Hebrews focuses on Jesus. The author is writing to both Jewish and Gentile Christians who are discouraged because Christ has not yet come (9:28; 10:23-25), and they are suffering persecution (12:3-13). He is urging them not to give up because God in Christ has accomplished his aim of redeeming all humankind, and a hopeful future lies ahead. He challenges them to have faith like those of old (Chapter 11) and to "run with perseverance the race marked out for us, . . . [fixing] our eyes on Jesus" (12:1-2, NIV).

In today's lection, several points about Jesus are made. First, the message that God had long been trying to get through to humanity through the prophets has now been made plain in Jesus, the Son of God himself (verse 1)! In him the message of God's redeeming love is not just spoken; it is embodied. Second, the One who had created the world would now inherit it. The crucified One was in power at the beginning and would reign again at the end. The future was bright. Empire would not have the last word. Christ is the "heir of all things" (verse 2).

Third, Christ the creator has become Christ the redeemer (verse 3). He has become flesh and dwelt among us and has died to save his people from their sins. (More of this in the Gospel reading.) Fourth, Jesus is God's glory (verse 3). The Almighty comes not in the form of a crusading warrior or mighty leader, but as a babe in a manger, a simple carpenter, a Galilean artisan who speaks with authority without throwing his weight around. His life is "the exact imprint of God's very being." God is like Jesus—humility not domination, love not power, compassion not control. He has come "not to be served but to serve, and to give his life a ransom for many" (Matthew 20:28).

Fifth, God through Jesus the Word also keeps things going (verse 3). The Word is the dynamic energy that holds the universe together, keeps things reproducing and developing, and enables everything to function in perfect order and symmetry. The earthly powers might hold the upper hand for now, but the ultimate control is in the hand of a Cosmic Power. And finally, Jesus has been exalted, not as our judge but as our mediator. He is seated at the right hand of God to make intercession on our behalf. He knows our tribulation, cares about our destiny, and will make sure God does not forget us.

Gospel: John 1:1-14

The cosmic theme continues in the prologue to John's Gospel. John the Evangelist proclaims, "In the beginning was the Word. . . . The Word became flesh, . . . and we have seen his glory" (verses 1, 14). The lection has three parts: the Word in creation, witness to the Word, and the Word becomes flesh.

The Word in Creation (verses 1-5)

The Word (Greek: *logos*, meaning divine wisdom, potent energy, creative power) is the dynamic love of God expressed in the process of creation. This is the origin of all that is. Life itself emanates from the heart of God, piercing the darkness with light. The light is too powerful for the darkness—the darkness of shadow, of ignorance, of superstition, of evil, and of death, for the Word is a God of newness, of illumination, of transformation.

Witness to the Word (verses 6-9)

This creating, loving Power is about to come into the world in a new, enlightening way. God sends a prophet to announce the inbreaking, to pave the way so people would be prepared to accept and believe. This prophet, John, was a forerunner, who pointed to the coming Light that would flood the world with illumination and make God's loving nature clear to all.

The Word Takes Human Form (verses 10-14)

The Light could have come as a blinding flash, a ravaging fire, or the glint of the sun on shining armor. Instead, he came as a man. The Word that had called the world into being now entered that world through a working class family living in an obscure village in a remote corner of the earth. One would think those would be honored and overjoyed to have the Almighty Word pay them a visit. But no, they did not accept this good fortune. Of course, some did receive and believe and were adopted into God's family in a new and special way. They were reborn, not through their own willpower, but through entering a personal relationship with the divine Word. This was made possible because that creative Word became embodied in the man Jesus, lived a normal human life, and showed us what the grace and glory of God were really like. Such a wondrous one as this could be no one but the Son of God.

It may sound presumptuous, but this rebirth fills us with a bit of that same dynamic energy that empowered Jesus. The Word can become flesh in us, too. This is no credit to us; it is the gift of God. We are called to live out the love and goodness of God just as Jesus was. As the Word flows through us to others, we may be rejected or accepted just as he was. There are some who will never be touched by God except through

> *Think About It:.* "In the beginning was the Word. . . . And the Word became flesh and lived among us, and we have seen his glory." What an astounding claim John is making! God the Creator, born to a teenage mother, baptized in the shallow Jordan, walked the dusty roads of Galilee, confronted the powers of Temple and empire, taught fresh truths, and had compassion on the multitudes. History has been changed by his coming. The hearts and lives of many have been transformed. Christmas is a celebration of this Christ event. How will you respond? Are you among those who do not know him? do not believe in him? pay more attention to tinsel and Santa Claus than to the Word become flesh? Or are you among those who receive, believe, become children of God, are reborn into a relationship with God?

us. This is an awesome privilege and responsibility. Christmas is about a gift given to the world through Jesus—but also through us! Will you share it?

Study Suggestions

A. A Joyous Beginning

Open by singing "Joy to the World." Ask the group what gives them joy this Christmas Day. Then name persons or groups in your community and around the world for whom Christmas joy may be difficult because of misfortune, loneliness, war, poverty, or natural disaster, and offer prayer for them.

B. Vision and Reality

Tell the story of the family who lost their farm. Relate it to Judah being driven from their land into exile. Share an experience of your own of loss or disappointment, and invite others to share theirs. Then read aloud Isaiah 52:7-10. Describe his vision that gave hope to a despondent people. Compare the promise of a deliverer coming to lead his people home with the good news of Jesus' coming to save his people from their sins. Ask: How do you think this prophetic oracle helped the exiles in Babylon? What gave hope to the family who lost their farm? What has sustained you in times of grief or devastation? What does the story and vision of Christmas do for us? How can we transform the tinsel and festivity of the holiday season into a lasting vision and hope that sustains us in times of tribulation?

C. Jesus Keeps Us Going

Draw a parallel among our times of desolation, Judah in exile, the Jews under Roman domination, and the Christians addressed by the Letter to Hebrews who were losing hope under persecution. Distribute several translations of the Bible, and have Hebrews 1:1-4 read aloud three times, each in a different translation. Pause after each reading to allow members to note impressions of Jesus that come to mind. Then ask them to share their insights. Explain the six aspects of Jesus described on page 40, and compare these with the group's list. Discuss: How does the view of Jesus in Hebrews compare with our understanding up to this point? Can we see why these aspects were emphasized to a people under persecution? What dimensions of Jesus' life and ministry are most meaningful to people in our time and circumstances? How have we found Jesus helpful in our down times?

D. The Word Become Flesh

Read John 1:1-14 and the interpretation of it presented on page 40–41. Invite members to share how the Word has become flesh for them—experiences in which Jesus became real to them, sermons or books that presented Jesus in fresh ways, or persons who told them about Jesus, embodied Jesus' love to them, or invited them to follow Jesus or give their hearts to him. Ask: Can the Word become flesh in us? If so, in what ways? (Point out that, while Jesus' incarnation was unique, he calls us to follow him, and his Spirit can fill our hearts and empower us to live and serve as he did.) What is God's Christmas gift to us? How can we share that gift with others?

E. Making a Joyful Noise

Stand and read Psalm 98 in unison. Notice how both nature and humankind join in this song of praise. Identify in one column on a chalkboard of sheet of paper the ways in which both the environment and human beings are being abused in our world—pollution, global warming, human rights violations, poverty, exploitation of women and workers, civilian victims of war, persons in prison, victims of crime, and so on. Then beside each item list a constructive way in which we can address this abuse. Stress that this is making a joyful noise with our deeds as well as our lips. Close with a prayer asking God to help us share the hope and joy of Christmas by working to meet human needs at home and throughout the world.

Lections for First Sunday After Christmas Day

Old Testament: Isaiah 63:7-9

*T*HESE moving verses are actually the first few lines of a much longer song (Isaiah 63:7–64:12). Like many of the psalms, it pours forth both praise and lament, trust and fear, joy and sorrow, as the past deeds of God for the people are recounted in light of the tragedy of recent events (destruction of the Temple and Jerusalem—see Isaiah 63:18). At many times in their past the Israelites had felt close to God. But not now. They long for that closeness again. The prophet, acting as an intercessor for the people, prays to God on their behalf.

Great Is Thy Faithfulness
This lament begins with "steadfast love" (which could also be translated as "faithfulness"). This theme is found quite often in the psalms. Just like the psalms, the prophet now will "recount" (identify, call to mind) once again those events from the past that prove beyond any doubt the faithfulness and goodness of God (see also Psalms 51:1; 89:1; 145:8). This song or prayer may have been composed or used for a festival or worship celebration. A common characteristic of those ceremonies was the retelling of the mighty acts of God on the people's behalf.

In the Beginning
The writer begins at the beginning—not Genesis, but when the Israelites became a people—the Exodus. That whole event was like the birth, the creation of Israel, when God set them apart as a chosen people, as dear and beloved children. They were often seen as the children of God (Exodus 4:22; Deuteronomy 14:1; 32:6). God had high hopes for these children—as most

parents do—that they would "not deal falsely," but rather would be faithful and loving in response to God's faithfulness and love toward them.

A God Who Suffers

God, like a loving parent, became their "savior" (verse 8b), their protector, the one who redeemed them from their afflictions. One has only to remember their sufferings in Egyptian bondage and how they cried out to God. God heard them and sent Moses to be their deliverer. But God did more than that. God entered into their life, was afflicted with them, and felt their pain. God suffered with them. This is the same God whose love enters into our life through Jesus, suffers and dies for us, and makes possible our reconciliation with God.

> **Think About It.** "God suffered with them." How can God be both almighty and subject to pain? Do you think of God as one who suffers? Is this a comforting or a disturbing thought? When you are suffering, is it helpful to think of a God who is suffering with you?

The image comes to mind of a parent who loves a child so much that anything that hurts the child also deeply hurts the parent. So touched by their pain was God, that God came personally—not through angels or the forces of nature—to be with them, to deliver and comfort them. Indeed, as a parent carries a child, so God had carried them "all the days of old."

Remember

One of the great gifts God has given us is the ability to remember (though sometimes there are things we wish we could forget). To remember means to make present again that which is past. This passage bids us to remember, constantly to name the many acts of God's faithfulness in our own lives and history, for that sometimes is the only way we can deal with a painful present. This is what we do each Sunday when we gather to study and worship—recount the faithfulness of God—so that we are empowered to face the future in trust and hope.

Psalter: Psalm 148

This is one of the Hallelujah Psalms (because it begins and ends with the Hebrew word *hallelujah,* which means "Praise the Lord"). As in Psalm 150, everything is called upon to praise the Creator—the angels in heaven (verse 2), the planets and stars (verse 3), even water and all creatures in it (verses 4, 7). The trees and creatures on land are not left out. Lastly, everyone—from kings to maidens—is called upon to praise God. For those with eyes to see and ears to hear, all of creation praises God. Whether we experience praise in the fall colors, a glorious sunset, the birthing of a calf, or the roar of a storm, the psalmist simply tells us, "Join in!"

Epistle: Hebrews 2:10-18

Today's Epistle continues last Sunday's emphasis on the Incarnation, that is, God with us (Emmanuel) through the person and work of Jesus. Like today's Isaiah reading, it tells us how God suffered with us though Christ.

The Greatest Pioneer

Jesus is the one through whom all things were created or exist (see John 1:1-5). Yet, Christ left that lofty position to become flesh and blood, a human being—so a path might be blazed back to God.

The author of Hebrews presents a strong Christology (doctrine of Christ), showing Jesus as pioneer, sanctifier, brother, conqueror of spiritual slavery and death, merciful and faithful high priest, atoner for sin, and partner in suffering and temptation. We do not know entirely what were the concerns and beliefs of this congregation but can assume they had some preoccupation with angels and other celestial figures. Angels are mentioned nearly a dozen times through this portion of the letter, and the devil (and things evil) appear more than once. We may freely suppose that this lofty and thorough Christology was presented to ensure that the congregation would "not drift away" (2:1) from God's word and salvation in favor of some lesser doctrine or practice.

> **Think About It:** Jesus is high priest, brother, savior, partner in suffering, and much more. What image of Jesus Christ is the most powerful for you? In what way do you relate best to who Christ is? When you pray, "in Jesus' name," what aspect of his nature is foremost in your mind?

Christ is the one who shows us the way back into relationship with God, giving his life to overcome the obstacle of sin. He made "expiation for the sins of the people," that is, he tore down the barrier of sin that separated God and humanity. He made a way across the great divide.

"I Understand"

When someone tells us he or she has cancer, we can listen intently and really feel that person's pain. But we cannot say we understand unless we have been through a similar trial. What we can do, though, is introduce him or her to someone who has. To have experienced the same thing makes all the difference. Our passage from Hebrews tells us that Jesus is the one who has been there and done that! He did not choose to stay above our suffering. To the contrary, he "in every respect" became as we are, even to the experience of death, so that we may know he understands us and all we go through.

But more than just understanding, we know that through Jesus Christ's intervention, salvation and freedom from spiritual slavery is ours. His "sacrifice of atonement" (2:17) destroyed "the one who has the power of death" (2:14) so we could live. He not only enters into our lives but also gives us saving strength to face and overcome whatever difficulties may confront us.

Gospel: Matthew 2:13-23

You might say that Herod was the real Grinch who tried, not to steal Christmas, but to prevent it altogether. He ruled from about 37 to 4 B.C. Even though he improved and greatly embellished the Temple, most people hated him. He was vain, ambitious, and paranoid. He dealt harshly with any threat to his power, including murdering his wife and several relatives, thus removing rivals to the throne. So, when Matthew 2:3 states that Herod was frightened when he heard of a messiah being born, and that all Jerusalem was also afraid, we know why.

The Flight to Egypt

After the wise men had departed from Herod and the Holy Family, Joseph had another dream, in which God warned him not to stay in Bethlehem because Herod was going to try to kill Jesus. Instead, he must flee to Egypt, where Herod was not in control. Jews had for centuries sought refuge in Egypt, and there were thriving Jewish communities there. The situation is reminiscent of the story of Moses, who came from Egypt and whose early life was endangered by another evil ruler—Pharaoh.

The Slaughter of the Children

From Matthew 2:7 we see that Herod skillfully extracted information from the wise men, from which he was able to determine the age of the child and the place of birth—Bethlehem. He even got them to promise to return if they found the child. But, also warned in a dream, they did not do so. When Herod learned that the magi had slipped away, he ordered the death of all children in Bethlehem two years old and under. There is no extra-biblical record of this event. We do not know how many children there were in that village; but from a Christian perspective, even one was too many to lose.

Think About It: Jesus was saved; the other children were sacrificed. How do you explain why, in the same situation, some are hurt and others spared? Is this a matter of chance, or fate, or evil intent? Or does God have a purpose in it? What was God's purpose in this event?

The slaughter raises difficult theological questions about why only one family was warned and the other children were left to be killed. For Matthew, the point centers on the fulfillment of prophecy (Jeremiah 31:15) that shows God unwaveringly ensuring the presence and redemptive work of the Messiah. Rachel, one of the mothers of the twelve tribes of Israel, is pictured as weeping while the tribes (her children) pass by her grave (at Ramah) as they are being taken into Babylonian captivity. Now Matthew hears Rachel weeping again—this time for the babies of Bethlehem. (Who is weeping for the millions of children dying today—from poverty, illness, war, and on city streets? How can God work through us to prevent this?)

Return From Egypt

Joseph received divine communication, again through a dream, that Herod was dead and that Joseph could take his family back home. We know Herod died about 4 B.C. This means that Jesus must have been born before that (sometime between 7 and 4 B.C.).

When Joseph learned that one of Herod's evil sons, Archelaus, now ruled over Judea, he decided to move his family to Nazareth in Galilee. Here Jesus would grow up. Once again Matthew sees this as fulfillment of prophecy: "He will be called a Nazorean." This is the only one of Matthew's fourteen formulaic quotations that ground these events in biblical prophecy that does not refer to an obvious passage in the Hebrew Scriptures. In fact, Nazareth is never even mentioned in the Old Testament.

Study Suggestions

A. Sing a Hymn

Begin by singing, "Great Is Thy Faithfulness." Use this as a springboard into reading aloud Isaiah 63:7-9, another song about God's faithfulness. Write: "Faithfulness is . . ." on the chalkboard or a sheet of paper, and have members complete the sentence.

B. Recounting

Recap what you know of the historical period of Isaiah 56–66 (about 538–515 B.C.). What concerned the returning exiles? What was their relationship with God like? What images of hope do you see in Isaiah 63:7-9?

Share a story from your own life concerning God's steadfast love for you (or ask a volunteer to do so). When you review your life, where do you see God's love and care for you? Worship and other devotional times are natural occasions for us to recount the faithfulness and goodness of God. Ask: How might the way we worship change if we were to see it as remembering the mighty acts of God for us and all God's people? How can remembering God's past faithfulness help us face the present and the future?

C. Questions and Exclamations

Have the group read Hebrews 2:10-18 and the explanation on page 46. Then have them read it again and place question marks beside words and phrases that raise problems, and exclamation marks beside verses that really stand out. Take turns sharing a question and an insight, discussing each one. Everyone should get a chance to offer one of each.

D. Support Groups

Read the " 'I Understand' " section under the Epistle lection (page 46). Ask: What life experiences do you have that could help someone else? (For example, loss of a baby, serious illness, divorce, feeling excluded.) Who has "walked in your shoes" far enough to be a help to you? Have you ever been part of a support group? (A support group's purpose is to bring people together who have had similar experiences—such as parenting teens, loss of a loved one, surviving cancer—so that group members can help one another.) What life concerns might need support in your church or community? How might you help get a group started?

E. Hold the Babies

The Matthew 2:13-23 passage contains some difficult issues. Before tackling it, read about it in one of the commentaries listed in the Introduction (page 9). Then ask: What is the moral and theological dilemma within the slaughter? How are we to understand this sacrifice? Given the brutality of Herod, why was only one family warned to flee? (Do not be concerned if you do not really have "the answer." There may not be an easy one.) Also discuss the present-day "slaughter of the innocents"—from handguns, landmines, domestic abuse, preventable poverty-related diseases, child soldiering—and ways Christians might respond and help.

Tell the Dr. Seuss story, *How the Grinch Stole Christmas*. Despite all the Grinch did, Christmas still came. Who or what are some of the modern-day Grinches that would keep us from experiencing Christmas? (Consider commercialism, busyness, injustice, conflicts and divisions, and so on.)

F. Summarize

Two significant themes that weave through our lections are suffering and salvation. Review the passages and commentary to note where these appear. Ask: How do you see suffering and salvation intertwined? What is the relationship between them? Does the suffering of one justify the salvation of another? How can suffering become redemptive?

G. Praise the Lord

Close by having everyone recite together Psalm 148; then do a circle response to this incomplete sentence, "I praise God this Christmas for . . ." After each person shares, say together, "Praise the Lord!" Or, using colored magic markers on a large sheet of paper, invite each member to put up a word or symbol representing her or his praise to God.

EPIPHANY

Lections for the Epiphany
of the Lord

Old Testament: Isaiah 60:1-6

*T*HERE are two central themes in this passage: the glory of God and the call to Jerusalem to rise and reflect the brightness of that glory. The poem begins, "Arise, shine," a call to become light in response to the light of God shed abroad in the world. This is an eschatological (future-looking) moment, a fulfillment of God's purposes. It begins with light, just as in the beginning of time when God said, "Let there be light."

The bitterness of defeat at the hands of Babylon and the despair that settled over both the exiles and those who were left behind in Jerusalem made it seem as if total darkness covered the earth. In this darkness, the prophecy of the light of God shining on Jerusalem seemed even more brilliant and intense. Out of a moral and spiritual darkness came a brilliant new vision, like a spotlight shining on one small part of a darkened theater. The nations would be attracted to this light and come to Jerusalem. What a sad contrast this is to today, when this city is the scene of continuing conflict and violence!

Think About It: God's light always shines in the darkness. When have you had dark times in your life? What were those times like? What dark spots exist in our world right now? What gives us hope in the midst of such darkness, whether personal or global? What is our greatest source of joy? What message of light does God have for us as we face the darkness?

One of the continuing themes in the later books of the Hebrew Bible is the sense that the world will be attracted by the splendor of God and be drawn to Jerusalem. We are reminded of other passages that speak of God's people being a light to the nations, or Jesus saying, "You are the light of the world. A city built on a hill cannot be hid" (Matthew 5:14).

52

Take a Look

Verses 4-6 begin with the command to "look around." The image is of a mother who sees her children coming home, just as mothers today look for the arrival of children for Christmas or other important occasions. The mother is radiant with joy and anticipation over the return of the children. When you consider that the time span here is much more than the span between one Christmas and the next, that mother Jerusalem had not seen her children for nearly sixty years, imagine her joy at seeing them coming home!

With the returning multitudes came wealth. This wealth of the nations pouring into Jerusalem was another common image for the glory of the coming reign of God. In that time, the wealth began with the "abundance of the sea"—the great maritime trade. We know from both history and archaeology that the Phoenicians particularly had far-flung trading routes, carrying goods from Egypt and northern Africa as far as Spain and (probably) the British Isles, and then transferring them to caravans to trade with the great empires of Mesopotamia. In verse 6, we see a reference to wealth coming in camel caravans from the great mythic sources of wealth in the Arabian peninsula.

The glory of God was reflected in these riches coming to Jerusalem; even the camels seemed to come willingly (a miracle, given the nature of camels), carrying gold and incense for the throne and the altar. And the flocks are not driven by shepherds, but almost seem to run voluntarily to the altar to be sacrificed. This is truly an eschatological vision!

Psalter: Psalm 72:1-7, 10-14

This was a prayer for the king and a reminder of his duty to the poor and oppressed. The responsibility of government (then embodied in the king) is to administer justice, care for the poor and needy, and overthrow the oppressor.

Justice and righteousness are signs of the reign of God and should be reflected in the life and reign of any leader of God's people. We see the call for justice repeatedly in the prophets; here we find it also in the book that was Israel's hymnal or prayer book. A regular part of worship is the reminder that God calls for justice and concern for the poor on the part of God's people, especially their leaders.

Notice how the message unfolds. Where there is justice and righteousness, one finds *shalom* (peace, harmony, well-being, and fulfillment for all). Verses 2-7 and 12-14 stress that *shalom* depends on how the poor are treated. The *only* responsibility of the king named in this psalm is to bring justice to the oppressed and to care for the needy, whose "blood" is "precious . . . in his sight." This God expects of all governments, including our own.

53

Epistle: Ephesians 3:1-12

A fascinating feature of Pauline literature is the "bunny trail," a digression of thought. Some of Paul's most important ideas are in these diversions. Ephesians 3:2-13 is one long bunny trail, with the idea in verse 1 not picked up again until verse 14.

God Has a Secret

God had a long-time secret that now has been made known—the Gentiles are also heirs to the promise! They are members of the same body of Christ as are Jewish believers. The barriers are down. God's grace is now seen to be for all humanity.

One of the basic human sins is contempt for persons different from ourselves. Our language expresses "us" versus "them," with a clear contempt for "them." So there were in the ancient world Jews and Gentiles, Greeks and barbarians. Many peoples even today have a name for themselves that means "human beings" or "people," implying that all others are subhuman. In our day, there has been a division between communist and noncommunist; other barriers exist between races, nations, classes, genders, and sexual orientations. Whoever is different is treated with contempt, and so we reassure ourselves that we are important or better.

There Is Power Here

The great power in the Christian message is this: We are all included in God's love. God loves those sinners whom we judge inferior, just as much as ourselves, who sin by discriminating against others. Paul, who calls himself among the "least," delivers this important message.

> **Think About It:** Our society still holds to an "us against them" mentality. Whom do we judge inferior? Does anyone hold you in contempt? Is this attitude justified? How does this message in Ephesians hold both judgment and hope for this situation? God's purpose is that all peoples are one in Christ, that no difference can separate those whom God brings together. God's grace reaches everywhere—into all the dark places of hatred, contempt, and false superiority that give rise to the "isms," prejudices, and phobias of all time.

In Christ there is a free approach to God, no matter where we find ourselves. We cannot draw closer to God without drawing closer to one another. This is true spatially, but also in terms of attitude and openness to those who are different. Just as in Isaiah's vision all peoples are drawn to God's altar, so does Ephesians proclaim that "through the gospel [groups heretofore divided are now] members together of one body, and sharers together in the promise in Christ Jesus" (3:6, NIV).

Gospel: Matthew 2:1-12

In the story of the Epiphany (meaning "manifestation" or "appearance," and referring specifically to God's self-revelation in Christ), Matthew gives Jesus' life a geographical and historical setting. He came into a real world, where Herod was the king.

The Magi

In this world, the magi came from the East and asked, "Where was the king born?"—a key question for Matthew. The magi were following a star and did not really need to ask for guidance. But Matthew knew that Jesus came from Nazareth and Scripture says the Messiah would be born in Bethlehem. This story is important because it says he *was born* in Bethlehem. The words *born king* mean the "king by right," born of the royal line, the legitimate heir of David. On another level, it also refers to the one who would rule in a heavenly realm.

The magi were Persian or Babylonian priests, experts in astrology and dream interpretation. They studied the stars and believed that the appearance of a new star meant the birth of a king. They were pagans (non-Jews) who had followed the bright light of that star on the long journey across the desert.

King Herod

Herod (verses 3-8) was "king by might," a half-Jewish usurper who had conquered his own people with the Romans' help and now ruled as a Roman puppet. He was not popular and lived in constant fear of rebellion and assassination. So Matthew is describing a clash between two claims to being king. Herod had the power and office, but Jesus was *born* to be king. This bothered Herod; and when Herod was bothered, so was all Jerusalem. It was not safe to be around Herod when he was in one of his paranoid moods. (Review last week's lesson for a more lengthy description of Herod.)

The religious leaders helped the magi by interpreting the Scriptures for them. They pointed out that Scripture (Micah 5:2 and 2 Samuel 5:2) said the Messiah would be born of David's line, in Bethlehem of Judea, the city of David. The magi followed their own light, but Scripture added to the light they had. The magi came asking "where?" in a sense of wonder and excitement. Now Herod asked "where?" with fear and murder in his heart.

Follow the Star

The magi followed the star to Bethlehem, where they found Jesus and offered him precious gifts. Gold was appropriate for giving to a king. Frankincense

> *Think About It:* Jesus was king by right, the answer to God's promise. Where do we look for ultimate truth today? What form does asking "where" about Jesus take today? What does it mean to seek Jesus? What convinces us to make him Lord of our lives?

and myrrh were rare and incredibly expensive aromatic gums. We need not speculate about any symbolic meaning of the gifts to know they were extremely valuable and fit for a king.

What Matthew Means

For Matthew, Jesus was the fulfillment of God's promise to Israel. He frequently added the line, "This was spoken by the prophet. . . ." The elaborate genealogy in Chapter 1, which traces Jesus' ancestry back to David and Abraham, is a way of showing how Jesus fulfilled God's promises. Matthew's story of these pagan priests demonstrates that Jesus was also the fulfillment of all human longing for salvation and peace.

Jewish tradition expected a procession of the nations to Jerusalem to worship YHWH, a prophecy noted in Isaiah 60. Matthew wrote to a Jewish audience. Without actually saying specifically that Jesus was the Messiah, Matthew nevertheless pointed out that in the visit of the magi, the nations were already beginning to come.

Study Suggestions

A. Reflect on a Christmas Hymn

Sing the "Gloria in Excelsis Deo" (or the entire hymn, "Angels We Have Heard on High"). Remind the group of the hymn and what the words mean. Invite them to stand and use their bodies to create movements or gestures to represent the moods of glory, joy, and praise expressed in the hymn.

B. Explore "Glory" in Isaiah

Read Isaiah 60:1-6 and explain the historical context of the passage. Ask: What are some images or metaphors in this passage that suggest God's glory and call forth attitudes of joy and praise? What is the significance of the nations streaming to Jerusalem, bringing their wealth with them? What does this say about God's glory? What does it suggest about the way God's glory reaches the Gentiles? Is this an image of power, worship, or service? What did it mean to the Jews in exile to say, "Arise, shine; for your light has come"? What does it mean for us today?

C. Get in on God's Secret

Read aloud Ephesians 3:1-12, and summarize the background and interpretation on page 54. Discuss: What is God's mystery or secret mentioned here? What is the human sin to which God's secret is opposed? How is it manifested? How does God's secret overcome that sin? If we took God's secret seriously, what might we have to change as individuals, and as a church—either our local church or our denomination? How is God's glory revealed in this passage? How does this differ from the way Isaiah expresses it? What does this passage call us to do? Be specific in identifying present-day divisions in the church and the human community that God's grace can heal and that God's people must strive to overcome.

D. Look at Kings (and Queens)

This is still another way of looking at the glory of God. Read Psalm 72:1-7, 10-14, and the accompanying commentary. Ask these questions: What is the chief duty of a king or national leader? What does this suggest about the role and responsibility of government, particularly in a society like ours that often invokes the Bible to justify political positions? If we took this seriously, what would be the chief aim of government, and what priorities would it adopt? (Consider areas like immigration, social welfare, criminal justice and prisons, housing, and the minimum wage.) What can Christians do to influence the policies of our government in this regard?

Then read Matthew 2:1-12. Ask group members what they recall about the description of Herod from this lesson and the previous one. There are two kinds of kings mentioned in Matthew: a king by might and a king by right. In this story, which is which? What is the importance of being "born king"? What makes a person a "leader by right" today? Can you give examples of both kinds of leaders in today's world?

E. Tie It Together

All four lections talk about the glory of God and how it is revealed. Ask: What is *glory* and how is it revealed in each lection? (Some synonyms for glory are brightness, splendor, eminence, radiance, and holy presence.) What does each passage suggest about the way we are expected to live?

All four passages also talk about how the message of God's glory reaches the outsider. Discuss: How is this described in each passage? What does this suggest about the way we live? How do these lections speak to you about your discipleship? What do these lections call you to do or to be?

F. Celebrate God's Glory

Read responsively Psalm 72:1-7, 10-14, a hymn about God's glory and message to the nations. Close with prayer for all religious and political leaders, that they may be faithful to God's standards of justice and righteousness.

Lections for Baptism of the Lord
(First Sunday After the Epiphany)

Old Testament: Isaiah 42:1-9

*T*HIS lection is one of the four servant songs found in Isaiah 40-55. The songs describe one who is called by God, who suffers for the sake of loyalty to God, and who is a "light to the nations." In the language of the royal court of Isaiah's day, the servant was an official of the king who announced the king's judicial decisions to be sure the will of the king was understood. Most Bible scholars believe that the servant is a personification of Israel, the people of God, rather than a particular person. But Christian interpreters also see here a reference to Jesus and his ministry. In this song, the servant's task is to live out God's commitment to justice.

Here Is True Religion

Justice (mish'pat) is a key term in the Hebrew Scriptures, meaning either "true religion" or "justice." Hebrew tradition suggests that justice *is* true religion: caring for the poor, the dispossessed, the oppressed, and the resident alien.

Think About It: Working for justice brings glory to God. To what is God calling you? Is justice for the poor and oppressed a call from God to which you can respond? What needs to be done for justice in your community? Where might you begin?

This idea was first expressed in the Torah (first five books of the Hebrew Bible), for example in the Holiness Code of Leviticus 19. Just so, the servant is called to bring justice to those who do not have the power to bring about justice for themselves. The Spirit empowers the servant with the strength and will for that purpose.

Servants work quietly and patiently. They do not impose a way of life on anyone; rather they demonstrate what it

58

should be. They do not fail or become discouraged because they are called and sustained by God. There is strength, encouragement, and the ability to pick up and begin over, because they know that God is with them. Even though the sum of their work may seem discouraging, they do not give up because they know that God will see them through and will ultimately bring about the justice for which they work. Part of the servant's task is to support and encourage those who are in despair (in contrast to current practice that blames the poor for their plight).

God Acts to Save

In verses 5-9, the prophet lifts up God's saving acts in creation. God gives light and life and breath—this is the first act of salvation. In response to God's act, Israel is called to be a light to the nations, a "covenant to the people," to all humanity. The covenant is both a gift of grace and a call to ministry and mission. God's gracious purpose is that Israel bring justice to all the nations, to be the light of hope and meaning and justice that shines in the world's darkness. Specifically, God's people are called to open the eyes of the blind to help humanity see God's light and truth and to bring out the prisoners. This could be a reference to the exiles in Babylon, but can also refer to the redemption of all who are confined in prisons of oppression, poverty, superstition, ignorance, or fear.

The call is authenticated by the Lord's own name. YHWH is the God of the ancestors, of Abraham and Sarah, Jacob and Rachel, Moses and Miriam. Israel is to worship YHWH alone; they are not to give glory to other gods. Coming full circle, one way to give glory to YHWH is to work for justice for the entire creation, including all peoples.

Psalter: Psalm 29

This is one of the oldest psalms, perhaps a recasting of an ancient hymn to the Canaanites' weather and fertility god, Baal. It begins with a vision of the heavenly council, in which all the angelic beings are invited to acknowledge YHWH as king. The psalm reflects a time when Israel believed there were many gods, including those worshiped by neighboring nations, but that YHWH was the supreme and only god who mattered. "Worship" and "give glory" both mean "bow down," that is, to acknowledge YHWH alone as God.

Verses 3-9 describe a powerful storm blowing in off the Mediterranean. The voice of YHWH (thunder) is mentioned seven times—a way of proclaiming that God's power is absolute. The poem is probably a polemic (attack) against Baal, and the message is: "You just think Baal is powerful. It is really YHWH who rules the forces of nature!"

God's reign has profound implications for justice, specifically economic and ecological justice. Creation exists to glorify God. When we act as if it exists solely for our benefit, then pollution of air and water, hazardous waste, death of species, and depletion of the ozone layer are some of the results.

Epistle: Acts 10:34-43

This passage comes in the middle of the story of Peter and Cornelius, which begins with Cornelius's vision of God telling him to send for Peter. Cornelius was a Roman officer, a Gentile, a part of the army of occupation— and therefore Peter's oppressor and enemy. At the same time, Peter had a vision telling him not to count anything unclean that God had declared clean, even if it seemed to violate the law. When messengers came from Cornelius, Peter sensed they were bringing God's call to him. The oppressed are to minister to the oppressor. Peter, not Paul, went to the Gentiles first.

Ministry to All

When Peter arrived and heard about Cornelius's experience of God, he responded that "God does not show favoritism" (verse 34, NIV). Because God's plan is the salvation of all humankind, Jews and Gentiles are equal in God's eyes. Peter then told the story of Jesus' life and ministry, which he had witnessed in person. The climax was the injustice done to Jesus by crucifying him and God's amazing power in raising him from the dead— which Peter had also witnessed.

> **Think About It:** God declares "clean" those whom we would find "unclean." Whom in our society would we willingly exclude from the church? What does Peter's experience say to us about excluding anyone?

Finally, Peter said, the promises of God are fulfilled in the forgiveness of sins and the giving of the Spirit. Early in the history of the church, probably by the time Acts was written, it was believed that the gifts of forgiveness and the Spirit were given in baptism. With Cornelius, the gift of the Spirit came first, as a sign that Peter should not deny baptism and fellowship to these Gentiles. Others may experience forgiveness first and then seek baptism. But for all, both are necessary. God works in perfect freedom, not bound by any human understanding. And God continues to push the church beyond the boundaries of its own comfort, to reach out to others and to become a light to the nations.

Peter's Synopsis of the Gospel

In just a few sentences, Peter shared the essence of the gospel with Cornelius and his household. His synopsis included key Lukan themes, such as the presence of the Holy Spirit; the apostolic witness to Jesus' life, ministry, death, and resurrection; and the fulfillment of prophecy. No doubt Peter elaborated (see 10:44), but first he painted the whole picture in concise summary.

Gospel: Matthew 3:13-17

That John baptized Jesus is one of the most solid facts in the Gospels. It is likely that, for a time, Jesus was John's disciple, since baptism implied becoming a follower. (The words "after me" in 3:11 refer to discipleship, not chronology.) This was a source of embarrassment for the early church, because they knew Jesus was more important than John. Matthew reflects that embarrassment by saying that John did not want to baptize Jesus, who was more important than he, and did so only because Jesus insisted.

Ancient Baptism
Baptism was not new; Jews already practiced various models of ritual cleansing. Pools and cisterns used in ritual washings have been identified in both public places, such as the Temple, and communities such as Qumran, along the Dead Sea.

The difference in John's baptism was eschatological. That is, it had implications for the coming reign of God and the place of repentant persons baptized into it. It sealed converts from the judgment to come. The "brood of vipers" (3:7) would be destroyed in the wrath of judgment like snakes in a fire, but the righteous would be saved.

Fulfilling Righteousness
Jesus insisted that he be baptized "to fulfill all righteousness." *Righteousness* here means "the will of God"; *fulfilling righteousness* means, therefore, "doing God's will." Jesus' baptism was carrying out God's will. This helps deal with the question: Since Jesus was sinless, why was Jesus baptized if John's baptism was for forgiveness of sins? The issue for Matthew was not about Jesus' sinning or not sinning. In fact, John's protest provides a way for Matthew to say: "This is not about forgiveness of sins," but about "fulfilling righteousness," that is, fulfilling God's will.

The Gifts of God
The heavens opened, a voice expressed approval of Jesus, and the Spirit descended in the form of a dove. These were all gifts of God—and signs that identified Jesus as God's Son. In the days of the second Temple (Jesus' era), Jews believed that these gifts would all appear in the days of the Messiah. So, Matthew is saying, here is the Messiah. The dove may also symbolize new creation in Jesus. Remember that the Spirit brooded over the waters of creation (Genesis 1) like a bird brooding over her eggs to bring forth life. So the new creation began with the

Think About It: Jesus submitted to baptism to fulfill the will of God for his mission and ministry. What does your baptism mean to you? How do you see it as God's call to mission and service?

dove/Spirit brooding over the baptism and bringing forth new life through Jesus.

The heavenly voice spoke in the words of Scripture, a combination of Psalm 2:7 and Isaiah 42:1. These words made Jesus' identity public: this is the Son of God. The age of Messiah had begun! The fulfilling of righteousness, submitting to God's will in baptism, was something done by God's own Son. The baptism was a sign of obedience to God, not of sin or weakness. Rather, Jesus was strong enough to be obedient precisely because he was the Son. Because Jesus was confident in his own identity and relationship to God, he could take on the attitude of weakness and obedience for the sake of the world.

Jesus' Baptism and Ours

There are important parallels between Jesus' baptism and Christian baptism. Jesus was obedient in receiving baptism, and so are we. Jesus received the gift of the Spirit in baptism, and so do we. Jesus was declared Son of God when he was baptized; in our baptism we are declared to be children of God, born anew through water and the Spirit. Jesus' baptism was the beginning of his call and struggle for faithful obedience in mission and service; our baptism is our call to ministry through the church to the world.

Study Suggestions

A. Pray Together

Examine the baptism liturgy in your hymnal or worship book and pray together the thanksgiving prayer for the water. Sing the baptism hymn, "When Jesus Came to Jordan to Be Baptized by John." This prayer and hymn remind us of God's mighty acts in history and in our lives.

B. Think About Baptism

Two of today's lections deal with baptism. Read Matthew 3:13-17 and the commentary on pages 61–62. Ask: What did Jesus' baptism mean to him and to John? What does it mean for us? What does our baptism mean? How can it have meaning, even if we don't remember it? What did it mean that the Spirit descended on Jesus?

Read aloud Acts 10:34-43 and review the exposition. Note that, in the verses immediately following this passage, the Spirit descended on Cornelius and his family, and Peter baptized them. Ask: What did that mean? What does it mean that we are baptized "by water and the Spirit," as the ritual says? How do we see the Holy Spirit acting in our lives?

C. Examine Notions of Partiality

The Acts passage begins with Peter's revised understanding about God's partiality (or lack of partiality). Peter began his prayer time with one notion that some persons were more valuable to God than others and came away with quite a different understanding. (See Acts 10:9-16.) His visit to Cornelius substantiated this change of heart.

Invite participants, in pairs, to recall their earliest prejudice or misjudgment of some person or group. Ask them to consider what their impression was, where it came from, and what made them change their minds (if they did). Be sure each person gets a turn, but do not insist that pairs discuss this with the whole group unless they wish to. As a group, consider how an understanding of God's inclusiveness influences your notions of partiality, exclusivity, or prejudice.

D. Consider Isaiah's Call for Justice

Read aloud Isaiah 42:1-9 and consider the commentary. Ask: What do you think of the identification of the servant with Israel? with Jesus? By extension, we can identify the servant with the church, which means we have the same calling to bring forth justice. How does that feel? Do you agree that "true religion is justice"? Why or why not? What are some ways we can practice justice? in the life of the congregation? (Note that there is a difference between giving food and clothing to the poor and working with them to confront the causes of poverty.) What are some ways we can work with the poor for justice in our community? nation? world?

E. Think About Justice and God's Glory

Psalm 29 is about God's glory revealed in a great storm. Read the psalm and the commentary on it. Ask: What is the relationship between God's glory, God's rule, and our care for creation? What are the practical implications for the ecology and the economy of God's glory in creation? What can we do in small ways (like car-pooling, recycling, avoiding styrofoam) to work for justice in the economic and ecological spheres?

F. Summarize

One theme in today's readings is that the God of justice is the God of all. Ask: If we take this idea seriously, what are we called to do or to be? What impact will that call to justice have on our understanding and treatment of others?

G. Celebrate God's Gifts

Invite class members to close their eyes and listen carefully. Then read, slowly and with feeling, Psalm 29. After they open their eyes, ask: What images did you see? What insights did you get into God's power and glory and God's blessings on people? Distribute paper and crayons and invite persons to express in pictures their feelings in response to this psalm.

Lections for Second Sunday After the Epiphany

Old Testament: Isaiah 49:1-7

*T*HIS lection is another servant song, in which the servant is again identified with Israel—and, by extension, with the church, God's people in every time and place.

The Servant Called

In verses 1-3, the servant addresses the nations with a profound description of his own call to mission and ministry. The Lord called him; in fact, God named him in the womb—for service. In biblical thought, a name says something significant about the nature and character of a person. The name referred to in verse 1 was probably either "Israel" or "servant."

One is also known by the words one speaks, and the servant is chosen to speak the word of God. The poet uses military imagery to describe the force of God's word. It is like a sword with tremendous cutting power. It is like an arrow that drives home to the mark. Finally, he says, God "hid" him, protected him in secret (like a sword in its sheath or arrows in a quiver), until the time came for his service to begin.

> **Think About It:** "One is known by the words one speaks." How are you known? Do your words honor God?

The Servant Honored

Because his calling and mission are so important, the servant feels himself to be a failure. He has not lived up to all the expectations God had for him, and his ministry seems to be in vain. When he looks at his lack of success, he feels he has given everything he has—and all, he thinks, has been for nothing.

The servant's experience transcends time. Here, as well as often in the psalms, what begins as a lament turns to praise and confidence. Even though he seems to the world to be a failure, through the eyes of faith he sees his life completely under the rule and guidance of God. This is all the assurance of success he needs.

> **Think About It:** The servant despairs over his apparent failure, yet he finds ultimate reward in God. How do you measure success? When things go badly for you, are you able to find strength and confidence in your relationship with God? How much of your life and feelings about your own worth are tied up with the way the world measures success?

The Servant a Light to the Nations

Verses 5-6 lift up a theme we see many times in Scripture. When people feel like failures and complain that tasks are too much for them, God gives them more to do. Here, God says, "I've decided it isn't enough for you to bring Israel back to me. Be a light to all the other nations also." God's will is that salvation should reach to the ends of the earth, not just to one people. This message hearkens back to the covenant made with Abraham long before, that all people will be blessed because of him. This descendant of Abraham will bring the light of God's love to all people on earth. (Is it any wonder that the Christian church reads this passage and thinks of Jesus?)

The Nations Pay Homage

In verse 7 we see another familiar theme: all the world will come and pay homage to God and to the despised servant, Israel. God is the Redeemer and the Holy One. God's holiness is revealed negatively in judgment and positively in redemption. As a result, the representatives of the nations will come to God's holy altar and honor the servant for the sake of God. This prophecy was fulfilled in Jesus, the servant Messiah. The task of carrying out this mission is given to his followers.

Psalter: Psalm 40:1-11

The psalmist waited patiently for God, and that waiting was not in vain. God heard his cry and saved him, setting him on a solid foundation for his life. The one who trusts in God is blessed (fulfilled). True satisfaction does not come from success, or wealth, or anything except depending on God and doing God's will. Such is the firm foundation.

Verses 9-10 describe the psalmist's public witness to God's salvation. In response to God's grace and faithfulness, he spreads the word. He does not keep his experience of God a secret, but instead proclaims it to the congregation. The words *faithfulness, salvation,* and *steadfast love* all speak of

God's covenant love and saving works. They also declare God's call to be faithful in response to God's love. Steadfast love means not only loving God, but also loving all God's children and serving their needs.

Epistle: 1 Corinthians 1:1-9

The Corinthians were Paul's most frustrating church. Corinth was a Roman military colony and one of the most cosmopolitan, free-swinging cities of the Empire. The church there faced all kinds of theological and ethical problems and carried on a lively correspondence with Paul about them. In this and the next two lections we get a glimpse of what life there was like—and how people dealt with issues still pertinent for us today.

Who Is the Church?

Paul wrote to "the church of God that is in Corinth." There is only one church of Jesus Christ, but it is located in many places. This location was in Corinth, the "sin city" of the Roman world. Paul wrote to "those who are sanctified in Christ Jesus, called to be saints." All in the church are sanctified by Jesus Christ and called to be saints, in other words, set apart for service to Christ and commissioned to be a part of the church.

The New Testament knew nothing about belonging to a church by voluntary association. We think we make a decision about joining the church. The New Testament says God calls us to be in the church. To be sanctified is to receive the gift of God's love and allow it to grow in our lives and be expressed in ministry and mission.

What Is the Church?

Paul followed the traditional form of a letter. After the greeting and blessing, he gave thanks for his readers. Here, however, the thanksgiving may be ironic. Paul's hope for strength and blamelessness for the Corinthians may be another indicator of the concerns he would soon share. Paul gave thanks for the very gifts he would later criticize—eloquence, knowledge, and tongues. It may be that the Corinthians had boasted about these gifts when they wrote to Paul, so he responded to what they said. Verses 4-7 may need to be read tongue-in-cheek. What was certain, though, was that, whatever gifts the Corinthians had, they were signs of the grace of Jesus Christ and not cause for personal aggrandizement or undue pride.

> **Think About It:** We are called to be the church, not as volunteers, but by virtue of our life in Christ. Why are you in the church? Because you joined or because God called you? To what did God call you? What gifts did God give you for living out that call? What does "salvation by faith" mean to you? Is it something that depends on your faith or on the faithfulness of God?

66

God and the Church

The God who calls the church is faithful. The implication is that the God who calls is also the one who sustains us. We can depend on the One who calls. "Salvation by faith" is really salvation by the *faithfulness* of God.

Gospel: John 1:29-42

This passage is a series of testimonies about who Jesus is and what it means to be a disciple.

John the Baptist

In verses 29-34, John the Baptist makes three statements about Jesus. First (verse 29), he says that Jesus is the "Lamb of God who takes away the sin of the world!" Several Old Testament images help us understand this phrase. The Passover lamb (Exodus 12:1-13) was a sign of God's love and faithfulness. The lamb was killed and the blood smeared on doorposts as a sign that Israelites lived in this house, so they would be saved from death. As the story goes, when YHWH passed through Egypt to take the firstborn animals and human beings, the Hebrews who displayed the blood were "passed over" and spared destruction.

The Suffering Servant was described as a "lamb that is led to the slaughter" (Isaiah 53:7). This song from Isaiah has long been used by the church to describe Jesus. Jesus' willingness to be put to death by the enemies of God's love and justice reveals to all the extent to which God will go to show us his reconciling love. Taking away sin gives us freedom to live and to enter fully into fellowship with God.

Second, John refers to Jesus as Son of God (John 1:34). In the Hebrew Bible, "Son of God" describes the king as one faithful to God's will. It is also a reference to the messianic king. In John's Gospel, the Son of God is one who reveals God's loving nature. This title also explains what John the Baptist meant when he said that Jesus ranks ahead of him, because "he was before me."

Third, John said that Jesus would baptize with the Holy Spirit and that the one on whom the Spirit descended would be the one to redeem Israel. John testified that Jesus was this one. Because John the Baptist was probably the greatest man in Palestine in his day, his word carried great weight with all who heard him.

Jesus' First Disciples

John's Gospel says that Jesus' first disciples had been disciples of John. John pointed them to Jesus and "gave them up." One of these was Andrew, a Galilean fisherman, who had been following John in Judea. After talking with Jesus, he went to find his brother Simon and brought him to Jesus. How did he do that? By saying, "We have found the messiah." What a witness!

Jesus immediately gave Simon a new name, Cephas (Aramaic *kepha*), which is also translated Peter (Greek *petros*). Remember that in Hebrew thought, a name said something significant about one's character. A name change signified an important shift in one's essential nature. So, this change was not just a matter of convenience, but a sign of conversion. Simon was changed and received a new name. *Kepha* and *petros* both mean "rock"—sturdy, tough, dependable.

> **Think About It:** John testified to three significant roles of Jesus. Who do you say Jesus is? What is your witness to him? Do you introduce people to Jesus? Does the church want persons to "join the church" or to "join Jesus," the head of the church? If Jesus were to change your name as a result of your conversion, what would it be?

Andrew's Gift

Several times in John's Gospel, Andrew appears bringing people to Jesus. That seems to be Andrew's gift and calling. What a wonderful model of discipleship, to introduce people to Jesus—to bring them together and then stand back and let the relationship develop. Is this something you could be doing?

Study Suggestions

A. Reflect on Calls

Two of our lections are about God's calls. Read aloud Isaiah 49:1-7 and 1 Corinthians 1:1-9, and review the commentaries. Ask: Who is called to what in these two passages? What does it mean to be called by God? Are you aware that God calls you? If the servant mentioned by Isaiah really stands for Israel and, by extension, the church, are you called to the same ministry as the servant? How do you feel about that? Is it enough simply to say that God calls us into the church? Or does God call us to mission in our baptism? Is that convincing enough for us? What more do we want?

Consider inviting the pastor or another church professional to talk with the group about her or his call to ministry and then respond to questions about what a call means and how one recognizes a call. Also explore the similarities and differences between the call of all Christians to ministry and the call to specialized forms of service.

B. Consider God's Faithfulness

Regarding Isaiah 49:1-7, ask: What are our standards of success? How do we know when we are successful? Can we consider our relationship with a faithful God as success enough? Is faithfulness in the face of apparent failure really a success? Is that enough? Why or why not?

With reference to 1 Corinthians 1:1-9, identify the gifts for which Paul first praises the Corinthians (and later criticizes them). Discuss: Does the situation in Corinth sound like any place we have been? What does Paul say to the Corinthian church about success and faithfulness? Does the God who calls us also sustain us? How do we know? We talk about "salvation by faith" as if it somehow had to do with our faith. What difference does it make in our understanding if we talk about "salvation by the faithfulness of God"?

Read Psalm 40:1-8 and the commentary on pages 65–66. Ask: How does the situation of the psalmist reflect an understanding of God's faithfulness? How are we called to respond to God's grace and steadfast love?

C. Think About Witness

Read Psalm 40:9-11 and John 1:29-42. Ask: What is the witness of the psalmist? How does he witness? What is the witness of John the Baptist? How does he express his witness? Finally, what is the witness of Andrew, and how does he express it? How do you respond to each of these testimonies? Which would be easiest for you to share with others? Which would be difficult? Why? (Draw on the background information on pages 65–66 and 67–68.)

Witness sometimes has a bad connotation. Talk about why this may be so and whether these reasons are justified. Ask: Is wearing a gospel T-shirt or a WWJD (What Would Jesus Do?) bracelet a sufficient or effective witness? Or is it important actually to tell people who Jesus is and what he means in our lives? How do we witness in our lives? What about Andrew introducing people to Jesus? When was the last time you introduced someone to Jesus?

D. Summarize

This session's major theme is faithfulness, both God's faithfulness to us and our faithfulness to God and to our call. Consider: If I take to heart my call to ministry, not as a volunteer but because of my inclusion into the church of Christ, what will I have to change? How will I be different? What is God's claim on me? Am I open to it fully?

E. Celebrate God's Faithfulness

Read Psalm 40:1-11 responsively, reflecting on God's faithfulness in the relationship with the psalmist and the power of the psalmist's witness. Sing, "If Thou But Suffer God to Guide Thee." Close with a prayer for strength, and for help in not being "lacking in any spiritual gift."

Lections for Third Sunday After
the Epiphany

Old Testament: Isaiah 9:1-4

*W*HEN kings were crowned in Israel, poems were written for their coronation. This is one of those poems. A new king had come to the throne after defeating a foreign enemy, bringing in a time of peace and national security. But the question is: Is the poem written for a king of that time, or is it a reference to an ideal king, somewhere in the future? Or could it have a dual purpose?

Hail to the King

There is no reason to doubt that this king is a real king, an "anointed one." The word for *anointed* in Hebrew is the word we transliterate "messiah." The king is born, figuratively speaking, on the day of his anointing as king. It is a new life for him. He is no longer just an ordinary man but the chosen and anointed son of YHWH. Think of the hopes we invest in the inauguration of a new president. That's how Israel felt about the new king. Of course, their hopes were often disappointed, just as are ours. But, if this new king were actually Hezekiah, then Israel's hopes were to be fulfilled to a great degree.

The Power of Words

Many of us remember thrilling to the words spoken by John F. Kennedy at his inauguration: "My fellow Americans: ask not what your country can do for you—ask what you can do for your country." Or

> **Think About It:** We are often disappointed by our leaders; but if God is our ruler there is great joy for the nation. Do you regard God as your ruler? as leader of our nation? If so, does this thought bring joy to you? to the nation? How would the lives and priorities of our nation and its citizens be changed if we truly thought of God as our leader and put God first?

we remember Dr. Martin Luther King, Jr., saying over and over, "I have a dream." Those words have power far beyond the lives of the men who spoke them, and far beyond the situation in which they were spoken. So it is with the words of Isaiah: part of the joy is that the king had defeated a foreign oppressor and forced him out. The yoke of the occupation and the rod of the oppressors have been lifted; the nation could rejoice at last.

The Anointed One

And so, on his anointing, the child "born for us" is named. The names for the wonder child, who is also the anointed king, are words of joy and hope that never lose their power to thrill and command (9:6). We no longer are excited about King Hezekiah, but we still thrill to the titles, whether we hear them read in Scripture or sung in Handel's *Messiah*. The words ascribed to an ancient king are fulfilled in Jesus!

We Add Meaning to the Poem

For Isaiah, the thrust of the poem was rejoicing and hope over the coronation of the new king, probably Hezekiah. But Christians, almost from the beginning, have also seized on these words as a message about Jesus, the anointed Messiah of the line of David. These words evoke in us the expectation and hope for the coming of Christ. We place on Jesus the joy and anticipation of this passage and thus give it a new layer of meaning. This is a legitimate way for Christians to interpret the text. But we also need to remember its original meaning—which does not detract from our Christian understanding, but actually enriches it.

Psalter: Psalm 27:1, 4-9

We often hear this psalm at funerals and find comfort in its reminder to have faith in the face of fear. Fear, after all, is the opposite of faith. This is important: doubt is *not* the opposite of faith. That would make faith a matter of ideas and logic. No, doubt and questions are expressions of a searching, growing faith. Fear, falling away from relationship with God, is the sign of a lack of faith.

Many have said that the widespread anxiety of our time is the most serious sign of our loss of faith, because it means we have no awareness of the power of God in our lives. The psalmist, on the other hand, was confident of his relationship with God. He had been fearful, but his faith had overcome his fear. How did that happen? He focused on his relationship with God. With his eyes and heart fixed on God, he no longer had room for fear.

Epistle: 1 Corinthians 1:10-18

Paul was dealing here with a familiar problem—factions in the church. There was no common mind among the Corinthians, only divisions. The issue on which they were split was personal. They may have had some different understandings of the faith, but the big problem was allegiance to different individuals.

Who Is Your Favorite Preacher?

There were three great missionaries (Apollos, Paul, and Peter) associated with the Corinthian church; and the members had taken sides, depending on their favorite preacher. "I belong to Paul." "Well, big deal, I belong to Peter, and he's more important." There was even one faction that claimed to be above all the petty strife: "I belong to Christ." Sounds like a spat in our churches over the preacher who just left and his or her style of ministry, or how we really prefer the pastor who was here fifteen years ago. It is that kind of factionalism that Paul is arguing against.

Chloe, Apollos, and Cephas

We can only speculate about some of the people mentioned. Chloe's people obviously had Paul's ear. They were the ones who reported to him about the quarreling (verse 11). Otherwise, we don't know who they were. Apollos, mentioned in Acts 18:24–19:1, was a Jewish Christian from Alexandria, "eloquent" and "well-versed in the scriptures." He was mentored by Priscilla and Aquila and was well received as he traveled and spoke to believers. Cephas was Paul's usual name for Peter, but there is no record that Peter had actually been to Corinth. Perhaps he and his message were revered from afar.

Arguments Against Factions

Why are divisions in the church such a problem? The first reason is that these factions put people in the place of Christ. When we say, "I belong to Peter," we say that Peter is more important than Christ. Second, since Christ cannot be divided, it is a scandal for Christ's *body* to be divided. Paul criticizes everyone who would cause divisions, but especially his own followers. How can one make a human interpreter of Christ more important than Christ himself, particularly when the interpreter himself insists on putting Christ first? That's why he made the ironic comments, "Was Paul crucified for you?" and "Were you baptized in the name of Paul?" "Keep some perspective here," he pleads.

Well, I Did Actually Baptize

Then Paul went off on a "bunny trail" about how, thankfully, he did not baptize at all, since baptism had led to division. Then, he qualifies his state-

72

ment and names those he did baptize. He is not belittling baptism; it is crucial for our relationship with Christ. But, for the most part, he left baptism to others, while he focused on preaching.

Gospel: Matthew 4:12-23

This passage describes the beginning of Jesus' public ministry. John the Baptist had been put to death; and Jesus had withdrawn to Galilee, away from the places in Judea where he and John had worked together.

The Word to Galilee

Jesus withdrew to Galilee, not because he was afraid of Herod Antipas, who had put John to death, but because he had a different vision of the future. There was agitation all over Judea for a king, for someone to avenge John's death. Jesus' vision of the Kingdom was one of nonviolence. He was not interested in revenge, not even for the death of his cousin and friend.

So Jesus settled in Capernaum, on the north coast of the Sea of Galilee. Since the conquest of Israel in 722–721 B.C., Galilee had been associated with Gentiles. The mission to the Gentiles was important to Matthew. He referred to Isaiah 9, which speaks of the king bringing peace to Galilee. For Matthew, this Scripture was enough to justify Galilee, rather than Jerusalem, as the center of Jesus' ministry. Just as in the great song of Isaiah, so in the dawn of the reign of God, there would be light in the spiritual darkness of Galilee.

Jesus' message is a positive one: repent, for God's realm has come near. This is not the negative, "repent, so you won't go to hell," that we often hear. It is a call for a response to God's action. God is making a new world. Get a new sense of direction and purpose and become part of that new world. Repentance is not only about remorse but, more important, about a change of direction.

The contrast of light and darkness is a familiar theme in describing this life direction. Jesus, in fulfillment of the Scriptures, will usher in an age in which the repentant will move toward the realm of light, and away from darkness, the shadow of death. The light had dawned because Jesus had arrived.

Calling Disciples

The call of fishermen to become disciples is significant, because it is the beginning of the church. Jesus took the initiative; he sought out these men in the midst of their work. The call was both a command and a promise. The command was to follow. The promise was to become "fishers of people." This was more than an allusion to the way they made their living.

In many cultures, both Jewish and pagan, "fishing for persons" was a way to talk about the deity's work of salvation and to invite human beings to become part of that saving process. So the promise was about taking part in God's work—the same promise as was offered to those who repented. Thus,

> **Think About It:** Jesus initiates his call to us. How did you come to believe? What was the call that led you to invest your life with Jesus and to believe in his good news? How are you currently living out your discipleship?

this is not just a story about Peter and Andrew, James and John. It is about every person being called to be a disciple. It is about our call through baptism to become Jesus' disciples.

Following Jesus

Peter and his friends were probably middle class. They owned their own boats; they had hired servants. But they left everything to follow Jesus. He issued a powerful appeal that made disciples. And it made a real difference in their lives.

How do we become disciples of Jesus Christ? It is not a great mystery. We simply follow him. We may not learn any great secrets or receive any great light. We do not even know at the outset where we are going; we find that out along the way.

Study Suggestions

A. Explore the Power of Words

Read aloud Isaiah 9:1-6 with passion. Ask: What feelings do these words stir up in you? What memories do they elicit? What is important about these words for us? Then summarize the background on this passage (pages 70–71). Ask: Does knowing this change the way you understand the passage? Does it lessen or heighten the power of the words? Why? What about the section, "We Add Meaning to the Poem"? Do you think this was the way the process of interpretation worked? Or did Isaiah really have Jesus in mind when he wrote the words? What difference does your answer make to your faith?

Play a recording of Handel's great chorus, "For Unto Us a Child Is Born," from the *Messiah*. What feelings, memories, and longings does this music evoke? Invite members to express their feelings through impromptu drawing, movement, or dance.

B. Discuss Factions in the Church

Ask: Who is (was) your favorite preacher or pastor? What did you most like about him or her? Do we normally choose sides over which preacher we like best? What does choosing sides do to the unity and ministry of the church? How can these divisions be overcome? Where should our primary loyalty lie?

Read 1 Corinthians 1:10-18 and the background information on pages 72–73. Discuss: What was the problem with which Paul was dealing? What

74

did he say about it? Why were the ironic statements about Paul being crucified and being baptized in his name so important to the point he was making? Why is it essential that we remember Christ is the center of the church?

C. Explore Fear and Faith

Read aloud Psalm 27:1, 4-9, and consider the background (page 71). Ask: When you heard this text read at funerals, what was your response? How do we experience being hid in God's shelter in time of trouble (verse 5)? Have you ever thought before about how fear, rather than doubt, is the opposite of faith? Do you agree or disagree with this statement? Why?

D. Get on God's Side

Read Matthew 4:12-23 and the background material on pages 73–74. Ask: What was Jesus' message to Galilee? What did he mean by repentance? How is that different from the way we usually understand repentance? What was the heart of his call to the fishermen? How is this different from the way we have usually thought about it? How might we respond to his call to discipleship today?

E. Tie It Together

Two of the common threads that weave through these readings are the contrast between light and darkness and the matter of allegiance. What do the metaphors of light and darkness represent? God acts in human history to combat the forces of darkness and to bring persons to the light. Jesus Christ offers that light. We must decide whose light we will follow: Will we follow a Paul? an Apollos? Or will we follow the Messiah who conquers the darkness?

Ask members to write what for them is darkness (for instance, living with debt, experiencing loss, struggling with obsessions). Then have them consider what form their allegiance to Christ might take that would allow that darkness to be conquered (for instance, surrender of control, the will to overcome, the security to admit to some difficulty, a readiness to trust). Participants need not discuss their writing unless they so desire.

F. Celebrate Being on God's Side

Play "For Unto Us a Child Is Born" from Handel's *Messiah*. Invite silent prayers for all members to be open to the light of Christ. Close by quietly uttering the words: "Jesus said: 'Follow me, and I will make you fish for people.' "

Lections for Fourth Sunday After the Epiphany

Old Testament: Micah 6:1-8

*T*HE setting is a court case, one in which the hills and mountains have been called to serve as the jury. The suit has been brought by God against Israel for breaking the covenant. Israel has complained that God is responsible for all the disasters that are happening. God's point is that if calamity comes as a result of breaking the covenant, then God is not unjust.

God Makes a Case

You can almost hear the hurt and pleading in the opening question of verses 3-5. "What have I [God] done?" Then follows the reminder of God's saving acts in the covenant (verses 4-5). YHWH passed over the houses of the Hebrews (Exodus 12), and they were not only saved from death but also led out of Egypt to freedom. Neither were they left alone in the wilderness. God sent them leaders: Moses, Aaron, and Miriam. Even Balaam's curse turned into a blessing (see Numbers 22–24).

"What happened from Shittim to Gilgal" was the crossing of the Jordan River under the leadership of Joshua after the Hebrews' period of wandering in the wilderness. As in the Exodus event at the Sea of Reeds, the power of God

> **Think About It:** God knows that we know better. Can you remember a time when you knew you had sinned, that things were not right with God, and that it was your fault? What convicted you? How did you feel? What did you do? How did things work out? We call this awareness of sin a sense of guilt. In our time many contend that such guilt is unhealthy because it contributes to low self-esteem. What do you think? When are guilt feelings appropriate and constructive and when inappropriate and harmful?

once again miraculously stopped the flow of the water so the tribes could cross on dry ground. There they celebrated the first Passover in the land of promise (Joshua 3–5).

Presented as a rhetorical question from the Israelites, verse 7 calls to mind human sacrifice. Practiced by the non-Hebrew religions around them, some Israelites during the time of King Ahaz and King Manasseh took on this heinous practice themselves. It was repugnant to God (see 2 Kings 16:3 and 21:6). God knew that the people knew better (Micah 6:8).

Through Micah's prophecy, God called upon the people to remember the stories of God's activity in their past history. *Remember* means more than just "call to mind." It's a matter of identifying with the stories, internalizing them, and living out the promise and the commitment they contain.

The People Reply

Against so clear an argument, there was no excuse. So Israel pleaded: "What can we do to make things right? What does it take to please God?" The examples they raised all had to do with Temple worship. Do we need more sacrifices, even human sacrifices? Because the Passover had saved Israel's firstborn, they belonged to God and believed they had to be redeemed with a payment. Did God now want his own back? Ultimately, the question remains: Can human beings do *anything* that will lead God to accept us?

The Ultimate Answer

God is more interested in the way people live their lives than in ritual. God wants *mish'pat* (justice), *ḥesed* (loving kindness), and *halak* (the walk with God). *Justice* means we work for fairness and equality for all, especially the weak and powerless. *Loving kindness* means grace, compassion, and openness to all persons. *Walking with God* means honoring God in our hearts and putting God first in our lives. It means living the way God wants us to live.

Psalter: Psalm 15

The questions in verse 1 are followed by a series of answers in verses 2-5. The "tent" refers to either the Tabernacle or the Temple. If this is a psalm of David, it is the Tabernacle, the "tent of meeting," since the Temple was not built until after David's death. The questions assume we do not deserve to live in God's presence; we can do so only by God's gracious permission.

The answers in verses 2-5 are not requirements. This is *not* a "do list" (if you want to be able to enter God's presence, this is what you have to "do"). Rather, they speak of how the character of God's people is shaped by the character of God. These people are not sinless, but their lives are in tune with God. They are trying to live faithfully. When they do the right thing, they show God's character to the world. Their relationship with God is expressed in their everyday actions. "[Those who do] these things will never be shaken" (verse 5).

Epistle: 1 Corinthians 1:18-31

These verses continue last week's discussion—church factions. A second problem with factions is that they involve us in differences of interpretation rather than in the word of the cross.

Good News, Bad News

We'll do the bad news (for some) first. Regardless of how highly we may regard wisdom and careful thought, the Christian message is not about these attributes. Rather, it is about the cross—not a piece of wood or a sentimentalized adornment or even a gruesome execution. The cross is the symbol of Christ's suffering. The good news, then, is about how God is saving the world through the crucifixion and resurrection of Jesus.

We might expect that the opposite of foolishness would be wisdom; instead Paul says it is "power" (verse 18). The power of God is *not* measured by the apparent defeat of the cross. And believers are *not* saved by a new wisdom, but by a new power. Wisdom can teach us a lot *about* God, but it cannot bring us into a saving relationship *with* God. We can learn a lot about God without ever knowing God.

Think About It: Human wisdom and power do not carry much weight with God. What is it that God expects from us, whether we are a slave or a merchant, a secretary or a CEO? What kind of life is God calling us to live? What are some examples of wisdom and power in our day? How can they be held accountable to the gospel? How can we use what wisdom and power we have been given in the service of Christ?

To both Jews and Greeks—and for many today—the notion of a crucified God was utter nonsense. Yet this was what Paul preached. That very nonsense, he said, is both wisdom and power to those whom God calls. Christ is God's power and wisdom—not an intellectual wisdom but the wisdom of trust, discipleship, and salvation.

Here's How It Works

In real life, there is the Corinthian church—and our church. The Corinthian church had a few members who were wise, powerful, or of good family. The majority were slaves or freedmen who worked hard to stay alive. In the church, Paul says, those differences do not matter. The only thing that matters is God's call.

God expects the church to be like Jesus. Does that mean we have to die to save others? No, only Christ could do that. What God expects is that we use the gifts we have been given. If we are in Christ, act like it!

Gospel: Matthew 5:1-12

The Beatitudes mirror what we said about the psalm—not prescriptions, but descriptions. They are not statements about how we have to live *if* we want God to love us. They are statements about how we live *because* God is in relationship with us. We are being molded into lives like this by walking with God.

This life with God has two dimensions. One is ethical. Day-to-day life must reflect the ethic of compassion. The Scriptures are clear about the demands of discipleship on those who claim to be believers. The other dimension is eschatological—concerned with the coming reign of God. We anticipate the final Kingdom and participate now in the realm of God ushered in by Jesus Christ.

Privileges of the Reign of God

Technically, a beatitude is a statement about privilege. Wait a minute! Hunger, poverty, grief, and persecution are privileged situations? Yes, but not in and of themselves. For example, the "poor in spirit" (Luke says simply "poor") are blessed, not because they are poor, but because they live in God's realm, and that life changes their lives. The blessings (comfort, being filled, receiving mercy) are objective reality—gifts of God's grace. Probably persons would never be open to receiving those gifts if they had not first been hurt in some way. We usually ask for help only when we cannot help ourselves any more. Beatitudes are the marks of the church. They describe the way Christians are. This is what it means to be and to live as God's people.

Ethics, Too

There is also an ethical dimension to the Beatitudes. The community that is blessed does not just sit passively, waiting for and then enjoying God's blessings. Rather, we live *as if* the rule of God were present in all its fullness. By the way we live, we translate these words into reality.

The Beatitudes are true because of Jesus Christ; they are blessings on disciples who live in authentic Christian community. It is not true that everyone who mourns will automatically be comforted; we know that is untrue from experience. Those who will be comforted are those who live in Christian community, where the caring is genuine and the community is lifted by the power of the Resurrection.

It's for the Church

The Beatitudes are not addressed to individuals, but to the community of faith. In every congregation, we find persons such as the ones the Beatitudes describe. Their very presence among us is a sign of God's blessing. But we also need whole congregations who manifest these qualities, both within their common life and through their corporate witness in the world. The Beatitudes are a call for all of us to live more of the blessings ourselves.

> **Think About It:** The Beatitudes are addressed to the community. Who in your community of faith really lives these Beatitudes? What does that life look like? Are those qualities you wish you had in your life? How do you "get" them? Does your congregation as a whole exemplify these characteristics? Why or why not?

A Counter-cultural Teaching

We can live the way described in the Beatitudes (which is counter-cultural) because we know that God's promises are not empty. God will make them happen. But this is not a pattern for success, nor a scheme for getting ahead, solving our problems, or even "making it" in the realm of God. That's why the Beatitudes are counter-cultural. Our culture demands success measured in money and power; the Beatitudes pose a direct challenge to that. We live in this new way in spite of whatever happens to us. To be a success or failure in the eyes of the world is not an issue for these promises. It is who we are, not what we achieve, that matters.

Study Suggestions

A. What Kind of Life: 1

Read aloud Micah 6:1-8. Discuss: What is the setting for this text? What is the point? How does the writer set it up to make a point? What kind of life does God expect us to lead? After examining the background material on pages 79–80, ask: How does this background add to our understanding of the way the writer sets up the text? How does it add to our understanding of the point? What insights do you get about the kind of life God wants us to lead? How do you assess the quality of your life in terms of these standards? List consensus responses on chalkboard or a sheet of paper.

B. What Kind of Life: 2

Read 1 Corinthians 1:18-31. Ask again: What does this text say about the kind of life we are called to lead? What is the most important aspect of this understanding of the Christian life? What does the text say about being in opposition to popular culture? Are Christians always meant to be just a little "outside" the culture? How do you experience and deal with this tension? What does God expect from us? Review the Epistle commentary on pages

78–79. Ask: What can we add from this to our understanding of how God wants us to live? Add responses to the list.

C. What Kind of Life: 3

Read Psalm 15. Point out that verses 2-5 are answers to the question in verse 1. Ask: What kind of life do these verses describe? How do they add to our understanding of the way God wants us to live? How can anyone live this way? Note that this is only possible by the grace of God. Review the commentary about these verses on pages 77–78 as a description of life in God's presence. Discuss: How does this understanding help us think about the way God wants us to live? What is the difference between meeting the requirements and living out God's character in the world? Add responses to the growing list.

D. What Kind of Life: 4

Read Matthew 5:1-12 and the background material on pages 79–80. Ask: What does it mean to say that the people described here are in privileged situations? How are the Beatitudes the marks of the church? How are they expressions of a faith and relationship that is distinctly counter-cultural? What does it mean for both individuals and congregations to live against the culture? How can the church be a source of power and guidance for living this kind of life? Add new expectations to the list.

E. Remember

Each of the passages asks us to recall important stories or practices from the past, some faithful and good, others that were abominations. Read the commentaries and note some of these remembrances (the Exodus and first Passover, the wrongful sacrifice of children, worship in the Tabernacle, the Crucifixion). Briefly indicate why each event is worthy of remembrance. Then invite members to recall their own foundational memories and their importance in helping us live as God calls us to live.

F. Tie It Together

All four texts have spoken of the way God wants us to live. Review your list of responses. Then ask: How can we live the kind of life they describe? What power and resources are available to help us? What passages in the Scriptures have you read that offer the promise of power to live the life God wants of us?

G. Celebrate

Ask the group to read their list again. Observe a time of silence and a brief prayer of thanksgiving for God's gift of life and Christ's call to faithful discipleship. Close by singing the hymn, "Are Ye Able?"

Lections for Fifth Sunday After the Epiphany

Old Testament: Isaiah 58:1-9a
(9b-12)

*M*ANY biblical scholars believe that the Book of Isaiah is made up of three separate works, differentiated by style of writing, theological insight, and historical setting. Today's lection comes from the chapters commonly termed Third Isaiah (56–66), which were written during the postexilic period, when the people were returning from Babylon.

Unlike the mood of preceding chapters, however, optimism concerning the return to their homeland and the rebuilding of the Temple had given way to disillusionment. Third Isaiah chronicles divisions within the community during the period 520 to 500 B.C. The rebuilding of the Temple had been disrupted and delayed. Pilgrims who had returned to help restore the fortunes of Israel's former glory days had suffered obstructions and interference from the people then inhabiting the land.

Authentic Religion

Isaiah 58:1-12 illustrates one of the controversies concerning religious practice within the Second-Temple community where strict observance of sabbath and ritual was increasingly emphasized. Deep divisions emerged among the leadership concerning the requirements of the covenant. The cultic rite of fasting was practiced with zeal. Those who had been lax in observing the law were severely chastised.

But the trumpet that announced the fast (Joel 2:15) had become the shout of the people. Their brazen arrogance is exhibited in Isaiah 58:3: What is the point of fasting if God refuses to look? Where is the gain in humbling ourselves before God if it brings no tangible benefit? Why go to church if there's no material payoff? For the people, living out the covenant had been reduced

82

to the rote performance of religious acts to look good in the eyes of others and secure favors from YHWH. The spiritual fire in their hearts had died out, and nothing was left but the outward form of religion.

God lays bare their motivation—to serve their own interests. Their devotion would enhance their reputation; such public display would allow them to point fingers, to fight among themselves, to oppress others. Pious, shallow religiosity had replaced right relationships with God and within the community.

A Hollow Ritual

The hollowness of their rituals had become offensive to the very God they were seeking. God announces a new kind of fast that better expresses the demands of the covenant—one of self-denial and compassion. They are to break the yoke—the burden—of the poor, the homeless, the dispossessed. The word *yoke* alludes literally to the restraint placed upon a beast of burden. But it would also be understood in this context as the political, economic, or religious power and control exerted over others. A true religious observance would not be pretentious or render another powerless.

> **Think About It:** A true fast would not be pretentious or render another powerless. Do any of your personal rituals, claimed to be good, render someone else powerless or contribute to someone's misfortune? Are they done to meet the expectations of others, or out of genuine love for God? Do you leave a service of worship more deeply committed to lifting the burdens of others through acts of compassion, justice, or service? What is the acid test of real devotion?

It is through the practice of justice, not ritual, that the covenant is fulfilled, says Isaiah. The conditions are specific and personal: share your bread, your house. Care for your family. Satisfy the needs of the afflicted. Clothe the naked. Treat your workers fairly. Free those imprisoned unjustly. Only then will YHWH recognize the fast or other religious practices. Only then will God satisfy the people's desires with good things. Only then will the people be counted as faithful. Only then will the restoration and healing of the once-exiled community be complete.

Psalter: Psalm 112:1-10

This psalm follows the themes of today's Isaiah passage. The "upright" are not those who observe religious ritual to the letter; they are characterized instead by their commitment to justice and compassion. This commitment produces an inner strength that is their "light," their joy. They will be able to withstand adversity. They will be "remembered forever," an incomparable tribute for the people of ancient Israel.

The psalm addresses those who "fear the LORD," and displays the influence of the wisdom tradition, which equated faithfulness with concrete, measurable results. Those who obeyed God would be blessed: "their horn is exalted in honor" (verse 9), while those who turn away would "gnash their teeth and melt away," (verse 10). The overthrow of evil, in this understanding, was accomplished through the destruction of those deemed "wicked." These images may be uncomfortable for today's reader, familiar with Jesus' mandate to "love your enemies." They stand, however, as examples of the wisdom tradition's clear-cut approach to righteousness; faithfulness (and God's response) could never be ambiguous.

The form of the psalm is an alphabetic acrostic. Every verse following "Praise the LORD!" (verse 1) begins with the letters of the Hebrew alphabet in alphabetical order. This structure creates challenges for both writer and translator. For example, the NRSV attributes graciousness, mercy, and righteousness (verse 4) to "those who fear the LORD." The NIV renders this, "Even in darkness light dawns for the upright, / for the gracious and compassionate and righteous man." But the RSV reads, "the LORD is gracious, merciful, and righteous."

Epistle: 1 Corinthians 2:1-12 (13-16)

Wisdom is the central issue in this lection. It is not, however, an extension of the wisdom tradition represented in Psalm 112. The issue addressed by Paul in First Corinthians concerns the place of human wisdom in light of the wisdom of God. Paul is not denying the place of human intellect in matters of faith. Instead, he puts human wisdom in its proper perspective—not as an object of faith, but in service to the central Christian message: "Jesus Christ, and him crucified" (2:2). The Spirit enhances human wisdom in order that believers may come to know (not just know about) God's purpose and power. Faith is not the product of human wisdom or intellectual endeavor. Faith, as a response to the gospel, is based solely in the power and love of God.

The Greek Intellectual World

Paul's humility regarding his oratorical prowess belies his mastery of the tools of Greek exposition. Skilled as a writer and speaker, Paul could hold his own against the great thinkers of his day. In a society steeped in philosophy and the pursuit of wisdom as an end unto itself, the key was to shift the focus from "lofty words" (2:1) to the message of the cross. In the preceding chapter Paul recognizes the "foolishness" (1:18) of such a message to those who rely solely on human understanding. Human wisdom alone will never "get it." What forms of human wisdom obscure the gospel message today?

For today's reader, the impact of "crucifixion" upon the hearers of Paul's day is lost. For them the inadequacy of human wisdom was uncovered by the very repugnance conveyed by the word *crucifixion*. That One divine should suffer and die by such abhorrent means was beyond comprehension in the Roman world. "Crucified" (2:2), in its Greek construction, implies that the Crucifixion, while linked to a specific historic occurrence, is an ongoing reality, a perpetual death. What is inconceivable to the human mind reveals the nature—and paradox—of God's wisdom. Can human reason today really explain why good people suffer?

Gospel: Matthew 5:13-20

The image of the Sermon on the Mount—Jesus climbing the hillside, addressing the crowd of followers—is a familiar one. The words are familiar too, especially the Beatitudes, often learned—or memorized—in childhood. Many scholars think, however, that this picture is less than accurate. The "great instruction," they believe, was not a public address, but an intensive course in living under the reign of God meant for the Twelve—Discipleship 101. It was not intended to create a moral theology, or set of rules, but a fresh way of experiencing God's covenant law.

Matthew frames Jesus' teachings to be accessible to those who will later teach them in the growing community. Their very phrasing provides for ease in memorization. "Blessed are those who mourn, for they will be comforted." Luke's parallel is the "Sermon on the Plain" (Luke 6:20-49), which includes woes as well as blessings.

Salt and Light

Today's lection, which focuses on the marks of discipleship, begins with the example of salt losing its saltiness. Salt loses its flavor by being diluted or absorbing impurities, so it no longer serves its intended purpose. In the Hebrew tradition salt stood for sacrifice, loyalty, a shared relationship, purification, seasoning, and preservation—all qualities of faithful discipleship. Salt does not serve itself, but exists to enhance the other. So with the disciples. If they do not embody these qualities, they are not serving the purpose to which Jesus is calling them, so risk being discarded.

Disciples are also to be light. In Mark 4:21 and Luke 8:16, similar light sayings follow the parable of the sower, accentuating the promise to the disciples that the Kingdom's secrets will be revealed to them. Matthew uses the metaphor to highlight the ultimate expression of discipleship—sacrificial service. True discipleship stands in sharp contrast to the darkness outside God's realm and sheds light on the world around it. When those in darkness see

> *Think About It:* True discipleship sheds light on the world around it. How are we salt and light in our corner of the world? What kind of response do we receive?

the light, they see the goodness—not of the disciple—but of God. Good works are rooted in obedience to God's will. The light of discipleship points beyond human action to God. For this to happen we must not hide our light, but openly and gladly bear witness by word and deed.

Jesus and the Law of Moses

"Do not think that I have come to abolish the law . . . but to fulfill" (Matthew 5:17). These words were perhaps as confusing to the Twelve as to today's Christian who sees Jesus' teaching as the harbinger of a new covenant. Indeed, much of Jesus' instruction seems to contradict, or at least challenge, the law as it had been understood. The seeds of truth were present in the old covenant, but it remained for Jesus to bring them to fruition. Jesus' confrontations with the Pharisees centered on interpretation of and faithfulness to the law. Paul would also face controversy in the early Jewish Christian community as to the authority of the law for Gentile converts.

The New Testament uses the verb *plersosai* (fulfill) in several ways. It can mean "to clarify the true meaning of" or "to end, conclude, or make complete." Paul referred to Jesus as the *telos* (end, goal) of the law. To fulfill the law is not, then, to rewrite or even to reinterpret it; it is to move beyond observing the letter of the law to discerning and doing the will of God, which is at the heart of the law.

Study Suggestions

A. Sing

Open with a hymn about the realm of God, such as "I Love Thy Kingdom, Lord" or "Seek Ye First the Kingdom of God." Pray together for strength to live under the rule of God as faithful disciples.

B. Examine Salt and Light

Spend a few minutes brainstorming a list of uses for salt—adding flavor, making ice cream, melting ice. (Or, provide a bowl of unsalted popcorn for the group to taste; then ask them for their impressions.)

Ask: Why do you think Jesus used such an example to define the place of a disciple in the world? Read aloud Matthew 5:13-20, and discuss the information about saltiness on pages 85–86. Ask: How can individual disciples (or the church) lose their essential qualities and cease serving their intended purpose? What happens in the world when we allow our witness to become bland? How can Christians, individually and corporately, retain our saltiness? (Here stress prayer, worship, study, risk-taking, mutual support, and other means of grace.)

Ask group members to share experiences of seeing a small or solitary light in a dark place (a night-light, looking down from a plane flying at night, a flashlight or candle when the power goes out, the beam from a lighthouse). If you are meeting at night or the room can be darkened, turn out the lights and light a match. Ask: What feelings are evoked by the presence of such a light? How does this parallel our experience of living and witnessing for Christ in an alien world?

Or, light a votive candle and cover it with a bowl; ask members to share their impressions. Ask: What does our light (witness) reveal about our faith? about God? about our impact? How do we protect ourselves against taking credit for our good works? Work as a group or in pairs to create contemporary metaphors for discipleship, other than salt and light, then present them in the form of pictures or skits.

C. Compare and Contrast

Form three groups, each to study one passage. Using the passages and the corresponding material above, discuss the following: false religiosity versus genuine faithfulness (Isaiah 58:11-12); human wisdom versus God's wisdom (1 Corinthians 2:1-16); the letter versus the spirit of the law—the salt and light of good works (Matthew 5:13-20). Then bring the groups together to share their insights. After each group has reported, ask: What do these passages tell us about God? about ourselves? about faithful living? How do emotionalism, intellectualism, and legalism manifest themselves in our lives and thereby block effective witness? How can we truly discern God's will in today's world? as individuals? as the church? (Consider the sources of Scripture, tradition, reason, and experience.) What things stand in our way? What are the marks of true discipleship?

D. Study the Psalm

Read Psalm 112 together. Ask members to give a one-word or sentence description of its message. What themes or images do you find in this psalm that are similar to those in today's other lections? Work together to compose an acrostic psalm (each line beginning with a different letter, in alphabetical order), using the words *salt* and *light*.

E. End With Commitment

Ask: What do the lections today require of us in our personal discipleship? What do the lections call us to be? Using the discussion material from Activity B, pray for a commitment (individually and as a group) to maintain our saltiness and to let our light shine. Then stand in a circle holding lighted candles and sing "This Little Light of Mine" or another hymn of commitment and witness.

Close with a prayer for strength and guidance in becoming more faithful disciples.

Lections for Sixth Sunday After the Epiphany

T Old Testament: Deuteronomy 30:15-20

THE origin of the Book of Deuteronomy is described in 2 Kings 22 during the reign of Josiah, in 622 B.C. Under his grandfather Manasseh, worship life had been corrupted by the erection of pagan shrines and the practice of sacred prostitution (see 2 Kings 21). Astrology and soothsaying had replaced the laws of Moses as guidance for living. During the repair of the Temple, the high priest Hilkiah discovered a "book of the law," which persuaded Josiah to start a renewal movement to remove heathen altars, idols, priests, and immorality, and to focus worship again on YHWH and his Temple. The consistency of these reforms with the teachings of Deuteronomy points to it being the very "book of the law" that was found by Hilkiah. It advocates practices based on the teachings of the eighth-century prophets Amos, Hosea, Micah, and Isaiah. The book could have been written by an underground group of their descendants during the reign of Manasseh and hidden by them in the Temple to be "discovered" and brought forth at a later, opportune time.

The Call and the Choice

Deuteronomy presents a clarion call to God's people to devote themselves solely to the worship of YHWH, who had brought them out of Egypt and into the Promised Land, and to observe the covenant entered into at Sinai. Using the form of a farewell speech by Moses, it describes standards for life and worship to be followed out of gratitude and devotion to YHWH. While written centuries after Moses, it seeks to represent his mind as interpreted by the prophets and understood by seventh-century reformers and, as such, speaks God's word to people of all times.

The name *Deuteronomy* is a Greek word that means "second law," referring to the fact that the book (Chapters 12–26; 28) is a later version—expanded and revised—of the law code found in Exodus 20–23, which is called the Book of the Covenant (Exodus 24:7).

In today's lection, Moses puts the choice clearly: Follow God's way, obey the commandments, worship YHWH alone, and you will be blessed with prosperity and a good life; continue in idolatry and immorality, and you will experience misfortune and death. Therefore, "choose life!" This is a choice people face in every age—the age of Moses, the age of Josiah—and our own.

For Deuteronomy the issue is sharply defined and the results certain. To choose life is to do God's will, which brings divine blessing in the form of material reward. To remain in the ways of sin and death will result in divine judgment experienced as misfortune and calamity. The righteous will prosper; sinners will suffer. While experience does not bear this out—evil often brings reward while the innocent encounter injustice—this idea continues to influence us. Discuss the validity of statements like: blame the victim; he brought it on himself; the poor deserve to be poor; pull yourself up by your own bootstraps; somebody up there likes me; God helps those who help themselves; and I prayed and God healed me.

Think About It: Moses says, "Choose life!" What are the choices between "life" and "death" we face today? What are the idolatries (false values) and immoralities (dehumanizing behaviors) that tempt us away from God's way? Is it always true that to "choose life" brings blessing and prosperity? What instances do you know of when bad things happened to good people, and vice versa? How do you explain this? What are some reasons for choosing God's way regardless of the consequences? Are there rewards other than material ones that might be even more fulfilling?

Psalter: Psalm 119:1-8

The first stanza of this psalm echoes Deuteronomy's call to keep the law and to walk in godly ways. But the psalmist is struggling with this. Those who devote themselves to God are blameless; no fault can be found with them. But he is still wishing that "my ways were steadfast" (verse 5, NIV), so that "I would not be put to shame when I consider all your commands" (verse 6, NIV). He's willing to learn, though, and will praise God as he moves along (verse 7). In the meantime, he asks God not to give up on him, since he really is trying to observe the divine decrees (verse 8).

Does this psalm give voice to your prayer, too? Do you sometimes feel it is really hard to lead a faithful life and doubt that you are worthy? Do you wonder if your "ways are steadfast"? fear you might be "put to shame" for your wavering? think God might forsake you in favor of others who are better Christians? If so, this psalm is for you. And something else that is for you—that the psalmist didn't have—is the word of grace that comes from Jesus, "You are forgiven!"

Epistle: 1 Corinthians 3:1-9

The "life-and-death" choice posed in today's Epistle lection is between the way of the flesh—manifested in jealousy and quarreling—and the life of a spiritual people—expressed in harmony and cooperation. The Corinthians do not yet qualify as being spiritual, as their bickering over which leader to follow (see commentary for Third Sunday after Epiphany, pages 72–73) demonstrates. Although Paul had given them a diet of milk (the basics of gospel teaching), apparently they had not yet matured sufficiently to tolerate a diet of solid food (advanced instruction in the faith). They are still squabbling like infants.

Self-centered Versus Self-giving

Here, as elsewhere in Paul's letters (see Galatians 5:19-20), the way of the flesh is not limited to physical or sexual sins, but refers to all self-centered attitudes and desires. The spiritual life, by contrast, is grounded in self-giving, other-regarding, God-centered love (see 1 Corinthians 13). But he must first make clear that leaders are servants who submerge their egos in the common venture of building up the body (see Chapter 12). He and Apollos aren't concerned about who got there first, who gets the credit, who has the largest following, or who is most eloquent. They are teammates, working together toward a common goal—the nurture and development of the church. And

> **Think About It:** "We are God's fellow workers." Do folks in your church think of themselves as God's servants, planting and building to nourish and support one another in a common mission? If not, what blocks this image from view? Is it big egos, apathy and dependency, or a contentious spirit? If you do relate and work together in unity, what makes this possible? And what "milk" or "solid food" is now needed to help you continue your ministry?

Paul would dearly love it if these brawling, obnoxious Corinthians would follow their example. "For we are God's fellow workers; you are God's field, God's building" (3:9, NIV).

In one church a well-meaning layman installed a new communion rail without getting permission. Imagine everyone's consternation on Sunday morning! Most were furious and could not rest until they discovered who did it and forced him to remove it. Ask: What went wrong here? How might this have been handled differently? How would you have reacted? What next steps would you have taken? What "milk" or "solid food" did they need? What should be planted and what water should be poured so God can give the growth in this church, which is "God's field, God's building?"

Gospel: Matthew 5:21-37

Gospel lections for this Sunday and next contain six antitheses, each with three elements—a statement from the Law, a reinterpretation that moves it from the external to the realm of motivation and attitude, and some startling, challenging examples. This revitalized Torah focuses on a religion and ethic of the heart and demands total commitment. It is a righteousness expressing the spirit not just the letter of the Law.

Antithesis I: Murder (verses 21-26)

"You shall not murder," says the Law. Just as serious, says Jesus, are harboring resentment, making demeaning insults, and vicious name-calling. If you have offended another child of God, before you come to worship first go and be reconciled. You cannot make up for soured relationships with a sweet offering to God. Those who claim to honor God but "murder" others with hate, prejudice, or cutting remarks, are liable for judgment. In a pagan world the church must be different from the vindictive, dog-eat-dog society around it. Only through a community of caring, forgiveness, and respect will others see the love of God.

Antithesis II: Adultery (verses 27-30)

"You shall not commit adultery," says the Law. But exploitation and dehumanization of women are equally bad, says Jesus. Any attitude or behavior that violates the sanctity of marriage or its partners is sinful. While in actuality the lecherous eye and roaming hand are driven by a sinful heart, any member of the body—and the person as a whole—come under judgment when they abuse a child of God. In Jesus' day, the woman was blamed for adultery and could be stoned (see John 8:1-11). Jesus instead places the onus on the man. What does this say about moral issues we face today, such as pornography, domestic abuse, use of women to sell products, and casual sex?

Antithesis III: Divorce (verses 31-32)

Divorce is permitted under certain circumstances, says the Law—especially if you're a man. But I hold you to a higher standard, says Jesus. Divorce may force a wife to give her body to another man, just to survive. Remarriage breaks the lifelong marriage vow. Thus both are committing adultery. When you make a commitment to love, honor, and cherish, it is "'til death us do part." When you violate that promise you are violating the sanctity, both of marriage and of persons created in God's image. What should be the church's stand on divorce today? remarriage after divorce? the moral laxity and gender inequity of our time? How can we keep a balance between maintaining the sanctity of marriage and preventing the harm of abusive relationships?

Antithesis IV: Oaths (verses 33-37)

Oaths are to be honest and true, says the Holiness Code (see Leviticus 19:12), and you are obliged to fulfill them—especially if made to God. But Jesus says no oaths are necessary. For a person of integrity, one's word is sufficient. Just always tell the truth, and you will have an unimpeachable reputation for honesty. Again, morality is a matter of inner character, not outer form. Righteousness is not meeting legal or social expectations; it is an expression of being right with God. When admen, lawyers, politicians, and spin doctors tailor the truth to sell a product, free a client, blur the issues, mislead the public, integrity is a scarce commodity. How do we discern truth from falsehood? decide what to believe? persuade another we are telling the truth?

In all these sayings Jesus calls us to base our behavior, not on conformity to outer expectations—from law, custom, religious teaching, or moral injunction—but on the integrity of character rooted in our relationship with God. As Martin Luther put it, "Love God, and do as you please."

Study Suggestions

A. Prayer and Psalter

Open with prayer, ask for guidance in finding God's word for the group in studying this week's lections. Read in unison Psalm 119:1-8. Discuss: Which phrases stick in your mind? Do these words express how you sometimes feel? What is it like to be constantly striving to live up to high standards? What kind of guilt feelings are healthy, and what sort are not? What is God's word of grace to us in this situation? Divide into groups, asking each to create a "space sculpture" made up of bodily poses frozen in place, to express their feelings in response to the psalm.

B. Background

Read aloud Deuteronomy 30:15-20. Explain the origin of Deuteronomy, the situation under Manasseh, Josiah's reform, and the call to loyalty put into the mouth of Moses but also strongly influenced by the prophets. Re-read verses 19-20, Moses' challenge to choose life. The deuteronomist possessed a particular view of Israel's history: Faithfulness brought prosperity, which led to arrogance, idolatry, and immorality. This invited God's punishment in the form of invasion and conquest. Prophets then arose to pronounce judgment and call for repentance. This brought about repentance and renewal, a return to God's way of morality and faithful observance of the law. Then the cycle began all over again. Deuteronomy represents the renewal phase under King Josiah. Ask: What signs do you see of a similar cycle in American history? What stage do you think we are presently in, and why? In light of this, what might God be calling our nation to do at this point in history?

Notice that it was this same challenge to faithfulness, and the guilt at failing to live up to it, that was troubling the psalmist. Ask: Were you raised with high expectations that fostered guilt feelings? If so, how have you dealt with them? If not, what provides guidance for your behavior and decisions? How do we distinguish between guilt feelings and actual guilt? Do we need to be held accountable and challenged to improve? How can the church best do this?

C. Jesus' High Standards

For a fresh perception of what Jesus is saying, read the Gospel lection from a contemporary translation—Phillips, *The Living Bible*, Cotton Patch, or the Contemporary English Version. Explain the form—six antitheses, each with three parts. Divide into four groups, each to discuss one antithesis and the commentary about it. Have each group report back their responses to these two questions: To what present-day issues does this passage speak? How would our lives, church, and society change were we to obey Christ?

D. Two Cases

Read 1 Corinthians 3:1-9 as a first case study. Explain the situation in the Corinthian church, referring back to the discussion on factionalism in 1:10-18. Highlight Paul's emphasis on the contrast between "flesh" and "spirit," readiness for "milk" versus "solid food," servant leadership, and working together toward the common goal of building up the body of Christ. Discuss how these themes might relate to the current situation in your congregation. Then present the second case, that of the conflict over the communion rail built without proper permission, and discuss the questions posed on pages 90–91.

E. Summary

Close by identifying common themes, such as: God's high standards for our behavior; the need for grace and forgiveness; our need for periodic challenge and renewal; the call to choose; morality as conformity to the expectations of others versus heartfelt commitment based in a personal relationship with God. Review any agreements the group may have made for accountability and offering grace to one another. Close by singing, "I Want a Principle Within," and saying the Lord's Prayer together.

Lections for Seventh Sunday After the Epiphany

T Old Testament: Leviticus 19:1-2, 9-18

THIS is the "you have heard that it was said to the people long ago" reference Jesus makes in this week's Gospel lection. Leviticus is mostly a collection of civil, liturgical, religious, hygienic, and moral requirements that Israel was called upon to observe. It was drawn together around 400 B.C.—eight centuries after the Exodus—when the people were returning from exile and beginning to establish their identity, rebuild their Temple, and restore their national life. For this they naturally turned to the tradition stemming from Moses. The prophets had helped them see that their misfortunes had stemmed from their breaking of the covenant, through idolatry, injustice, and foreign alliances. Determined that this would not happen again, they gathered together this set of rules and laws to govern their community in order to demonstrate their loyalty to YHWH. The focus of the book is on forming a people with a unique way of life that will distinguish them then and always from all other peoples around them.

> *Think About It:* "A unique way of life that will distinguish them from others." What distinguishes you from those around you? Do you observe standards that set you apart? How can we balance the need to be friendly, respectful, and caring of others, with the call to live holy lives?

The rationale for a distinctive way of life is found in two verses—19:2, "You shall be holy, for I the LORD your God am holy;" and 19:36, "I am the LORD your God, who brought you out of the land of Egypt." This code of laws had been given them by a holy God who had made himself known to Moses in a burning bush and on a holy mountain. It was this same YHWH who had freed them from slavery, guided them in the wilderness, and

94

brought them into a land flowing with milk and honey. They had disobeyed, strayed, and played too long, at their peril. It was long past time to return to their God, and this new law code would show them how.

Israel could start with the Ten Commandments, most of which—and more—are restated in Chapter 19. Honor your parents; keep the sabbath (verse 3). Worship no idols (verse 4). Make proper offerings (verses 5-8). Leave gleanings for the poor (verses 9-10). Do not steal, lie, or make false oaths (verses 11-12). Do not cheat your neighbor or employee (verse 13). Do not insult the deaf or trick the blind (verse 14). Treat others justly and impartially (verse 15). Do not pass on unkind gossip or accuse or stand idly by while another is unjustly punished (verse 16). Do not hate, criticize, take revenge, or hold grudges (verses 17-18). In sum, "You shall love your neighbor as your-

> *Think About It*: "Time to return." Might you have "disobeyed, strayed, and played too long"? We all need to be reminded from time to time of who and whose we are. Think back to the time you made your original commitment to God. What has happened since? Have you always been faithful? Where are you now in your journey of faith? Is it time for a fresh accounting? What promises may need to be dusted off? What help do you need to renew your commitment?

self." Why? Because, says YHWH, "I am the LORD," the Holy One who redeemed you from bondage.

Here we see a call to integrity, generosity, respect, justice, fairness, concern for the poor, and positive relationships. No wonder Jesus said, "I have not come to destroy the law but to fulfill it" (see Matthew 5:17).

Psalter: Psalm 119:33-40

Psalm 119 is an acrostic poem—each stanza of eight verses starts with the succeeding letter of the Hebrew alphabet, and within each stanza each line begins with the same letter. Each verse contains a different synonym for the law (statute, commandment, decree, way, promise, ordinance, precept), which shows the care and precision with which the work is crafted. No doubt a person with such dedication would be very steadfast in internalizing and observing the law.

This stanza could well have been written by one of the returning exiles, intent on knowing and keeping the law of YHWH spelled out in Leviticus, which would form the basis for life in the restored community. He (or she) wants to learn the law from God, to observe it, understand it, follow in its path, put it above personal benefit, and become more vital by turning from empty pursuits. In view of his commitment to the law and goodness, the psalmist asks God to fulfill God's promises and to remove all penalties and to grant blessing to the faithful.

Epistle: 1 Corinthians 3:10-11, 16-23

Paul here continues his emphasis in last week's lection on Christian leaders as servants and colleagues who work together to build up the body of Christ. Each receives gifts from God for use in the construction—some, like Paul, to lay the foundation and others to come after and build the structure upon it. But he does seem to lay claim to being the captain of the team, naming himself the master builder and cautioning others to be careful to follow the form he has designed (verse 10). This is justified, though, because the foundation is none other than Jesus Christ himself (verse 11), so any variation from this standard would put the whole building at risk. The church needs to be grounded in the Christ Event.

> **Think About It**: "The foundation is none other than Jesus Christ." Some churches were founded by a charismatic pastor. For others a dedicated, sometimes wealthy, family has long been the mainstay. Some grew out of splits over doctrine, a controversial pastor, or a divisive vote. Some have catered to a particular social class, neighborhood, or ethnic group. On what is your church founded? Has the community built on it remained true to it or moved in another direction? How can we discern whether to remain bound to the past or to move out into an unknown future? How do we know which structure is truly built on the foundation of Jesus Christ?

Whoever follows Paul must realize that the community (the "you" is plural here) is God's holy temple, inhabited by God's Spirit. Any leader who undermines its unity and integrity will have to answer to God (verses 16-17)! Paul next addresses the leaders who had moved in after him and were disrupting the harmony of the Corinthian church and disturbing their faith. They seem to have been teaching a form of Jewish Hellenistic wisdom theology, which drew on Greek philosophy and claimed possession of special knowledge and spiritual power, thereby distracting believers from a central focus on Christ. He tells them they are mistaken (deceived) to think that their intellectual arguments give them special status. Rather, they must stay with the basics of the gospel and not embellish them (verses 18-19). He buttresses his claim that worldly wisdom cannot compare with the light of God's truth by quoting from Job 5:13 and Psalm 94:11 (verses 19-20).

Finally, he speaks again to the Corinthian members, admonishing them not to attach themselves too tightly to particular leaders or cliques, or even special doctrines about life and death, present and future. They must ever remember that it is they, not the leaders, who are the church, and that the church is Christ's and therefore God's (verses 21-23).

Gospel: Matthew 5:38-48

We continue with the final two antitheses in Matthew's compilation of the teachings of Jesus. These are probably the most difficult of all.

Antithesis V (verses 38-42)

"An eye for an eye and a tooth for a tooth," says the Law. (See Exodus 21:23-24; Leviticus 24:19-20; Deuteronomy 19:21.) Retribution for wrongdoing must not be excessive or extreme, but measured. This is not retaliation or revenge; it is justice. This rule puts a curb on the common practice of "a life for an eye"—killing a person in anger for even a minor offense. But no, says Jesus, do not make matters worse by assailing the one who has harmed you. He then gives four concrete examples:

1. Turn the other cheek. A right-handed fist to the jaw would land on the left cheek, but a demeaning back-handed slap would strike the right. The intent would be to shame not injure—an insult inflicted on an inferior to induce compliance. The poor and outcast were used to this kind of treatment from their overlords. But if they voluntarily turn their cheek to take a second blow, they are in charge. Rather than meekly accepting further humiliation, they can assert their dignity by taking the initiative. In rejecting retaliation, Jesus is not counseling passive submission, but rather a passive resistance to evil that retains one's self-respect.

2. Give your cloak as well. (See Exodus 22:25-27; Deuteronomy 24:10-13, 17; Amos 2:7-8; Ezekiel 18:5-9.) Many Galilean peasants were deeply in debt, having lost their farms to wealthy, absentee landlords. If they were to be taken to court and lose, as those who cannot afford a lawyer often do, a garment might be all they could give as collateral for the fine. In defiance of their unjust treatment, Jesus is saying, if they demand your outer garment in payment, strip off your underwear, too, and stand there in the nude! To thus shock the sensibilities of the rich and powerful just might awaken them to the injustice they are inflicting. But if not, at least the poor debtor would be making a statement and thereby feel empowered.

3. Go the second mile. The Roman soldiers occupying Palestine could freely order their subjects to carry their packs—but only for a mile. Jesus does not urge people to resist or rebel against this. Instead, he advises them to surprise their oppressors by showing some spunk, seizing the initiative, and thereby claiming their dignity.

4. Give and lend to those who ask. A peasant would have little to give or

lend. One can just see the smile on their faces as they pull out their pockets to demonstrate their poverty. They have already been taken for all they are worth, so to offer to give more would be a wry but devastating comment on an unjust system. Again, Jesus is showing how we can avoid degrading submission by resisting injustice with both humor and self-respect.

Antithesis VI (verses 43-48)

The tradition says, "Love your neighbor (Leviticus 19:18) and hate your enemy." But Jesus says, love and pray for your enemies. That's what God does with his unlimited gifts of sunshine and rain. If you only love and salute your family and friends, you are no different than pagans and exploiters. Be like God; be righteous and holy (Leviticus 19:2). Thus, just as in today's Leviticus passage, the culmination of Jesus' ethical teaching is grounded in the holiness and goodness of God.

Jesus sets a high standard. In showing us these various ways to love neighbor as self, he rejects violence, upholds the dignity and worth of all persons, and points us to the justice and love of God as the model and source of all goodness.

Study Suggestions

A. Identify Major Themes

Ask the group to read all four passages silently, look for key themes, and share what they find. Note that three of the four deal with the law: Leviticus gives a list of laws, the Psalm expresses devotion to the law, and in Matthew Jesus infuses the law with fresh meaning. First Corinthians emphasizes Christ as the foundation of the church and the basis for dealing with rivalry and pride in human wisdom. Except in Leviticus the motivation for right conduct comes from within. All use interesting literary devices—Leviticus grounding the call to obedience in God's holiness and redemption, the psalmist using a sequence of Hebrew letters and synonyms for law, Paul using the analogy of building, and Jesus contrasting the old with the new.

B. Provoke New Thoughts

Ask: What is good and bad about laws? If Jesus Christ is our foundation, do we as Christians really need laws? Why did the returning exiles need the laws of Leviticus? How does law help form identity and nationhood? What kind of law could one long for and delight in, like the psalmist? How would the scribes and Pharisees likely have reacted to Jesus' treatment of the laws of old? What about the peasants and fishermen? Would some laws have helped manage the dissension in the Corinthian church? Do books of church law help congregations order their life?

C. The Church's Foundation

Discuss the questions in the "Think About It" paragraph on page 96. Recall the story of how your church was founded. Around what persons(s) or principle(s) is it organized today? Is it still true to its original purpose? Is it time for a change? How can you discern where God may be leading? How can you balance respect for the past with response to present needs and future possibilities?

D. You Have Heard . . . , BUT I SAY. . . .

Call for volunteers to pantomime Jesus' four examples of preserving one's dignity through nonviolent resistance—the other cheek, the second mile, removing the undergarment, and giving what is asked. After each, ask the participants how they felt in their roles, and ask the group what they think of this approach to resisting evil. Then raise these questions about loving our enemies: Is it practical? possible? effective? faithful? When has it been tried? Will it work for nations or only individuals? Is violence acceptable in self-defense? What is the difference between passive submission and nonviolent resistance? Have you ever been in a situation where you had the opportunity to love your enemy? How did you respond? How do you feel about what you did? Remind them that the Hindu Gandhi once said that the difference between him and the Christians was that he believed that Jesus meant it.

E. Winding Up

Challenge members to continue thinking about these issues, to raise the questions about your church's past and future with the appropriate committees, to try practicing respect for opponents in everyday relationships, and to cultivate the psalmist's love for God's word. Depending on what issue caught fire, close by singing either "The Church's One Foundation," "Dear Jesus, in Whose Life I See," or "Take Time to Be Holy."

Lections for Eighth Sunday After the Epiphany

Old Testament: Isaiah 49:8-16a

CHAPTERS 40–55 of Isaiah are generally thought to come from a disciple of the eighth-century prophet whose thought is contained in Chapters 1–39. He lived two centuries later among the discouraged exiles in Babylon, and his mission was to give them new hope. They felt abandoned by YHWH and believed the gods of Babylon had overpowered him, but still longed for the comforts of Zion (Psalm 137).

> **Think About It:** "They felt abandoned." When in your life have you felt abandoned, isolated, or rejected? Was it when you had just moved, changed jobs, lost a loved one, experienced a separation? Did God seem distant? What gave you comfort and hope? Where did you turn? How did you recover a sense of God's presence?

Along came the second Isaiah to offer the people consolation and encouragement (40:1-2). In Chapters 40–48, he speaks of their coming deliverance from Babylon; and in 49–55, he promises their return to their homeland. Cyrus the Persian will be YHWH's chosen instrument to liberate his people. Once their captors have been subdued, God will lead them homeward across a magnificent highway through the desert wastes, like a shepherd guides his sheep (40:3-11). The false gods of Babylon will be powerless to prevent this (44:9-17), and the pronouncements of their priests and seers will prove empty (47:1-15). The power of YHWH will supersede them and bear his people to safety (46:1-7).

YHWH, the only true and living God, loves his people; and even though they have rebelled in the past, he will now have mercy on them, graciously forgive them, welcome them back (55:6-7), and give them another chance to serve him (44:22; 48:11). He is not just doing this for their benefit, though, for they are to be the means of bringing all nations to bow before God

100

in belief and adoration (45:22-23; 55:1-2). Second Isaiah is the foremost exponent of monotheism in the Old Testament and a forerunner of Jesus in describing God's tender mercy and grace.

The Suffering Servant

The agent of God's redemption will be his suffering servant, whom Bible scholars have variously identified as Jeremiah, Isaiah himself, the nation Israel, a faithful remnant, and God's holy people. But the prophet's description of him as God's faithful servant who suffered to bring people to God convinces Christians that Jesus has to be the true and only fulfillment of this profound prophecy.

Today's passage spells out the servant's mission. His prayer has been answered, and he has received God's help and commission—he will fulfill God's covenant (verse 8) by delivering the captives from darkness. On the journey home he will find them pasture, shelter, water, and a pathway through the mountains (verses 9-11). God's people will come from all directions (verse 12). "All nature sings and round them rings" because God has had mercy on his hurting people (verse 13). They thought he had deserted them; but even if a mother were to abandon her baby, God would never forsake his people (verses 14-15). He has written their names on his palms with indelible ink (verse 16).

Psalter: Psalm 131

The writer of this psalm of confidence expresses no pride or pretense. No claim is made of being a great thinker. There is no speculation of lofty ideas (verse 1). Whatever turmoil, it is now passed and gone. The psalmist's soul is content, like the satisfied child the psalmist is holding (verse 2). The writer calls on the people, with whom the psalmist feels a close affinity, to share in this trustful reliance on the God of the covenant. The psalmist wants them to find the peace of God that has become so meaningful (verse 3).

> ***Think About It:*** "I have calmed and quieted my soul" (verse 2). What is currently troubling your soul? Are you disturbed by new ideas? controversy? rejection? violence? Think of a baby asleep in your lap. Why is the baby not upset? Because the baby is being held close. Think of God holding you close (or writing your name on the palm of God's hand, as Isaiah put it). Does this thought give you peace? Can you share this contentment with your people?

Epistle: 1 Corinthians 4:1-5

To the previous claim of being a servant of Christ, Paul adds the duties of steward. As servant he would do his master's bidding; as steward he is responsible for his message. A servant performs the master's errands; a steward manages the master's household. As servant Paul traveled widely, spreading Christ's message and building his church; as steward he has the additional authority to expound and interpret that message, to be sure that the mysteries (depths) of faith are properly understood and communicated. For both responsibilities the qualification is to be worthy of the Master's trust. Paul's concern is not to convince the Corinthians of his faithfulness but rather to claim authority in his controversy with the local leaders who were undermining their faith.

These divisive teachers had been challenging his authority. Paul here contests their right to judge him. He knows he is guiltless, but he is not appealing to his own clear conscience or any human standard of evaluation. Rather he points to a higher authority—to God alone. Paul also warns his accusers to beware of sitting in judgment. When Christ comes all will stand under his judgment. He will make plain our innermost thoughts and motives and give to each the approbation or censure we deserve. Here Paul is echoing Jesus: "Do not judge, or you too will be judged" (Matthew 7:1, NIV).

Think About It: When a disagreement occurs in your church to what authority(ies) do you appeal? The Bible? precedent? a mediator? a rule book? a higher denominational figure? a process of negotiation? prayer to discern God's leading? Would you ever resort to Paul's warning to beware of God's final judgment? What effect would this have on the feelings of those involved and on the final outcome?

Today, sincere Christians disagree over whether homosexuality is a chosen lifestyle or an inherent orientation. Some appeal to Scripture describing it as a sin and an abomination, and pass judgment on those who practice it. Others say the verses referring to men's degrading sexual exploitation of young boys are irrelevant to today's loving, committed, same-sex covenant relationships. They further argue that Jesus' call to love our neighbors takes precedence over Old and New Testament prohibitions and ancient cultural customs. This controversy threatens to divide the church, as did another issue in Corinth. How can people who differ so strongly live together in the same household of faith? Does appeal to any authority resolve these kinds of conflicts? Is Paul's appeal to let God be the final judge relevant here?

Gospel: Matthew 6:24-34

The collection of Jesus' teachings commonly called the Sermon on the Mount were originally given for the instruction of those who had left all to follow him. Matthew later directed these sayings to the local church with which he was associated, which had become a more settled, well-off community. In this context, the sayings took on the character of the wisdom teaching common in the day and were shared with a wider audience. Today, because many of the sayings are difficult to apply literally in modern society, we tend not to take them too seriously. But let's look again at what Jesus is saying and ask how they speak to contemporary issues of society and lifestyle.

Addictions and Anxieties

Today's lection begins with a statement that assumes the background of slavery (verse 24). One present-day parallel is addiction. Nearly all Americans are addicted to something—tobacco, alcohol, drugs, work, fashions, food, TV, music, shopping, you name it. Jesus' hearers were addicted to wealth and possessions. If you are devoted to God, he says, there can be no room in your life for any addictions—most especially money. What is the appropriate attitude toward money of a disciple of Jesus?

Behind the issue of addiction is that of anxiety, to which the rest of the passage is devoted (verses 25-34). We become enslaved to the thing we think will make us secure and help us overcome worry—worry about being alone, hungry, in pain, in want, abandoned, or the ultimate anxiety, facing our own death. Whatever preoccupies us in our mad scramble for security becomes our god—for the moment or for a lifetime. Jesus says, Wait a minute. Stop and look around. The birds and flowers aren't anxious, and they are cared for. God knows their needs and provides for them. So why not trust like that? Our perpetual worry puts us in the same class as the Gentiles (read "atheists").

Put God First and Don't Worry

Our priority must be our commitment to the reign of God and what God considers good. Put that first, and everything else will fall into place (verse 33). We are supposed to be people of faith. Loosen up—and trust! Don't worry about tomorrow; your anxiety can't change what will take place then. Take things a day at a time; whatever trouble may be just over the horizon, with God we can handle everything (verse 34).

John Wesley said, "Earn all you can; save all you can; give all you can." He took this quite seriously and lived on the same frugal annual budget throughout his life, while giving increasing amounts to charity as his income grew. As a disciple of Jesus, what are the appropriate allocations of your resources for: housing, food, clothing, insurance,

Think About It: "Do not worry about your life" (verse 25). What are we anxious about/addicted to? What is the basic fear behind that? Is Jesus' advice to be like the birds and flowers and just trust God to take care of us realistic? How do we balance trust in God with appropriate precaution and preparation for a rainy day? What would it mean for us really to put commitment to God first in our life? How would that affect our budget and expenditures? Is it possible that a lot of our anxieties might then drop away?

103

savings, and charitable giving? How do we distinguish between necessities and luxuries? How much is enough? Are our answers dictated more by our addictions, our anxieties, or our trust in God?

Study Suggestions

A. Word Reaction

Distribute paper and pencils and give the group a quick word reaction test. Have them number from one to ten. Read out the following words, one by one, asking members to write the first word or phrase that comes to mind in response: *Abandonment. Servant. Controversy. Authority. Judgment. Sexuality. Addiction. Money. Anxiety. Trust.*

B. Abandonment and the Suffering Servant

Ask members to call out their responses to the word *abandonment*. Notice the feelings behind their words. Ask: What experiences evoked those feelings? Give the background of Second Isaiah. Read aloud Isaiah 49:8-16a. Compare the sense of abandonment felt by Judah with that expressed by class members. Then recount God's promise of restoration, to be led by his suffering servant. Ask for responses to the word *servant*. Compare those to the role of God's servant in bringing his people home and to the ministry of Jesus. Ask: How has your faith in God helped you deal with feelings of abandonment and depression?

C. Controversy, Authority, Judgment

Ask for responses to the word *controversy*, and identify related feelings. Ask: In what controversies have we recently been involved? How did these make you feel? How were they dealt with? Recall the controversy in the Corinthian church between Paul and the false teachers. Read 1 Corinthians 4:1-5. Then ask for responses to *authority*, commenting on the feelings they imply. Discuss the questions in the "Think About It" on page 102, plus: What part did judgmental attitudes play in the controversies you have shared? What authorities were turned to for help in resolving them? Were they helpful? Ask for responses to *judgment*. Would Paul's advice not to pass judgment now but to leave everything to God's ultimate judgment have been helpful in our controversies? Invite responses to *sexuality*, pose this issue as described in the last full paragraph on page 102, and discuss the questions in that paragraph.

D. Addiction, Money, Anxiety

Ask for responses to *addiction* and what addictions members think are most widespread today. Read Matthew 6:24, and discuss the similarity between slavery and addiction. Call for responses to *money*, and discuss whether participants think Jesus was right in posing addiction to wealth as a primary rival to God for our loyalty and commitment. Invite and discuss their responses to and feelings about *anxiety*. Read Matthew 6:25-32, and discuss the first three questions posed in the "Think About It" paragraph on page 103.

E. Trust

Read Matthew 6:33-34, invite responses to *trust*, and discuss the last four "Think About It" questions on page 103. Also ask: When so much is available to us and advertisers put so much pressure on us to buy, how can we give priority to God's reign and righteousness? What practical measures might we take to follow Wesley's three-point formula? Invite members to share what stewardship practices they follow to guide what they give, earn, and spend.

F. Close With Scripture and a Hymn

Close by reading the NRSV translation of Psalm 131. Note the feminine images in the text. Invite members to close their eyes and image themselves as babies lying in their mother's arms. Close by first humming, then singing softly either "On Eagle's Wings" or " 'Tis So Sweet to Trust in Jesus."

2-21-23

Lections for Transfiguration Sunday

Old Testament: Exodus 24:12-18

*T*HE lectionary for the last Sunday after Epiphany (which precedes Ash Wednesday, the beginning of Lent) always contains an account of Jesus' transfiguration on the mountain. The revelation of God's glory and power is a theme throughout the lections for today. The Old Testament reading, from the Book of Exodus, looks to another "mountaintop experience," that of Moses as he prepared once more to meet God face to face in order to receive the tablets containing the Law.

This was not Moses' first trip up Sinai. It had been on the holy mountain that Moses first encountered God in the burning bush. It had been on the holy mountain that God's own name was disclosed to Moses: YHWH, meaning "I AM WHO I AM," or "I WILL BE WHAT I WILL BE." It had been on that occasion that Moses learned God's awesome identity—and discovered his own, as the one commissioned to challenge Pharaoh in God's name. Today's verses follow an interesting encounter where Moses, Aaron and his sons, and the elders, not only see God and survive, but share in a meal in God's presence (Exodus 24:9-11).

Think About It: "Moses learned God's identity and discovered his own." What encounters with God have you had in which you discovered something about both God and yourself? What is the connection between knowing God and knowing oneself? Can there be a true revelation of God that does not expose us? Can one really know oneself apart from God?

Moses and Company at Sinai

The instruction to Moses and his company was to "come up to the LORD . . . and worship at a distance" (24:1). At this point, we see evidence that this longer passage may be the conflation of several different accounts of the same event. After camping at the base of the mountain, Moses, Aaron, and the others "went up" (verse 9). Then Moses was again invited to approach the Lord on the mountain. Next Moses and Joshua, who would one day assume the position of leadership in the covenant community, "set out" (verse 13) while the elders waited (verse 14). Aaron and Hur were left to deal with the issues of the community (hence the forging of the golden calf reported in Exodus 32).

Then Moses "went up" by himself (24:15). (We never see him come down to go up again.) According to verse 15, Moses alone was the one set apart for this encounter with YHWH; but others apparently saw God, too (24:9-11). This was either one trip reported by several sources, or several encounters with God reported as one story.

Moses on the Mountain

The summons to Moses, like the covenant itself, was initiated by God. Beginning at verse 15, Moses entered the cloud in which the presence of YHWH had settled on the mountain. No details are given concerning the six days (an allusion to the ordinary days of the week) Moses had to wait for God to speak. The image is one of silence and stillness, majesty and awe. On the seventh day (the sabbath) God called to Moses. The clear message is that God is in charge. The place of the revelation, the call to covenant, the waiting, the glory—all speak of the sovereignty of YHWH: "I WILL BE WHAT I WILL BE." (Chapters 25–31 of Exodus give the details of that visit with God.)

Moses remained in the presence of God's glory for "forty days and forty nights" (24:18). The number *forty*, which occurs frequently in Scripture (the days of rain in the story of Noah, the years in the wilderness, the days of Jesus' fast and temptation), connotes a long passage of time, not necessarily exactly forty.

Psalter: Psalm 99

Along with Psalms 93 and 96–98, Psalm 99 is considered an Enthronement Psalm that would be used during the Feast of Tabernacles, the celebration of the fall harvest. "The LORD reigns; let the nations tremble" (99:1, NIV) seems to anticipate the very experience of Peter, James, and John when they enter the glory of God's presence on the mountain. Some scholars suggest that a truer translation would be, "YHWH has become king." Again the theme of God's glory being revealed is accentuated. God speaks in "the pillar of cloud" (99:7); the call is given to worship "at his holy mountain" (99:9).

Holiness is attributed to God three times, in verses 3, 5, and 9—verses 5 and 9 functioning as a refrain that breaks the psalm into two sections. Verses 1-5 extol YHWH's rule; verses 6-9 address YHWH in a just and forgiving relationship to the people. God's universal dominion is illustrated by the trembling of the people and the shaking of the earth.

God is enthroned upon the cherubs (winged creatures with human faces and animal bodies). Cherubs decorated the ark of the covenant, which housed the stone tablets delivered to Moses, as well as the Holy of Holies within the Temple. The ark itself was looked upon as YHWH's footstool. The Temple, as the resting place of the ark—the Law—is the figurative "holy mountain" where the Law was first given to Moses.

Epistle: 2 Peter 1:16-21

This is Peter's post-Resurrection witness to the glory of God revealed in Jesus at the time of his transfiguration upon the mountain. By asserting his participation as an eyewitness to this glory, Peter's authority and that of his teaching are established. This is emphatically stated in verses 20 and 21, which ground true prophecy in the revelation of God as opposed to human interpretation. In the next chapter Peter disputes false teachers, describing them as "springs without water and mists driven by a storm" (2 Peter 2:17, NIV). As an eyewitness to the divine unveiling of Jesus, Peter's prophecy may be regarded as authentic and superior to that of his opponents.

The apocalyptic imagery in Matthew's account of the Transfiguration is not the emphasis in Peter's recollection and recounting of the event. The appearance of Moses and Elijah, the radiance of Jesus' face and robe, the cloud and the brightness of God's glory, are not the central features of his testimony. Peter emphasizes not what was seen, but what was heard. "He received honor and glory . . . when that voice [of God] was conveyed to him" (1:17). Peter was a witness to the message of God concerning Jesus, "This is my Son, my Beloved, with whom I am well pleased" (1:17). Peter was a witness to the moment of Jesus' exaltation.

The Gospel accounts of the Transfiguration connect Jesus with God's unfolding plan of salvation, as evidenced by the presence of Moses and Elijah. Jesus was shown to be the Messiah, the fulfillment of God's promise. In Second Peter, the Transfiguration is connected not only to the distant past and the Resurrection. Jesus' return is assured through remembrance of his exaltation on the mountain. The Transfiguration is a witness to this future glory, as a "lamp shining in a dark place, until the day dawns and the morning star rises in your hearts" (1:19). The Transfiguration is the lamp that reminds the church of the future reality of Christ. It provides comfort and confidence for daily living, and hope in the coming glory.

Think About It: God's prophetic message about the Son is to claim your attention like a lamp claims the darkness. Does Christ occupy such a position of prominence and attention in your life? How does he make himself known to you?

Gospel: Matthew 17:1-9

Matthew's account of Jesus' transfiguration bears striking similarity of detail to today's lection from Exodus. There is a six-day interval. There is a high mountain. God's voice is heard within an overshadowing cloud. And while it is not included in the verses read today, Moses' own face shines in response to his encounter with YHWH (Exodus 34:29). With both Moses and Jesus, God's glory is revealed upon the mountaintop.

Features of the Transfiguration account also appear in descriptions of both Jesus' resurrection and ascension (particularly Luke 24:4 and Acts 1:9-11), including shining robes and the ascent into a cloud. There are sixteen mentions of such garments being worn by heavenly beings in the Book of Revelation alone. These signify an encounter with God's glory (usually expressed in images of light), as well as the limits of human language in articulating an experience of the divine. The images are apocalyptic or the revelation of the hidden things of God disclosed in vivid, larger-than-life language and symbolism. Jesus himself refers to the experience as a vision (Matthew 17:9), another feature of apocalyptic literature.

And His Face Shone Like the Sun

The Greek word *metamorphothe*, rendered in the NRSV as "transfigured" (17:2), provides a challenge to interpreters because its meaning is ambiguous. The English understanding of *metamorphosis*, as change or transformation, can be misleading. As an apocalyptic vision, the transfiguration of Jesus' face and clothing was not a change into something new, but rather an uncovering of who Jesus really was. Peter, James, and John witnessed, if only for a moment, the glory of God revealed in the Son. This was the true Jesus.

> *Think About It:* The disciples fell down in awe in the face of God and their call to discipleship. Why would they be awestruck? What would they be afraid of? Are your faith and commitment to Christ that passionate? What emotions do you feel in the presence of Christ?

This mountaintop experience occurred on Jesus' way to the cross. The words, "This is my Son, the Beloved; with him I am well pleased" (17:5), emanating from the bright cloud of God's glory, echoed the words spoken at Jesus' baptism (3:17). From the beginning of his ministry, Jesus was the Beloved. Now, as he neared its end, the disciples heard the urgent command, "Listen to him!" They fell down in awe, recognizing that they were face to face with God and with their own call to discipleship, the call to pick up their own crosses (16:24), which immediately precedes the account of the Transfiguration.

Jesus' Companions

Peter, James, and John represented the inner core of the Twelve. Peter's confession of Jesus as Messiah preceded this Transfiguration experience. On the mountain, Jesus was revealed as the Son of Man. Peter's desire to make three dwellings discloses he was unaware that this vision would last but a moment. As God had touched human existence with divine glory, now Jesus touched the disciples as he raised them up and reassured them, "do not be afraid" (17:7).

Moses and Elijah, representing the Law and the Prophets, affirmed Peter's confession of Jesus as the fulfillment of messianic hope. Their presence unveiled the continuity of God's plan of salvation. In the verses that follow this section, Jesus addressed the question of Elijah's return (as prophesied in Malachi 4:5-6) before the coming of the Messiah. Jesus had stated earlier that Elijah had returned in the person of John the Baptist (Matthew 11:14).

Jesus charged the three disciples to keep silence. Indeed, how could they possibly share what they had seen (but could not fully comprehend) until the ultimate revelation of God's glory, when "the Son of Man has been raised from the dead" (17:9)?

Study Suggestions

A. Open With a Song

Open by singing "Christ, Whose Glory Fills the Skies." Pray that God's glory may be revealed in your study and that your group members may be inspired to glorify God during the coming week.

B. Go to the Mountaintop

Using Bibles, commentary, and members' knowledge of Scripture, outline the Moses story up to the time of receiving of the Law at Sinai. Ask: Why do you think God chose Moses to receive the divine revelation?

Have someone read aloud Exodus 24:12-18 while the others listen and try to picture the scene. Ask them to tell the story from the perspective of Joshua, Aaron, the elders, and the people. Discuss: What do you think the experience was like for Moses? How was he changed by this encounter? How would you define glory? Note that glory has both visible (brightness, splendor, radiance) and emotional or spiritual (honor, fame, grandeur) significance.

Ask participants to remain silent for two minutes, then discuss: What did you feel and think about? Did it seem like a long time? What would it be like to sit in silence for six days in God's presence? Why did God wait so long to speak? In our busy lives, how can God get through to us? How can we find more quiet time for listening to God?

C. Examine the Transfiguration

After reviewing the Gospel commentary, form two smaller groups. Ask one to compare Matthew's Transfiguration account (17:1-9) with those of

Mark (9:2-8), and Luke (9:28-36), and the other to compare it with 2 Peter 1:16-21. Have both identify similarities and differences. Then come together to share insights.

D. Take the Apostles' View

Assign the roles of Peter, James, and John to three group members, with each to tell the story from that character's perspective. Have the rest think of themselves as the other disciples, hearing the story afterwards at the foot of the mountain. Ask them: After hearing what happened, how do you feel about Jesus? toward Peter, James, and John? about your task as disciples from now on?

Now re-read verses 9-13, and discuss Jesus' response to the disciples. Why did he not want them to tell what they had seen and heard? Are there times when it is best to keep quiet about what God is revealing to us? How do we know when to speak and when to remain silent?

What other Jesus stories can you think of involving touch? (See Matthew 8:3; 8:15; 9:20; 9:29; 14:36; 20:34; and other verses.) In each case: What effect did the touch of Jesus have? What effect does touch have on our relationships? What guidelines govern touching in your group or church? Through what medium may we feel the touch of Jesus?

What other stories include the message "do not be afraid"? (See Matthew 14:27; 28:10; Mark 5:36; Luke 12:4.) In each case: What were they afraid of? How did Jesus calm their fears? What experiences of ours correspond to this? When is fear an appropriate response?

E. Summarize

Point out that the common theme in the four lections is the transformational power of God's presence. Ask participants to share times when they felt they had seen God "face to face." Ask: What was this experience like? Was it transformational? If so, how? Noting the proximity of the Transfiguration to the disciples' call to a commitment to Christ, do you feel you are called to do or be something more? Explain.

F. Close With Praise and Commitment

Read Psalm 99 in unison. Invite members to stand in a circle, join hands or hug (touch), and offer prayers of thanks for ways God becomes known to us, and for commitment to more faithful discipleship.

LENT

Lections for First Sunday in Lent

*T*Old Testament: Genesis 2:15-17; 3:1-7

ODAY is the first Sunday in Lent, a period of forty days between Ash Wednesday and Easter (not counting Sundays) during which Christians traditionally have devoted themselves to prayer, fasting, self-examination, and repentance in preparation for Holy Week and Easter. Today's readings recount pivotal events in God's unfolding salvation history, beginning with the temptation of Adam and Eve in the garden and continuing through Jesus' temptation in the wilderness. The Lenten season invites reflection on who we are as human beings in relation to God. This week's lessons move us from the sin of the first Adam to the free gift of grace offered by the second Adam, Jesus Christ.

The Beginning of Life

In the Judeo-Christian tradition, the human saga begins with an account of the origin of our need for salvation: the fall of humankind. The creation has, in Genesis 2, already been called forth from chaos and given form. The garden, with its variety of flora and fauna, is "up and running." Today's lection begins with the place of human beings in creation. The human creature's name 'adam, being taken from the word for soil or ground, 'adama, has a Hebrew understanding similar to that of "earthling." The creature has a God-given purpose, to "till and keep" the garden.

> **Think About It:** "The tree of the knowledge of good and evil." What do you think this tree represents in human experience? Why did God want to keep this knowledge from us? Is it the knowledge itself or the attitudes it evokes in us that is the problem? Did gaining this knowledge make humans free?

With the task, the humans are given a certain freedom within the garden; everything they could ever need is at their disposal. God encourages, "freely eat"

114

(Genesis 2:16), having personally planted an easily accessed "tree of life" (2:9) at the garden's center. The only prohibition, the "but," comes in verse 17; the creatures are forbidden to eat from the tree of the "knowledge of good and evil." To eat from this tree is to die (in Hebrew, literally, "on the day"). Human task and human freedom, assigned by God, do not include the attainment of such knowledge. The fruit of this tree is reserved for God alone.

"You Will Not Die. . . ."

Today's passage skips the creation of the "helper" (2:18), the one (perhaps better expressed as) "corresponding to him," and moves to the beginning of Chapter 3 and the introduction of the serpent. The serpent appears without warning. There is no explanation for why the serpent is there, nor any indication of its purpose. In both NRSV and NIV, the serpent is described as "crafty" (in Hebrew 'arum, a play on the word "naked," arummin); in other versions as "cunning" or "subtle." Notice the number of verbs associated with God in Genesis 2; God forms, breathes, makes, takes, plants, and commands. God acts in decisive ways with purpose.

Think About It: The creature has a God-given purpose. What is God's general purpose for all human beings? Do you feel that God has a special purpose for you? If, so, what is it, do you think?

The serpent, on the other hand, confounds God's purpose merely by questioning and contradicting God's instruction. There is no exertion of power or force; through distortion of God's word, the serpent's work is accomplished. By simple speech, the serpent is able to turn the humans from their created purpose—as well as from their freedom—in an attempt to make them equal to God. The innocence of their relationship with God ends with the knowledge of their nakedness (3:7). They are now capable of knowing shame and fear.

Psalter: Psalm 32

This selection—along with Psalms 6, 38, 51, 102, 130, and 143—is a "penitential" psalm, although the joyful anticipation of God's forgiveness is expressed throughout. "Happiness" is equated with the forgiveness of sin. Understandably, Paul quotes the first two verses of Psalm 32 in Romans 4:6-8.

Verses 1 and 2 are in the form of a beatitude, "Happy are those. . . ." This feature, as well as the inclusion of other words and phrases—sin, night and day, teach (which shares a common root with "law" or "instruction"), way, wicked, righteous—echoes Psalms 1 and 2. The distinction is made, however, that righteousness depends not on sinless living, but on divine forgiveness. The righteous are still subject to sin, but their "sin is covered" (verse 1).

The words associated with sin—transgression, iniquity, guilt—in the first five verses (as well as the effects of sin—the body wasting away, the groaning, the drying up of strength) are not repeated after the declaration of God's grace (32:7). The psalmist addresses God directly: "I acknowledged my sin to you . . . and you forgave the guilt of my sin" (verse 5). This realization becomes the psalmist's witness. The call to gladness, the call to "shout for joy" (verse 11) is not a proclamation of personal righteousness, but an invitation to others to witness God's grace for themselves.

Epistle: Romans 5:12-19

The relationship between sin and grace is the major focus of Paul's Letter to the Romans. Today's lection relates the action of Adam in the garden with the saving grace of Jesus Christ, the "new Adam." It is the relationship between death and life, between an old world and a new world. In Paul's understanding, sin and death are powers that entered the world when Adam turned away from God's purpose. Sin was a reality before the giving of the law (5:13); the law, Paul asserts later in the Epistle, accentuates the power of sin. Only through Christ is the new reality of grace and justification realized.

The Nature of Sin

More than a list of specific wrongdoings, sin is not an action, but a power that has taken control of human life since Adam. Sin is the state of separation between God and humankind. For Paul, original sin is not something passed physically from generation to generation; rather, it is a power that "came into" the world at the time of the Fall and to which all humanity is subject. "Because all have sinned" (5:12), "all . . . fall short of the glory of God" (Romans 3:23).

> **Think About It:** All have sinned and fall short of God's glory, but Christ redeems the fallen. Do you think of yourself as a sinner? as falling short? as redeemed? as saved by grace? Is sin part of human nature, or something we willfully do?

One Man's Act

As Adam ushered in the power of sin, so Christ ushers in the power of grace. Paul uses a familiar Greek rhetorical device of arguing from the lesser to the greater. Having discussed the all-encompassing nature of sin, he moves to a discussion of the reign of grace initiated by Jesus Christ. Sin is no match for the power of God's grace, which entered the world through "one man's act of righteousness" that "leads to justification and life for all" (5:18). Grace is not a reward for righteous behavior; grace is God's free gift that overcomes the power of condemnation by the power of justification and righteousness. Human beings are not asked to choose between sin and grace; both are realities of the human condition, universal in scope. The power of grace, however, ultimately prevails because it is the power of God freely given.

Gospel: Matthew 4:1-11

This lection (see also Mark 1:12-13 and Luke 4:1-13) tells another story of temptation, that of Jesus following his baptism. The Spirit led Jesus into the wilderness to experience temptation by the devil. This was the purpose of his desert sojourn. Jesus' responses to the tempter's taunts and questions reveal his clear understanding of his God-given purpose. Contrast this with Adam's passing-the-buck response to God in Genesis 3:9-12. Jesus knew who he was and acted in accordance with that knowledge.

The Devil

Scriptural treatments of evil and temptation are varied. In Job's prologue, Satan (a Hebrew figure) is presented as a member of the heavenly court acting as a legal prosecutor. First Chronicles 21:1 presents the image of an opposing counsel. This role of accuser or adversary gives way in the New Testament to an image of "the devil" (*diabolos* in Greek), who oversees the dominion of evil. How this change in understanding occurred is not made clear in Scripture. The devil's aim is to destroy humankind through temptation.

After forty days and nights, the biblical connotation of a prolonged period of time, Jesus was "famished" (Matthew 4:2), a very human condition. In spite of his hunger Jesus would not, however, call upon any superhuman powers to ease his discomfort. Adam was surrounded by plenty and encouraged to "freely eat," ultimately choosing the only forbidden fruit to satisfy his hunger to be like God. Jesus, on the other hand, would not abandon his purpose as God's servant in the face of his own need. "One does not live by bread alone," he answered, quoting the word of God from Deuteronomy 8:3. His response, like his need, exemplified his true humanity.

The Devil Works His Tools

The actions and responses of Adam and Jesus are strikingly dissimilar, but the tools of the tempters are identical. No physical force is used. The serpent and the devil manipulate God's own words to lure Adam and Jesus away from their true purpose in relationship to God. "He will command his angels" (4:6), he taunted, quoting Psalm 91. By jumping from the pinnacle of the Temple, wouldn't Jesus be providing God a chance to display power and fulfill prophecy? "Do not put the LORD your God to the test" (from Deuteronomy 6:16), was Jesus' only response.

Matthew is fond of placing significant events in Jesus' life on a "very high mountain" (the Sermon on the Mount, the Transfiguration, the final parting from the disciples). Here Jesus was offered the ultimate "reward." From this high place, Jesus was shown the world's kingdoms and offered the very thing for which Adam had striven—equality with God. But Jesus could not be swayed. He turned the tables on the devil and commanded him, "Away!" When he quoted again from Deuteronomy (6:13), "worship the Lord your God / and serve only him," the devil departed without another word.

A Victory, But Not the End

The tempter, seeking to destroy humankind by leading them away from God, was dismissed by Jesus' definitive statement of God's absolute sovereignty. His power over the devil was rooted in his understanding and acceptance of his place—of humankind's place—in relation to God. Knowledge of God's word and obedience to God's will allowed Jesus to persevere against temptation. Jesus had not seen the last of the devil, to be sure; but the age of grace was dawning in the world.

> **Think About It:** Jesus has not seen the end of the devil, but grace abounds. How do you experience temptation? Do you ever feel as if you are involved in spiritual warfare? What do you do? How does your faith hold firm? Where do you turn for help?

Study Suggestions

A. Open With Singing

Sing a hymn that speaks to temptation, such as "I Need Thee Every Hour." Pray the Lord's Prayer, asking group members to reflect on the phrase, "lead us not into temptation, but deliver us from evil." (Some change the first clause to, "help us to resist temptation." Is this what is meant? If not, what?)

B. Talk About Temptation

Ask members to jot down three things that tempt them. After several moments of reflection, invite members to share. Are these tempting things tangible (money, food, possessions), or intangible (power, attention, control)? Which temptations are stronger? Which are harder to admit (to ourselves as well as to others)? Define *temptation*. How can temptation be overcome?

C. Compare Christ and Adam

Form two groups, assigning the Old Testament lection to one and the Gospel lection to the other. Ask each small group to read and discuss its story (using background material and "Think About It" questions on pages 114–15 or 117–18). Have each group prepare to share a dramatic reading or a pencil drawing of its story. When each group has presented, compare them using the following questions: What is the setting of each story? What are the similarities and differences between the tempters? between their methods? Who is in power in each story? What is the source of the power? What are the similarities and differences between Adam and Jesus? Why are they significant for us today? Is humankind still seeking equality with God? In what ways? How are we to deal with the temptation to reach beyond our assigned role?

D. Examine Spiritual Warfare

Some persons experience calamity or temptation following an intense exercise of prayer or other Christian practice. They believe these events represent the struggle between good and evil. Discuss: Do we believe in the idea of spiritual warfare? Do we find that faithful acts are challenged by periods of trouble or distress? How do we faithfully address difficulties?

E. Consider the Epistle

Ask someone to read Romans 5:12-19 aloud. Ask: who (or what) is really in charge of the world—according to this Scripture? according to your own perception? After summarizing the background material, ask: How does Paul understand sin? How do the realities of sin and death co-exist with the realities of grace and justification? If God's grace is the greater power, how do you explain the continued presence of sin in the world? What does it mean to be living in the age of grace? How does the image of Jesus as the "new Adam" give encouragement to those seeking to withstand temptation?

F. Reflect on the Season of Lent

Ask participants to share their impressions of Lent. Discuss: How do you observe Lent? How can the Lenten season become an opportunity for Christians to celebrate the reign of grace in light of the reign of sin? Read and discuss Psalm 32, highlighting the psalmist's equation of "forgiveness" with "happiness and joy." How can we use this understanding in our witness and invitation to others?

G. Summarize and Conclude

The themes of temptation and sin run through each of today's lections. Ask: As a result of examining the grace of God available to us as sinners, do you feel led to act or believe differently? What do you feel God is calling you to do or to be in your own exercise of faith? How do you handle temptation? What clues do Jesus' responses to the devil give as to the resources to draw on? How can you place your trust in God to see you through times of fallenness and temptation? How can group members support one another during this Lenten period to become stronger spiritually? End by saying Psalm 32:5-7 together as a prayer.

Lections for Second Sunday in Lent

Old Testament: Genesis 12:1-4a

*T*ODAY'S Old Testament lection, despite its brevity, marks one of the most significant events in God's salvation story—the call of Abram/Abraham. This was the beginning of a journey for one elderly, childless couple that has since come to signify an epic voyage for all humankind. God's call, God's promise, and Abram's "yes" set a new course for the relationship between Creator and created. To this foundational covenant we can trace the origins of three of the world's major faith traditions—Judaism, Christianity, and Islam—all having a common father (Abraham) and mother (Sarah) who were blessed by God to be a blessing to the nations.

Introducing a First Family

In Genesis 11:26-31, we are told that Abram was the son of Terah, that Abram took Sarai as his wife, that Terah and his family set out from Ur of the Chaldeans (southern Iraq) to journey to Canaan (Palestine), but only got as far as Haran (northern Iraq) where they settled down and Terah died. We are also told that Sarai and Abram had no children. It is significant that this detail is included in the genealogy here, for without an heir Abram would have ended the line of his ancestors. Childlessness would rob the family of a future, without which there would be no hope. For, failing to produce a child, Abram and Sarai were living with the disappointment and shame imposed on them by the culture of that time, for which heirs who could carry on the family lineage were all important.

In light of their situation, however, they had established a life within their community in the midst of their extended family. This was the context in which they expected to live out their remaining years in relative peace and prosperity. But God had something else in mind for them.

120

The Call of Abram

The actual call event is not detailed. Unlike Moses, who met God in a burning bush, Abram's encounter was conveyed without supernatural signs, without special effects. God simply spoke, and Abram obeyed. Without question, without hesitation, without needing to know God's name or credentials, or his ultimate destination, Abram picked up his life and, with his wife and his nephew Lot (12:4b), he went as he had been told by God. What had happened up to this point in his life was inconsequential; for from this moment on Abram's life truly began.

> **Think About It:** Abram and Sarai were already old when called to go somewhere new, and yet they packed up their belongings and went. What would it take for you to respond to a call from God so totally? What kinds of choices or moves would correspond to this change for you? What would cause you to hesitate or resist? What might convince you to respond as Abram and Sarai did?

The Response of Faith

Abram's response was the embodiment of faith; his future was the embodiment of hope. What was once barren, God promised, would become fruitful. This promise empowered Abram (and all his descendants in faith) to leave behind what was secure, familiar, and comfortable in order to embrace the unknown possibilities of God. Abram thus became the very model for stepping out in faith. His nomadic journey across the desert wastes of the ancient Near East symbolizes the faith pilgrimage of every believer. The gift of faith was not for Abraham's family alone. (Abram's name was changed to Abraham when the covenant was established; see Genesis 17:1-8.) God's promise provided a blessing for all humankind through God's blessing bestowed on one man who was willing to risk everything to say "yes" to God's call.

Psalter: Psalm 121

Psalm 121 falls in the collection of "Songs of Ascents" (Psalms 120–134) sung by pilgrims "going up" to Jerusalem for the great festivals (including Passover and the Feast of Weeks or Tabernacles). Characteristic of an Ascent, Psalm 121 begins by directing the pilgrim's eyes upward, toward Mount Zion, where YHWH would be encountered. The lifting of eyes also signifies dependence on God, creator of heaven and earth and source of help and hope.

God is the keeper of Israel, offering shelter and comfort. In eight short verses a form of *keep* appears six times. As Israel is so often instructed to "keep" (observe, honor) the ways of God, so God will "keep" (protect, guide) the people. Israel's keeper is ever vigilant, stopping "neither [to] slumber nor sleep" (verse 4). This is, perhaps, an allusion to Elijah's showdown with the priests of Baal, taunting them with the notion that "no show" Baal must be sleeping (1 Kings 18:27). There is no need to awaken the keeper of Israel; by day or by night, they can be confident that no harm will befall them.

Epistle: Romans 4:1-5, 13-17

Abraham's response to God's call is also the focus of today's Epistle lesson. Paul expounds Abraham's faith, quoting a later passage from Genesis 15:6: "Abraham believed God, and it was reckoned to him as righteousness." Abraham was made righteous, Paul asserts, not because of his work, but through his faith. The believing itself, however, should not be interpreted as Abraham's work, or the reason for his designation as righteous. Righteousness is not a reward for belief. Abraham is declared righteous through God's grace in response to—not because of—his faith. Righteousness is a gift that only God can bestow.

Faith as Obedience

Faith here is not a religious attribute; it is trust in God's promise. Faith is the receiving and keeping of God's word. As such, it is the arena of God's gracious activity. The power and prerogative are God's alone, the God who "gives life to the dead and calls into existence the things that do not exist" (Romans 4:17).

> **Think About It:** God's grace is not dependent on human action. What is the proper connection between faith and right living? What is the difference between a Christian and a good person? Does God accept all, or only those who believe and obey? Can God's grace be resisted?

The section omitted from Chapter 4 (verses 6-12) focuses on the question of circumcision in regard to faith and righteousness. Abraham believed, and was reckoned as righteous, although as yet uncircumcised. God's grace is not dependent on human action. Circumcision was the sign—the seal—of Abraham's righteousness. Circumcision here represents the law. Righteousness does not depend on fulfilling the law, but on faith alone.

Faith of Our Father

The promise made to Abraham's descendants is not transmitted through the Law. Thus Abraham is the spiritual father of all who believe, so they too might be reckoned as righteous (4:11). For Jews, he is "ancestor according to the flesh" (4:1), as implied in the Genesis promise. But for Gentiles as well, he is father in faith, the model for the believer.

Today's lection picks up at verse 13 with a discussion of the primacy of faith over law, a central issue in Romans. Chapter 7 will deal specifically with faith as the prerequisite for understanding the law. That faith itself is not a good work cannot be overly stressed in this passage (or in Paul's understanding of their relationship to one another). It is God, not the believer, who "justifies the ungodly" (4:5) and makes right living possible.

Gospel: John 3:1-17

Nicodemus provides a stark contrast to Abraham. Abraham believed God's promise and acted on it. Nicodemus, on the other hand, although a faithful and representative leader of the Jews, understood faith as the result of what he could discover and validate through investigation and deliberation. He had seen the verifiable evidence (through the miracles) that God was present in Jesus. Cautiously, by night, Nicodemus approached Jesus. He showed none of Abraham's daring. He was unable to step out on faith but needed proof.

The stage is set for the encounter between Nicodemus and Jesus in the last verses of the preceding chapter. Nicodemus had come to believe in Jesus during the Passover festival. And Jesus already knew what was in Nicodemus's heart (John 2:23-25). A hesitant believer, Nicodemus, as a member of the Sanhedrin, was literally a ruler. His cautious approach to Jesus, though apparently in earnest, revealed the inadequacy of his faith.

Born From Above
Nicodemus's faith, tied to what he considered plausible, rendered him unable to grasp the fullness of God present in Jesus. Indeed, it would take another act of God for him to comprehend what Jesus was talking about. It is not enough to be born physically. To see the realm of God one must be "born from above" (3:3). This was incomprehensible to Nicodemus. The Greek *anothen* can mean "from above," "again," or "anew." Nicodemus interpreted it to mean "again." His literalism in regard to entering again into the womb further illustrates his reliance on tangible, observable facts.

His religion prevented him from experiencing the radical newness of God's activity, likened by Jesus to the wind (*ruach* in Hebrew, *pneuma* in Greek). Both languages use the same word to mean "spirit" or "wind," creating a play on words impossible to reproduce in English (see Ecclesiastes 11:5). Nicodemus's understanding, being born only of the flesh, limited his ability to see beyond the physical into the realm of the Spirit. Jesus reminded him that the effects of the wind were visible, even if the wind itself was not. So it is with the things of the Spirit. To embrace the newness of God, one must be born through the Spirit. Being born of water would later come to signify Christian baptism.

By an Act of God

This pouring out of the Spirit "from above" (like Abraham's designation as righteous) cannot be accomplished through human action. Jesus could only know these heavenly things because he was from God. John stresses throughout his Gospel (1:18; 5:37; 6:46; 14:7-9) that only Jesus had seen God. It was through his "lifting up" (crucifixion), resurrection, and ascension, that the work of the Spirit was made known. The things of God were revealed only through Jesus' sacrifice and ultimate glorification. For John, this was a continuous action of ascent that led to the gift of eternal life for all who believe.

Think About It: John 3:16 may be the best-known verse in the Bible, but what does it mean to you? What does it mean that God gave a beloved child for us? What has been your experience of the new birth? Is it a one-time experience, or does the renewing wind of the Spirit continue to blow in your life?

For God So Loved the World . . .

The focus shifts to God in verse 16. The purpose of Jesus being "lifted up," in both his crucifixion and the glory to follow, was to manifest God's love for the world. God sent the Son into the world in order to reveal divine love and through that love save creation.

Study Suggestions

A. Sing and Pray

Sing a hymn of stepping out in faith, such as "Where He Leads Me I Will Follow." Pray for the strength to respond to God with the faith of Abraham. Pray for the courage to say "yes" to God.

B. Explore Abraham's Call

Read together Genesis 12:1-4a and the information on pages 120–21. Ask members to think of a one-word description of Abraham's life before his encounter with God and another of his response to God's call. List these on the chalkboard or a sheet of paper. Ask: How do you characterize the call? the response?

Ask for two volunteers to roleplay the ensuing conversation between Abram and Sarai as they try to decide how to respond to God—setting the story in the present. Ask: Is God's call to us as radical as the call to Abram and Sarai? Would we be willing to do what they did? What were the obstacles they would have encountered? How do these compare with the barriers to faithful living we face? Define faith in the context of this story. Is this the same way we understand faith today?

124

C. Examine Faith in Paul

Read Romans 4:1-5 and 13-17, skimming the omitted verses. Clarify verses or concepts that members find hard to understand. Drawing on the information on pages 122–23, discuss the questions in the "Think About It" paragraph, plus the following: What is faith according to Paul's account of Abraham's story? If faith precedes righteousness, why isn't faith a work of the believer? Can we believe our way into righteousness?

Use this passage (and Genesis 12:1-4a) to develop a definition of faithful living based on Abraham's response to God. This might include elements of trust, obedience, and reliance on God's grace. Ask: Why is Abraham the father of all who believe?

D. Study the Gospel

Ask members to recite John 3:16. Ask: Why is this verse so beloved? What does it add to understandings of belief and faith discussed in the other three lections? Call for two volunteers to read the parts of Jesus and Nicodemus. Discuss what it means to be "born from above." Invite members to share what being "born again" means to them. Ask: Who initiates the action in this birth from above? Discuss the "Think About It" questions on page 124.

Compare Nicodemus's response to God's radical newness with that of Abraham. Ask: Is our response to God, as Christians today, closer to that of Abraham or Nicodemus? Can we learn how to step out in faith? How can we as a group support one another in this effort?

E. Summarize

Common themes in today's lections include answering God's call and obedience to God's will. Abraham and family went out not knowing; Nicodemus, not knowing, came to Jesus to seek direction. Invite members to tell of times when they "went out not knowing," or prayed for help or discernment in deciding on a step of faith. Experiences like changing jobs, moving to a new community, entering or leaving a relationship, or a congregation starting a new ministry, might be cited.

Then ask: When we accept God's call to step out in faith, with the promise of blessing but no assurance of the outcome, what must we give up? What do we gain? Is submitting to God's will or plan for our lives something to be discussed in terms of gain and loss? If not, what are the criteria for faithful decision-making? What new steps of faith might today's Scriptures be calling us to take?

F. Close With the Psalm

Pray Psalm 121 together, lifting your souls to the One who was lifted up. Ask the Keeper of Israel to empower you to respond in faith to God's call.

3.14

Lections for Third Sunday in Lent

Old Testament: Exodus 17:1-7

*I*SRAEL'S experiences in the wilderness provide us with images of a people in need of a God who saves. Wandering, hungry, and thirsty, the newly forming people of God encountered situations that could only be resolved by faith. The Israelites had traveled roughly 250 miles through the desert from Egypt to their present location at Rephidim, about 25 miles northwest of Mount Sinai. "The whole congregation of the Israelites journeyed by stages, as the Lord commanded" (17:1). This suggests a nomadic existence, in which the people camped for a while, grazed their flocks, and then moved on.

Reasonable Rebellion

The people's sojourn in the wilderness, which had been about two months long at that point, depicts a people reaching physical, emotional, and spiritual bankruptcy. Not only did they want water they also needed it. YHWH had promised a land flowing with milk and honey (Exodus 3:8). In their needy state, the people rebelled. Although their murmuring against Moses seemed to stem from their thirst, hunger, and fear, it also revealed a theological crisis. Though God had already promised to protect and provide for the people at all times, their complaints questioned the sufficiency of God.

Think About It: "Is the LORD among us or not?" When have you been pushed to the limit and wondered if God had deserted you? Is God present with us whether we are aware of it or not? whether we are blessed or not? whether our prayers are answered or not? What assures us of God's presence and guidance during dark times?

The question, "Is the LORD among us or not?" (17:7) implies a dichotomy or fallibility within God. Could God be both compassionate and passionless, simultaneously a promise-maker and a promise-breaker? The children of Israel

126

demanded an answer from Moses. In the midst of this rebellion, Israel's faith-lessness allowed God to reassure them that the promise of sustenance was both spiritual and physical. Their immediate needs were met miraculously with manna, quail, and water. The rebellion may have seemed reasonable, but their faith was seriously lacking.

Quarreling and Testing

In naming the locale Meribah ("quarrel") and Massah ("test"), Moses also identified the faithlessness of the people. Rather than giving thanks for the manna and quail, the people contended that Moses had deceived them and that God had abandoned them. Moses in turn pleaded with God, "What shall I do with this people? They are almost ready to stone me" (17:4). The wonder and triumph of God's acts of salvation were all but forgotten.

Geologists have shown that the desolate region of Horeb contains sources of water that seep through the crevices of the eroded rock cliffs. Moses, who years before had tended his father-in-law Jethro's flocks in this region (Exodus 3:1), knew the terrain. Water was available, but it was not as abun-dant as it was along the irrigation canals of Egypt. God provided all the water that was needed. So it was that the people drank. God's saving acts had guided them and taught them to soften their hearts.

The real test here was not the people's demands of God, but came from a God who was seeking an obedient and faithful people. They had to learn from experiences like this that, "one does not live by bread alone, but by every word that comes from the mouth of the LORD [YHWH]" (Deuteronomy 8:3b). God wanted his people to learn to live faithfully. Life at the mercy of the elements in the desert required complete dependence on the grace of God. The people needed to be willing to accept deliverance and to trust God's providence for their very survival.

Psalter: Psalm 95

This is an "enthronement psalm," in which the worshiper is invited in three movements to give praise and thanks to God (95:1, 2, 6). Our confi-dence in God is assured because of what God has done in the past, and God's present activity charges and ignites the soul for faithful obedience. Nevertheless, the psalmist is not naïve to the historic lack of faith and easily swayed opinion of God's people. Worshipers are reminded of Israel's sin at Meribah and Massah: stiff-necked people who doubted God's ability to meet their needs. In an otherwise celebrative psalm that seems to end abruptly and ominously, the people are told, in effect, "Do not let this happen to you." Rather, like simple sheep out to pasture, they are encouraged, "O that today you would listen to [God's] voice" (95:7b).

Epistle: Romans 5:1-11

These verses call forth a sense of abiding gratitude for the gift of grace God provides through Christ. Humanity's justification (being made right) before God rests on Christ's gift of himself. Paul here captures the essence of humankind's dependence on God's sovereignty and grace. Despite our infirmity and sin (separation from God), God's great love moves Jesus to give his life so we may be reunited with God and saved from divine judgment.

The Right Love

Married couples can recount the time and place when they found the "right love." The right love that finds us, as described in this lection, comes from the sure hope we receive from God through the Holy Spirit (5:5). Hope is realized because Christ's love is the source of peace and the avenue to grace. "We rejoice in the hope of the glory of God" (5:2b, NIV), and through God's goodness we know our sin is forgiven. Paul presents life as it is. God's promise is not that hate will never be present, but that love will overcome it.

> **Think About It:** Hate will be present, but God's love overcomes it. When have you encountered hate? How did you respond? feel? How can our actions and attitudes contribute to overcoming hatred?

The "right love" enables us to contend against the present evils of this world, which pale in comparison with God's glory (8:18). "While we were still weak, at the right time Christ died for the ungodly" (5:6), and therein lies our hope.

The Right Death

Suffering and disappointment influence Christian life. We typically raise questions about God's love in tragic circumstances. We view death morbidly, as an ending rather than as a transition of life. Jesus' death for the sins of many proves that God loves us. His right death is one that sacrifices, redeems, and reconciles us to a God whom we may have doubted or abandoned. Jesus removed death's sting. His death is the right death to establish the right relationship with God for the forgiveness of sin.

The Right Relationship

Justification comes via the judgment of God. The Old Testament reference to "making right" a relationship sought vindication of a wrongly accused person. The Israelites were guilty of abandoning God many times, and God punished them; but his mercy was always available when they repented. God's just act of restoration becomes an act of judgment, deliverance, and redemption.

Conversely, Paul describes justification by faith as an unmerited gift of God for anyone who believes. The sinner is absolved from sin and reconciled to the Creator. This right relationship is one that is bestowed on us through

Christ's sacrificial love, that we might be saved from God's anger (5:9). And having been reunited with God, we are saved to life eternal through his resurrection (5:10).

Gospel: John 4:5-42

The spiritual nature of John's Gospel emits a strong personal witness of Jesus as *Logos*, "the Word made flesh," the Son of God. But he is also the very stuff of life (bread and water). This encounter with the woman at the well exemplified Jesus' nature as both human and divine. The confluence of Jesus' human need for water with the woman's spiritual need for a fresh start created an opportunity for a life-changing event.

Human and Spiritual Needs
People come to a place of worship for comfort, healing, and renewal. Jesus had made his way to Sychar (ancient Shechem) near Mount Gerizim, the Samaritan place of worship. This was a radical thing to do, as "the Jews have no dealings with the Samaritans" (verse 9, KJV). He came to Jacob's well, a revered and historic place. Abraham, Jacob, and Joshua had visited here; and Moses had instructed the people to hear the word of God there, announcing blessings from Mount Gerizim and curses from Mount Ebal as consequences of keeping or breaking the covenant (Deuteronomy 27:1-13). This was a sacred place for Jews and Samaritans alike. Jesus, however, elevated the importance of attitude over place in worship. More important than the place of worship was the honest heart of the worshiper.

Divided for centuries by racial and religious conflict, Jews and Samaritans avoided contact whenever possible. But Jesus, weary and parched, saw that the woman approaching him was needy, spiritually and morally, and responded with a gift he called living water. The water of life is a proper description for Jesus. He was for her, and is for all who believe, a life-giving fountain that nourishes the soul. He brings succor and salvation to all who thirst for healing and wholeness, for "those who drink of the water that I will give them will never be thirsty" (John 4:14a).

Water of Life
Jesus placed this salvation into a context that was foreign to the woman and is to many of us. Worshiping God in spirit and truth (or integrity) requires a willingness to enter into a personal relationship with God in penitence and humility (4:23-24). Thus, in vital, transforming worship, the water of life makes us new and whole.

The Samaritan woman wanted this water. When Jesus suggested that she call her husband, her candid answer allowed him to perform a spiritual

129

healing. He confronted her with her true situation, opening the way for a confession that freed her of doubt and guilt. John says later, "You will know the truth, and the truth will make you free" (8:32). The water of life frees us for heartfelt worship and engagement with a loving God.

Food for the Soul

John shows Jesus in need; he said to the woman, "Give me a drink" (4:7).

> **Think About It:** "Jesus' nourishment came through fulfilling God's work." What special work has God called you to do? How does the fulfillment you gain from this compare with the satisfaction of a good meal? Should one always take priority over the other, or can we feel good about turning the energy gained from eating and drinking into committed service?

By asking the woman to meet his physical need, he opened her to receive a gift at a much deeper level. In meeting her spiritual need, he too was fulfilled. The disciples were perplexed by his refusal to eat. He turned this into an opportunity to teach them that more important than satisfying physical hunger was one's commitment to serving God's purpose. Jesus' nourishment came through fulfilling God's work (4:34) and nurturing others to participate in the harvest (4:35-38).

Ripples of Belief

Having sown these seeds of belief in the Samaritan woman, Jesus saw his ministry extended. Her report inspired other villagers to seek the living water for themselves and to find faith in Jesus as the Savior of the world.

Study Suggestions

A. Learn Desert Ways

Using a map or atlas, examine the route of the Exodus. Recall what the people were carrying and the haste with which they left Egypt. Review Exodus 17:1-7 and read earlier chapters to get the context. Ask: What were the traveling conditions? What did the people think they needed? What had they received so far to sustain their needs? What was their response to these gifts?

B. Quarrel and Test

Invite group members to imagine themselves on the sixty-first day of a backpacking hike through the desert. (Ask any who are familiar with desert terrain to describe it.) Ask: How many of you are tired and cranky by now? are tired of eating the same thing? are worrying where the next water source will be? are wishing you had never left the Nile delta?

Read aloud Exodus 17:1-7. Discuss: What were the Hebrews' motivations during their desert sojourn? Were their fears and complaints justified? If your hiking guide told you everything would be fine, would you be completely reassured? How does this expert advice compare with Moses' assurances to the Hebrews?

Ask the group to put the main point of this story in one sentence. Could it be: Trust God to meet your basic needs? Miracles are proof of our faith? Moses was a powerful leader? Don't try to test God? Don't quarrel among yourselves? Or what? Test all their statements in light of their faith experience and other central themes of Scripture. Which statement seems most consistent with other biblical teaching and with the way God works in our lives?

C. Be Justified by Faith

Read aloud Romans 5:1-11. Review the interpetation on pages 128–29. Share your own experiences of the "right" love, death, and relationship. Compare your experience with Paul's teaching in this chapter. In verses 1-5, Paul introduces a hierarchy of circumstances that lead to hope. Ask: What is suffering? Is it more than unavoidable difficulty? What value have you found in suffering? Does knowing that Christ suffered and died for us convince you of God's love? How does recognizing God's love affect your faith? How does your faith shape your response to God's love?

D. Seek and Share the Water of Life

Review John 4:5-42 and the commentary on pages 129–30. Briefly summarize the sequence of events. Then examine the twists and reversals in the story. Ask: What behavior seems unexpected or uncharacteristic of the characters? Do you note any changes or shifts in perspective? If so, what is the consequence? Again, have group members state the main point. Is it: Jesus breaks down barriers of prejudice? Jesus knows our hearts? Spiritual needs are more important than physical ones? Jesus satisfies our spiritual thirst? When Jesus saves us we want to share our joy? Or what? Test the statements against central biblical teaching and your own faith experience. Which statement best meets both standards? What does this story say to you about God's grace? Jesus' purpose? your need? your faith? your response?

E. Examine God's Care

Review your discussions of today's lections. Ask: What kind of care does God offer? Have you ever questioned the sufficiency of God's care? Have you ever felt abandoned or fearful that God's care would not be available? Do you ever insist on being self-sufficient rather than availing yourself of God's care? What has doing this taught you about God and about yourself?

F. Close With Worship

Stand and read Psalm 95 responsively. Invite members to offer sentence prayers in response to today's study. With eyes still closed, ask the group to extend their hands in the shape of a cup and sing together, "Fill My Cup, Lord."

Lections for Fourth Sunday in Lent

Old Testament: 1 Samuel 16:1-13

*T*HE anointed king of Israel stood as the representative of God before the people. The king, however, was not God. The people demanded a king, yet they did not fully understand what they were asking. On the surface it looked like their neighbor nations got along better with a clearly designated leader, but this led them away from reliance on God and into dependence on arms and alliances. God accommodated their weakness; and kingship theology developed from the time of Saul, reached its height during the reign of David, and began to decline with the arrogance and excesses of Solomon and his successors. The kings conquered territory, accumulated wealth, practiced injustice against the poor, and corrupted the worship of YHWH with Canaanite customs. While in the eyes of the world they were successful, God had a different perspective. The meaning and purpose of a worthy king as defined by God was: "The LORD does not see as mortals see; they look on the outward appearance, but the LORD looks on the heart" (16:7).

Samuel's Mission

Samuel was a vital leader in Israel's history. Between the theocracy of the prophet Eli and the newly established kingdom of Saul, Samuel's role was significant to the future. He anointed first Saul, later David as God's chosen kings. But Samuel's demeanor was problematic. He was slow to denounce Saul, reluctant to follow God's direction, and upon his visit to Jesse's house was anxious to anoint any one of Jesse's sons. God, however, had decided on David, Jesse's youngest son. (David followed Jacob and Joseph as younger brothers who succeeded to national leadership.) Samuel's fear of Saul made him question God's decision. Still the mission was accomplished; Samuel anointed the unlikely and unexpected David as king.

David was the eighth son of Jesse, according to First Samuel, but was the sev-

Lections for Fourth Sunday in Lent

enth of seven sons, as recorded in 1 Chronicles 2:13-15. Only Eliab, Aminadab, and Shammah (Shimea) are mentioned in both accounts. Seventh of seven, David's family position, suggests perfection, a common motif in hero tales.

The Messianic Family

What an intriguing lineage! When we look at David's line, we find some questionable or undesirable individuals: Ruth, Tamar, Rahab, and others. But God was not concerned. The way David's ancestors or our family members live is irrelevant to God, if any of us are to be used as instruments of change. The Bible is filled with misfits and throw-aways whom God refines into usable servants. God sees a purpose that is hidden from us. God looks to the heart. David would be judged, not by his pedigree, but by his faithfulness to God in what he did as king. God established David's lineage in the messianic family.

> **Think About It:** God looks upon the heart to judge our fitness and faithfulness. What do we look at in assessing desirability and making choices? How can we discern God's purpose? What criteria do we use in selecting leaders? What does God see when looking into your heart? If it is not right with God's will, how does God want you to change?

Oil and Spirit

The New Testament sacrament of baptism and the anointing of kings in the Old Testament are similar in some ways. David's kingship was inaugurated by the anointing with oil and sealed by the descent of the Spirit of the Lord (16:13). The connection between John's proclaiming that he baptized with water, but sealed the baptism with fire (Matthew 3:11-17), closely mirrored the prophet's anointing of the king and the Spirit of God descending upon the chosen one.

Psalter: Psalm 23

The imagery in this familiar psalm excites our senses and helps us recognize the level of comfort and protection God truly provides. We place our confidence and hope in the affirmation that God is all we need. Just as a shepherd gives food, water, shelter, protection, and comfort to the sheep, so God provides abundantly for us. The divine Shepherd enriches our entire existence, making life better, more secure, and more hopeful for all the sheep "who dwell in the house of the LORD."

Epistle: Ephesians 5:8-14

The trio of good, right, and true (5:9) reminds us of 1 Samuel 15:22 ("Has the LORD as great delight in burnt offerings and sacrifices, / as in obedience to the voice of the LORD? / Surely, to obey is better than sacrifice, / and to heed than the fat of rams") and other prophetic verses in which obedience from the depth of the heart is placed above religious order, rites, and performance. Paul unpacks a number of theological idioms when addressing the discussion of light over darkness, most important that Christ is the light.

Children of Darkness

Darkness forms a compelling landscape on which we place everything opposite to light. Darkness contrasts with the faithful journey of Christians who walk with, or before, God in trust and obedience. The function of darkness is to protect evil works. Children hide things under a bed or in a closet. Similarly, children of darkness hide secret deeds in their hearts or under the cover of night. But they are offered hope and salvation by the words, "For once you were darkness, but now you are light in the LORD" (5:8, NIV). Children of darkness are the potential children of light! When the Light shines on it, darkness is transformed into light.

Think About It: Children of darkness are the potential children of light. God sees in an ungodly person or situation the possibility of becoming godly. Do we? Are persons and situations usually either all dark or all light? Does how we view others make a difference in how they respond? Was there a time when we were children of darkness? How were we changed? How can darkness become light for us?

Children of Light

The writer understands the dualistic belief systems in the Greco-Roman world. Using the contrast of light and darkness, which suggests the dualism of good versus evil, he urges renunciation of the ways of paganism (darkness) in favor of faithfulness (light). The shameful, hidden behavior, repudiated as ways of darkness in verses 3-6, must be replaced by living out what is "good and right and true." True children of light neither associate with the children of darkness (5:7), nor participate in "impurity of any kind" (5:3).

Lest they become discouraged, the Ephesians are reminded that although they were once in darkness, they are now in the light (5:4, 8). What they need to "find out what is pleasing to the Lord" (5:10) is a relationship with God. This new life is possible and is better than what they have known. Our renunciation of darkness opens our hearts to receive the illumination and inspiration of the light of God.

Death Be Not Proud

The "sleeper"—one who is dead spiritually—is called to a radical change—from death to life! The song, "Sleeper, awake! / Rise from the dead, / and Christ will shine on you" (5:14), represents the power of Christ over death. The awakening is a rising to new life. Christ's light dispels the

134

darkness and sin in our lives and empowers us to live in new ways. Death and darkness recede in the presence of God's searching, transforming light.

Gospel: John 9:1-41

In one of the few instances of a healing or miracle in this Gospel, John presents a story with layers of meaning, contrasting the blindness of those who could see with the insight and vision of one born blind.

Who Sinned?

The action began with Jesus and his disciples encountering a blind man begging beside the road. Apparently the disciples already knew him and his condition, since they commented that he had been blind from birth. What they didn't know, though, was who had sinned. Working from their worldview that illness and disability were the results of sin, they looked for a nonphysical reason for the man's blindness. Jesus used their question to confront the inaccuracy of this notion, offer an opportunity to see the greatness of God, and confront the religious authorities with their own shortsightedness.

The Healing (and Confusion) Begin

The man was not consulted about his wishes; Jesus simply initiated the first step in the restoration process. He made mud to smear like ointment on the man's eyes and told him to take the second step—to wash in the pool of Siloam. Then able to see, the man returned center stage, and Jesus became a secondary character. First the neighbors and acquaintances, then the Pharisees and villagers, began questioning and speculating about what had happened. In spite of the man's open acknowledgment of Jesus' involvement, they just could not believe what they were seeing. So they asked him again, then ran to get his parents.

For Fear of the Authorities

The man's parents were asked to verify that he was born blind, but they could not account for the healing. Fearful of expulsion from the synagogue, they replied, "Our son is of age; ask him." In much the same way we would expect Jesus to do, the man took on the establishment: "Do you want to hear it again?" Whatever else may have been unclear, the healed man knew that Jesus was from God. The religious authorities squabbled and sputtered about the healing, which had been done on the sabbath and which they could not explain. They did not want to hear that someone who had challenged their authority and broken sabbath law was a prophet (9:17), had disciples (9:27-28) and stature (9:29), and possessed a clearer vision of religious propriety than they (9:39-41).

135

Jesus Again

In the absence of a good solution, the religious leaders expelled the man from the synagogue, just what his parents feared would happen to them. Jesus then returned a welcome to the banished man. He confirmed the man's observations and pointed out the same irony the man had earlier noted—the one who was blind had vision enough to see God, while the ones who had sight were blinded by law and tradition from seeing God's glory.

> **Think About It:** The blind man could see and the religious leaders were blind. Can you think of circumstances like this today? From Jesus' perspective, what is sight and what is blindness? What blinds us to the glory and grace of God?

Jesus next confronted the Pharisees about the second part of their double condemnation; first the man (9:30-33), then Jesus (9:40-41) berated them for their spiritual blindness. This provides an answer to the disciples' initial question in verse 2. "Now that you say, 'We see,' your sin remains" (9:41). The sin was neither with the blind man nor his parents, but with those blinded by pride of position and those whose beliefs blinded them to the work of God before their eyes.

Study Suggestions

A. See Who Would Be King

Kingship is an important step for Israel. The shift from theocracy (ruled by God) to monarchy (ruled by royalty) is an extremely important one. Israel had begun to forget that they were a theocracy. Look back to 1 Samuel 8 for a synopsis of God's opinion of Israel's request for a king. Then read aloud 1 Samuel 16:1-13, and review the commentary on pages 132–33, to see the beginning of a long procession of kings. Ask members what they remember about the anointings of Saul and David. What were the differences? How did God select David? What were the criteria? God had Saul anointed, became sorry for doing so (15:35), and chose someone else. How does this square with God's call to and use of unlikely persons to fulfill God's plans? On what basis might God reject a person whom God had chosen earlier?

B. Search Darkness for Light

Read Ephesians 5:8-14 aloud, and review the commentary on pages 133–35. Discuss: What does the dark/light metaphor signify? What truth does it convey? In what circumstances is the writer offering this insight? The dark/light motif has cosmic implications: the battle between the forces of good and evil, life and death. Ask: What do these implications mean for us? Is our faith affected by these cosmic, eternal dimensions? Do we experience a similar battle in our lives?

Ephesians 5:3-5 refers to the practices of darkness in everyday terms and points out that we do shameful things, hoping no one will find out. Ask: Is it possible to conceal our acts of darkness? Do we think these actions will never be exposed? Is it appropriate to expose another's darkness? Does our faith require it? What would be the cost? What are some practices of the light? How are we actually empowered to live in the light?

C. Open Your Eyes

Summarize the sequence of events in the healing of the man born blind, based on John 9:1-41 and the commentary on pages 135–36. Identify the key elements in the story: the healing was done on a sabbath; religious leaders were supposed to be the visionaries in the faith; disease and disability were thought to be the result of sin; and the irony of the blind seeing and the sighted being blind.

Now look more closely at the actions of each set of characters. Invite different group members to take on the role of the blind man, Jesus, the disciples, the Pharisees, the parents, and the crowd. Analyze the action from each point of view. What insights does this bring? What truth about faith is made clearer? What does this story tell us about our own ability and willingness to see the work and glory of God? about our adherence to blind tradition or practice? about our need to be more insightful and observant of God's will?

D. Be Healed

Jesus did not ask the man if he wanted to be healed, but he did ask him to participate. Discuss: Can we be healed against our will? Do we allow Christ to heal us? Can we participate in our own healing? block it? From what kind of blindness do we most need healing?

E. Summarize and Conclude

All the lections for today deal with our need to change, to be changed by God, or to accept changes brought by God. Ask: How do we handle change? Are we open to change if we have more or better insight? What are the blocks to change in us and in our situation? Is faith something that should not be changed? In closing, read Psalm 23 in unison; sing the hymn, "The Lord's My Shepherd, I'll Not Want"; and pray for openness to accept God's call to change.

3·28
Hope for new life

Lections for Fifth Sunday in Lent

Old Testament: Ezekiel 37:1-14

*P*ROPHETS of Israel figure prominently in the salvation plan of God. The surrender of Jerusalem by Jehoiachin to the Babylonians in 597 B.C. initiated the prophetic call of Ezekiel, a young priest in training. Ezekiel represented Israel's hope for restoration and a new beginning. This week's passage offers us a vision and interpretation of Israel's condition as a nation and the people's predicament of faith.

A Valley of Bones

The possibility of a resurrection of dry bones, which was revealed to the prophet in his vision, describes the return of God's glory and the political and religious reawakening of Israel. Considering the vision, a graphic scene of death and utter destruction, all possibilities of restoration appeared hopeless (37:1-10). Yet God's message to Ezekiel provided the errant people with renewed hope. God was not defeated; it was Judah's own sin that had caused their devastation. The vivification of this new, embryonic community was brought about by one who had endured criticism and ridicule because of unfulfilled prophecies.

> *Think About It:* Name some situations in your life or church or our society that are comparable to a valley of dry bones. What caused the dryness or death? Has it been restored? Why or why not? To what do you attribute the change? Was there anyone like Ezekiel involved, who saw the situation for what it was and named the cause and the cure? How was God manifest? How can we address such situations in ways that restore life and hope?

The people recognized God's presence through the healing and uniting of restored character and purpose.

Body and Spirit

The valley in Ezekiel's vision is one of unparalleled devastation and hopelessness. The fallen warriors lie unburied, a great shame in the ancient world, because all the women also had been destroyed and none remained to bury the dead. God commissioned the prophet to view the valley of dry bones, commanded them to assemble, and brought them to life again. The critical element lost in the despondent community of faith was a hope beyond exile. The people were dead and dry as bones dispersed upon a desolate battlefield. The vision given to Ezekiel provided hope and direction for resuscitation of a people.

Ezekiel's mission related to both physical and spiritual renewal. "Mortal, can these bones live?" asked God (37:3). Ezekiel did not know, but God immediately offered an answer to what was probably a rhetorical question. Ezekiel was to address the bones and tell them that God's spirit or breath (*ruach*) would restore life.

Fulfillment of Purpose

The function of prophecy at this crucial moment in Israel's history is epitomized by this passage explaining the estranged, then mended, relationship between God and humanity. When we are lost and cut off from the land of the living, God can "open our graves" (37:13) and bring us back to life.

Ezekiel's mission was threefold: (1) the opening of the graves signified the awakening of a politically and religiously dead people to renewed national and spiritual life; (2) the covenantal clause, to "put my spirit within you" (37:14), anticipated a higher moral and spiritual life than the nation had previously possessed; (3) the promise of a land, "your own soil" (37:14), provided new hope to God's people. They would return home at last.

Lent can be a time of spiritual dryness when we are called to examine our hearts, repent of the sin that has caused it, and look forward to the new vitality of Easter. God can breathe life into our spirits and move us from a "weariness in well doing" to a renewed commitment to active discipleship.

Psalter: Psalm 130

This is a "songs of ascents," which may refer to its literary form but more likely to its occasion. Pilgrims on their way to Jerusalem ascended nearly 2,700 feet above sea level, or 4,000 feet above the Dead Sea.

The psalm refers to "depths," a concept made more poignant by the dramatically hilly terrain of the area. Here the depths refer to agonizing separation from God. Life without God is unbearable; yet the psalmist knows to wait and, in waiting, to find hope (130:5-6). It is God's choice whether to respond to our sin and sense of abandonment; if God should "mark iniquities, . . . who could stand?" (130:3). But the psalmist ascends. He knows that

God will "redeem Israel from all its iniquities" (130:8) by "steadfast love" and "great power" (130:7).

Epistle: Romans 8:6-11

What kind of life do we possess? Paul's insightful description of the conflict between flesh and spirit presents us with one of life's most probing dilemmas: Where are our limitations and boundaries for living? This passage proposes that we all live either in the flesh (self-centeredness) or in the spirit (God-centeredness). Whichever path we travel, it is our inner state of mind that guides our outward actions.

Things of the Flesh

Our first task is to decipher the language. What we commonly refer to as "our flesh"—our physical nature with its needs and desires—is not what Paul is addressing. Rather, he means by flesh our self-serving state of rebellion and sin. Paul refers to having one's "mind on the flesh" as being "hostile to God," defiance of God's law, and the inability to please God (8:7-8). Setting one's mind on the flesh brings spiritual death (8:10), or separation from and antagonism to God our maker. This separation leads to a willful refusal to live according to God's will and purpose and sets in motion a downward spiral of self-rejection and estrangement from others. "Those who are in the flesh cannot please God" (8:8) because we are too busy pleasing ourselves.

> **Think About It:** Those who are in the flesh cannot please God. This does not mean that our bodies and desires are unacceptable to God, but rather that when we focus on ourselves we leave God out. From this standpoint, how is it with our souls? With what are we preoccupied—our needs and activities, or God's purpose for our lives?

Ezekiel depicts those who have failed to please God as being without flesh. As a result of their sin (separation from God), they are symbolically reduced to a collection of dry bones. But the prophet proclaims that God will give them a new spirit so the covenant can be ratified in their hearts. Several centuries later, Paul contends that the children of God are still in the same state, though God's Spirit remains available to bring about restoration and renewal.

Things of the Spirit

Paul tells the Romans that, through the vivifying power of the Spirit, there is a way to a new and better life. Opening one's mind to the Spirit of the resurrected Christ represents a new beginning, transforming all

140

thought and action from self-centered to God-centered (8:11). Only through focusing on God in Christ are we able to fulfill "the just requirement of the law" (8:4).

Nevertheless, it is not the law that saves, but Christ. Paul is emphatic about the enveloping, nurturing, life-giving presence of the Spirit. He describes that presence in several ways: "you are in the Spirit"; "the Spirit of God dwells in you"; you can "have the Spirit of Christ" (8:9); "Christ is in you" (8:10); and "the Spirit of him [God] who raised Jesus from the dead dwells in you" (8:11).

Gospel: John 11:1-45

The raising of Lazarus marked a turning point in the ministry of Jesus. This last sign was a double-edged event that brought many persons to belief but also launched the plot to kill Jesus (11:45-53). From that moment, Jesus curtailed his travel. He retreated to Ephraim (11:54), spent another week in Bethany (12:1), then headed to Jerusalem for his last days (12:12).

John highlights the way Jesus made his message known with signs—the first his changing water into wine, the last the raising of Lazarus. Jesus was life incarnate and brought life to all he encountered. Every human contact up to the point of raising Lazarus included offering persons a fuller, more wholesome, more joyful life, though not everyone was willing to accept it.

Lazarus Was Taken Sick

Jesus and his disciples were "across the Jordan" (10:40) when word came that his friend Lazarus was seriously ill. As is characteristic of John's Gospel, Jesus is shown to know already what had and would happen and what was its larger meaning. "This illness does not lead to death; rather it is for God's glory" (11:4). The language sounds familiar: remember the man who was "born blind so that God's works might be revealed" (9:3)? Jesus tarried two more days before heading to Bethany.

Lazarus took a turn for the worse. While Jesus' disciples debated with him over the attendant risks of returning to Judea, a place of danger (11:8), theologically Jesus was preparing them for what was about to happen. Knowing that his life was nearing a climax, Jesus taught them about the necessity of living in the light (11:9-10). As usual, they did not understand. In the meantime, Lazarus had died and was buried, probably on the same day, as was the custom. Jesus delayed his arrival to ensure that Lazarus would have already been buried. The two-day delay, plus the time it took for the message to reach him and for him to reach Bethany, would have brought him to Lazarus's town on the fourth day after burial.

141

Burial Customs

John assumes his readers know the burial and funeral customs. Jewish belief held that the soul of the deceased lingered with the body for three days; hence the fourth day of death finalized the process (11:17, 39). Usually, the corpse was wrapped in a shroud, and a binding held the jaws in a closed position (11:44). Designated mourners would join the grieving family and friends and make a loud lamentation (11:19, 31, 33, 42). Family members would not leave the house for the seven-day mourning period except to visit the tomb (11:20, 28-31); so it was atypical that first Martha, then Mary, left the house to meet Jesus at the edge of the village.

Lazarus Awakened

The family followed local custom; but with Jesus' involvement, the usual gave way to the unusual in order that all might "see the glory of God" (11:40). The first hint of what was to come occurs when Martha met Jesus. We do not know if her statement is plaintive or accusatory, but Martha knew that Jesus had the power to save (11:21-22). He engaged her in an affirmation of resurrection, both for Lazarus and for all, by the power of God. Martha returned and pulled Mary aside. Mary began her conversation in the same way as Martha had; presumably Jesus repeated his assurance (11:28-32).

Then, the message became available to all. For the sake of the crowd, it was offered with drama and emotion (11:33-42). Lazarus was called forth from the tomb. Jesus had saved! (The Greek word for *save* conveys a total restoration of wholeness.) But Jesus would pay with his life, as freely given as his tears of love for Lazarus.

Study Suggestions

A. "Dry Bones" Will Live

Invite group members to sit quietly with eyes closed, while you slowly read Ezekiel 37:1-10. Ask them to immerse themselves in the mental image of this great valley and to see the result of God's prophecy. Then invite them to describe any new insights or appreciation for this vision.

Now ask members to review the rest of the passage (verses 11-14) and the commentary on pages 138–39. Discuss what this vision meant to the people of Judah. What was their political and spiritual condition? Examine the threefold purpose of Ezekiel's mission. Pay particular attention to the restoration and the indwelling of God's spirit. What metaphor or metaphors would be descriptive of our yearning and need for spiritual renewal?

B. Look at Bones with Flesh

In Ezekiel, the bones took on flesh as a sign of restored vitality and faithfulness, while Paul in Romans 8:6-11 uses the image of flesh as a sign of faithlessness. Spend a few minutes sorting out the metaphors. How is the image of "flesh" used differently in these passages? What do you think Paul means by saying that those who "are in the flesh cannot please God," when it pleased God to restore the dry bones with flesh? Are Ezekiel and Paul saying the same or different things? Discuss the difference between being self-centered (living in the flesh) and God-centered (living in the spirit).

C. Look at Bodies With Spirit

In Ezekiel, God's Spirit restored life to "death valley." In Romans, Paul tells the congregation that they live in the Spirit and the Spirit dwells in them. Review the commentary, then ask: What does it mean for us to have our mind on things of the flesh or on things of the Spirit? What is the consequence of knowing the difference but of continuing to "live in the flesh"?

D. From Death to Life, Again

Now it is an individual's turn to die and be restored. Review John 11:1-45 and the commentary on pages 141–42. Recap the sequence of events. What new ideas or insights emerge? Consider the main themes of this passage (life and death, Jesus' power to save, the possibility of resurrection, the love of Jesus for others, and so on). How do they inform, shape, or transform our faith?

E. Lazarus, Come Out!

Form three groups and assign to each group one of these passages that deal with resurrection and its consequences: John 11:11-16, 38-44, 45-48. After reviewing their verses and the commentary on pages 141–42, ask each group to answer these questions and report back: What was the purpose of raising Lazarus? For whose benefit did it happen? How was Jesus regarded for this miracle? What does the event mean to us?

F. Summarize

One recurring theme in today's lections is God's power to make life overcome death. Recap the ways in which this theme has been expressed in each of the readings. Discuss: How does your faith push you to seek renewal? What are the ways in which God restores you when you your soul feels dry or dead? What is God calling you to do or be through these Scriptures? How does a study of these passages restore your spirit?

G. Come Out of the Depths

Invite anyone who wishes to describe a recent "depth" from which he or she needed (or needs) rescue. Read aloud Psalm 130 together, sing the hymn "O Breath of Life," and pray for renewal of spirit and rededication of life during these days of Lent.

Lections for Passion/Palm Sunday

Old Testament: Isaiah 50:4-9

*T*HE prophets of Israel contended with a rebellious people. Second Isaiah, written around the time of the Babylonian Exile (597–539 B.C.), addressed an antagonistic community released from exile. The message was one of hope, promise, and encouragement. Yet the prophet was humiliated and rejected. His predecessors' messages of judgment and doom had been unwelcome, even though they had later been proved right. Now he was experiencing the same prejudice and abuse. As he continued to convey a message of hope for the future, Isaiah was persistent and constant with his convictions and faith in God. Regardless of the suffering he was encountering in his ministry, he did not lose heart; he remained secure in God.

The Servant of Israel

This passage is the third of four servant songs in Isaiah 40–55. Various scholars interpret the servant to be the prophetic author himself, a national leader such as Zerubbabel, a composite royal figure, and a symbol of the people of Israel as a whole. But unlike the nation of Israel, the servant did not turn away from God, even in the face of terrible treatment.

This song of the suffering servant reminds us of the prophet's plight in very physical terms: "the tongue" (50:4), "my ear" (50:4), "my back" (50:6), "my cheeks" (50:6), "the beard" (50:6), and "my face" (50:6) were all involved in his ministry—hearing and speaking God's message, receiving abuse of his enemies, conveying his staunchness of purpose.

In Semitic thought there is a close psycho-physical relationship; these personal references imply a deep, intimate investment of the servant in his mission. The beard, for example, was a sign of male pride. To have the beard cut off, left unkempt, or pulled out was a sign of mourning but also of humiliation. That the servant was at least figuratively beaten and abused, but

144

continued resolutely in his call and mission, was both a telling witness to his courage and strong condemnation of those to whom he was sent.

Israel as the Servant

If the servant was not a specific person but a figure representing the nation as a whole, it is clear that there had been a grievous breach in its relationship with God. The servant speaks of weariness (50:4), rebellion (50:5), insult (50:6), disgrace and shame (50:7), contention and adversaries (50:8), and guilt (50:9). In all, they had through their exile experience (and perhaps among themselves) been a beleaguered but stiff-backed people.

Weary, torn, dejected, and scorned, the prophet proclaimed a message of encouragement. His principal concern was to help those who heard his voice believe that God was still going to make

> **Think About It:** God makes a difference through people who make a difference to others. Why did the prophet persist in trying to convey a message of hope to a people who were rejecting and persecuting him? What difference did he finally make? What empowers you to persist when you meet resistance or rejection? What message do you have to share with friends who may or may not be receptive?

a difference in their lives. He said this because he believed that God was making a difference through him. He had been given the "tongue of a teacher" that knew "how to sustain the weary with a word" (50:4). He knew also how to listen to the word of God, since "God has opened my ear" (50:5).

Thus, the servant signaled a quantum change. One of the gravest fears from the Exile was that God had abandoned the people and their covenant. Not so, said the servant. Even though the sin of the people had marred the relationship (50:1), "he who vindicates me is near" (50:7).

Psalter: Psalm 31:9-16

Psalm 31 is a prayer of praise and thanksgiving for God's deliverance from enemies. The psalmist moves from deploring his tragic circumstances to imploring God to rescue him. It is included this week because it could well have been on Jesus' lips during the agony of his passion. Verses 9-13 expound on the psalmist's dire plight: he is in "distress' and "grief" (31:9), "sorrow," "misery," weakness, and waste (31:10). He is "the scorn of adversaries," a "horror to neighbors," and "an object of dread to acquaintances." Even "those who see me in the street flee from me" (31:11). Then, in verses 14-16, he moves to voice confidence that deliverance will come to those who trust in God. The steadfast love (ḥesed) of God will overcome all human pain and weakness.

Epistle: Philippians 2:5-11

Paul's ministry in Philippi began during his second missionary journey. Along with Silas and Timothy, he founded this congregation, the first European Christian community, with whom he established life-long bonds of friendship. This intimacy was based in their continued diligence in the gospel. Paul greeted them as "sharing in the gospel" (1:5); and whatever might happen it would advance the gospel (1:6). First he encouraged them to remain steadfast (1:27-30), harmonious (2:1-2), humble (2:3-11), and obedient and selfless (2:12-18). His central concern was that they remain faithful to the gospel of freedom and not be led astray by the Jewish Christians. These persons remained strict proponents of Jewish customs and beliefs and sought to persuade Gentile Christians that they must be circumcised in accordance with the law before they could be considered bona fide Christians.

Be of One Mind

The letter was a rallying cry to continue "of one mind" in service to the Christ whose death had made them free. Rather than allowing factionalism and pride to dominate their relationships, they must strive for unity and humility, following the example of their Redeemer, who left the heavenly realm, became human and a servant, and submitted to an ignoble death. This profound theological truth is expressed in a great hymn of salvation— likely in use in the early church before Paul included it in this letter—that lauds Christ as Servant Redeemer (2:5-11). They must conduct their lives in imitation of Christ's humility. "Let the same mind be in you that was in Christ Jesus" (2:5).

> **Think About It:** Paul assumes that it is entirely possible for the Philippian congregation to have the same mind as was in Christ. Is it really possible to be of the same mind as Christ? Was Paul speaking only of Christ's humility, or of other dimensions of his mentality as well? What might persons become if they had the mind of Christ? How can this mind be in us?

The Hymn

The hymn introduces six aspects of the revelation and work of God in Christ: divine pre-existence (2:6), the humility of incarnation (2:7), the humility of Jesus' death (2:7b-8), his exaltation (2:9), his universal adoration (2:10), and his new title, *Kyrios* (Lord—which takes on a cosmic dimension, 2:11). Paul here expresses what Christ gave up for our salvation, how he manifested God's nature and love among us, and why he deserves our grateful praise.

The early church declared that Jesus was equal with God, yet willingly emptied himself to become a servant. The verb meaning "emptied" (Greek: *kenosis*) points to leaving behind his divine attributes or powers in order to carry out God's saving mission on earth. Christ's self-deprivation for a time then results in God's raising and honoring him, so that his name (personhood) may be humbly acknowledged by all as reigning over all creation (2:6-8).

Gospel: Matthew 27:11-54

Today's Gospel lection is part of Matthew's account (26:14–27:66) of the final days of Jesus' life, beginning with the betrayal by Judas (26:14-16), and continuing with the last Passover (26:17-30); the anticipation of Peter's denial (26:31-35); Jesus' prayer in Gethsemane (26:36-46); the arrest (26:47-56); Jesus before the various authorities, with asides about Peter's denials and Judas's suicide (26:57–27:26); and the move from accusation through crucifixion, death, and burial (27:24-66). Today's portion begins with the questioning by Pilate and concludes with Jesus' death. Let us look at the several characters in this drama of Christ's passion:

Pilate

Pilate was the governor of Judea from A.D. 26 to 36. Matthew presents him in an essentially favorable light as one trying to find a way through a thorny situation. (Other historians are less kind.) First Pilate tried to help Jesus see the seriousness of his situation (27:11-14), then attempted to divert the crowd's wrath to Barabbas (27:15-23). Pilate's wife warned him (to no avail) to get out of this muddle (27:19). His ceremonial handwashing (27:24) might have assuaged his own feelings, but he allowed Jesus to be flogged and handed over to the soldiers.

The Crowd

It is by no means clear that the rabid mob calling for crucifixion was composed of the same persons who days earlier proclaimed Jesus the Son of David. By the time they came before Pilate, they were nearing a riot. Following Jesus to Golgotha, they shook their heads, a sign of mockery (27:39), and taunted Jesus with his own teaching (27:40). Expecting, perhaps hoping, for a moment of high drama, they conjectured about whether Elijah would appear (27:46-49). They believed Elijah to be the helper of the oppressed.

The Soldiers

The cohort in Palestine was just over 1,000 troops, quite a crowd if it did indeed gather around Jesus. The soldiers, having some sport with Jesus, took his clothes and substituted for them the robe, crown, and reed, all symbols of a figure of power to whom they had pledged their allegiance (27:27-31). After shameful treatment, they briefly returned Jesus to his own bloody clothes. Usually, convicts were stripped naked before being nailed to their cross. So it was with Jesus (27:35). At least one soldier saw his own belief turned upside down. Terrified at the earthquake at the moment of Jesus' death, the centurion testified, "This man was God's Son!" (27:54).

Simon of Cyrene

Cyrene was the capital of the Roman province, Cyrenaica, or modern Libya. An African bystander, Simon, was pressed into service to carry the cross (27:32). The Gospel of Mark identifies him as the father of Alexander and Rufus, apparently well-known figures in the early church.

> **Think About It:** Just about every class and category of person was present for some portion of the Crucifixion. If you had been present, knowing only what they knew, with whom might you have allied yourself?

The Bandits

Jesus asked the religious authorities if they had come to arrest him as if he were a bandit (26:55), even though he was behaving peaceably. Then he was crucified, a form of execution reserved for persons convicted of insurrection. Two bandits were put to death with him (27:38). Even in the midst of their own torment, one found the energy to mock Jesus (27:44).

The Religious Authorities

Jesus had already appeared before the high priest (26:57-68). Even false witnesses could not seal the accusation until the council settled on blasphemy (26:64-66). On the strength of this charge, Jesus was brought before Pilate. Seeing no guarantee in achieving the result they wanted legally, the religious authorities turned the crowd into a near riot (27:20). They joined the passersby and the bandits in deriding Jesus on the cross (27:41-43).

Study Suggestions

A. Passion/Palm Sunday

Today's Gospel reading, for the Sunday before Easter, describes the events in the last week in Jesus' life from Matthew's perspective and reminds us of what was to come during Holy Week.

B. Place Yourself in the Action

Ask group members to read Matthew 27:11-54, noting who does what as the Crucifixion event unfolds. Have individuals locate themselves in the story, not to replace the biblical characters, but to join them. Caution them to try to think about the event without the benefit of centuries of hindsight, but as first-hand witnesses. Use the commentary on pages 147–48 to summarize the key players' involvement. Ask them to imagine to whom they might relate and why. Ask for volunteers, each representing one of the characters, to engage in a conversation about these momentous events. Ask each to respond to these

148

questions from his or her angle of vision: What happened? Who is this Jesus? Why did you do what you did? How do you feel about it afterward? What do you think the future holds? What personal insights come from inside of the story? Then open it up to comments and reactions from the rest of the group.

C. Find Comfort from the Servant
Read aloud Isaiah 50:4-9, and review the commentary on pages 144–45. In looking back at the suffering servant, the early church saw in him a messianic figure. Jesus was assaulted and mocked by religious leaders, who should have welcomed him. Ask: What was the servant's situation? What happened to him? Why? What images of hope do we find in this message? Then examine the passage again with the Messiah in mind. How does what happened to Jesus compare with the experience of the servant? What do these insights tell us about our own discipleship? What might be required of us? Would we be prepared for a call that led to suffering? to humiliation? to ridicule? to danger? to expulsion from our community?

D. Paraphrase the Hymn
Read in unison the ancient hymn in Philippians 2:5-11, and examine the commentary on pages 146–47. Look at the six Christological statements about Jesus Christ. Have the group members paraphrase this hymn. Ask: How does this portrait of Christ and his work impress our faith? What of it is difficult to understand or accept? What is most important to us who define ourselves as Christians?

E. Be of the Same Mind
Paul encourages the Philippians to be of the same mind as Christ. Attempt to reach group consensus on the meaning of: "let the same mind be in you that was in Christ Jesus." Discuss: Does this mean believing like Christ did? acting like Christ? thinking like Christ? being like Christ? Is the mind of Christ possible for ordinary people?

F. Explore Sacrifice and Suffering
All three key passages deal with sacrificial suffering. Isaiah centers on the suffering servant whose message offers hope of restoration to exilic Israel; the Epistle and Gospel recount Jesus' ultimate sacrifice and how it was appreciated and celebrated in the early church. Ask: If we take this knowledge seriously, what does it suggest for our own discipleship? our sense of identity as a Christian?

G. Summarize and Sing
Close by stating that this Sunday has a dual emphasis, beginning with the celebration of Christ's triumphal entry and ending on a somber note with the Crucifixion (which we know is not the end of the story). Then sing "What Wondrous Love Is This" or "Were You There?" and read Psalm 31:23-24 in unison as a benediction.

EASTER

Lections for Easter Day

First Lesson: Acts:10:34-43

*T*ODAY'S passage is like reading in the middle of a novel, in this case, Acts 10:1–11:18. In Acts 1, we saw how the risen Christ had commanded the disciples to be his witnesses starting in Jerusalem and spreading throughout the world (Acts 1:8). The Book of Acts is a record of how the disciples did just that, starting with the Day of Pentecost when many Jews from various nations heard and responded to the preaching of Peter. In today's passage the subject is Cornelius, the first Gentile convert in the new church of Christ.

Background—Visions

Scene 1. Cornelius was an officer in the Roman army. He was stationed in Caesarea, a city on the coast of Palestine (twenty-three miles south of Mount Carmel). He was a "God-fearer," that is, a devout person seeking to know and serve God. One afternoon, around three o'clock, an angel appeared to him, telling him to send for someone named Peter who was then in Joppa (a city also on the coast south of Caesarea). Cornelius sent messengers to do as the angel had said.

Scene 2. The next day, around noon, Peter was on a rooftop praying. He, too, had a vision that prepared him for the coming of the messengers and for a momentous event—sharing the gospel with Gentiles. But Peter's heart had to be prepared; that is, he could no longer regard Gentiles as profane and unclean. Through this vision and the hunger for God he saw in Cornelius, he came to understand that Gentiles also are loved by God, needed the gospel, and could be received into the church. So, in a way, this passage is a story of Peter's continuing conversion.

Peter's Sermon

This sermon is an excellent example of early Christian preaching. Most sermons in Acts cover the same points, if not in the same order: how God's promises of salvation found in the Hebrew Bible had been fulfilled in the birth, life, death, and resurrection of Jesus (10:37-43); the work of the Holy Spirit in all of this (10:38, 44); how Jesus had been exalted as Lord (10:36) and become judge of the living and dead (10:42); that Peter and the other apostles were witnesses to these things

> **Think About It:** Peter's heart and mind had to be opened to the new thing God was doing. He needed further conversion. His conversion would lead to a conversion in the church as well. Are multiple conversions needed in our Christian walk? What conversions can you recall in your lifetime? What new thing is God doing in you now? How do you still need to be converted? What conversions are needed in the church as we know it?

(10:39, 41, 42). The preaching concluded with a call to repentance, belief, and promise of forgiveness (10:43).

Through Jesus, God was bringing peace (10:36) between God and humanity, and now, as Peter realized, among humans. The Acts narrative is not a cold, aloof retelling, however; it is a telling that came from an eyewitness whose own life had been transformed. Such personal testimony carried great impact and authenticity. It was made even more powerful by Peter's acknowledgment that he had been wrong. He now realized that God accepts not only Jews but also those of all races and nationalities who honor God and live upstanding lives (10:35). Indeed, the God of universal love "does not show favoritism" (10:34, NIV)!

Peter concluded his address by sharing what this testimony meant for everyone—forgiveness from sin and a whole new relationship with God (10:43). The result was that the Holy Spirit came upon this Gentile household; they were converted and then baptized.

Psalter: Psalm 118:1-2, 14-24

This is the last of the *hallel* (praise) songs (Psalms 113–118), which were used especially during the Passover celebration. This is a joyous song of thanksgiving, perhaps led by the king himself, after a victory in battle. Verses 1-18 took place outside the Temple; 19-29 were sung inside.

The king calls the whole nation to give thanks to YHWH for yet another demonstration of God's steadfast love (*hesed*). In verses 1-4, first Israel (everyone), then the house of Aaron (the priesthood), then those who fear YHWH (the truly faithful) affirm the depth and breadth of God's *hesed*. Things had looked bleak (118:5-12), but God had delivered them (118:13-18). No wonder he tells them that "this is the day that the LORD has made" (118:24)!

Easter is surely a time for thanksgiving, for in Christ God has given us all a great victory over the enemy, death. It looked so bleak for Christ. He had been crucified and buried. But God raised him up! The rejected stone had become the cornerstone, the most important stone of all. So rejoice and be glad on this day (118:24)!

Epistle: Colossians 3:1-4

Paul wrote this letter to the church at Colossae, a town east of Ephesus in Asia Minor (Turkey), having heard about false teachers there who were saying that more than faith in Christ was needed for salvation. One also needed to worship other spiritual beings, as well as follow strict dietary rules. Paul wrote to affirm that in Christ God gives all that is needed for our salvation. To follow all these other things was actually to be led away from salvation.

Everything Is Different

In Colossians 3:1-4, Paul uses the imagery of dying and rising to refer to what happens when a believer is baptized. Baptism is dying with Christ. The baptismal waters become a tomb in which the old self is buried. Leaving the water symbolizes our being raised to new life in Christ (3:1).

> **Think About It:** In Christ, we become completely new. If you had to name one thing that sets a Christian apart from others, what would it be? How does being a Christian change our priorities? thinking? behavior?

Everything is now different; we are new creations (2 Corinthians 5:17)! We look the same, but we do not think or behave or believe as we once did. Our minds are set now on Christ, not ourselves; on godly concerns, not selfish concerns; divine values, not those of the world. The Christian, being a new person in Christ, is now more interested in giving than receiving; serving than being served; loving than being loved. These become the Christian's priorities.

False Teaching

Paul also addresses the false teachings that were disturbing his readers. Some thought Christ could not be human and also divine. Jesus died; but he is seated at the right hand of God. He had an earthly body, but it has been resurrected. In Jesus Christ, the boundaries of earth and heaven come together. Not only that, but weak, earthly mortals can enter this same glory.

Hidden With Christ

Turning to another false teaching, Paul addresses the notion of spiritual knowledge. Some false teachers presented the things they had been teaching as wisdom hidden except to the special few. Paul taught that true wisdom from the true God is not kept secret for only the favored few to know, but in Christ is freely available to all (3:3-4).

The Gospel Lection: John 20:1-18

This is John's account of the first Easter. Although Peter and John have a role here, the main character is Mary Magdalene. Note that it was a woman who was at the cross on Good Friday who came to the tomb on Easter Day (John 19:25; 20:1).

The Empty Tomb

Before sunrise Mary came to the tomb of Jesus (John 19:41). She was shocked to see that the massive stone, which had been rolled over the tomb's entrance to keep out bandits, animals, or disciples who might wish to steal his body, had been rolled away. She ran to tell "Simon Peter and the other disciple." Peter took the lead in running to the tomb; but "the other disciple" passed him, came to the tomb, stooped and peered inside to see only linen cloths. Peter, in character, boldly rushed in.

The body of Christ, as was the custom, had been wrapped in linen cloths (John 19:40) and laid on a rock shelf inside the tomb. Peter and "the other disciple" saw these cloths lying neatly on the shelf as if Jesus' body had simply passed through them—not torn away by bandits. The napkin that had been tied around his head (a custom to keep the mouth closed) was lying in place as well.

The "other disciple" is given credit as the first to believe that Jesus had risen (20:8), even though neither he nor the others understood yet that this was supposed to happen (20:9). To believe even before understanding or seeing the risen Lord is an indication of great faith. (As the risen Christ will say, "blessed are those who have not seen yet have come to believe," 20:29.) The two disciples returned home; Mary remained there crying.

I Have Seen the Lord

Weeping outside the tomb, Mary looked in and saw two angels dressed in white The angels asked Mary why she was crying. Her answer implied that she thought someone had stolen the body of Jesus, as if crucifying him was not enough. Suddenly, Mary became aware of a presence behind her. She turned to look upon Jesus, but did not recognize him, perhaps because he looked different or because she was not expecting to see him. He too asked why she was weeping. She thought he was the gardener who might know where the body had been taken.

Think About It: Mary came to the tomb still in a Good Friday world—grieving, depressed, discouraged. But she discovered that Easter had come! In the midst of your Good Friday days (days of sadness, disappointment, or loss), how has Easter (new life, hope, possibility) come to us? Where have we been surprised by the joy of Easter and the presence of a risen Lord?

Then Mary heard the voice that she thought she would never hear again.

And the voice spoke her name! She exclaimed, "Rabbi!" (teacher). She reached to embrace him. Jesus told her: "Don't cling to me." No longer could she cling to the old Jesus, to the way she had known him before. She must now learn to embrace him in a new way as the risen Lord who would return to God yet still be with them through the Holy Spirit. She was also to embrace a mission—to go and tell others that he is alive! Hers is the first Easter testimony: "I have seen the Lord."

Study Suggestions

A. Sing a Hymn
Recite together Psalm 118:1-2, 14-24. Share the information on pages 153–54 about this psalm. Then sing together the chorus, "This Is the Day," which is based on the psalm reading, or a favorite Easter hymn, like "Christ the Lord Is Risen Today."

B. Visions and Conversions
Summarize the background on the Acts reading, then have someone read Acts 10:34-43 aloud. God spoke to Peter and Cornelius through visions and dreams. Ask: What was God trying to tell them? What was the impact on Peter? on Cornelius and his household? on the church? Why would it have been difficult for Peter and the early Jewish Christians to accept that "God shows no partiality"? What groups do we have difficulty accepting into the church today? How has God spoken to you? Share a story from your own life of how God has confronted you with the need to change. Invite group members to tell briefly their own conversion stories.

Peter's sermon is a summary of the gospel. Have participants study and outline the main points together. Then compare their outline with that given under "Peter's Sermon" on page 153. ask: How would you sum up the gospel story in your own words? What are the most important points to include?

C. What's Our Mindset?
Explain the concept of mindset—the way we think and look at life; our worldview or basic perspective. Then invite someone to read Colossians 3:1-4 aloud. Ask: What does Paul say our mindset as Christians should be? What does he mean by "things that are above" and "things that are on earth?" What synonyms for these phrases are most meaningful to you? Sometimes we say of persons, "His work is his life," or "She lives for golf." Paul says that Christ is our life and elsewhere that "to live is Christ." Discuss what this means in practical terms of what we as Christians are called to devote our lives to.

D. Mary's Story

If there is a woman in your church with a gift for storytelling, ask her to come to the session and tell the story of Mary as found in John 20:1-18. Perhaps she could be costumed as Mary, tell her story, then let members ask her questions.

E. The Disciples' Story

First review the events of the first Easter. What happened? Who was involved? What new insights come to you now from the story?

Then use the senses to tell this story. Read the narrative one or two verses at a time, pausing to allow time for members to imagine what any of the Easter Day participants may have been thinking, feeling, or otherwise sensing. Ask them to consider questions like: What was he or she thinking? feeling? hearing? Why was he or she going there? Then ask each member to assume a bodily pose expressing the feelings of Mary, Peter, or John. As each in turn does so, invite the others to name the feelings they have embodied.

F. Summary

The readings from Acts and Colossians show us the power of the risen Lord and the message of Easter to change lives. The psalm calls us to give thanks for this wondrous work of God. And the gospel reading bids us, like Mary, to go and tell others, "We have seen the Lord." To close, ask group members to reflect on which character they most identify with this Easter. Is it Cornelius, hungering for contact with the risen Christ? Is it Peter, called to grow, change his mind, and share the good news? Is it Mary, either before Easter dawned, or once it had come? Then lead the group in a prayer of thanksgiving for Easter and all that it means.

Lections for Second Sunday of Easter

First Lesson: Acts 2:14a, 22-32

LAST week we studied Peter's sermon to Cornelius and his family and friends (Acts 10). Today and next Sunday we examine Peter's first sermon, which was preached in Jerusalem on the Day of Pentecost, a Jewish festival celebrating the grain harvest and the giving of the law at Sinai that attracted Jewish pilgrims from all over the Mediterranean world (2:5-11).

Jesus—His Life and Death

Peter was not addressing strangers (Gentiles) but fellow Jews, "Israelites." His sermon drew upon their heritage, the teachings of the Hebrew Scriptures, and explained how this Jesus of Nazareth was the fulfillment of the ancient promises (2:25-28, 31, 34). Jesus, Peter declared, was a fellow Israelite, but he was not just an ordinary man. The power of God flowed through Jesus, which was evident in the signs and wonders he performed. Surely the people knew this (2:22).

In verse 23, Peter returned to controversial and prophetic truth-telling. He reminded his hearers of the role they had played in having Jesus crucified by the Romans. Peter did not linger on this point, but stressed it strongly enough to make the next point: that God had been in no way constrained by their actions. In fact, Jesus had been raised because "it was impossible for him to be held in [death's] power" (2:24).

Human Responsibility, God's Plan

Peter emphasized that this death was the result both of human responsibility and human inevitability. "Those outside the law" (2:23) are the Gentiles, meaning in this case the Roman authorities. Even so, "you crucified

158

and killed" put the responsibility squarely in the hands of his Jewish hearers, among whom were some who had been in the crowd at the trial and who had witnessed the Crucifixion.

This accusation has led to anti-Semitism and even to outright persecution of Jews as "Christ-killers." Peter, a Jew himself, was certainly not advocating such thinking or action. An all-wise and all-powerful God was able to use the suffering and death of the Messiah to bring salvation and forgiveness to all the world. This was, Peter was saying, God's plan all along.

> **Think About It:** "This accusation has led to anti-Semitism." Can you see how negative New Testament references to "the Jews"—accusing them of contributing to Jesus' death—even though in that setting nearly everyone was Jewish, could have led to prejudice and persecution in later times? How can the New Testament be read to avoid this inference? What can you do to foster positive, respectful relationships with our Jewish neighbors?

Jesus—His Resurrection

But a dead Jesus could not bring this salvation. God brought him back to life (see also 1 Corinthians 15:4-8). Peter even quoted David (Psalm 16:8-11) as proof of the Resurrection (Acts 2:34-35). Few of the Jews' ancestors were held in greater esteem than David. So to appeal to him was an effective tactic. But Peter did more than that. "David," Peter said

> **Think About It:** Peter saw the Lord and his signs and wonders Do you use the signs as proof of Jesus' divinity? On what do you base your faith in Jesus as Lord? What signs and wonders has Christ wrought in your life? What will you tell others about Jesus to convince them to follow him?

in verse 29, "both died and was buried, and his tomb is with us to this day" (present in Jerusalem and a place of great interest to all Jews). David, a great hero and one in God's favor, could not do what Jesus did, but he prophesied the resurrection of the Messiah, who was one of David's own descendants.

Peter reinforced David's prophecy as one witness among many (2:32). He was saying to the assembly at Pentecost just what Mary had declared, "I have seen the Lord" (John 20:18).

Psalter: Psalm 16

This is one of the many songs of trust in the Psalms. The key theme is the absolute confidence of the psalmist in the love, care, and providence of God, no matter how present situations may call that into question. God is a "refuge," a mighty rock fortress, surrounding his life. He will not place his trust in any false gods (16:3-4), for that would be foolish. He chooses YHWH, just as he was chosen by YHWH (16:5-6), who (like Peter's concept of inheritance), has given him a "goodly heritage."

God has provided all he has needed. As Peter does with these same texts in Acts, the psalmist can do nothing but praise God who is always with him now (16:7-8) and in the future (16:9-10), trusting that he will not be abandoned or separated by death or Sheol (the pit or grave). In God alone is "fullness of joy" and "pleasures forevermore" (16:11).

Epistle: 1 Peter 1:3-9

First Peter was written to Christians in Asia Minor. Its main purpose was to encourage them in the face of persecution for their faith. They were reminded that Jesus himself also suffered, but in the end, through his resurrection, was victorious. They, too, were assured the victory.

A Context of Suffering

This letter was probably written between A.D. 70 and 90, after Paul's missionary travels and before widespread persecution of the early Christians. The social context of the Greco-Roman world was strongly patriarchal, and foreign religions were suspect. Conversion might lead to division within the family and a resulting disruption of the social hierarchy. Most of the letter tacitly reassured Christians that by imitating Christ (and obeying the authorities) they would survive the "various trials" brought on by their despised position in the culture. The writer was trying to establish the legitimacy of Christians and their faith so they would become accepted and no longer have to suffer unjustly.

A Living Hope

Christians are an Easter people. The Resurrection is at the very heart of our faith. Peter and others were witnesses to this, and it made all the difference. Having the courage of their conviction, members of the Christian community found hope in the face of opposition and persecution.

> **Think About It:** The Resurrection is at the very heart of our faith. What if there had been no Easter? no doctrine of the Resurrection in the Christian faith? What gave the early Christians the strength to endure persecution for their faith? What does it mean to you to confess that Jesus rose from the dead? Is it primarily the promise of life after death, or does life emerge out of death in everyday experience as well?

Peter assured his readers that they had an inheritance awaiting them, not subject to present circumstances, but reserved for them in heaven. The image is that of a heavenly "promised land." Nothing

160

could take this inheritance from them. The power of God guarantees and guards it!

Peter's language is reminiscent of Paul's first letter to the Corinthians. Using birth and death imagery (1:3), Peter moves to the next, eschatological (future-oriented) level to speak of the eternal inheritance, "kept in heaven for you" (1:4; see also 1 Corinthians 15:50-54).

So Rejoice

Having received the promise of this inheritance (1 Peter 1:3-5), which includes faith, believers are called to rejoice in this empowering gift. In the midst of present suffering, the Christian's faith remains firm (compare Matthew 5:11-12). Suffering is a context for faithfulness that leads them to believe in and love the risen Lord, though they have not seen him. In this stage of faith and hope, they find the "the outcome of your faith, the salvation of your souls" (1 Peter 1:9).

Gospel: John 20:19-31

Last week we saw how the risen Lord first appeared to Mary, who had been commissioned to go and tell. Peter and John came and found the tomb empty. But then Mary saw the Lord and ran back to tell the disciples. They gathered together again and were soon be able to say with Mary, "We have seen the Lord." This week's lection begins at evening on the first day of the week (20:19). Sunday became "the Lord's Day" because it was on this day that Jesus arose. So, for Christians each Sunday is an Easter.

A Day of Pain

We meet the disciples in "the house" (some say in the upper room they had used for the Passover meal). The disciples had to be greatly troubled. Who would not be under the circumstances? Added to their grief and pain was the fear that they would meet the same fate as Jesus. Peter's grief must have been greatest of all, for his last words concerning Jesus had been ones of fearful denial. Despite Mary's witness of having seen the risen Lord, they hid themselves behind locked doors.

A Day of Peace

Suddenly, Jesus appeared, offering the usual Jewish greeting, *shalom* (peace). But was this really Jesus?

There could be no doubt that this was Jesus—the wounds—in his hands, his feet, his side and brow. But before the disciples could believe their eyes, he gave them a commission—that repentance and forgiveness of sins should be preached in his name (see Luke 24:47). The post-Resurrection stories carry these common features: the disciples are mourning, Jesus appears, he greets them, they recognize him, and he gives them a command. Their faith is described in terms of seeing, believing, and receiving an assignment.

The command was threefold: to be sent as Jesus was sent (John 20:21), to receive the Holy Spirit (20:22), and to forgive sins (20:23). With the power of the Holy Spirit, the disciples were able to carry out this commission.

From Doubt to Faith

Thomas in Greek is "Didymus" and means "Twin," perhaps because he was a twin. He had not been present with the disciples when Christ first appeared. He refused to believe them until he saw and touched for himself. In Thomas's first transitional role, he represented the faith of "seeing *is* believing."

The next week, Jesus appeared again; and before Thomas could say anything, Jesus offered to provide the proofs Thomas required. We are not told if Thomas actually did touch Jesus; but if he had, that would have been a further sign of unbelief. Thomas answered with an immediate affirmation: "My Lord and my God!" (20:28).

Now the stage was set for the real transition—from seeing and believing to just hearing but believing. Jesus was mindful of all future generations of Christians who would come to faith without an eyewitness. "Have you [plural, not just Thomas] believed because you have seen me? Blessed are those who have not seen and yet have come to believe" (20:29). Both Jesus and the Evangelist were eager to get this message across (20:30-31).

Think About It: Blessed are those who have not seen but believe. What is the basis of our belief? Is it wrong to doubt? to have questions? Can doubt be understood as "searching faith"? Do we try to suppress our doubts or openly acknowledge them? What can we learn from Thomas about how to deal with doubt?

This transition implies the need for a new definition of faith in the absence of Jesus. Looking to the future, Jesus could see all those who would come to trust him "and have life in his name," even though never physically seeing him.

Study Suggestions

A. Begin With Easter Music

Invite the group to identify and sing one or more favorite Easter hymns, such as: "Cristo Vive" (Christ Is Risen); "O Sons and Daughters, Let Us Sing"; "Thine Be the Glory"; "The Strife Is O'er, the Battle Done"; "Easter People, Raise Your Voices." As an alternative, play a CD or cassette of Easter music, or invite a musician to play Easter music as participants arrive.

B. Telling the Good News

In Acts, Peter was preaching to his own people, to persons with whom he shared a common history. Read Acts 2:14a, 22-32, and review the commentary. Ask: What was the essence of Peter's sermon? What was the context in which he preached it? What was the significance of his message in its time and place?

Peter drew upon his solidarity with the people to tell them the good news. Invite group members to think about their own people, the ones who surround them, with whom they share much in common. Ask: What would be the best way to tell them the good news? Have you ever tried? What happened?

In small groups, ask members to share their own faith journey or testimony with one another—how they became a Christian, what Christ means to them, the struggles they have had, the growth they have experienced, and where they are right now. Have them discuss why (or if) faith sharing is difficult and how to get around the obstacles or the possible offensiveness sometimes associated with personal witnessing.

C. Peace in the Midst of Pain

Investigate the setting of First Peter, using the commentary on pages 160–61 for more information. Invite participants to try to imagine that they and their religion are the strangers in their immediate society. Ask: What might life have been like for those Christians in Asia Minor? What was the nature of the suffering they were enduring? What was the consequence of endurance?

Discuss: We are called to rejoice even in the face of suffering. Is that really possible? Have you ever been able to do that? In the midst of difficulty or time of pain, how have you felt? Where have you turned for strength? When have you experienced a sense of joy and peace?

D. Is Anyone Like Thomas, the Doubter?

Read aloud John 20:19-31, and study the commentary on pages 161–62. Examine the movement of the passage from "faith is seeing and believing" to "faith is just hearing but believing." Then ask: What is the commission Jesus gave to the disciples, and how were they to be empowered to carry it out? Can we identify with Thomas? Do we ever have doubts and questions? Do we experience this as troublesome or as "searching faith"? What can we learn from Thomas about how to handle them?

E. Celebrate a "Goodly Heritage"

The psalmist thanks God for the "goodly heritage" he has been given. Ask: What is our goodly heritage? What are the blessings we have inherited and wish to give thanks for? The psalmist also talks about God being his "refuge." Sing or recite "A Mighty Fortress," and invite group members to tell of their experiences of God as a fortress. Close by standing in a circle and offering sentence prayers in response to learnings gained in this session.

Lections for Third Sunday of Easter

First Lesson: Acts 2:14a, 36-41

*P*REACHERS often try to end their sermons with something that will strike home, that will put in a nutshell the essence of their message. Peter has done that in today's concluding passage from his powerful Pentecost sermon. Because people from many nations were all hearing the disciples speak in their own languages, they thought they must be drunk. So Peter began by assuring them that it was not wine that was behind this marvel, but rather the fulfillment of a promise from the prophet Joel (2:28-32) that an out-pouring of God's Spirit would lead to signs and wonders. He then proceeded in a persuasive manner to show how the coming of Jesus fulfilled several other messianic prophecies. The sermon had its intended impact. The people pleaded with Peter to tell them what to do, and he did so.

Lord and Messiah

The last sentence drove home Peter's point to the "entire house [nation] of Israel"—that the one he had been talking about was Lord and Messiah. These were two of the greatest titles by which Peter could refer to Jesus. *Lord* meant that Jesus was the one to whom they belonged, the one to whom they owed the highest allegiance and service. *Messiah* (or *Christ*, the Anointed One) was the one chosen by God to fulfill Jewish expectations and bring salvation into the world. These are titles that Peter's listeners knew well. Jesus was the fulfillment of long-held hopes and dreams, but the people still would have trouble accepting him.

The People's Plea

The power of Peter's testimony elicited a deep and convicting response. The people were "cut to the heart." They had heard truth in Peter's words and could only respond with a desperate cry, "What should we do?" It was not Peter's oratorical gifts that brought them to this point; after all he was but a fisherman. It was the power of God's Spirit that penetrated their hearts (2:33).

Peter's response was immediate. "Repent," he said first. Repentance would be heartfelt sorrow for their sins. It would also be a profound change of mind and heart and life. It would mean turning from a rejection of Christ to acceptance of him as Lord and Messiah.

Next Peter said the new believers must be baptized in the name of Jesus. This ritual act would incorporate them into the body of believers and signify that they belonged to Jesus, placing themselves under his authority and lordship. With heartfelt repentance and baptism would come forgiveness by God for their sins and the interior presence of God through the Holy Spirit. The good news was that this wondrous promise of forgiveness was not just for eyewitnesses like Peter and the others but also for them and their children and everyone near and far, in present times and all times (2:39; see Isaiah 57:19; Joel 2:32).

Astounding Growth

Over three thousand persons heard the good news that day and were baptized, making them a part of the new community of faith. This fits in well with the whole theme of Acts, that is, the wondrous and miraculous growth of the early church. It did indeed start in Jerusalem and would spread throughout the world. In fact, as we saw earlier, these new converts were from many different nations. It is likely that they went back home with this new faith, taking with them the good news of God's salvation in Christ Jesus.

Think About It: Do you recall when you first really heard and understood the good news of what God has done for you in Christ? How did you feel? What was your response? When have you found yourself "cut to the heart" and left asking, "What should I do?" Did you feel impelled to share this good news with others? Are you still doing so?

Psalter: Psalm 116:1-4, 12-19

This psalm of thanksgiving (like Psalms 30, 32, 34) was used during Passover (perhaps because of the mention of "cup" in verse 13, but also because of its celebration of God's deliverance). The psalmist begins by expressing his deep love for God and how God heard and helped him (116:1-4). In gratitude, he proclaims to all God's love and goodness (116:5-7). After returning to how God had delivered him from death (verses 8-11), the psalmist asks (as in Acts 2:37), "What should I do in light of all God has done for me?" (116:12-19). His answer is to go to the Temple and give public thanks and sacrifice to God.

Epistle: 1 Peter 1:17-23

Peter had been telling his hearers to rejoice in their salvation through Christ, even if they suffer now as Christ himself suffered (1 Peter 1:3-12). In 1:13–2:10 he challenges them to live a life of holiness.

Living in Reverent Fear

"If you invoke as Father" may refer to the Lord's Prayer, which begins with "Father." The faithful call upon God as a child would a parent; but God is also an impartial judge, as Peter had learned in his experience with Cornelius (Acts 10:34). Verse 17 may mean that inasmuch as they already know God as father and then as judge, they should live in appropriate "fear" of that judgment.

The text suggests that, if the people realize that the One who judges them is also a loving Father, their "reverent fear" may include a confident devotion. This is not fear as terror but as awe or respect, of realizing that we stand before a holy God. The reference to exile would first remind a persecuted people of the Babylonian Exile from which God had delivered the Jews long ago. In their context, exile would refer to the "not yet" time of waiting for the final salvation by Jesus Christ "when he is revealed" (1:13). In any case the message confirms our gracious relationship with God, who bestows on us love and hope, but also requires accountability and reverence.

A Costly Ransom

The incentive for holy living is the realization of how much our salvation has cost the Son of God. The image is that of a ransom for the release of a slave—usually done with the payment of money ("silver or gold") and sealed with a sacrifice (of an animal). But their release from slavery (to sin) was paid not by mere gold but by something far more precious—Christ's gift of his life. He became the Paschal (Passover) lamb (see Exodus 12:3-8, 21; 1 Corinthians 5:7), the sacrifice that sealed the liberation. Jesus himself talked of this (Mark 10:45). This redemption had been God's intent from the beginning. But they are the ones blessed by seeing the fulfillment.

> **Think About It:** "You were redeemed from the empty way of life handed down to you from your [forebears]" (1:18, NIV). What was "empty" about what they had learned from the past? Were there positive aspects of their heritage as well? What empty (and enriching) ways have we inherited from our forebears in the faith? How do we decide what to affirm and what to reject of what they have passed on to us? How does Christ redeem us (bring us back) from emptiness?

Our grateful response to Christ's great sacrifice that "purifies" us from our self-centeredness, is to become God-centered ("obey the truth," NIV) and to "love one another deeply, from the heart" (1:22). This love is not just sentiment, but rather a "genuine mutual love," that, like the love of Christ, is willing to sacrifice and even die for one another.

Gospel: Luke 24:13-35

The setting is still the day of Resurrection, not in Jerusalem, but on a dusty road to Emmaus. This is one of the best known and loved Resurrection stories.

Meeting a Stranger

The circle of disciples was larger than just the Twelve. Two of them, Cleopas and a companion, were sadly returning to their homes after the sabbath and the tragic death of Jesus. Their destination was the village of Emmaus, about seven miles northwest of Jerusalem. (Several possible sites for Emmaus have been identified, including one about twenty miles from Jerusalem; but there is no certainty about which, if any, is the correct one.)

As they walked along, talking about all that had occurred, they were joined by a stranger. Like Mary earlier, they did not know who he was. We are told that "their eyes were kept from recognizing him" at the beginning (24:16), but that "their eyes were opened" later after their meal together (24:31). Apparently God's agency was at work, or perhaps their grief blinded them for the moment. Just as their ancestor Abraham entertained angels unawares, so Christ was with them and they did not know it.

> **Think About It:** "Christ was with them and they did not know it." Why do you think they did not recognize him? Are there times when we are not aware of Christ's presence? What blocks our receptivity? What might help us recognize him more clearly and respond to him more faithfully?

Talking With the Stranger

Jesus initiated the conversation; Cleopas answered. We know little about him. Some early church fathers have identified him with the Clopas of John 19:25, though there is little evidence to equate the two. Cleopas assumed that this stranger had also come from Jerusalem and was surprised he was unaware of recent events there. "You must be the only person around who doesn't know what's going on," Cleopas said. The irony is that this stranger was, in fact, the only one who did know. The stranger responded with one word, "*Poia*?" that is, "What things?"

Recounting the Story

Cleopas then narrated the story of Jesus, how he was from Nazareth, God's messenger, and handed over by their leaders to be killed. Jesus was more than a prophet. They had hoped he was the Messiah, the one to bring redemption to the nation, the one who would fulfill the promises in Scripture. Cleopas perhaps echoed the language of Isaiah 41:14 and 43:14 regarding "the Holy One of Israel." Jesus then told them that these promises had been fulfilled, but not in the way they expected.

Cleopas mentioned, sadly, that it was even then the third day since these events took place. Recall the Jewish belief that the soul finally departed on the fourth day. Before this could happen, Cleopas told of angelic messengers who reported that Jesus was alive. The women and some of the male disciples discovered the tomb to be empty. Jesus did not give Cleopas an opportunity to interpret this mystery.

Jesus Revealed

Jesus began with a gentle rebuke for their apparent lack of understanding. Then it was his turn to tell the story of faith, starting with Moses and going through the messianic prophecies—"the things about himself in all the scriptures" (24:27). And though their hearts "burned within," they still did not recognize him—until he broke bread with them. As in some other post-Resurrection appearances, it was at a meal that they saw Jesus for who he truly was. Thus for Christians Holy Communion has become a time in which we seek to see and know once again who Jesus is and what he has done for us.

Study Suggestions

A. Offer Your Devotion

Begin by singing or reading together the hymn, "When I Survey the Wondrous Cross"—paying special attention to the last stanza—or, "On the Day of Resurrection," which tells the whole Emmaus story. Then pray together the Lord's Prayer.

B. Sermons

Read Acts 2:14a, 36-41 with special emphasis on the response of the people to Peter's sermon at Pentecost. Drawing on the commentary on pages 164–65, discuss: What is the main message of the sermon? What was its effect? What extraordinary things occurred after the sermon? Ask if group members have ever heard a powerful, compelling word from God through a sermon. If so, when? What was the message? What impact did it have on their lives? As an alternative, have someone read Peter's entire sermon from Acts 2, then invite response. Ask: What part spoke to you? What parts raise questions? Have the group state in one sentence the central message of the sermon.

C. Understand the Holy Life

Read aloud 1 Peter 1:17-23 in two or three different versions. Together list the key words and phrases on chalkboard or a sheet of paper. Be sure these terms are clearly understood. Consult a Bible dictionary for help in defining them.

Pay particular attention to these terms: *reverent fear, ransom (redeem* in NIV), *impartial judge, precious blood of Christ, sacrifice,* and *genuine mutual (Christian) love.* Ask: What does *reverent fear* mean? According to this passage, how do we show reverence for God? According to Peter, why is it important that God be an impartial judge? What does the word *ransom (redeem)* mean? Does it help you to understand what God has done in Christ? Have you ever had someone make a great sacrifice for you? If so, who and why? If we truly believe that Christ gave his life for us, what difference does it make in how we think and act? How do we define *Christian love*? What does it look like? How is it demonstrated? In what ways do we experience it (or not) in our congregation?

D. Tell Stories

The Luke reading really tells two stories; one by Cleopas and the other by Jesus. Form three groups. Ask everyone to review Luke 24:13-35 and the commentary on pages 167–68. Group One should concentrate on verses 13-24, Group Two verses 25-27, and Group Three verses 28-35. Each group should report on what happened in its story and how the story influenced the believers' lives.

Use the "Think About It" questions in the Acts commentary on page 165 to invite group members to tell when they first heard the good news about Jesus or experienced his love. Begin by telling your own story.

Arrange ahead of time for two class members (or others invited especially for this purpose) to come prepared to assume the roles of Cleopas and his companion, the two on the road to Emmaus, in telling their story of meeting the risen Lord. Or, write out the story as a script for three persons plus a narrator, as a brief readers theater. Practice with the readers at least once beforehand.

E. Summarize and Pray

The readings show the power of the risen Christ and of the spoken word to touch and change lives. Ask group members to reflect on the messages of transformation in today's Scriptures. Ask: If we take the Jesus story as seriously as did the early disciples, what transformation might be brought about in us? Close by offering prayer for all who believe and for those who have not heard the story. Then invite members to commit or recommit their lives to Christ.

Lections for Fourth Sunday of Easter

First Lesson: Acts 2:42-47

A PHOTO album is an ideal way of preserving and presenting a pictorial record of family activities or church events. Long before the advent of cameras, Luke, the writer of Acts, in his own way, did much the same thing by painting in these few short verses a portrait of the life and work of the early church in Jerusalem.

Blueprint for an Emerging Church

This passage, particularly 2:42, lays out in embryonic form what it means to be the church—both then and ever since. These first Christians involved themselves in teaching and learning, fellowship and worship, and communion. They also gave of their resources, served those in need (2:44-45), witnessed to their faith, and led others to Christ (2:47). Worship, education, community life, stewardship, evangelism, and service—all essential functions of a vital Christian congregation—have formed the heart of church life from that day to this.

Hunger for More

Last week's Acts reading reported on how over three thousand persons became part of the church all at once. Some of these converts stayed there at least for a period of time. They had just begun the journey and had a hunger to learn more about Christ. Empowered by the Holy Spirit, they spent time listening to the apostles teach and preach. They also participated in the fellowship of the gathered community. Most likely what the apostles taught was what they remembered about Jesus and his teachings (see John 14:26). The Greek word for this is *didache* (teaching). Some of these teachings would later be collected in a book called *The Didache*, others in the Gospels.

170

Wonders and Fellowship

Wondrous things happened in the early church. Persons were healed. Lives were touched and changed. Miracles took place, perhaps none greater than that this diverse group came together as one people. They had found a power greater than their differences. The Greek word for this is *koinonia*, meaning "fellowship," but more than that, a profound oneness or unity. In fact, they felt so close to one another that they sold their goods and made a common fund from which the needs of any and all could be met. No one was compelled to do this. It came as an expression of their love for one another. Such actions were truly miraculous.

Prayers, Food, Praise, Growth

The early believers did not separate from the Temple in Jerusalem until it was destroyed. In fact, they went there together at designated times throughout the day for prayers and worship. They also congregated in their homes, eating together and most likely also observing Holy Communion. Christians have always found strength and a renewed sense of unity by sitting in fellowship around a table. There's just something about eating together that brings people closer. And there was a sense of awe and expectation as this growing community worshiped and praised God together. There was something about them that was so attractive that persons, by the power of God (2:47), were joining them daily.

> *Think About It:* The early believers had vigorous and gracious discipline (verse 42). Do you have a personal rule of faith and life? Are you part of a covenant or sharing group that provides corporate discipline, support, and accountability to aid in spiritual growth? What can we learn from this early Christian community about ways the church must contribute to nurturing our spiritual lives?

Some point out that Luke's snapshots of the early church are idealistic. Maybe that's true. We know from reading the rest of Acts that the church would soon have problems and challenges. There can be no doubt, however, that something profound had happened to these people. They had been transformed. And through them and those after them the world would begin to be transformed as well.

Psalter: Psalm 23

This psalm draws on a very common experience in pastoral Palestine—herding sheep. In this poetic parallel, we are the dependent sheep, God the shepherd who meets our every need. Everything a shepherd does for the sheep—protecting them, feeding them, treating their wounds, leading them through dark valleys—God does for us, and more. God can lead us to the best grazing and to calm, refreshing streams. When we suffer from fatigue or discouragement, God restores our hope and vitality. When we face evil or death, God's presence provides comfort and strength (verses 1-4).

In verses 5-6, however, the image of God changes from caring shepherd to gracious host. God provides protection from enemies, royal treatment and bountiful blessing, lifelong grace and goodness, and eternal life in the gracious presence of God. (Further insight into this well-known and much-loved psalm may be found in the psalter commentary for the fourth Sunday in Lent, page 133.)

Epistle: 1 Peter 2:19-25

Today's verses from First Peter are set in the larger context of an emphasis on submission to and respect for authority—political, societal, familial, and, ultimately, divine authority. Peter was urging his readers to use their freedom responsibly and to live exemplary lives so as to make an upright witness and give no cause to their detractors for criticism or persecution. In this connection he counseled Christian slaves to respect and obey their masters, even when they were treated unfairly (2:13-18).

In the stratified class system of Peter's day, slavery went largely unquestioned. Nor did Peter challenge it in this passage, probably because Christians, a tiny persecuted minority, were in no position to take on a major institution of the Roman Empire. Instead, the background of slavery was used to make quite a different point.

Christ Our Example

Trust in God and awareness of his presence enables us to withstand unjust treatment when we must endure it (2:19). By no means should Christians, slave or otherwise, behave in such a way as to deserve punishment (2:20a). To be persecuted for our goodness is pleasing to God (2:20b). In this we are called to follow Christ as our example (2:21). As Isaiah described the suffering servant (Isaiah 53:9), he suffered unjustly even though innocent of any wrongdoing (1 Peter 2:22). When humiliated and abused he did not seek revenge, but instead returned good for evil, entrusting the outcome to the justice of God (2:23). He took onto

Think About It: "We are called to follow in his footsteps." As Christians we must live in such a way as bring no dishonor on the cause of Christ. Must we submit to injustice when we have the means to resist such evils, unlike the slaves in the first century? When is it justified to "stick up for our rights"? How can we discern when to acquiesce and when to protest nonviolently? Compare Peter's advice here with that of Jesus in Matthew 5:38-48, as described in the Gospel commentary for the seventh Sunday after the Epiphany (pages 97–98).

his own body the worst that humankind could offer, and his suffering and death has made it possible for us to overcome evil and live above reproach (2:24).

Secure and Free

But for Christ, Peter continued, we would still be like wayward sheep. But, thanks be to God, he has brought us into his fold for guidance and protection (2:25). Thus, even though our outward circumstances may enslave us, in our souls he has made us free—free from bondage to sin, free from submission to intimidation, free from fear of death, free to live our lives in his service and according to his will.

Gospel: John 10:1-10

Jesus was a master at using objects and illustrations from everyday life to convey his teachings. This passage (and most of John 10), tells how he used the images of sheep and shepherd to help explain his relationship with his followers. In a society of farmers and herders, the relationship of a shepherd with his sheep would have been very familiar.

The Good Shepherd (10:1-6)

Drawing upon these images, Jesus began by saying who he was not. His hearers knew well that sheep were very vulnerable animals for which the shepherd must offer extensive care. They were also well aware of the typical analogy of the king or leader as a shepherd (Psalm 23) and Jeremiah's condemnation of the unfaithful shepherds (Jeremiah 23:1-4).

A lazy, careless, or bad shepherd (leader) would neglect or endanger the flock (the nation). Jesus, the good shepherd, was not like the many would-be shepherds or leaders of the past (or the many false messiahs of his time), or like the Pharisees who had challenged his healing in John 9. So many of these "shepherds" tried to fleece the flock, using them for their own advantage and gain. The "sheep" knew that these false shepherds could not be trusted. Jesus may have had in mind Ezekiel 34, which condemned the leaders of Israel who had been bad shepherds, exploiting and endangering the flock.

The Gate of the Sheep

Jesus is not given to stealth; he comes into the fold by the gate, which is open and visible to the gatekeeper. (Sometimes large flocks had a gatekeeper to watch over the fold at night.) Folds were sometimes attached to a house or an extension to a house and had a separate gate. Some were just stone enclosures out in a field. Sometimes a shepherd who had no gatekeeper would lie down at the entrance to the fold to keep the sheep from getting out or wild animals from getting in. So literally the shepherd could be the gate. The gatekeeper knows the shepherd by sight and lets him inside.

The sheep also know the gatekeeper and recognize his voice. Stories have been told of shepherds coming together with their flocks at a watering hole and then easily separating out their own sheep simply by calling them. Sometimes shepherds even gave their sheep names. Likewise, Jesus knows his sheep by name and calls them, and they know his voice. They know whom they can trust.

Thieves and Bandits

Some who heard did not understand. Jesus' primary audience may still have been the Pharisees addressed in John 9. Their failure to understand was not just a matter of intellect but of heart. They could not or did not wish to see the truth in him. But to interfere with Jesus' work was to interfere with God's work, to steal away God's goodness to the nation. The thief or bandit cared only about his own agenda; the good shepherd and good gatekeeper cared about those entrusted to them, and that was the difference between them. Jesus says much the same thing in John 14:6, "I am the way. . . . No one comes to the Father except through me." He may also have had Psalm 118:20 in mind: "This is the gate of the Lord; / the righteous shall enter through it."

> **Think About It:** Jesus calls his own and leads them out. There are so many would-be shepherds (leaders) out there seeking us to follow them. Can you identify some? How can we discern the voice of Jesus in all this noisy clamor?

The images Jesus used have a movement. The shepherd and gatekeeper not only protect and lead the sheep but go well beyond. The bandit (also a term for anti-Roman messianic pretenders) seeks to "steal and kill and destroy." The good shepherd comes to bring abundant life (10:10).

Study Suggestions

A. Prayer

In Acts we see that one of the things the early Christians did each day was to pray together. Begin by inviting members to name prayer requests. Observe a time of silence, then lead the group in prayer, mentioning each request in turn, and pausing after each and at the end for silent intercessory prayer.

B. The Church Then and Now

Read aloud Acts 2:42-47, and review the commentary on pages 170–71. Together list the characteristics of the early church as Luke identifies them. They are: hunger for learning, a sense of fellowship or oneness, breaking bread, wonders and miracles, prayer, worship and praise, giving of their material goods, and growth. Then ask: If the Christian community grounds itself in these practices, what will be the result? How well do we and our own church community engage in these Christian practices? Which areas need attention and improvement? What can you do about this?

Those who had just been baptized and become part of the church had a yearning for learning and growing in their faith. Why is this important? What can we do as Christians in the church today to help one another grow in our faith?

C. Facing Suffering

Read aloud 1 Peter 2:19-25 and draw on the commentary on pages 172–73 in summarizing Peter's message to Christians suffering unjustly. Review 2 Peter 2:11–3:12 to better understand the broader context. This is a complex passage written for a society different from our own. Ask: Do you agree with Peter's instructions? What is the context and what are the societal givens? How was the submission of Jesus to his suffering similar to (and/or different from) the persecution Peter says they should endure? Compare Peter's counsel here to Jesus' words in Matthew 5:38-48. How do we as Christians respond to unjust treatment?

A question we often hear today is, What would Jesus do (WWJD)? Peter seems to be saying, "Look at what Jesus did, how he faced and endured his suffering. Follow his example." Discuss: Can we actually follow that example? At what points is this difficult? Is this the best guideline for faithful Christian living? Where else can we turn for guidance? How has Jesus been a model or example?

D. Sheep and Shepherds

Have someone read aloud John 10:1-10 and Psalm 23. Review the commentary on these passages on pages 171–72 and 173–74, and discuss the significance of these pastoral terms: *shepherd, gatekeeper, sheep, fold.* Ask: What similarities do you notice between the two Scriptures? What is the significance for you of this teaching of Jesus? How do you react to being compared to sheep? How are we like (and unlike) sheep? How has God been like a shepherd to us?

For many today shepherding is an unfamiliar occupation. Divide into groups, assigning some to rewrite Psalm 23 using experiences from their everyday lives, others to draw pictures on sheets of paper of images from their experience that convey the feelings about God contained in the psalm, and others to prepare a skit to dramatize their relationship with God. Then ask them to share what they have come up with.

E. In Closing

Each of the main texts reflects life, perhaps an idealized life, in the early Christian church and points out some of the challenges Christians face. Ask: What are these challenges? How would the faithful practice of learnings from this week's study help equip our church to be the church? us as individuals to grow in faith?

Sing or read a hymn like "The Lord's My Shepherd, I'll Not Want" or "Dear Jesus in Whose Life I See." Pray for the church, for believers, for challengers of the church's status quo, and for strength and guidance to live out what has been learned in this study.

Lections for Fifth Sunday of Easter

First Lesson: Acts 7:55-60

*T*HE context of these verses is the trial of Stephen, the first Christian martyr. Stephen was chosen for service as a deacon (Acts 6:1-6) along with seven other men who were commissioned to "wait on tables." (The Greek word *diakonia*, from which our word *deacon* comes, is translated as both "ministry" and "service." Ministry is service!) Of that group, Stephen was singled out as "a man full of faith and the Holy Spirit" (6:5). More than just a waiter serving widows, he "did great wonders and signs among the people" (6:8).

Members of the synagogue argued with Stephen; but , because "they could not withstand the wisdom and the Spirit with which he spoke" (6:10), they charged Stephen falsely with blasphemy and brought him before the council. Of all the charges, one was particularly important: Stephen dared to say that God's love was open to all people. This proclamation was a threat to those who wanted to keep the circle of God's love closed and to determine just who would be allowed in and who kept out.

> **Think About It:** Stephen dared to say that God's love was open to all people. Who does the church today say is not welcome? Is God's love closed to anyone?

The Power to Go On

Acts 7 is Stephen's speech in his own defense. After rehearsing the long history of God's dealing with Israel, he saw "the heavens opened" and Jesus standing at the right hand of God (7:56). This gave him the assurance that love still was triumphant and that the power that raised Jesus could raise him as well. So he shouted out his testimony! But the crowd "covered their ears" (7:57), refusing to listen any longer. When he said that he saw Jesus standing at the right hand of God, the members of the court rushed on him. The Greek literally means they savaged him like a pack of dogs.

176

A Death More Cruel Than Usual

All violent death is cruel, but death by stoning is worse than most. The victim was thrown into an open pit. Probably he would be stunned or hurt by the fall. Then the crowd began to throw stones at him—not little pebbles, or even fist-sized rocks, but the largest stones they could pick up or roll. The stoning would continue until the victim was buried under a mound of stones. For the disciples to remove Stephen's body from that mound and give him a decent burial was an enormous act of courage.

> **Think About It:** The leaders of the community covered their ears rather than consider Stephen's witness. What are some recent examples of covering our ears and refusing to listen to a witness from God? When have you felt that your witness was being rejected by others? Since, as the saying goes, "you can never be sure through whom the voice of God may choose to speak," how can we make sure that every voice gets a fair hearing?

Prayer

"Receive my spirit" is a common prayer at death. Jesus had prayed from the cross, "Father, into your hands I commend my spirit" (Luke 23:46). Stephen's prayer was similar, except that he offered up his spirit to the "Lord Jesus," his Savior and Lord. Finally, perhaps with his dying breaths—again like Jesus' words, "Father, forgive them for they know not what they do"— Stephen prayed that the sin of his death would not be held against his executioners. These words seem almost strange to a culture devoted to "getting even" or "exacting justice," which often means the same thing. How could he forgive those who were killing him because of what he believed?

Psalter: Psalm 31:1-5, 15-16

Verse 1 is key to understanding the others: the psalmist puts his trust in God. The phrase "in your righteousness deliver me" was crucial for Martin Luther. He had always thought of righteousness as God's legitimate anger and judgment at sin, until he came to understand the truth in this verse—that God's righteousness was essentially love. This insight changed Luther's life and led to the Protestant Reformation.

The psalmist asks for rescue from either suffering or persecution because of his faith. Verse 5a is familiar, because Jesus quoted it on the cross (Luke 23:46). In Jesus' case it was a commitment for dying; here the psalmist makes it a commitment for living to God. The word *spirit* can also mean "breath" and is synonymous with *life* here. The psalmist is confident because of God's saving activity. Psalm 31 can teach us how to die in quiet confidence in God's love. It can also teach us how to live, trusting and committing our spirits to God.

177

Epistle: 1 Peter 2:2-10

Peter reminds his readers that Christ is the foundation stone on which to build a life. His argument cites a series of passages from the Hebrew Bible, almost as if there were a common list circulating in the church.

Built on the Rock

That Christ was rejected shows a major difference between the world's values and God's values. God chose as valuable a living "stone" that the world rejected. Peter reminds the church that we, too, are to become living stones, a spiritual house, a holy priesthood. Since the house is a temple where sacrifices are offered, we are to offer spiritual sacrifices, lives of holiness. The Christian life is based on what God has already done in Jesus Christ; it is also about what God is doing in the lives of his followers.

The Old Testament citations are from Psalm 118:22, Isaiah 8:14, and Isaiah 28:16. Together, they make a cumulative point. Christ is both the cornerstone and a stumbling stone. For those who believe, he is the foundation of their faith; for those who do not, he is a scandal. God's act calls for a response in faith. On whom do we bet our lives? Faith is not only believing but also living and following.

The Glory of the Church

First Peter 2:9-10 is among the greatest passages in Scripture. Imagine a community of converted slaves, Jews who had been cast out of the synagogue, a few merchants or traders, some free artisans. None of them had any power, status, or religious standing. Yet Peter says to them, "You are a chosen race, a royal priesthood, a holy nation, God's own people" (2:9). The world may not see them as of much value, but look what God thinks of them! And, these persons are not chosen just for glory, but for witness. They are all those things so they can witness to all God has done in, for, and through them for the world.

> **Think About It:** You are a "royal priesthood." Priests guide people to God. Royalty are people of privilege. It is our privilege to lead people to God. Is it a privilege to point people to God? How do we do this? How could we do it better?

"Not a People" to "God's People"

The citations from Hosea 1:10 also point up the difference between what they were and what they became. "Not my people" refers to those who were Gentiles, unacquainted with the Jewish tradition. Now as Christians (but not Jewish Christians) they had become "God's people"—new members of the faith community and inheritors of the promises given to the "chosen race." From "not a people" to "God's people" is quite a leap.

178

Gospel: John 14:1-4

These words are a part of the "farewell discourse," the winding up of Jesus' life with his disciples. They begin with the comforting words we often hear at funerals. Here, Jesus is urging the disciples to stand firm in the face of his death.

The Father's House

The "Father's house" does not mean heaven in this context. Rather, it is a reference to Jesus' intimate relationship with God. The Father's house is not about location, but about relationship. Within the relationship of love between Father and Son, there are "many dwelling places" or "rooms" (NIV)—opportunities and situations in which Jesus' followers may enter into that love. Jesus' words about going and preparing remind us that, in John's Gospel, it is only Jesus' return to God that makes it possible for the disciples to enter into relationship with both Son and Father.

"You know the way to the place where I am going" (14:4). Thomas misunderstands this and asks for clarification. The "way" here is not a destination or even a route for which we might need a road map, but Jesus' reference to himself.

I Am

One of John's literary devices is the series of meditations on Jesus beginning with the words, *I am* "the English translation of what scholars believe is the hidden name of God, YHWH. (See Exodus 3:13-15.) Thus, these statements say two important things about Jesus. First, he is God. He takes the divine name and uses it for himself. Second, these metaphors can help us understand this God whom we experience as both Father and Son.

Truth and Life

"I am the way" (John 14:6). We have seen that "way" is about relationship, about a life lived obediently and freely in the will of the Father. "Truth" and "life" are two further metaphors that help us see how Jesus is the "way." The truth about Jesus is that he is the incarnation of God. (See John 1:1-18.) As the Word made flesh, Jesus shows us the truth about the God of love and compassion. Jesus as "life" manifests the vitality of God that empowers us to truly live.

> **Think About It:** Jesus promised to take his believers to himself in a place he had especially prepared. Is it a place in this life or only in the next? Is it a literal place, a spiritual state, or a redeeming relationship?

No One Comes to God But By Me

This is a hard saying for some of us because of its exclusivism. What about others who practice their faith but don't believe in Jesus? Are they cast aside?

On the one hand, we may be uneasy about the literal understanding of the passage. We experience God as being more open and inclusive than this verse suggests. A God of infinite power and steadfast love, who is revealed as Father (and Creator), Son (Jesus Christ), and Holy Spirit (divine presence), could certainly be revealed in whatever way God chooses. So, we look at the original context and remember that these verses constitute the statement of a religious minority in the Mediterranean world.

On the other hand, there is something to be said for the claim. Verses 6-7 say, "This is who we are. We are the people for whom God has been revealed in Jesus Christ. Our Scriptures, which contain a record of the source of our truth, confirm this, as do our traditions and creeds." If we know the God of Jesus, we know that God through Jesus.

The way we interpret this saying determines how we relate to Jews and Muslims, Hindus and Buddhists, and millions of others in our world who do not experience God through Jesus Christ. As believers we walk a fine line between crusading arrogance and affirming our legitimate distinctiveness.

Study Suggestions

A. Think About Stones

Bring to the session a handful of stones. Some may even be polished and used as jewelry or other ornaments. Show them to the group. Ask: What are some qualities we associate with stones? (hard, heavy, smooth, sturdy, impenetrable, destructive, permanent) For what are they useful? (building, paving, protecting, dividing)

B. Reflect on Stones in This Scripture

Read aloud 1 Peter 2:2-8. Ask: What do these images say about Jesus Christ? How do the qualities we associate with stones (see Activity A) help us understand Peter's metaphors about stones? If the Christian life is about faithful living, what does the image of the stone suggest about the way we relate to Christ? What resources in the church can help us "build on a rock"? What resources can help us become "living stones"?

C. Think More About Faithful Living

Read aloud Acts 7:55-60 and Psalm 31:1-5, 15-16, and the commentary on both passages on pages 176–77. Ask: What clues do the experiences of Stephen (service, witness, courage) and the psalmist (prayer, commitment, trust) give us for living faithfully? In what specific verses do we find these clues? How could we develop these clues into a pattern of faithfulness in our own lives? How can we support each other in this endeavor?

180

D. Deal With the Tough Question

Read aloud 1 Peter 2:9-10, and review the commentary on page 178. Ask: What does this message about being chosen to be God's people suggest about who we are as Christians? How does Christ transform a negative past into a positive present and a promising future? What does this suggest about what God calls us to be and do?

Now read aloud John 14:1-7 and the commentary on the way, the truth, and the life. Ask: If "the way, the truth, and the life" are about relationships and a journey, rather than a destination, what does this say about how we live as Christians on a day-to-day basis? about the point of being Christian?

E. Deal With Another Tough Question

Reflections on the texts from both Acts and John raise another tough question: What does "no one comes to the Father except through me" mean? Are there other ways to God? Does a God of infinite love and power limit access to salvation? Apart from Jesus, do we know God as Father? Does this verse mean that God might be known apart from Jesus, but only through Jesus do we know God as the loving Father of the Son? If Christianity is the only way, what implication is there for Christians and for non-Christians? Is this claim exclusive or inclusive? How does this claim affect our approach to mission?

Now consider your church and the universal church. Discuss: Who is included in the church? Who is excluded? Is the congregation truly representative of the population of the community? If certain groups in the community are not represented in the congregation, is this evidence of who is excluded? Who might not be welcome? To whom would we not intentionally reach out? What is the connection between faithful living and being open to all persons?

F. Celebrate the Faith

Read 1 Peter 2:9 aloud in unison. Read it together again, this time with "pizzazz" (great expression). Read it a third time and insert the name of your congregation after the word *you* each time it appears in the text. Sing in closing "Help Us Accept Each Other."

Lections for Sixth Sunday of Easter

)

First Lesson: Acts 17:22-31

*P*AUL began his speech at the Areopagus (either the city council or at the place) by telling the Athenians he could tell they were very religious. He had been around the city and noticed all the temples and altars, including one to an unknown god. There is a legend in the writings of Diogenes Laertius, telling how, during a plague, Epimenides the Cretan told the Athenians to turn sheep loose on the Areopagus. Wherever the sheep lay down, there they should be sacrificed to "the appropriate god," that is, to the unknown god who was causing the plague. Paul may have seen an altar like this.

Think About It: Paul began by mentioning the unknown god. If you were addressing a group who were hostile, skeptical, or merely bored or indifferent, how would you go about attracting interest and establishing rapport? Would you try to shock, startle, befriend, identify, or what? Have you ever had such an experience, either with an audience or a small group of acquaintances? What did you do? What do you think of the way Paul started off? Was he trying to "win friends and influence people," proclaim the gospel, or both?

In any event, Paul told the Athenians he could reveal to them the nature of this unknown god. This was a daring statement. Earlier we have been informed that the Athenians liked to spend their time in hearing something new (verse 21). So Paul had his audience set up. What did he tell them about this unknown god?

Creation

First, Paul said, God made the world and everything in it. Therefore, God does not live in human shrines or need anything from human beings, since God is the source of all that is. Second, God made all nations from one common humanity. Third, God determined national boundaries and fixed the times the nations would live in them, which refers to Deuteronomy 32:8. The Greeks also believed their place in the earth came by divine appointment. Perhaps Paul was trying to speak to his sophisticated Greek audience in terms they already understood.

Relationship With God

Humans were created to seek after God, yet God is never far away. "In him we live and move and have our being" is a line from a poem attributed to Epimenides, the Cretan already mentioned. The second quotation, "For we too are his offspring," is from Aratus (born 310 B.C.), who was from Cilicia, Paul's native province. The two quotations sound even less like Paul, for they ring of pantheism (the idea that God is everything, and everything is God). The Paul we read in his letters makes a much sharper distinction between God and humanity.

The Heart of the Matter

Paul then turned from his philosophical argument to the heart of the matter. The present time, he said, is a time of crisis. God has overlooked our ignorance in times past, but now God calls us to repentance. Why? Because the Day of Judgment has been fixed. "A man" God has appointed will judge the world. Paul's reference to "a man" reflects ideas found in Matthew, Mark, and Luke. There Jesus refers to himself as a "Son of Man" who will be God's instrument for judging the world. (See, for example, Matthew 25:31.) The sign that this will happen is that God raised this "man" from the dead.

The Athenians liked to hear something new, but not this "resurrection" business! They did not care about the body and wanted to escape from it, not to find it in the life to come. Nevertheless, some asked to hear more; and others, including two prominent citizens—one a member of the court of the Areopagus—became believers (verse 33).

Psalter: Psalm 66:8-20

The psalmist here praises God for saving him from death. The tests and trials we face are not necessarily punishment, but they may be God examining us in order to affirm us (as with Job). The key is not in the testing but in God's deliverance. Verses 13-20 remind us that the psalmist is in worship, praising God for what God has done in his or her life. God has not removed God's steadfast love. Several words and phrases here remind us of the Exodus from Egypt, so the psalmist may be singing the "old, old story" of God's saving power. That old story from the past has now become real in the psalmist's life.

183

Epistle: 1 Peter 3:13-22

How do Christians hold to the promise of God's blessing and also deal with those who are hostile to the faith?

Dealing With Hostility

If we are steadfast in holding to the good, Peter says, we don't need to fear ultimate harm. That does not, however, mean there won't be unjust suffering. There are clear references here to the teachings of Jesus. *Blessed* is the same word that is used in the Beatitudes (see Matthew 5:11-12, with its teaching on the blessedness of being persecuted for righteousness). To "sanctify Christ as Lord" (verse 15) uses the same verb as the Lord's Prayer (the Lord's name be *sanctified* (hallowed, made holy). It's all right, Peter says, to defend yourselves against those hostile to you, but do it gently. "Keep your conscience clear" (verse 16) means, "be sure they are slandering you for your goodness, and not for evil you have done."

Rejoice in Suffering

We can actually rejoice in suffering, Peter says, if we do it because of goodness. If we suffer as Christ suffered, we can also be a part of Christ's redemption. About 100 years after Peter wrote this letter, there was another outbreak of persecution in the area where his readers lived. Polycarp, the Bishop of Smyrna (ca. A.D. 69–155), was tortured and killed because he was a Christian. All through his sufferings, he kept praising God for God's goodness and for the privilege of being allowed to suffer for Christ. He truly rejoiced in his suffering and was a powerful example both to his church and to the non-Christians who witnessed his suffering.

Reminders of the Faith

Peter reminds us of an ancient article of faith present in the Athanasian and Apostles' creeds; that is, "he descended to the dead" and preached to the spirits in prison. The *Preaching of Peter* has an account of the Resurrection in which Jesus is led from the tomb by two angels. A voice comes from the heavens asking, "Have you preached to the spirits in prison?" to which Jesus replies, "I have." The power behind this story is that no one, even those who died before Jesus, is beyond God's saving love.

> **Think About It:** "It is better to suffer for doing good, if suffering should be God's will, than to suffer for doing evil." Have you ever felt that any of your suffering was God's will? Have you ever had to suffer for doing good?

Baptism Again

Peter refers to the ark of Noah and those saved from the Flood. That event, he says, is like baptism, a saving act. When Peter says we are saved in

184

baptism, he does not mean there is something magical about the sacrament, but that baptism is a part of God's power for our salvation. The response to God's saving act is the "appeal to God for a good conscience" (verse 21), which means a commitment to live out our baptism in the world.

Gospel: John 14:15-21

There are two important truths about love in this passage:

1. Loving Jesus and keeping his commandments go hand in hand.
2. God abides with (is present with, lives with) those who love God.

Love and Commandments

In John's Gospel, *commandments*, *word*, and *works* are all synonyms that refer to everything Jesus says about God. So "keeping my commandments" means far more than living by all the ethical rules. It means being faithful to what we know about God.

Love and the Father

This passage contains three promises, all rooted in the mutual love between the Father, the Son, and the disciples:

First, the coming of the Advocate (verses 16-17). The Advocate, sometimes called the Paraclete, is another name for the Holy Spirit, particularly of those functions the Spirit shares in common with Jesus. Here that function is to reveal the truth—not abstract truth, but truth about Jesus. It is truth about who Jesus is (the Word made flesh) and what Jesus does (save his people). The Holy Spirit will help the faithful recall this truth (verse 26).

Second, the promise of Jesus' own return (verse 18). *Orphan* is a metaphor used to describe disciples without a master. Jesus' disciples were soon going to be orphaned in that sense. We often talk about Jesus' second coming, but also about Jesus being with us all the time. A hymn such as "In the Garden" is an example of the latter. But notice: Jesus cannot return unless he leaves first. The Advocate, or the Spirit, is the power of Jesus present with us *while Jesus is absent with the Father.*

Third, the promise of Jesus' presence with the disciples (verses 20-21). This sounds like a contradiction of the second promise. But, as we have seen, the Spirit is the power of Jesus present with us while Jesus is absent.

> *Think About It:* Jesus said the world would not see him, but the disciples would. What do you believe about Jesus' absence? about the Second Coming? Does it make sense that Jesus can come if he has not first gone? Have you "seen" Jesus? How do we experience the presence of the Holy Spirit in our life?

The disciples (and we) can love Jesus even after he is gone. We love him by keeping his commandments, that is, by being faithful to what he taught us about God and by making that truth about God known to the world. Jesus presents the relationship between keeping commandments and loving God from both sides. Those who keep the commandments are those who love. Those who love will keep the commandments. In some ways, it is much harder to be faithful to what Jesus taught us about God than it is to live by a set of rules (another way to understand the commandments).

The Ultimate Relationship

John teaches that the disciples (and Jesus' faith community) can be in relationship with the Father and the Son after the Resurrection and Ascension, but this relationship only exists within a community of faith. Once more we see that there is no rugged individualism about faith in the New Testament. It is always a faith of the community, rooted in the community, nourished in the community, lived out in the community. Jesus makes the promise to the community, not to individuals—the pronouns are *all* second-person *plural*.

In this model of love, the relationship between Jesus and others can grow beyond that first community and include us. The relationship depends on the presence of the love of God in the life of the community. That love is present wherever those who love Jesus keep his commandments.

Study Suggestions

A. The Second Coming

Begin by asking the group to stand and recite the Apostles' Creed. After they are seated, repeat the statement, "from thence he shall come to judge the quick and the dead." Ask: What do you think this means? Do you expect Christ to come again? How do you respond to those Christians who keep pointing to current events as signs that the end is near? Now read Acts 17:22-31 and refer to the "Heart of the Matter" paragraph on page 183. Ask: What does Paul say will happen in the Judgment? How does this compare to what we hear being said about judgment in the church today? Who does Paul say will judge the world on God's behalf? Is the knowledge that Jesus Christ will be the judge cause for hope or fear? Why? How will Christ judge us?

B. Other Crises

Read Psalm 66:8-20 and 1 Peter 3:13-22. Ask: What kinds of crises are these writers talking about? What is the cause for each? What is the source of hope in each? What does Peter mean when he says to rejoice in suffering? (See "Rejoice in Suffering" on page 184.) Is this the same as "praising God if it kills you"? Or is it something deeper? Does sharing in Christ's redemption mean that we have to suffer like Christ before we can be saved?

C. Glory in the Faith

Read 1 Peter 3:13-22 and "Reminders of the Faith" on page 184. Ask: How does this Scripture speak to these familiar questions: Can the people who lived before Jesus be saved? What does it suggest about God's plan—and power—for salvation? What does the statement "he descended to the dead" or "he descended into hell," which appears in the Apostles' and Athanasian creeds mean to us?

D. Focus on the Faith Community

Read John 14:15-21 and the commentary on pages 185–86. Ask: What does Jesus mean by "I am in my Father, and you are in me, and I am in you" (verse 20, NIV)? The "you" in each case is plural. Do we experience Jesus as being in the midst of our faith community? in this group? Why are U. S. Christians prone to think of their relationship with Jesus individually rather than corporately?

E. Think on the End of the World

Look again at John 14:15-21 and the "Love and the Father" paragraph on pages 185–86. Remind the group that Christians speak calmly about Jesus' return or second coming. For someone to return, one has to have been absent. Yet we also speak about Jesus as always being present. How can Jesus be present and be away at the same time? How do we know he is there?

F. Consider Relationships

React to this statement: "I can worship God as well on the beach, in the mountains, or on the golf course as I can in church"? Is this true? Read John 14:15-21 again and "The Ultimate Relationship" on page 186. Ask: Is it true that we can have this relationship with God and Christ only in the gathered, worshiping community? Why or why not? Does the Bible indicate where a relationship with God must take place? If specific boundaries exist, can those persons who are "out of bounds" have a relationship to God? Why or why not?

G. Closing

Sing a hymn of Jesus' presence, such as "Abide With Me," or "We Meet You, O Christ." Repeat again the Apostles' Creed, including the words, "he descended to the dead." Pray for Christ's continuing presence and guidance in the coming week.

Lections for the Ascension
of the Lord

First Lesson: Acts 1:1-11

*L*UKE and Acts are two volumes by a single author. Both are addressed to Theophilus, meaning "friend of God." This could be a general term, suggesting that the book is dedicated to all believers. But Luke 1:3 refers to him as "most excellent," implying that he was a real person of some status—either a pagan seeker whom the writer sought to inform, or a believing official who needs further instruction.

Luke first reviews the Jesus story—his deeds, teachings, suffering, resurrection, and command to wait for the promise of the Spirit (verses 1-5). Then he describes the Ascension (verses 6-11). The gathered disciples still think Jesus is a political messiah who will restore an earthly kingdom. Jesus chides them for wanting to know too much and trying to anticipate events. Only God can know such things. Jesus has better news. They will be given the power of the Holy Spirit and will be sent to the Jews, Greeks, and throughout the world to represent the risen Christ! Then it happened: "He was taken up" (verse 9, NIV). They were dumbfounded! But suddenly two messengers appeared to assure them that Jesus would be back.

On the Mount of Olives in Jerusalem stands a church and a tablet marking the spot from which Jesus ascended. The people who put them there long ago believed, with countless others, that the Ascension was a literal, historical event. At this point in the Christian Year, Christians annually celebrate this happening.

For many the literal Ascension is an article of faith. If the Bible says it happened this way, it most certainly did. Even though since Copernicus we no longer believe in a three-story universe, with a flat earth suspended between heaven and hell, we retain the image that these are dwelling places—one up where God reigns, Jesus ascended, and good people go, and one down where Satan waits to punish the bad.

Other Christians prefer to think of heaven and hell as spiritual conditions rather than actual places. Heaven is the condition of being in relationship with God; hell a condition of separation. In this view, what do we make of the Ascension? If Jesus didn't really vanish into the clouds, why observe the Feast of the Ascension at all?

> **Think About It:** What do you believe about the Ascension? What is its meaning for us? Why should we celebrate it today?

For persons of both persuasions, the significance of Ascension Day is threefold: (1) At the Ascension the power of the Holy Spirit was promised. Even though the visible Jesus is gone, his Spirit is with us and gives us strength. (2) At the Ascension we received our commission. We are to bear witness that Jesus is Lord—of our lives and of the world. (3) At the Ascension we are told that God is in charge of history and the ultimate end is sure. We cannot know when Christ will reappear to assert his authority, or how, but that he will do so there can be no doubt.

Psalter: Psalm 47

This psalm is read on Ascension Day because it sings of the enthronement of YHWH. Written after a successful battle, it gives credit to God and celebrates his sovereignty over the nations (verses 2-3, 8). The people are summoned to praise God's majesty with clapping (verse 1), trumpets (verse 5), and song (verse 6-7). They are grateful that through this victory God has assured their inheritance (verse 4), shown his love (verse 4), and brought them together as Abraham's descendants to demonstrate his and their dominance over all "the shields [armies] of the earth" (verse 9).

> **Think About It:** Do you think of Jesus as a conquering military hero? Can you understand why persecuted Christians would take comfort from the thought that their crucified Lord, gone to be with God, would soon return in triumph to subdue "nations under our feet" (verse 3)? Do others sometimes get you down to the point that you think, "Just you wait; when the Lord comes you'll get yours!"? How does this relate to the "love your enemies" emphasis of Jesus?

The primary theme of this psalm, though, is not vengeance, but the homage due to God as sovereign over all the earth and all of history. This is the assertion of the Ascension as well.

Epistle: Ephesians 1:15-23

Like a piece of music, this passage begins quietly with the gentle violins of prayer and thanksgiving and builds up to a great crescendo with the crash of drums and a ringing declaration of Christ's universal power. The writer—either Paul or one of his disciples—first expresses gratitude for his readers' exemplary faith and love (verses 15-16). Then his prayer moves to intercession as he asks God to deepen their understanding of the hope (soft), rich heritage (louder), and majestic power (louder still) of God's work on their behalf through Christ (verses 17-19). But the climax is still to come. This work involves nothing less than Christ's resurrection from death and his ascension to reign with God on high (verse 20—resounding)! The Son of God is exalted above all kingdoms and powers of this time and all time (verse 21—deafening)! He reigns—

> **Think About It:** "For the sake of the church, . . . the full and final completion of his mission and destiny." Does the church as you know it seem like the fulfillment of Christ's ministry? We tend to see the church's shortcomings—shabby buildings, squabbling congregations, feeble commitments, uncertain leadership. What is there about the church that shines through all of this to be seen as the body of Christ, the ultimate accomplishment of his earthly mission and the culmination of his exalted reign? Is this rhetoric or reality?

but not for his own benefit or glorification. His honor and glory are for the sake of the church, his body, which is the full and final completion of his mission and destiny (verses 22-23—awesome stillness).

Paul's point is that the Ascension is not only about Christ, but also about us—the church, his body. As he gave himself in service so must we. As he stood for justice and against oppression so must we. As his physical body was broken by the earthly powers, so must his body the church be willing to die to manifest God's reconciling love. As it was his destiny to be exalted so, ultimately, is ours. The church is the body of Christ—human yet godly, broken yet raised, humble yet exalted. In the words of a familiar collect: "Make her valiant to give up her life to humanity, that, like her crucified Lord, she may mount the path of the cross to a higher glory" ("For the Church," by Walter Rauschenbusch, in *Prayers of the Social Awakening*, Pilgrim Press, 1909).

Gospel: Luke 24:44-53

This is Luke's first account of the Ascension. The resurrected Jesus has suddenly appeared among his disciples with the words, "Peace be with you." This frightens them because they think they are seeing a ghost. So he has to show them the nail wounds in his hands and feet and have them touch him to be convinced that it is really he. They are glad but also dubious. Sensing this, he eats a piece of fish as additional proof (verses 36-43).

The disciples had had high hopes for Jesus. His compassionate healing, challenging words, remarkable miracles, and courageous confrontation of power—all had led them to believe that he was indeed the long-awaited Messiah. But it had all come to such an awful end—death on a cross. Then came the surprise of his sudden reappearance. They were still reeling from all that had happened in the last few days. No wonder they were still hesitant to believe that Jesus, their friend who was dead, was now alive again.

You Have Seen; Go and Tell

So Jesus begins a final teaching session. "If you haven't gotten it by this time," he seems to be saying, "I'll give you one more chance. I am both the fulfillment and the interpreter of your Scriptures. I am the Messiah who died and rose to bring salvation to you and all people. I am now commissioning you to go everywhere and share this good news. You have seen; now go and tell. But first, stay here awhile to receive the promised power from God that will enable you to do what I am asking" (verses 44-49).

Now they go out the city gate, down through the Kidron valley, and up and over the Mount of Olives to Bethany. There he gives them a final blessing, walks away, and disappears into the mountain mist. They are awestruck for a while then turn and go back down the hill and into the city, laughing and singing happily. From that time on they spend much time in the Temple in worship and praise (verses 50-53). They are not grieving that Jesus is gone; rather, they are glad to have been with him this last time, challenged by the task of continuing his mission, expectant about the gift God will soon bestow on them, and drawn to the Temple to prepare their hearts to receive it.

Think About It: "You are witnesses of these things" (verse 45). The word *witness* here has a double meaning. To witness means to see and also to tell. Watch carefully, and then tell what you have seen. Share your experience. Witnessing about Christ is not preaching at people, telling them what to believe and do, or coaxing them to make a decision. It is simply sharing what Christ has done for us. What have we witnessed of what Christ has done? To whom will we witness about this?

During the closing prayer in a youth Sunday school class, I raised my hand when the teacher asked who would like to follow Jesus. I had no idea where this would lead, but "my heart was strangely warmed." I was on the mountaintop with the Lord, and when I came down I could not contain my newfound joy and enthusiasm. He had appeared to me and then he was gone. He had called me and I had said yes. And the glow of his presence remained—and continues to this day, though admittedly there have been ups and downs. I witness now to what I witnessed then—the presence and guidance of the Spirit of Christ in my heart and life.

What has been your Ascension experience? How do you share it?

191

Study Suggestions

A. Setting the Stage

Remind the group that Ascension Day in the Christian Year is observed on the fortieth day after Easter. It concludes the post-Easter period and points to the approach of Pentecost ten days later. It highlights the changed relationship of Jesus to his followers—from friend and teacher to sovereign Lord. The responsibility now falls on them—and us—to carry on his ministry by being his witnesses.

B. Confronting the Doubts

Raise the issue stated earlier about whether we can believe the Ascension story literally. Invite an honest expression of views. Ask what value the Ascension might have for us if we don't take it literally, and explain its three-fold significance as stated on page 189.

C. Reviewing Luke's Stories

Point out that Luke-Acts is a two-volume work. Ask two volunteers to read Luke 24:44-53 and Acts 1:1-11 one after the other. Note the differences in emphasis of the two accounts. Ask: Why were the disciples slow to believe? How were they changed by what happened at the Ascension? How would this affect what they became later?

D. Talking About Witness

In both accounts Jesus commissions the disciples to be his witnesses. Discuss the two meanings of *witness*—seeing and telling. Ask: What have been your experiences with witnessing? Have members share what they have witnessed—their experiences of meeting and being changed by Jesus—and how they witness about this to others (share their faith stories).

E. Praising the Exalted Lord

Read in unison Psalm 47. Explain that this is an enthronement psalm after a military victory. Discuss the parallel between this celebration of YHWH's dominion over the nations and the ascended Lord's sovereignty over all creation. Also discuss the contrast between Jesus the suffering servant and Christ the regnant king. Ask: How do these fit together? Which do you relate to best? How has the church manifested these dimensions down through history? Ask two small groups to do a "sculpture" of each dimension by taking bodily poses, then asking the groups for responses on what they see and feel.

F. Being the Church

As someone reads Ephesians 1:15-23, play some music in the background, such as Ravel's "Bolero" or Randall Thompson's "Alleluia," that corresponds to the rising and falling moods of the passage, as noted on pages 189–90. Point out that this passage climaxes with words of praise to the ascended and reigning Christ. Also stress that this is not for his own honor or benefit, but for the sake of the church, the body of Christ. Discuss: Was the formation of a church the ultimate end of Jesus' ministry, or was it the saving of souls? To what extent is the church a fitting representation of the body of Christ? In what ways is the church called to embody Christ incarnate in Jesus? How can the church as institution give faithful expression to (embody) the healing, saving, reconciling spirit of Christ? Give examples from your own experience of the church.

G. Celebrate the Ascension

Close by singing "All Hail the Power of Jesus' Name" or "Crown Him with Many Crowns" and inviting sentence prayers for your church body to become a more faithful manifestation of the spirit of Christ.

Lections for Seventh Sunday
of Easter

First Lesson: Acts 1:6-14

*T*HIS is Ascension Sunday, the Christian celebration that marks the return of the risen Christ to God. This passage, which overlaps with the lection for Ascension Day, is Luke's report.

When? When? When?

The lection begins with the disciples asking if this is the time for the Kingdom to come. Jesus' followers have been asking that question ever since, particularly when times are hard and we get discouraged. Jesus' reply is important for us. Basically, he said, "That's none of your business. God is taking care of that. Here's what you *should* be concerned about. . . ."

> **Think About It:** Only God knows the times set by God's own authority. Why do you think we keep trying to predict the time, when Jesus was so clear that we are not to know? Is it that we misinterpret other biblical signs? are anxious for our reward? want to see evildoers get their just deserts? are pessimistic about the way things are going? or what?

The Promise of Power

Probably all of us like power. We might like to have a power position at work, or chair a church committee, or just be able to command quiet in our family room. Jesus told the disciples they would receive power—but it was not this kind of power. Rather, it was power to witness. With this power also came a set of marching orders. When the disciples received this power, they would witness to Jesus in Jerusalem (their own neighborhood), Judea (their sphere of influence), Samaria (the places where "those other people" live, the ones we don't like), and throughout the earth.

The text reports Jesus was lifted up and a cloud took him out of their sight. What does Ascension mean for the Christian faith? One meaning is that Jesus had returned to God, that he was in "glory" with God. A cloud, in the Hebrew Bible, was a representation of the hiddenness of God. By his ascension in the cloud, Jesus was now received into the divine presence.

Back to Business

In the New Testament, whenever people "in white robes" appear, something is going to happen. Here there is a promise and an implied message. The promise was that Jesus would return. The implication, "So, don't just stand around here looking at the sky. Get on with God's business." And so they did.

The disciples went back to Jerusalem, to the upper room, probably the same room where they had eaten the Passover some weeks before. There they began to get ready for the promised power. The eleven are named—Peter and the rest. But they were not the only ones there in the upper room, just as they may not

> *Think About It:* "Don't just stand there; do something!" In the spiritual life, we move back and forth between moments of inspiration and our daily routine. Both the uplifting mountain-top and the hard work of faithful living are spiritual. The trick is to channel the energy from one into the other. When are you tempted to continue gazing heavenward when there is work to be done? When do you hear Jesus say, "Get on with God's business"? What rhythm have you worked out between prayer and action?

have been the only ones at the Last Supper. There were the women (who had been Jesus' disciples in Galilee), his mother and brothers, and others. While they waited, they spent their time in prayer, in remembering the teachings of Jesus, and in building a sense of community among themselves.

Psalter: Psalm 68:1-10, 32-35

This psalm portrays YHWH as a God of battle. Verse 1 reminds us of Numbers 10:35, the song of the ark of the covenant (the chest that carried the tablets of the Law, the jar of manna, Aaron's rod, and so on). The psalm, therefore, may have been sung in a celebration about the ark. These opening verses also remind us that righteousness is not morality, but living in dependence on God.

In Canaanite literature, the god Baal rides upon the storm, bringing wind and rain. Verse 4 says that God rides on the clouds and brings the rain. That is, YHWH claims authority over Baal's domain. In verses 5-6, God is the ideal ruler, who cares for the poor and marginalized, who have no power to

195

take care of themselves. So God not only rules in the areas claimed by other gods, but also is the model for the ruler. Thus, government need not be a four-letter word. The true function of national leadership, according to the Bible, is to provide care for those who cannot care for themselves.

Epistle: 1 Peter 4:12-14; 5:6-11

Peter promised his church that they would be able to face the rough times that were coming. Why? Because they knew that glory and power belonged to God. Nations and emperors may think they have the ultimate power; indeed, they may have the power to persecute, even kill, the faithful. But ultimate power belongs only to God. So the church can stand firm, knowing we are supported by the greatest power in the universe.

The address, "beloved," reminded the church that they were loved—by Peter, who showed his love in this letter and also by God. Verse 13 is one of the letter's great themes—Christ's suffering is the example for their suffering *and* the ground of their salvation. Now, given the realities in their world, they shared in Christ's suffering. Because of this they could rejoice. Later, when they would come to share in Christ's glory, they could rejoice exceedingly!

God Cares About You

One of the great messages of hope in Scripture is that God cares about us—personally! The great God Almighty loves us and cares for us more deeply and tenderly than human parents care for their children. "Cast all your anxiety on him, because he cares for you" (5:7).

> **Think About It:** How do we talk about God in human terms? What do we say about God's rule? Is it only "pie in the sky by and by," or is it a reality in time and space? When we talk about God's rule, we are not talking about power and authority, but justice and hope.

Notice the warnings about how faithful people respond to both present danger and coming judgment. They need to be alert and sober. *Sober* does not mean abstaining from alcohol, though that might not be a bad application. Being sober, rather, is a lifestyle in contrast to the licentiousness of the world (and of the believers' past life). That is, live as if you were really serious about God being in your life and caring about you.

Expectations of Suffering

Finally, 1 Peter 5:9 reminded the Christians to stand firm because they were not the only Christians who were suffering. There is a *koinonia* (community) of suffering. These Gentile Christians were caught between cultures. Some of the ethical admonitions in First Peter are rooted in Greco-Roman culture. The congregation had to live in the tension between Christian and Gentile ideals. The persecution one suffers, Peter says, includes others in the Christian community. Stand fast as an example to others, and draw strength from their example as well.

Gospel: John 17:1-11

These verses are part of what is known as Jesus' high priestly prayer, included in John's Gospel where the Synoptic Gospels (Matthew, Mark, and Luke) have Jesus asking God to remove the cup of suffering from him. It speaks of the relationship between the Father and the Son and how it takes form in the life of the church.

Jesus' Prayer for Himself

In verses 1-8, Jesus was praying for himself and his work. The "hour" to which he referred was his time of departure. It involved crucifixion and death, but also glorification. Indeed, it was in the act of crucifixion that Jesus is glorified.

The "hour" is the ultimate purpose of Jesus' work and revelation of God. So he prayed that the Son might be glorified. There is no agony in the garden here, such as we find in the Synoptics. Instead there is a gentle request to God to bring to fruition all that he has done.

> **Think About It:** In what seems a contradiction, Jesus was glorified through torture and death. What can this mean? What does it suggest about faith? Can this help us find meaning in our suffering?

Glorification

In Jesus' death, resurrection, and ascension, God would be glorified. (Read: God's good purpose would be served.) God would be known as the Father of Jesus. (That is, the blessing on all that Jesus had done would be in the gratitude humans would give to God.) The "hour," on one level of meaning, was the fateful time when Jesus was betrayed, judged, tortured, and killed. But on a deeper level, the "hour" was the time when God's glory was revealed through torture, death, and resurrection. What human beings meant for a victory over one who disturbed their world turned into God's victory over sin and death.

Eternal Life

Because of his death and resurrection, and because of his relationship with the Father, Jesus was able to give eternal life to those who believe. But eternal life does not mean the same thing in John's Gospel that it means for many of us. Eternal life does not mean living forever in heaven, but rather knowing God as Father through the Son. *Eternal* is a quality of life that begins now and continues throughout the relationship of love between God, Christ, and faithful community.

The Power of the Name

Jesus also said that he was revealing the Father's name. In Hebrew thought, to know the name of someone or something was not only to know the essential core but also to have power over that person or thing. To change a name meant a significant change in the character of a person.

What name of God did Jesus reveal? Father, or *Abba* in Aramaic. This

> **Think About It:** Exclusively male images of God trouble some persons because they imply that God is male. What meanings do you associate with "Father"? What images of God are most meaningful to you?

name does not mean "Father," spoken in reverential tones. Rather, it is more intimate, tender, and loving; it is more like "Daddy," with the trust and adoration that a two-year-old puts into the word when she or he sees Daddy coming up the walk. Incidentally, the child puts the same meaning into "Mommy."

In verses 9-11, Jesus began to pray for his followers. He prayed that he would be glorified in the community; that is, that his identity would be made known in them, just as God's identity had been made known in him. How does your community of faith make Jesus' identity known to the church and to the world?

Study Suggestions

A. Reflect on Power

Read Acts 1:6-14 and the commentary on pages 194–95. Ask: What does it mean to have power in business? in politics? in the church? What kind of power does Jesus promise to the disciples? (Note that these disciples were a larger group than just the Eleven.) Power to do what? What marching orders come with the power? If we took both the promise and the orders seriously, how might that change the way we do things in the church?

Read the "Back to Business" and "Think about It" paragraphs. Ask: What can we learn about power from the actions of the disciples here? How do we channel inspiration into daily discipleship?

B. Explore Ultimate Power

Read 1 Peter 4:12-14; 5:6-11; and Psalm 68:1-10, 32-35. Review the commentary on pages 195–97. Ask: What do these verses suggest is the source of ultimate power? What does ultimate power mean in this context? What kind of power is it? How is the power expressed in nature? in the political realm? (Refer to the commentary on the psalm.) How is ultimate power expressed in God's relationship with the church? How is God's care for us an expression of God's power?

C. Think More About Caring

Choose a painting of Jesus' crucifixion or a crucifix. Have the group look carefully at the art. Ask: How is this cruel death a sign of God's glory?

Read aloud John 17:1-9. Ask: What does John say about Jesus being glorified? Is it a contradiction to say that torture and death are ways to reveal God's glory? Why or why not? Refer to the "Glorification" paragraph. What form does that glory take? How is this understanding of glory different from the way we usually think of glory (for example, a war hero covered with glory)?

D. Explore Naming

Examine "The Power of the Name" paragraph. Ask: Why was it important that Jesus reveal God's name? Can you think of some examples in the Bible where a name says something significant about a person? where a name change reflects a change of character? (Look up in a Bible dictionary the names *Jacob, Peter, Ruth,* and *Naomi,* for example.) Ask members to share what their names mean to them, and, if they have changed their name, what that felt like.

If God's name, as revealed to us by Jesus, says something important about the nature of God, then what kind of God do we have here? Discuss the name *Abba.* What is important about this name? What does God's name say to us about God's nature? about our relationship with God?

Ask: If a child is raised in a home without a father or has an abusive relationship with the father, what will this name suggest to him or her about God as Father? How do we help all persons claim an intimate kinship with God as a loving Parent, especially if their own parental relationships have been unloving? Is God "Mommy" or "Daddy" to you? Would you like that kind of relationship? What would it take to have it?

E. Go Back to Business

Look again at Acts 1:6-14 and the "Back to Business" paragraph. What did the "men in white robes" say to the disciples about getting on with life? How did the disciples respond? How is that advice appropriate for the church today? If we take our kinship with God and the power God has given to all disciples seriously, how might our lives be transformed?

F. Praise God's Glory

Sing or read together the hymn "Thine Be the Glory" or "Christ, Whose Glory Fills the Skies." Pray for lives that bring glory to God.

Lections for the Day of Pentecost

First Lesson: Acts 2:1-21

MOST Christians who visit Jerusalem will go to Mount Zion and be taken to a large medieval room. There they will hear their guide say something like this: "This is not the actual room, but this is believed to be the place where Jesus ate the Last Supper with his disciples and the Spirit came on the church at Pentecost. This is holy ground for you Christians, and you should take off your shoes." And Christians will feel like removing their shoes, for it does seem like holy ground.

The Spiritual Tongues

It was on that holy ground that the Spirit fell on the Day of Pentecost, some fifty days after the Resurrection. The disciples (a larger body than the Eleven) were gathered in the upper room, and something happened. There were what seemed to be tongues of fire and a sound like a rushing wind. The Holy Spirit had come, and wind and fire were metaphors that only weakly described the reality they experienced. The best they could say was that "it was something like that." Then, under the power of the Spirit, they began to speak in "other tongues" (NIV). The native tongue of Jesus' disciples was Aramaic. At Pentecost, they were able to speak in the languages of various visitors in Jerusalem. The visitors could not understand how the disciples, who were Galileans, could speak in languages they would not have understood themselves.

The Gathered Community

Because it was Pentecost, one of the three major Jewish festivals at which all Jewish males were supposed to be present, there were many visitors in Jerusalem from all over the Mediterranean world (see verses 9-11). On the one hand, the crowd thought the disciples were drunk; on the other hand, the crowd essentially said, "We come from all over the world; and yet each of us can understand in our own language. What's going on here?"

Peter responded to the charge of drunkenness in two ways: (1) a reminder that the wine shops were not even open at this time; and (2) a more serious appeal to the prophet Joel about the Spirit of God being poured out on all humanity, even on those who in many cultures were thought too insignificant for God to deal with.

A Bold Power

What does all this mean? It is clear that the disciples felt a new sense of power—power that changed them from quiet, hesitant believers to bold witnesses to the Resurrection. This power, they said, came from the Spirit resting upon them. It was like the power we feel in a "violent wind" or recognize in a fire. The fire may suggest that power needs to be channeled into uses God intends, or else it can run out of control and become destructive and deadly. In any case, the Holy Spirit was present in the experience identified by the metaphors of fire and wind.

> **Think About It:** "The disciples felt a new sense of power." The Holy Spirit transformed them from disciples (learners) into apostles (ones sent, witnesses). How do we experience the power of God's Spirit in the life of the church? Can we be both learners and witnesses at the same time?

A Promise Fulfilled

It was probably not the first time the disciples had felt the presence, or the power, of God's Spirit. But this time was different. This was the power that Jesus had promised them! This was the power that would give them the calling, the gift, and the strength to witness to God both in their own communities and to the very center of the world, to Rome itself.

Psalter: Psalm 104:24-35

Through the marvels of astronomy and space travel, it is now commonplace, in our own living rooms, to see such wonders as the four moons of Jupiter, the surface of Mars, meteor showers, and human beings inhabiting a space station orbiting Earth over two hundred miles in space. When viewed through the eyes of faith, we see these as reminders that all of creation is a witness to God's wisdom.

In Canaanite mythology the sea was a god of chaotic power. Israel also saw the sea as a symbol of chaos. The psalmist says that God orders that chaos. The stormy waters become life-giving springs and rivers (verses 6-13). Leviathan, the great sea monster, sports in the water, like God's bathtub toy. The psalmist was an "environmentalist," who wanted nothing to interfere in the operation of the world as God intends it. We live in God's world, and what we do affects that world.

Epistle: 1 Corinthians 12:3b-13

What does the Spirit *do* in the church? Paul gives a partial answer by talking about the Spirit's gifts to the church. There are varieties of abilities, ministries, and tasks, all of which are gifts of the Spirit. Whether we repair the church roof, cook in the kitchen, teach Sunday school, lead committees, run a homeless shelter, or demonstrate against injustice, it is the gift of the Holy Spirit—given to us for the common good. Each talent, ministry, and job is valued; in the church there is never ground for boasting about our contributions.

Nine Gifts of the Spirit

Wisdom and knowledge are important gifts in themselves. But here Paul talks about the *utterance of wisdom and knowledge*. This means teaching, whether standing in front of a class, or teaching by example, caring, or confrontation. *Faith* is the gift to trust in God. Some of us develop rational beliefs propounding doctrines or fashioning theological systems. But faith involves trusting God for daily bread, staking our very lives on God's providence and steadfast love. Faith also leads to *healing* and *miracles*.

Prophecy is not about forecasting the future. It is insight into the will of God for the current situation. A prophet looks beneath the surface and sees the meaning of trends. The *discernment of spirits* has to do with reading and testing the motives and intentions of others, so we are not taken in by those who would manipulate or stir us up. It serves to warn the church of the danger of being used.

Ecstatic speech was a common religious expression in Paul's day in churches and in pagan religion. But where it is present there should be *interpretation*. Paul insists that no one is to utter ecstatic speech unless there is someone to interpret. Why? The gifts of the Spirit are for the building up of the church, which cannot happen if no one can understand what is being said. Further, Paul recommended restricting ecstatic speech to private devotion rather than public worship (1 Corinthians 14:13-19).

The Body and the Spirit

The *body* here means the church, the body of Christ. Spiritual gifts are for the sake of the church. Paul presents this metaphor of the body to remind his readers that, however different our gifts might be, we are all part of the same body; and our gifts serve that community in different and interdependent ways.

We all come into this one body through baptism and are baptized into the church on an equal basis. There can be no cultural, gender, or social distinc-

202

tions; there are only those who drink of the one Spirit and become part of the church.

Gospel: John 7:37-39

This lection picks up the thirst-and-water theme of the woman at the well story we explored on the Third Sunday of Lent. It would be well to revisit that in conjunction with today's study. There, Jesus offered the woman "living water" to quench her spiritual thirst. Here he extended the invitation to "anyone who is thirsty," and promised that "out of the believer's heart shall flow rivers of living [running] water" (verse 38).

Quenching Thirst

Jesus said "on the last day of the festival" that he was the one who could quench thirst—the ultimate thirst. The festival was Sukkoth (Tabernacles), which celebrated both God's act in history (the years of wandering in the dry, dusty desert) and God's act in the present (thanksgiving for the recent harvest).

In Jesus' day, this was an eight-day celebration, centered on the Temple. At night, four huge lamps were lit. They gave out so much light that no part of Jerusalem was completely dark. A highlight of each day's worship came when the priests went in a solemn procession to the Pool of Siloam to draw water. The procession included the singing of the "hallel" (songs of praise from Psalms 113 to 118), flute playing, dancing, and the waving of branches. From the Temple to the pool was a great enough distance that all the psalms could be sung, and there could be quite a spectacle.

The water was brought back to the Temple and poured out on the altar as an offering. This act was a prayer for rain and for the promise of a good harvest the following year. It was also a reminder of the water that had flowed out of the rock in the wilderness (see Exodus 17:1-7 and Numbers 20:2-13) when the people had complained of thirst and Moses had interceded with God. On that last day, Jesus looked around at the water rituals and invited anyone who was truly thirsty to come to him for "living water."

Anyone who grew up on a farm in years gone by will be familiar with the contrast between rainwater collected in a cistern from off the roof and fresh water coming from a flowing well, fed by an underground spring. In hot, dry weather a cup of the fresh, cool spring water is indeed a treat! Cistern water meets the need of the body for moisture, but it is not fresh and satisfying to the spirit. Jesus promised living water through the gift of the Spirit who was to come.

As Yet There Was No Spirit

This blunt statement does not mean the Spirit did not exist before Jesus' death. Clearly, there are indications of the working of the Spirit in the

Hebrew Scriptures. Power can exist without our being able to access it. For example, solar power has always existed, but it has only been in the last few decades that humankind has developed the technology to harness that power to serve an increasing variety of functions.

> **Think About It:** Jesus promised "living water" would flow from "the believer's heart," if only one would accept it. What is the thirst for living water? How is this water given to us? How does this water change our lives?

So the Spirit has always been present—but it had not yet been given to the church in all the fullness of Pentecost. Jesus had not yet been glorified; that is, he had not yet been crucified, resurrected, nor had he ascended to God. Only since then has the gift of the Spirit become a reality in the church. In John's theology, the Spirit is given to the church by the crucified and risen Lord.

Study Suggestions

A. Celebrate Pentecost

Put an array of candles on a table or worship center (as many as possible). Light the candles as someone reads aloud Acts 2:1-21. Ask: What properties of fire make it a good symbol for the Holy Spirit? What does fire do? What does wind (also a metaphor for Pentecost) do? (Be sure answers include negatives, such as wind in tornadoes or fires that destroy homes or kill people, as well as positives.) Why is wind a good symbol for the Holy Spirit? If you had been present on that first Pentecost, what do you think you would have experienced in the upper room? What might you have experienced out on the street?

B. Look Deeper at the Holy Spirit

Refer to the commentary on Acts. Ask: What kind of power came to the disciples at Pentecost? From where did it come? How were the disciples changed? What was the first thing they did with their new power? What were the results, both good and bad? Have you ever seen, in person, a dramatic work of the Holy Spirit? (Invite persons to share their experiences.) What was your reaction?

C. Look at Some Gifts of the Holy Spirit

It's fine to talk about all the wonderful things that happened at Pentecost, but what about today? Ask: How do we experience the Spirit at work in the church? (Trust this question. When the silence falls after you raise it, be patient. Wait a full two or three minutes. Then quietly ask the question again. Wait to see what happens. Remember, sometimes we have to wait for the Spirit.)

After some discussion, read 1 Corinthians 12:3b-13. Remind the group that this passage is about what the Spirit does in the church. (See the commentary on pages 202–203.) Paul wrote this passage to the Corinthians in the first century, but it is equally true for us today. Have members name the various gifts and list them on chalkboard or poster paper. Ask: What is important about each of these gifts for the church today? What gift does Paul suggest is most important? (1 Corinthians 13:13)

If you know of workshops on discovering spiritual gifts, this session might be an opportunity to connect persons with this expression of spiritual formation.

D. Connect Creation With the Spirit

Read Psalm 104:24-35 and the commentary on pages 201–202. Ask: What is the connection between the Holy Spirit and this expression of creation? (Note that Jewish wisdom literature suggests that God's Spirit was involved in the work of Creation.)

E. The Spirit—One More Time

Read John 7:37-39. Ask members to recall times when they were really thirsty and what a good, cool drink felt like. Relate this passage to the woman at the well story in John 4.

Read the background material on the Feast of Tabernacles, and relate it to the question of the Spirit in this text. Ask: What does Jesus say about quenching thirst? Look again at the statement, "As yet there was no Spirit." Ask: Does this statement mean that the Spirit did not exist before Jesus' time? If the Spirit did exist, what might the statement mean? How does the Spirit exist in us?

F. Rejoice in the Spirit

Form a circle around the lighted candles. Sing "Breathe on Me, Breath of God" or "Spirit of the Living God, Fall Afresh on Me." As participants watch the candles, offer a prayer of thanks for God's gift of the Spirit, for the gifts of the Spirit present in this circle, and for God's power to use them in witness and service.

SUNDAYS AFTER PENTECOST

Lections for Trinity Sunday

Old Testament: Genesis 1:1–2:4a

*T*HERE was already something "in the beginning." God was working with the formless void, the darkness, and the "deep." The "deep" is *tehom* in Hebrew, the same word for the Babylonian monster of chaos. God creates by bringing order out of chaos. The Spirit of God was brooding over the water. One way to interpret that image is to say that the Spirit rested over the water like a giant bird brooding over her eggs. A psychological understanding would be to say that the Spirit brooded, that is, pondered and considered, what to do with this chaos, darkness, and formless void.

"Then God Said . . ."

And then God said, "Let there be light." This is the biblical way of talking about the Big Bang, pouring light out into the darkness and beginning the process of bringing order out of the chaotic mix of atoms that existed in that first flicker of Creation. There is no reason to say that modern science and the Bible contradict each other on the question of the origin of the world. They say different things because they speak from different times and cultures and because they ask two different questions.

Modern science wants to know *how* the world came into existence; the biblical narrative wants to know *why*. But there need be no conflict between the two as long as scientists do not try to claim that God was not involved, which they cannot prove, and Christians do not try to say that what science observes is wrong. Here we are most interested in the biblical answer: "The world as we know it came into being because God wanted it so."

> **Think About It:** Do science and the Bible clash for you in the Creation story? What more do you want to know about the world and the Creation story? What do you believe about God and Creation?

208

God Created . . .

God created by saying the word, which is also an ordering of chaos. The biblical author makes clear that the world came into being by the will of God. By separating light and darkness, God ordered them and gave even darkness a meaning. God named the night, which means that God identified what *night* is, and asserted control over it. The order of day and night is part of the basic ordering of the cosmos. The same process is true for the work of the second and third days; God orders Creation by a word and names what God has done.

God Created Humanity in God's Own Image. . . .

Next God turned to the creation of humanity. "Let us make humankind in our image, according to our likeness." The "image" and "likeness" of God probably mean the same, since Hebrew literature is so fond of parallels and doublets.

The key issue is that humanity is created in the image of God. There are aspects of the human being that are godlike! And since humanity is created male and female, we have to take seriously the feminine nature of God. We believe that God transcends gender, but the limitations of language mean we have to be intentional about saying so.

"That's the Best Thing I Ever Did":

So God proclaimed after humankind was created. Consider that statement a blessing on humanity, on human sexuality, on human freedom and ingenuity, on the human capacity for love and relationship, and on all the other things that make us human. Consider that statement a blessing on the image of God found in all of us.

Psalter: Psalm 8

What are our thoughts as we stand looking at the heavens on a clear night? There is Jupiter shining brightly, dominating the eastern sky. The stars are spread from horizon to horizon. How many years it takes one of our little spacecraft to get to Jupiter! And that is only the first step on a journey to the stars! This surely is something of what the psalmist felt when he looked at the stars. *Why should you even pay attention to humanity, God? What is there about us? Yet you made us only a little less than yourself.* Glory and honor are attributes of God, so this is not a light statement the psalmist makes.

God has given humanity dominion over all creation. We become partners with God in caring for the created order. Think again about the Creation story and about bringing order out of chaos. Part of our responsibility is to continue to order creation, to keep it in balance. What happens in one place affects all others. How do we help sustain order and harmony in our world? Are the gifts God has given us sufficient for the task?

Epistle: 2 Corinthians 13:11-13

Paul had trouble with the Corinthian church. Most of Second Corinthians addresses the problems. It's about finding unity, making peace with Paul, and preparing the offering for Jerusalem.

Paul began his farewell words by repeating what he had said over and over. Put things in order. Pay attention to what I've been saying. Work out your differences and learn to live in peace. The "saints" were all the people in the church where Paul was, perhaps Ephesus. "Saint," in Paul's letters, is not someone who is holier than others, but one who is part of the community of believers, a follower of Jesus, someone who is "on the way."

Meet the Trinity

At least meet the important part of the Trinity for today, since this is Trinity Sunday. Paul's benediction names all three persons in the Trinity. The early church experienced God in different ways. They experienced God as Holy Spirit, who awoke in them a hunger for God and guided them to hear about Jesus and become a part of his church. They experienced God as Savior and Lord in Jesus the Christ. And they experienced God as the Creator of heaven and earth and Father of Jesus Christ. Out of their experience they came to use language such as Paul used in this benediction.

God Language

A word about language is appropriate here. First, we are two thousand years removed from Paul, and many things have happened since. One is the development of Christian theology, especially in the great councils of Nicaea (325) and Chalcedon (431), where the doctrine of the Trinity was developed. Those councils said that God was both three and one, three persons in one Godhead. Whenever we speak of one person in the Trinity, we speak of all three.

Second, we often refer to the Trinity as God, Jesus, and the Holy Ghost, or Creator, Christ, and Holy Spirit. This makes Jesus Christ and the Holy Spirit seem subordinate when they are not. What the traditional language captures in "Father, Son, and Holy Spirit" is the relational aspects: God is described by Jesus as *Father*; God is incarnate in the *Son*; God as *Holy Spirit* is present with us.

> **Think About It:** What language do you use for God? Does it disturb you to hear others use different God language? What does the idea of the Trinity mean to you?

However careful we are about our language making God open to feminine understandings, we have not said all there is to say about God until we recognize the intimate interrelatedness in God as divine Father (Parent), Son, and Holy Spirit.

Gospel: Matthew 28:16-20

Jesus directed the disciples to go to the mountain. We don't know what mountain because, for Matthew, a mountain is a matter of theology, not of geography. The mountain is the place where God reveals God's self. The location of the mountain is not important. What is important is the revelation of God.

My Lord Spoke

When we say God reveals God's self, we have already said something about Jesus as God, because it is clearly the risen Christ the disciples met on the mountain. This was an extraordinary experience, and Scripture says some doubted what they saw. Then Jesus spoke: "All authority in heaven and on earth has been given to me." This was the glory of the Son. No wonder they fell down and worshiped! Jesus of Nazareth, their teacher and friend, was the ruler of the cosmos. Imagine (again) all those stars, and picture the Jesus you learned about as a small child ruling over all of them and billions more we cannot see.

Make Disciples

These disciples were instructed to go to all nations and disciple them. They were not only to call individuals to faith, but to do so as part of the community. They were to be disciples and to *live* their faith within the Christian community. We cannot be disciples alone. We have to gather together as the body of Christ to do that. It is in this unity and kinship that we find support, nurture, accountability, and vision to help us move along the path of discipleship.

Matthew says that, even seeing the risen Jesus, "some doubted." Matthew understands discipleship to allow for being "of little faith" where there are always some elements of doubt, even in the act of worship. This doubt is not about skepticism. Rather, it is about risk. What path do we follow? How risky is it? Am I willing to take that risk? Can I count on God to be with me in the risk-taking? The mission to disciple the world is given to a worshiping, yet doubting, community of disciples.

> **Think About It:** Some of the disciples doubted. Is doubt really about risk-taking? What if I doubt God even exists? Is that a matter of ideas, or of a willingness to "act as if" God were real? Can doubt be seen as "searching faith"? What is at stake in matters of doubt and faith?

211

Baptize Them in the Name . . .

. . . of the Father, Son, and Holy Spirit. Again we have the Trinity, this time in the most basic rite of the church. Baptism is the sacrament of initiation, the point at which we move from the outside to the inside of the community of faith. This is true regardless of the age of the person being baptized. To be baptized in the name of Father, Son, and Holy Spirit means that we come into the community under the power and sponsorship of all three persons of the Trinity, of the complete Godhead. For the church, our name for God is "Father, Son, and Holy Spirit."

In the instructions for baptism contained in an early church document called the *Didache*, we find that the temperature of the water, the mode of baptism, all the physical elements are secondary. What is *not* optional is the use of the formula: "I baptize you in the name of the Father, and of the Son, and of the Holy Spirit."

Teach Them

The disciples were given authority also to teach all nations "to obey everything that I have commanded you." The teachers did not have to decide the content; Jesus had already done that. The disciples' task was to call believers to obedience to the Christ who saves and who promises to be with them to the end of the age.

Study Suggestions

A. Look at the Trinity

Display paraments, banners, or other worship elements that include symbols of the Trinity. If these are in the sanctuary, start your session there. Ask: How do these symbols express the reality of God for you? When you hear the word *Trinity*, what comes to mind?

B. Reflect on Experiencing God

Read Genesis 1:1–2:4a and Psalm 8. Display pictures of space taken using the Hubble telescope, from *The National Geographic, Scientific American, Discover,* or similar magazines. Ask: What does the writer of Genesis say about the relationship between God and the cosmos? (Tip: This is not an easy question. Allow time for silence and reflection, even if it takes a while. Trust your question and the group; when answers start coming, they may come thick and fast.) What does the psalmist see in the world around him that gives him clues about God and God's relationship with humanity? Read the commentary on these two passages on pages 208–10. Ask: How can we relate the discoveries of science and the revelations from faith to each other?

Discuss the image of God. Ask: What does it mean to say humanity is created in the image of God? When is a human being most godlike? Do you think God has a feminine nature? a masculine nature? What images of God are most meaningful to you?

C. The Church Experience of God

Read in unison 2 Corinthians 13:11-13; review the commentary about it. Refer to the Apostles', Nicene, and Athanasian creeds as found in your hymnal or worship book. The structure of these creeds says something about how we experience God, with a paragraph about the Father, another about the Son, and a third about the Holy Spirit. Ask: What does each paragraph say about who God is and what God does? about the relationship among the persons in the Godhead? about how you understand God personally? Engage group members in writing their own creed, with a sentence about each person in the Trinity.

Stress the importance of language when talking about the Trinity. The language of the creeds is centuries old and was developed to address issues at a very different time in history. Ask: Does the language of the creeds still speak to us? Why or why not?

D. Discover God in a Familiar Passage

Read aloud Matthew 28:16-20. Ask: What does this passage say about the Son as God? about the authority of the Son? about your own marching orders as a believer? Include background from the commentary in the discussion.

Stress the importance of doubt in the life of faith. Review the section, "Make Disciples." Ask: Why does Matthew think of disciples as being "of little faith"? What is the difference between doubt as skepticism and doubt as risk? Does this distinction help us understand the importance of questioning in the life of faith? How? In your experience, has doubt been a kind of "searching faith"?

E. Your Baptism Commitment

Baptism marks us as disciples; confirmation reaffirms the commitment made at our baptism. How are those claims evident in our lives? Is this Great Commission part of our baptismal commitment?

F. Affirm the Faith

As a closing act of worship, sing "Lord, You Give the Great Commission"; then say together one of the church's ecumenical creeds (the Apostles', Nicene, or Athanasian creed).

Lections for Sunday Between May 29 and June 4

Old Testament: Genesis 6:11-22; 7:24; 8:14-19

*T*HE Flood story is similar to the ancient Babylonian myth, which tells the story of a man named Utnapishtim, who, like Noah, receiving a warning from the god Ea that a deluge was coming, built an ark and was saved. The Hebrew version of the story differs from the Babylonian one in the strong religious and moral lesson it teachers and in its monotheistic foundation— one God rather than many. There is an archeological basis for both these and other Near Eastern flood stories. In 1929, evidence was found of a flood occurring around 4000 B.C. in the Persian Gulf area that inundated much of Mesopotamia.

The minor inconsistencies in the Genesis story—differences in the numbers of clean and unclean animals (compare 6:19-20 and 7:14-15 with 7:2-3) and in how long the flood lasted (compare 7:11 and 8:14 with 7:12 and 8:10, 12)—are due to the way the Genesis editor combined the J (Jahwist—ninth century B.C.) and P (Priestly—fifth century B.C.) documents. The story is a dramatic tale of how God's anger against humanity for their sin and corruption brought about the obliteration of the entire race, except for one righteous family.

The story is not complete with today's lection, however, for the sequel (Genesis 8:21–9:17) relates how God had mercy on humankind by entering into a covenant with Noah. The preceding stories of the disobedience of Adam and Eve (Genesis 3), the murder of Abel by his brother Cain (4:1-16), the bloody vengeance of Lamech (4:23-24), and the wickedness of the Nephilim (6:1-4), show the increasing decadence of the human race at that time. They had taken advantage of God's patience and refused to repent, so they needed to learn a lesson. Hence, the Flood. Human sin and disobedience are not just one-time occurrences. They are ongoing, so God's judgment must continue. The Flood is not a one-time expression of God's judgment, but rather symbolizes God's eternal concern with righteousness and determination to judge all humankind in terms of how well it measures up to the divine standards of morality.

God's Covenant With Noah

Accompanying continuing judgment was God's unlimited grace, represented by God's rainbow covenant with Noah—and with the whole earth (Genesis 9:13) and every living creature (9:16). The rainbow (9:13), symbol of God's grace, replaced the war bow, sign of God's vengeance. The deluge of punishment was over—at least for the time being; God promised a brighter future. And just as the animals were saved by being taken into the ark, they were to be included in God's eternal covenant as well (9:15). God's redemption is not only for humans but for all of creation. The basic, persistent message of the Bible is the story of God's effort to rescue his creatures from the effects of sin and disobedience and bring them back into a redeemed relationship with God.

The thrust of the Noah story, then, is that, through the righteousness of one man, the entire race can be saved. From a Christian perspective, the redemptive life of Noah points to Jesus, the righteous Son of God. In him, "God's grace and the gift that came by the grace of the one man, Jesus Christ, overflow[ed] to the many!" (Romans 5:15, NIV). Noah's is one of a series of divine covenants recorded in the Bible—each conveying God's caring love and requiring human response and responsibility. The final covenant came with redemption through Christ Jesus, which we discuss in this week's Epistle lection.

Psalter: Psalm 46

The theme of water prominent in the Noah story continues in this much-loved psalm. It is divided into three parts, two of which conclude with an uplifting refrain celebrating YHWH's protective presence (verses 7, 11). The God of Zion will shelter his people during the cataclysms of nature (verses 2-3) and human history (verses 6, 9).

> **Think About It:** "God is our refuge and strength, a very present help in trouble. . . . Be still and know that I am God!" (verses 1, 10). Where have we heard these verses before? What effect did they have? How does God speak to us through these words?

In the first section (verses 1-3), the stormy waters burst forth, jarring the mountains and disturbing the earth. Through all this God is near. The second stanza (verses 4-7) depicts the city of God, the home of the Almighty, as the source of serenity and strength. Here the water (of life) is not turbulent but flows gently from the Temple in a pleasant stream. The inhabitants can live in peace and contentment, even though the surrounding nations are in turmoil and revolt against the reign of God. In the final section, all are asked to survey the wondrous works of YHWH. God has destroyed God's enemies and put an end to war. God's peaceful rule has begun. All must bow in awe and recognition of God's sovereignty over the earth.

Epistle: Romans 1:16-17; 3:22b-28 (29-31)

Here Paul expounds his central teaching—the salvation that comes through faith. His argument runs like this: I stand by my message, for it tells both Jews (the in-group) and Gentiles (the out-group) they can be saved by faith (1:16). Those who believe in God's goodness will receive the gift of faith, which will help them live righteously (1:17).

Both Jews and Gentiles are sinful; none can live up to God's perfect standard (3:22b-23). But what they cannot achieve by themselves, God gives them—justification (made right in the eyes of God) and redemption (brought back from a sinful life) through Christ (3:24). His death shows the extent of God's great love, God's readiness to forgive, and the sacrifice God makes to bring humanity back into relationship with God (at-one-ment; 3:25). This demonstrates that God is good and wants to make us good, too, if we will but commit ourselves to Jesus (3:26).

Only Through Faith

We can take no credit for this. In our own strength we cannot obey the law or perform good works. We can only be made right with God through faith (3:27-28). God loves both Jews and Gentiles and wants both to trust in his love and be restored to a right relationship with him (3:29-30). This teaching does not reject the law but affirms and builds on it by showing that the loving God who gave the law also forgives us when we break it (3:31).

The Jews demanded observance of the law as the way to please God and earn God's acceptance. The Gentiles worshiped pagan deities, which often made no moral requirements. For the Jews salvation came through human effort, for the Gentiles through mystery rites, secret knowledge, or special offerings. None of these will work. Only

Think About It: How do we seek to please God? How do we feel when we strive to be good—and fail? What is the cure for feelings of guilt? Why is it hard to trust God?

through faith in God's loving act of sending his Son to reveal God's reconciling love can persons be restored to the heart and favor of God.

Gospel: Matthew 7:21-29

The Sermon on the Mount concludes with the ringing affirmation that it is not religious affectation but sincerity of life that counts. More important than saying the right words is doing the right things (verse 21). On the Day of Judgment, says Jesus, some will point to their eloquent preaching, some to works of healing and exorcism, and some to mighty achievements in the world (verse 22). But Jesus will reject them all as base persons (verse 23). Why?

He explains with a parable of two houses in a storm—one with solid footings, the other with a flimsy foundation. The former represents persons who have internalized Jesus' word and based their lives on it, the other those who have listened to his teachings but chosen not to live by them. The result is rewarding for the one but disastrous for the other (verses 24-27). This story is reminiscent of Noah's Flood, where the winds and waters destroyed the wicked, but those who had been doing God's will were saved.

> **Think About It:** Jesus reveals to us God's will for our lives—to love our neighbor, to stand for justice, to serve the poor, to give generously of ourselves and our resources, to forgive, to have mercy, to oppose oppression, to honor truth, to be sacrificial. We have heard all this from our youth up. The question is: Will we do it?

Matthew concludes this collection of Jesus' sayings with the observation that the people were deeply impressed with him because, unlike the ordinary religious leaders, he spoke from an inner authority (verses 28-29). There is a difference between the authority of position and the authority of conviction and authenticity. A Samoan proverb says: "The pathway to authority [the same Samoan word also means "power" and "leadership"] is through service." The scribes and Pharisees had the knowledge, the training, and the official designation as leaders, and they claimed their authority and demanded the attention and respect that went with their office. Jesus had none of this; he came to his own as one who served. In their interpretations of the Mosaic laws, the scribes appealed to many authorities. But Jesus HAD authority.

The people knew the difference. They tolerated the scribes because the scribes lorded it over them; but they loved Jesus because he went out of his way to help, serve, and love them. The scribes spoke with the voice of those who knew a lot about God; Jesus was the voice of one who knew God. This was the source of real authority.

Take Thou Authority

"Take thou authority," says the bishop in the ordination service. But can any words, even words spoken in such a sacred ceremony, really convey authority? Some traditions teach that only persons who have been ordained in the apostolic succession are able to interpret the Bible. The purpose of ordination is to identify individuals who demonstrate in their lives they understand the Scriptures, but is the interpretation of the Bible limited to the ordained? Is there a sense in which God says to each of us, "Take thou authority"?

What is our attitude to authority? Do we submit to those who have authority over us and dominate those under us? Do we do as the bumper sticker suggests and "question authority"? Do we claim our own authority as children of God who have the same access to God and truth as anyone else, regardless of position? Do we tend to respect more the authority of official position or the authority of authenticity and inner conviction? Is there a place for both? Which should take precedence when they are in conflict? When might this occur?

Study Suggestions

A. Find the Intentionality

Divide into four groups, each to study a lection (include Genesis 8:21–9:17 with the Genesis passage.), and discuss: What is the intentionality of this text (or, what, in essence, is God saying to us through it)? State its central message in one concise sentence. How would our lives change if we were to take this message seriously?

For starters, the intentionality of the Genesis passage might be: God judges, has mercy, and makes covenant with humanity. If we believe this we will try to do God's will, accept forgiveness when we fall short, and care for all God's earth and all God's people within the covenant. The message of Romans might be that we cannot please God through our efforts, so must trust Christ to accept us and help us to be good. To take this seriously would mean to stop striving, accept forgiveness, and live righteously in grateful response to God's grace rather than trying to earn it. Psalm 46 may be saying: In times of trouble, we can find peace and security in God's care. To believe this would be to pray to God and trust the outcome. In Matthew, Jesus may be telling us, "Take my words seriously or you will be sorry." To do so would mean to read the Gospels, commit ourselves to Jesus, and live simply and lovingly. Matthew's conclusion might be: Study Jesus' authority and seek to imitate it. Claim our authority but make sure it is based in a grace-filled relationship with God and our authentic convictions, not external status and recognition.

B. Report Findings

Have the groups write their intentionality statements on the chalkboard or a sheet of paper. Look for similarities and differences. Note that the Noah

218

story, the Psalm, and the Romans passage emphasize trusting God's grace, while Jesus stresses doing the word. Is this difference of emphasis on faith versus works a contradiction or a paradox? That is, are these ideas diametrically opposed, or are they two aspects of a deeper truth? Could the paradox be that we *are* expected to live up to God's standards, but in response to God's grace not in an effort to earn it?

Comment on the water element in all but the Romans passage, and ask group members to identify the different meanings of water represented—judgment in Genesis, God's power in Psalm 46:3, God's nurture in 46:4, and a test of faithfulness in Matthew.

C. Explore Implications

Ask: How can we know God's will? (Possible answers: Study Jesus' teachings. Pray for guidance. Seek the counsel of wise and faithful friends. Follow good examples. Consider the consequences.) How can we do God's will? (Possibly: Try hard. Follow the rules. Pray for strength. Seek others' support. Be willing to risk.) What happens when we fail? (Give up. Keep trying. Accept the consequences. Pray for forgiveness. Rely on God's grace.) Should we fear the Judgment? (Yes; we are sinners. No; we are saved by grace. Probably; it will motivate us both to faith and to good works.)

D. Share Experiences

Invite members to tell about times they have tried to know and do God's will, how they felt when they succeeded or failed, how others' reacted, and whether they were able to rely on God's grace to see them through.

E. Make Commitments

Call for reports on how lives would change if we took these passages seriously. Encourage participants to covenant together and with God to practice their faith in some of these ways and to report back weekly. Close by joining hands, offering sentence prayers for support and accountability, and singing "Spirit of the Living God, Fall Afresh on Me."

Lections for Sunday Between June 5 and 11

Old Testament: Genesis 12:1-9

*"I*N the beginning. . . ." These first words of the Book of Genesis are well known to Jews and Christians (as well as to many outside these historic faith communities). The first eleven chapters of the first book of the Hebrew Bible provide a majestic prehistory to God's unfolding plan of salvation for the human race. But the real story of the Hebrew people begins with today's lection: God's call to Abram (Abraham) and Abram's response. God's invitation to a covenant relationship provides the context and foundation for all that is to follow. Through God's word, Abram became the father of the faithful (a theme Paul addresses in today's Epistle lesson) for Jews and Muslims as well as for Christians.

Now the Lord Said, "Go. . . ."

God's choice of Abram and Sarai as the forebears of the faithful is never explained. It appears that Abram was a person of means, an established landowner enjoying his golden years in relative prosperity despite the lack of an heir. God spoke first of what Abram had to leave behind: the land of his birth (and thus his identity), family, livelihood, and ancestral homestead. The promise followed. Abram would be given territory; he would become a "great nation" with a "great name" that would bless "all the families of the earth." He was asked to exchange comfort, security, and familiarity for a challenging but glorious unknown. And without so much as a word, he went, taking his family and belongings with him. From a life as landed gentry he became a nomad.

So Abram Went

At age seventy-five Abram began his odyssey, leaving Haran (in northwest Mesopotamia) and setting out for Canaan. He arrived at Shechem, a thriving city in the land of the Canaanite people, and the oak of Moreh (the place of an oracle or soothsayer—an indication of local religious belief and practice). Once again God spoke. "This is the place," God declared, promising the land to the descendants of the obedient, childless, septuagenarian. Again, without question (not even "but what about all these Canaanites, Lord?"), Abram responded. Immediately, he built an altar (which he would do again as he moved south through the land, invoking "the name of the Lord"). This time his response was more

> *Think About It:* Abram responded to God's call without question, without hesitation. How do we experience God's call? How do we answer? How can we learn to say yes to God without first weighing the consequences? How can we be sure the voice we hear or the impulse we feel is really God's leading? Is unquestioning obedience always the equivalent of faith? When is consideration of outcomes and alternatives appropriate? What guidelines might we follow in making important decisions?

public—more political—than personal; his actions acknowledged that YHWH was the sovereign of this promised land. Then he moved on again, step by step, toward the Negeb desert—further indication of the nomadic nature of his new life.

Blessed to Be a Blessing

Much of the eleven preceding chapters of Genesis chronicles the cursed state of the nations. The call of Abram established the seed of a new nation, a chosen people whose relationship with this covenant-creator God would influence all the peoples of the world. Their lot in life would depend on their relationship to the God of this new people. In Abram and his descendants lay the possibility for a blessing universal in its scope. And so, the journey began—not just the journey of a faithful individual, but the journey of a people toward faith in God and the redemption of the world.

Psalter: Psalm 33:1-12

The themes of call (here the call to praise) and the response of the "righteous" to the trustworthiness of God's word echo today's Old Testament and Epistle lessons. God's word is "upright," God's "work is done in faithfulness" (verse 4); the righteous, then, can only obey and praise.

The psalm, written in the characteristic pattern of a summons to praise (verses 1-3, 8) and reasons to praise (4-7, 9-12), is both particular and universal in its address. "Blessed is the nation whose God is the Lord" (verse 12, NIV) recalls the promise to Abraham that his descendants would be blessed. The emphasis on "all the earth" and "all the people of the world" (verse 8, NIV) affirms that this blessing will extend to all creation. The psalmist declares the sovereignty of YHWH as God of Israel and all the earth. So, praise steeped in the assurance that God's promises are real is the faithful response to God's reign.

Epistle: Romans 4:13-25

Abraham's immediate, unwavering response to God's call provided Paul with a supreme example of the primacy of faith over law in his letter to the church in Rome. Paul's mission to the Gentiles (and the resulting conflict with the Jewish leadership of the early church) often centered on the tension between faith and a particular way of observing Jewish traditions. Could a convert become a Christian without first becoming a Jew? Was circumcision a requirement for new Gentile believers? Today's Epistle lection pursues this theme, focusing on the question: Who are the true descendants of Abraham?

The preceding verses in Romans 4 set the stage for today's lection. Paul asserts that Abraham was not justified by his observance of Mosaic law (which had not yet been given), but by grace. While *reckoned* is a term of commerce, it does not imply here that grace is in any way earned as the reward of faith. Abraham's faith is understood as a manifestation of grace— a gift from God "reckoned to him as righteousness" (Romans 4:2-3). More to the point of his argument, Abraham obeyed God and received the promise before he was circumcised in order that he might become the father of both the circumcised and uncircumcised (4:11-12), the "father of all of us" (4:16).

The Promise

God's promise to Abraham and his descendants is the connecting theme throughout today's passages. More than that, the promise connects the entire history of God's saving activity from Creation to the resurrection of the dead in the end times. Paul opposes the belief that the promise is in any way dependent on adherence to the law (4:13-17a) or to works, while Jewish tradition taught that the law itself was the bearer of the promise (2 Maccabees 2:17-18a).

Think About It: Paul referred to Abraham as "the father of all of us." Do we see ourselves as children of Abraham? How do Abraham's faith and our connectedness to all his children inform our belief as Christians? What is the relative importance for us of our connection with all peoples through Abraham and Sarah (and Adam and Eve) and our distinctiveness as followers of Christ?

The promise is "guaranteed" to "those who share the faith of Abraham," faith in the God "who gives life to the dead and calls into existence the things that do not exist." These, says Paul, are the true descendants of Abraham, who lived centuries before the giving of the law to Moses.

Does this imply that Abraham shared a belief (a pre-knowledge) in Jesus? This is not Paul's point. What unites the children of faith is belief in God's power and trust in God's love. It is faith that believes that God is able to do all that God has promised, that responds to God with an unwavering yes.

Gospel: Matthew 9:9-13, 18-26

Today's Gospel lection begins with another story of call and response. Father Abraham is not the subject of this account, but his children are. Matthew's Gospel is written specifically to the Jews in order to proclaim the resurrected Jesus as the fulfillment of messianic hope. The call to and response of Matthew the tax collector bear striking similarities to that ancient encounter between the divine and the human. Matthew's (Levi's) call and Jesus' controversial choice of dinner companions are also recorded in Mark (2:13-17) and Luke (5:27-32).

Follow Me

The story begins with the words of Jesus, "Follow me" (Matthew 9:9). Without hesitation, Matthew followed. Like Abraham, Matthew was a man of means. His response meant the leaving behind of prosperity and "business as usual." There was a twist, however; if Abraham stands as a paradigm of faithfulness, the tax collector stands as a synonym for the worst of sinners.

As a tax collector, Matthew probably colluded with Roman authority and the oppressive regime of Herod. Tax collectors were notorious extortionists and cheats; worse still, in Jewish understanding, they handled coins inscribed with pagan images. But it was precisely this worst-of-sinners who responded with immediacy, not weighing the consequences of his decision. Those who saw themselves as the truer children of Abraham, the religious insiders, were offended to the bone.

The response of the religious insiders to Jesus' table fellowship with "many tax collectors and sinners" (9:10) exemplifies Paul's message in Romans. The Pharisees' question to the disciples, "Why does your teacher eat with tax collectors and sinners?" implies that this was a common practice for Jesus. Jesus' acceptance of the religious outsiders threatened the status quo and self-understanding of those believing them-

> **Think About It:** Jesus called a blatant sinner to leave everything behind and "follow," the invitation dependent, not upon the worthiness of the guest, but on the grace of the host. And yet, in today's world, many hesitate to respond to God's call (or the fellowship of the church community) until they "get their act together." Do feelings of shame or unworthiness prevent us from embracing God's grace? What makes one "worthy" to become part of the church? Are sinners and insiders accepted on an equal basis in our church?

selves to be safely and securely on the inside. The Abraham model of faith-fulness, however, involved risk and boldness.

For Paul, as well as for the One who could raise up from stones new children for Abraham, authentic faith could not be reduced to strict adherence to the law. Authentic faith, the very manifestation of grace in the life of the believer, empowered an immediate, unwavering, affirmative response to God's call. Jesus confronted them with the word of God they had claimed as their exclusive province, "I desire steadfast love [mercy], not sacrifice" (see Hosea 6:6). Jesus would quote this passage again (Matthew 12:7); "Go and learn what this means," he told them.

The Faithful Approach

Today's lection continues with the healing stories of two daughters of Abraham (9:18, 22), one an insider (the child of the synagogue leader) and one an outsider (the woman who had been suffering from hemorrhages for twelve years), separated by law from the community because of her medical condition.

The healing of the child exemplified the power of God in Jesus to give "life to the dead" (Romans 4:17). The woman who hopefully and desperately touched Jesus' clothes, became a model of faithfulness. Under the law, all that she touched—including the healer—would be made "unclean" (Leviticus 15:19). She was "made well" (from the Greek *sozo*, elsewhere translated "save." More than her health, her inclusion in the community was restored.

Study Suggestions

A. Sing Together

Sing a hymn of faith and journey, such as "The God of Abraham Praise" or "Guide Me, O Thou Great Jehovah." Pray together for the courage to respond to God in obedience and faith.

B. Begin the Journey

Read the story of Abram's call (Genesis 12:1-9) together, then review the commentary on pages 220–21. Trace his journey using a Bible map or atlas. On a chalkboard or piece of paper, outline the call and the promise, then develop a list of the questions (or excuses) Abram might have offered God in response. Read verse 6 aloud. Ask: What future challenges are implicit in God promising Abram's descendants a land already inhabited by another people? Is this consistent with God's justice and compassion as we now understand it through Jesus? How does this influence events in that part of the world today?

Ask for a one-word reaction to Abram's silent, unhesitating response to God. Why did God choose Abram? Why did Abram obey? How has the world been blessed through his response? Are we as Christian children of Abraham's promise also blessed to be a blessing? How are we blessed? In what ways are we called to be a blessing? How are we responding to that call?

Discuss the questions in the "Think About It" paragraph related to discerning God's voice, unquestioning obedience, considering consequences, and guidelines for decision-making. Invite members to share their experiences with seeking God's leading in making decisions.

C. Examine Abraham's Faith

Read Romans 4:13-25 together, and study the commentary about it. Why did Paul use Abraham as a model for Christian faith? What characterizes a true "child of Abraham"? How can Abraham's faith help today's Christians to "hope against hope" (verse 18) in a world of overwhelming obstacles? Invite members to share personal stories of the triumph of faith against the odds. Begin with an experience of your own. Ask: Do you feel like one of Abraham's spiritual children? Why or why not? How is your faith similar to and/or different from that of Abraham? Do you feel connected to his other children (Jews and Muslims)? What commonalities do we share with them? How might this passage (as well as the Genesis passage) be used to foster interfaith understanding?

D. Explore the Gospel

Begin by reading Matthew 9:9-13 aloud. Then review the commentary on pages 223–24. What similarities exist between the call (and the response) of Matthew and that of Abram? What differences? How does this encounter, as well as the Pharisees' reaction to Jesus' table fellowship with sinners, inform our understanding of Paul's discussion of the true descendants of Abraham? Why does Jesus answer by quoting Hosea?

Read and discuss Matthew 9:18-26 and the commentary on page 224. Does the church today respond to outsiders with the compassion of Jesus or the judgment of the Pharisees? What particular groups or individuals come to in mind when we think about this question? Whom do we consider to be the "worst of sinners"? How do we treat them?

E. Close With Praise

Read Psalm 33:1-12 responsively, with half the group reading the first part of each verse, the other half the second part. Then, following the pattern of this psalm, have the group spontaneously create their own act of praise, alternating summons to praise (God's call, verses 1-3, 8) and reasons to praise (our response, verses 4-7, 9-12). (See commentary on pages 221–22.)

Ask participants to share briefly in turn how their lives would change if they were to follow God's summons immediately and without question. Close by praying for faith like Abraham's, faith to respond to God with immediacy and conviction.

Lections for Sunday Between
June 12 and 18

T Old Testament: Genesis 18:1-15

ODAY'S Old Testament lesson resumes the story of Abraham (Abram) at the time a fulfillment of another part of God's promise is being realized—the promise of a son and the beginning of the "great nation" by his progeny through whom the entire world would be blessed. Abraham's hospitality, extended to the unknown strangers, would seem to explain at least in part God's investment in him.

The preceding chapters, however, which are not included in the lection, give another picture of the revered patriarch and matriarch. While in Egypt, Abram lied to Pharaoh (who was taken with the beauty of the elderly Sarai!), telling Pharaoh that she was his sister out of fear for his (Abram's) own safety. Sarai's lack of faith in God's word caused her to present Abram with her maid, Hagar, in order that the concubine might provide the promised heir. Ishmael was born (and through his line, the Arabic people), causing Sarai in her jealousy to abuse Hagar. God changed their names; renewed the covenant with Abraham, now ninety-nine; and instituted circumcision as the seal of the covenant.

> **Think About It:** Lies, deceptions, using women as bargaining chips. Abram and Sarai were not perfect by any means. Given their ethical shortcomings, why do you think God chose them as covenant partners? Given our imperfections, why does God accept us as covenant partners? What is the relationship between faith and morality? between grace and goodness?

Hospitality

Today's lection focuses on Sarah's response to the message of the visitors in an account that serves in part as a lengthy explanation for the name of the long-awaited heir, Isaac: "he laughs." More important, however, it stands as a sign of YHWH's faithfulness to the covenant promise in spite of humankind's best efforts to negate it.

The welcome Abraham extended to the unknown travelers was a common response in his culture, and remains a part of Palestinian culture even today. The time of their sojourn, "in the heat of the day" (Genesis 18:1), implies an urgency to their mission, because travelers would normally be resting at that time. In verse 1, YHWH is identified as appearing, though that manifestation is not explicitly detailed. All three may represent the divine presence. It is also possible that the one who spoke (verses 9-15) was YHWH; the other two just in attendance. It is clear, however, that Abraham did not immediately recognize the visitors as divine beings.

As they shared the lavish meal prepared by their host, they asked about Abraham's wife by name, an indication of the nature of their visit. Sarah, who was eavesdropping, laughed at the incredulity of their message: "in due season," the term of pregnancy, she would bear a son (18:10). This was a restatement of the promise to Abraham delivered nearly twenty-five years before in Haran.

So Sarah Laughed

Sarah did not understand who these visitors (specifically referred to as angels in Genesis 19:1) were. YHWH was revealed as the speaker in 18:13, where Abraham was addressed directly by "the LORD," wanting to know why Sarah laughed. Fearfully, Sarah denied her response. "Is anything too wonderful for the LORD?" God's rebuke becomes the heart of the story: God's promise would soon be realized.

> **Think About It:** Sarah was about ninety years old by the time of Isaac's birth. She had good reason to chuckle over the prospect of becoming a new mother. What promises of God seem "too wonderful" or outlandish to be possible in our lives? Do we sometimes miss out on God's blessings by being too skeptical?

Psalter: Psalm 116:1-2, 12-19

Today's psalm provides an excellent follow-up to Paul's "boasting" in God, as well as to the fulfillment of the covenant promise made to Abraham. The psalmist acknowledges what God has done and proclaims complete reliance upon God's power. The entire psalm is a joyous proclamation of God's ability to do all that God has promised. In thanksgiving, the writer resolves to trust God with all future needs and troubles.

To "love the LORD" (116:1) is to submit oneself to God's sovereignty—to recognize a right relationship of creature to Creator. The response is decisive: "I will lift, . . . I will offer, . . . I will pay" (116:13-18).

Epistle: Romans 5:1-8

Today's Epistle lection follows the discussion concerning Abraham's faith being "reckoned to him as righteousness" (Romans 4:22). Chapter 5 begins with the bold assertion that we too are "justified by faith" and thus "have peace with God through our Lord Jesus Christ, through whom we have obtained access to this grace in which we stand" (5:1-2). This peace is cause for boasting, or rejoicing, even in times of suffering (a theme Paul develops further in Chapter 8) because it produces hope. This peace is the reality for those living fully under the lordship of Christ, where the power of love has overcome the power of wrath.

Boasting in God

"And we boast in our hope of sharing the glory of God" (5:2). Boasting has been addressed by Paul earlier in this letter. In Chapter 2, in fact, he warns against boasting. We are not to boast in our relationship with God or knowledge of the law—to do so is to boast of our own accomplishments, which is to pay homage to the world and its powers. This seeming contradiction has resulted in the RSV and NIV using "rejoice"

> **Think About It:** "At the right time Christ died for the ungodly." God's story of salvation is filled with ungodly characters, today's lections included. Abraham, Sarah, Matthew, Judas—each exhibited the human "weakness" for which Christ died. How do these ancestors in faith influence your own experiences of weakness? Do you see yourself in God's salvation story? If God accepted them, can there be hope for us?

(and other versions, "exult") for the NRSV's "boast" here.

Paul is not, however, condemning boasting in and of itself. It is the object of boasting that is at issue. Human existence is defined by God's restoration of true humanity in Jesus Christ who "while we were still weak . . . died for the ungodly" (5:6). Paul highlights our fallen nature and Christ's justification throughout the passage (and beyond). Such boasting is a statement of who (and whose) we are—creatures in a proper relationship to our Creator. Such boasting is a proclamation of our reliance on God to make our reconciliation possible. Through grace, we are given faith; through faith, we are justified and given access to God. This is our peace, our self-understanding, our "boast."

The Nature of Hope

Hope is the result of character; character comes from endurance, which is the result of the suffering in which we boast. Hope is characteristic of the Christian life. In essence, it is "realized eschatology," a vision that encompasses the present as well as the future. We do not hope in an unknown, unresolved end to God's unfolding salvation story. We already know the outcome of history, even while we await its consummation. God's love, poured into our hearts through the Spirit, claims us now and connects us with the past; and, more important, with the future reign of Christ. Such hope "does not disappoint us" (5:5).

Gospel: Matthew 9:35-10:8 (9-23)

The commissioning of the disciples for ministry is a common theme in Matthew's Gospel and the focus of today's lection. In Chapter 10, the Twelve who became Jesus' closest earthly companions are named (along with some of their less honorable traits). The message seems to be directed beyond the apostles (as they are addressed in this passage) to the greater body of disciples who will follow. This account serves to foreshadow the Great Commission recorded in Chapter 28, when the resurrected Lord instructs those who follow him to "make disciples of all nations" (28:19-20).

Harassed and Helpless . . . Sheep Without a Shepherd

This account of discipleship begins and ends with the activity of Jesus in relationship to the people of his world. His teaching, proclaiming, and healing (9:35), rooted in his deep compassion (9:36), were the marks of his ministry. The disciple's work must be centered in nothing else. The mission of the disciple cannot be separated or understood apart from the mission of the One the disciple seeks to follow. Jesus' ministry was a living out of the "good news" (translated also as "freedom"), a fulfillment of the prophecy of the Messiah whose work would be understood in terms of healing and restoration. Chapter 9 ends with the recognition that God, the "Lord of the harvest" (9:38), calls for more laborers.

Chapter 10 begins with Jesus sharing with the Twelve the authority to exorcise spirits and to heal infirmities of every kind. With this authority, Jesus granted them power to perform the same mighty acts God had worked through him. This is the only place in Matthew's Gospel where the term *apostles* is used in reference to the Twelve, although the concept of "sent on a mission" implied in this title is a familiar theme. A listing of disciples also appears in Luke 6:13-16 and Mark 3:16-19. The number *twelve* is believed to have been chosen to correspond to the twelve tribes of Israel more than as an exact accounting of those in Jesus' inner circle. In addition to the names, certain features of the individual men are identified. Matthew is the "tax collector"; Simon, the "Cananaean" (in some ancient texts, "zealot"); Judas Iscariot, the "one who betrayed him" (10:3-4). These designations highlight the unlikeliness of some of Jesus' followers, as well as the potential for betrayal in those who identify themselves as disciples.

From the commissioning Jesus turned to giving instructions for the journey. The mission was to proclaim to the lost sheep of Israel the "kingdom of heaven [that] has come near" (10:7). The specific instruction to "raise the dead" is mentioned in verse 8. As Jesus shared the good news with the Twelve "without payment," so the disciples were to carry out his mission without expectation of reward. To accept more than basic provisions for their labors was prohibited. This understanding is founded in the concept of hospitality exemplified by Abraham in the Old Testament passage and included in covenant law. Precautions against missionary abuse of hospitality are dealt with in the Epistles.

The Worthy

Jesus instructed the disciples, upon entering a town, to look for who is "worthy" (10:11). This does not imply the value judgment in today's connotation of the word. A more faithful translation would be "suitable." The implication is that the disciples should search out those who would be open to their ministry; those willing to receive the apostles and their message were those deemed worthy.

There was a sense of overall urgency in Jesus' preparation of the disciples. Sent as "sheep into the midst of wolves" (10:16), their road would be paved with opposition and rejection. The cost of discipleship—as the mission itself—was no less than that of the Master.

Study Suggestions

A. Open With Singing

After singing a hymn like "If Thou But Suffer God to Guide Thee," say: "Is anything too wonderful for our God?" Ask participants to call out some "impossible" things God has accomplished in human history. Make these into a litany, following each statement by saying together, "For this, we are thankful, O God."

B. Explore Genesis

Form members into three groups, with one skimming Chapters 13–17; the second, 18:1-15; and the third, 21:1-7. Then have each group tell its story, concluding with a group "sculpture" of body poses depicting the central emotion or theme of their passage. Discuss each section using the following questions: What is our response to this "sculpture"? How did God uphold the covenant promise? How did the people doubt or challenge God's promise? How would you characterize the relationship between the covenant partners?

Discuss Sarah's response. Ask: How would you respond to the possibility of a pregnancy at age ninety? Invite members to share personal experiences of God's power as revealed in seemingly impossible ways. Examples might include a call to ministry later in life, healing from an "incurable" condition, or a breakthrough when facing an impasse.

C. Examine Boasting and Hope

Read Romans 5:1-8 and the commentary on pages 228–29. Form two groups. Ask the first group to define *boasting* from present-day understanding, then list the things about which humans tend to boast. Ask the second group to do the same with *hope*. For what are we are likely to hope? Come together to share findings and compare them to Paul's understanding of "boasting" in God and "hope" as the reality for Christians. Ask: Do we tend to boast (exult, rejoice) in God as the source of our reconciliation, or in our own self-righteousness? Do we "hope" as though we believe in the final triumph of God's righteousness, or are we "wishing" that things will turn out right in the end? What is the difference between hope and optimism?

Ask participants to reflect silently on these questions: How has God's love laid claim on your life? What does it mean for you to proclaim that "Christ died for us while we were still sinners"? Invite those who are willing to share their responses. How might this understanding be used to invite persons who do not know Christ into the fellowship of the church? Does our congregation think of itself as a fellowship of forgiven sinners?

D. Boast With the Psalmist

Read Psalm 116:1-2, 12-19 in unison. What themes from the other lections are expressed there? Do you see boasting? If so, is it boasting in the accomplishments of God or of the faithful? What is the psalmist's understanding of the future? How might we define the psalmist's (pre-Christian) hope? As an act of praise and commitment based on verses 14-18, ask members to write responses to God in the form of their own "I wills."

E. Reflect on Discipleship

Ask group members, without looking at their Bibles, to call out the names of Jesus' twelve disciples. What is known about the better-known disciples? the less familiar ones? Why do you think Matthew included descriptions such as "tax collector" and "the one who betrayed him"? How does Romans' emphasis on justification by faith and Christ's dying for the ungodly influence our experiences of faith and discipleship? Using this passage (and the previous lections) formulate a definition for *discipleship*. What is the mission of a disciple? Has that mission changed for today's disciples? Describe your own mission as a disciple.

F. Close With Prayer

Pray together for a renewal of hope Christ's coming reign. Use the "I wills" act of praise and commitment composed in Activity D.

Lections for Sunday Between
June 19 and 25

T   Old Testament: Genesis 21:8-21

ODAY'S Old Testament lection continues the story of Abraham and Sarah following the birth of Isaac. This particular episode of God's salvation story can be difficult for modern readers because it seems to accept—if not condone—the ill treatment of the slave Hagar and her son Ishmael by the boy's own father, Abraham. Throughout the history of biblical criticism, scholars have sought to explain—if not condone—Sarah's resentment of her own son's half-brother. Abraham and Sarah's conduct violated the community standards of their day. The story stands as a reminder of God's mercy shown to the other nation of Abraham's lineage.

The Child Grew

Several clues about the story's time frame are given in the details. Abraham threw a feast to celebrate Isaac's weaning (still a practice in today's Middle Eastern world). This event could have taken place up to a child's third birthday (sometimes later). By this time, his half-brother Ishmael would have been approximately fifteen years old (a fact that will call other aspects of the story into question). Sarah was angered by the sight of the boys playing together (21:9). The word *play* (*shq*) itself has been interpreted in different ways; some scholars have suggested *mocking,* in an effort to explain Sarah's defensive response. There is, however, no evidence of abuse between the brothers. The verb form is another wordplay on Isaac's name, which means "to laugh."

Sarah's reaction, instead, seems based in her jealousy. This was the second time for the issue to be raised. In Chapter 16, Sarah (then Sarai) complained that Hagar, once Hagar had conceived, had looked upon her (Sarah) "with contempt." The role of a concubine was to produce an heir who would, in effect, be claimed by the wife as her own. (Implicit in her decision was Sarah's lack of trust in God's promise.) Abraham reminded Sarah that she was in charge of her servant. Hagar's beatings at the hand of her mistress had earlier caused her to run away. Sarah, as "queen of the harem," had great influence over her husband (who, in turn, had absolute authority over all members of his household). So Abraham, in spite of his distress, agreed to banish his own son along with Ishmael's mother, Hagar.

> **Think About It:** Beatings, concubinage, banishment, absolute authority. By our standards, Abraham was a tyrant and polygamist who sanctioned domestic abuse. How could he be a hero of faith? Does conformity to the customs of an alien culture in an earlier era invalidate the claims of biblical interpreters that call us to emulate him and other biblical characters? How can we discern which aspects of biblical stories to reject as sub-Christian?

The Promise Unbroken

Equally troubling is God's apparent consent to Sarah's cruel plan. God assured Abraham that the child (and thus the promise) would be protected. It was through Isaac and his lineage that "offspring shall be named for you" (21:12), but Ishmael would also become a "nation" in accordance with the promise. While it was Hagar who was weeping aloud, the angel who spoke to her told her that God had "heard the voice of the boy" (21:17). The name *Ishmael* means, "God hears." She was instructed not to be afraid and to comfort her son. The expression "God was with the boy [in Hebrew, *na'ar*]" (21:20) suggests an adolescent too young to bear arms. Again, God's promise had withstood the best human efforts to negate it.

The "Ishmaelites" became traders—nomads in the southern deserts (37:25), and Ishmael is honored by Muslims the world over as the forebear of the Arabs and the child of divine promise.

Psalter: Psalm 86:1-10, 16-17

"Turn to me and be gracious to me; / give your strength to your servant; / save the child of your serving girl" (Psalm 86:16). It is easy to imagine this psalm being spoken in prayer by Hagar as she watched Ishmael suffering from thirst in the wilderness. This verse shows that it is the weakest and most vulnerable whose complete dependence and trust are placed in God's power.

Psalm 86 is an example of a lament (complaint) that is composed alternately of petitions and reasons for God to respond: "Incline your ear . . . for I am poor and needy" (86:1) "Preserve my life, for I am devoted to you" (86:2). The petitions of verses 1-4 and 6-7 show the depth of the psalmist's agony, as well as a total reliance upon God's grace and mercy. The psalmist, confident in God's power, makes a bold statement of faith in how God is steadfast (86:5, 8-10, 13, 15) even in the midst of crisis. God has acted decisively in the past, delivering the faithful. God will so act again.

Epistle: Romans 6:1b-11

Paul's treatment of righteousness as a product of faith (which is a gift of God's grace) in Romans 4 and 5, gives way here to a discussion of new life in Christ. His discussion of dying and being raised with Christ is set in the context of Christian baptism and is the only mention of baptism in the Epistle.

Should We Continue to Sin?

Paul begins his discussion with a rhetorical (and radical) question: "Should we continue in sin in order that grace may abound" (6:1)? The idea of righteousness being "reckoned" through grace was an offense to Paul's critics, who understood righteousness as the reward for works. If piety did not win God's favor, why be righteous? Paul carried this logic to its extreme, asking if continuing to sin would not, then, provide more opportunities for God's grace to operate. His answer? "By no means!"

> **Think About It:** "For whoever has died is freed from sin" (Romans 6:7). Paul affirms that sin has no power over those who are united to Christ. Do we find that sin has no power over us? How do we explain our struggle with sin even after we have become Christian believers? How do we experience freedom in Christ?

For Paul, the believer's union with Christ meant that the power of sin had been broken. This union, expressed through baptism, he explained in images of death and life, slavery and freedom. To be baptized is to share in Christ's death—not physical death, but a death "to self" that results in "newness of life" (6:4). Our self-centered nature is replaced by a heartfelt desire to put God at the center of our lives.

Paul did not equate this new life with participation in the coming resurrection. They are separate realities. (Possibly some Corinthians had interpreted their baptism as a realized resurrection.) Baptism in Christ renews the life of the believer in this world and anticipates a sharing in Christ's resurrection in the life to come.

By No Means!

This "death to sin" and "newness of life" move the believer into a new reality where sin is powerless. The believer cannot live in union with Christ and remain under the power of sin. The enslavement to sin has ended (6:6). If we have died to sin, if we are alive in Christ, we have been "freed" (6:7). This freedom is not, however, license to "do our own thing," to continue in sin that "grace may abound"; it is the freedom to live in obedience to God, a theme Paul develops later in this chapter. Neither is this freedom a temporary condition; baptism has the power to become a "once for all time" event (6:10).

Gospel: Matthew 10:24-39

This passage continues the theme begun last week, a theme best understood as the "cost of discipleship." Jesus' instruction to the Twelve outlines the challenges his followers could expect to encounter. This echoes an overall theme of Matthew, whose Gospel is filled with examples of faithful versus faithless responses to Jesus and to the reign of God. This section in particular contains difficult teachings, which may tempt present-day disciples to assign its message exclusively to the time of Jesus and his contemporaries. Dividing the material into four sections can help make its points, and its unity, more accessible.

The Disciple and the Teacher
The first section (10:24-25) addresses the relationship of the follower to Jesus. If Jesus himself was equated with Satan, what reception could his followers anticipate? As Jesus had shared with the disciples the call and the power to act in his name, so, too, were the consequences of his mission transmitted to those coming after him. Jesus' followers would not escape the rejection he himself experienced.

Do Not Be Afraid
In the second section, verses 26-31, the command to have no fear appears three times. Unlike those whose message was delivered in secret (or to the elect), Jesus' message would be shouted "from the housetops" (10:27). The power of this world could not threaten the ultimate truth of the gospel. Those who could kill the body had no power over the soul. That power belongs exclusively to God, who cares for even the sparrows. Even the hairs of each disciple's head are numbered—no detail of life is unimportant to God.

Everyone Who Acknowledges Me
The third section speaks of the reassurance of God's protection. It reminds us that one's response to Jesus is, in fact, one's response to God. Verses 32 and 33 make the point clearly: Jesus is the mediator of God's will; he will acknowledge those who acknowledge him. He will deny in heaven those who deny him in the world. The disciple must respond in complete faith—there is no middle ground between confessing Christ and denying him.

I Have Not Come to Bring Peace

The last section, verses 34-39, is perhaps the most difficult: the paradox of the Prince of Peace who has come with a sword. More troubling still is the place where division will be most keenly felt—the disciples' own families. Jesus' message is so new, so radical, that it will challenge all pre-existing structures, even those most intimate and familiar. When this new order confronts the old, conflict and chaos result.

Jesus cites Micah 7:6 in verses 35-36, which recall Jerusalem's corruption and downfall. Jesus prophesies the impact of the gospel: "One's foes will be members of one's own household" (10:36). To "set against" (10:35) is literally to "divide in two." The "sword"—Jesus' radical message—will cut these family ties. The warning for those who love "father or mother more than me" is, in essence, a restatement of the first commandment. This saying of Jesus is remembered by early disciples who found that following Jesus led to separation from their fellow Jews.

The passage can be summarized by the call to "take up the cross" as the ultimate expression of discipleship. Often our "cross to bear" is a responsibility we must take care of anyway and not a truly sacrificial cross. But Jesus is saying here that the disciple must not just endure inconvenience, but rather, like him, willingly choose to sacrifice everything, including family and life itself, to be a true follower.

> **Think About It:** "Those who lose [give] their life for my sake will find it" (10:39). What has our discipleship cost us? Is there a cost we would not be willing to pay?

Study Suggestions

A. Sing Together

Sing a hymn of God's covenant faithfulness, such as "Great Is Thy Faithfulness" or "O God, Our Help in Ages Past." Ask participants to reflect silently on times God has delivered them from danger, threat, or misfortune—or enabled them to deal with it faithfully.

B. Study Ishmael's Story

Form four groups; assign one of the following characters to each: Abraham, Sarah, Hagar, Ishmael. Read the story aloud (Genesis 21:8-21), asking participants to listen as their character. First in the small groups, then all together, discuss: What feelings did each experience—about their character? toward one another? about God? Compare responses and insights.

As an alternative, act as host of a television talk show. Ask volunteers to assume the four roles and the remaining group members to be the audience. Let each character tell his or her side of the story while answering questions from the audience.

Using the commentary material on pages 232–33 (and Genesis 16), discuss Sarah's demand and Abraham's response. Ask: What is the main point of the Ishmael story? How might Sarah and Abraham be characterized? How was the fulfillment of God's promise threatened by the human responses? How did God uphold the promise in spite of human interference?

C. Explore New Life in Christ

Read Romans 6:1b-11 and the commentary on pages 234–35. Then discuss: What is the difference between freedom from sin and personal independence? Do we believe that sin has no power over us? How do we as believers experience both the deliverance from and the ongoing struggle with sin? What are the marks of a life made new in Christ?

D. Weigh the Cost of Discipleship

Read Matthew 10:24-39 and the commentary on pages 235–36. Working through the passage section by section, list together the costs and rewards of discipleship. Ask: Which are the easiest to assume? the hardest? What is involved in taking up one's cross and following Jesus? Name some disciples (from the time of Jesus and onward to today—such as Peter, Paul, the early martyrs, Wyclif, Hus, Luther, Susannah and John Wesley, Dorothy Day, Martin Luther King, Jr., as well as less famous disciples—who have taken up the cross. What was the cost for them? How do we understand taking up the cross in light of Paul's understanding of "dying to self" and "new life in Christ"?

E. Examine *Threat* and *Promise*

A common thread running through today's lections is the juxtaposition of *threat* and *promise*. Working in pairs, trace these ideas in each of the four passages. Ask: What forces threaten God's promise (or God's people) in each? How is God's power (and promise) triumphant in each situation? What message is there for Christians living today? What threatens us? How do we personally experience God's presence, power, and promise?

F. Make It Personal

Ask members to think about times when God seemed absent or when their responsibilities threatened to overwhelm them—when they have "been expelled to the wilderness" or had to "take up a cross." Invite any who wish to share how they worked this through. What part did (does) God play in these times?

G. Close With Devotion

Read Psalm 86:1-10, 16-17 responsively. Read verse 7 aloud; invite members to reflect on their own "trouble" in life. Pray for the strength to declare with the writer, "you will answer me." Invite participants to memorize verse 15 as a reminder of God's power to deliver.

237

Lections for Sunday Between June 26 and July 2

Old Testament: Genesis 22:1-14

*P*ERHAPS no other episode in the life of Abraham is as perplexing as today's lection from Genesis. God commanded Abraham to offer Isaac, the fulfillment of the ancient promise, as a sacrifice. Again, the divine promise was in danger. This time, however, it was YHWH who seemingly threatened to undo the promise that Abraham's lineage would continue through Isaac. Once more, the faith of the "father of many nations" was to be tested; would he choose the gift—the cherished son of his old age, or the Giver—the One to whose call he had responded and with whom he was in covenant?

"Here I Am"

In Chapter 21 the long-awaited son was finally born. Abraham's joy, however, was to be short-lived. By the first verse of Chapter 22, the test had begun. At God's call, Abraham responded: "Here I am." God instructed Abraham to take his "only son" (not a denial of Ishmael, but an emphasis upon Isaac as the beloved) to Moriah and give him as a burnt offering. His response was as immediate as his initial response in Haran. "So Abraham rose . . . and went" (Genesis 22:3).

The reader is told from the onset that this was a test; the text is unclear as to the level of Abraham's under-

Think About It: God required the ultimate sacrifice of Abraham and Abraham obeyed, not counting the cost. Do you think God was really asking this of Abraham, or did he misunderstand God's will because child sacrifice was a common cultural practice in that time? Does God test us this way? What sacrifices (hopefully not nearly so dire) has God required of us? What was our response? Once the decision was made, did it still seem a sacrifice?

standing of God's purpose. When he told his servants to wait, adding that "we will come back to you" (22:5), he may have been proclaiming his faith that God would provide another way. Perhaps he expected another miracle (as Isaac's birth had been to a man of one hundred years). Perhaps he was lying to the servants as well as to the son, who was given the burden of carrying the wood for his own sacrifice.

The next voice to be heard was that of the child calling out to his father. Again, Abraham answered, "Here I am" (22:7). The drama of the moment cannot be overemphasized: the "lamb" himself was asking where they would obtain the animal for the sacrifice. Again, the thoughts of Abraham's heart are not revealed. When he answered that "God himself will provide the lamb" (22:8), he may have been protecting his son from the painful truth. Or he may have been holding out hope that God would somehow spare the boy's life.

God Will Provide

The child made no sound when his fate became clear. The final steps were taken for the sacrifice. (The sacrifice of children was a practice throughout Mesopotamia during this time; some scholars argue that this account is used to express God's disavowal of such barbarism.) At the last second, God's angel intervened. Abraham responded a third time, "Here I am" (22:11). His "fear" (awe or reverence, expressed here as uncompromised devotion) had been recognized and rewarded. YHWH had provided a ram for the sacrifice, and Abraham's son was thereby saved.

Abraham's answer to Isaac had proven prophetic. Indeed, God had provided. The promise (and thus the future through this child) had been secured. And so, the place of sacrifice was renamed as testimony: "The Lord will provide" (22:14).

Psalter: Psalm 13

Today's psalm is another complaint or lament, with a movement toward hopefulness in God's steadfast love. Such a lament is as much a statement of faith and trust as it is a cry for help.

How Long . . . ?

Four times in the first two verses the psalmist cries, "How long . . . ?" The cry is an accusation, "Will you forget me forever?" The writer feels deserted by God, whose face is hidden. This abandonment has caused pain in the soul and sorrow in the heart (13:2). As the absence of God causes suffering, the lamenter petitions God to come near. "Consider and answer me. . . . Give light to my eyes" (13:3), meaning bestow life itself—something only God can provide.

The end of the psalm anticipates God's intervention. The final claim, that God has "dealt bountifully," affirms that the prayer has been answered.

Epistle: Romans 6:12-23

Continuing the discussion of freedom from sin and for obedience, this week's lection explores the very nature of sin in Pauline theology. He is speaking not of "sins"—a series of wrongs committed by the individual, but of "sin"—a locus of power that stands against righteousness. In Chapter 6, Paul outlines three sets of opposing realities—sin and righteousness, freedom and slavery, wages and gift—to prove his points.

Righteousness and Sin

The concept of sin as a power is clearly shown in verse 12. Sin threatens to "exercise dominion" over a person's "mortal body." Under the power of sin, human beings are susceptible to becoming (through the corruption of their human faculties) "instruments of wickedness" (verse 13). Christian life exists in the arena of Christ—the arena of God's grace. This occurs in the context of this world, a world subject to the power of sin.

> **Think About It:** We are "freed from sin and enslaved to God." As Americans, we think of freedom as part of our birthright. What is the difference between this political freedom and the freedom Paul is talking about? Can we have one without the other? Do we understand our freedom as license to do as we will or as freedom to live in accordance with God's will?

Freedom and Slavery

Slavery was a reality in Paul's world and provided a clear analogy for Christian life. For Paul, freedom and slavery were more than abstract concepts; they were references to specific, all-or-nothing human realities. In Paul's understanding, human beings were either "enslaved" to sin or to God. There was no middle ground.

Freedom, too, was understood in the same absolute terms. Being "set free" from sin (6:18) transformed the believer into a "slave of righteousness." Individual liberty as an end unto itself is a modern concept, which finds no home in Paul's theology. The difference between serving sin and serving righteousness is the final outcome. Sin brings death; righteousness gives eternal life.

Wages and Gift

In the midst of the series of opposites, Paul poses a question that, in essence, restates the question that opened Chapter 6: "Should we sin because we are not under law but under grace?" The answer is the same: "By no means!" (6:15). In closing, Paul stresses the importance of the human will.

Throughout the Epistle, Paul has repeatedly asserted that righteousness is the result of faith; faith made possible only through God's grace. Grace cannot be earned. Righteousness is not the "reward" or the "wages" of faithful living. Sin, on the other hand, pays a very specific wage to those enslaved to its power: "the wages of sin is death" (6:23). By contrast, God "gives" eternal life "in Jesus Christ our Lord." Eternal life cannot be earned; it can only be given. The question of enslavement is the choice between slavery to life or to death.

Gospel: Matthew 10:40-42

This lection closes Matthew 10 and Jesus' teaching on the risks inherent in taking up one's cross and following him—a discourse on the nature and cost of discipleship. The chapter ends on a more positive note, anticipating that the rejection the disciples can expect to receive in Jesus' name will be tempered with experiences of acceptance, welcome, and fellowship. Not all will turn away from the messengers or the message. Those who receive the disciples will receive Jesus himself as well as the One who sent him. Such acceptance, Jesus declares, God will see.

Matthew's account of Jesus' discipleship training differs significantly from that offered by Luke (10:1-11, 17-22). While Luke chronicles the resulting mission, Matthew's concern all along has been with the preparation. Thus, the teaching seems more poignantly directed toward future disciples, as well as his contemporaries in the inner circle. It stands as a clear call to disciples in today's world—complete with warnings of difficulties to come as well as anticipated rewards.

Whoever Welcomes You Also Welcomes Me
The disciple risks losing the bonds of family in the act of taking up the cross. In the context of the mission, however, Jesus points to the creation of a new kind of family, united in the sending and welcoming of missionaries in his name. This statement is consistent with Jesus' definition of family as those united by their commitment to God's will (Matthew 12:46-50).

The preceding passage (10:34-39) foreshadowed the divisions—even within the closest of families—that would mark the journey of those taking up the cross. Those seeking to preserve the status quo above the gospel message were deemed unworthy to take up his mission. Only those willing to risk everything, including their lives, could hope to find their true lives (true self, true soul) in him. Discipleship requires nothing less than total dedication.

The good news for the disciple, however, is the presence of the divine inherent in the mission. To welcome the disciple is to welcome Jesus himself; to welcome Jesus is to welcome God (10:40). Scholars disagree concerning the subject of verse 41. Both NRSV and NIV use "prophet" and "righteous person" as designations for the followers of Jesus. Other translations accept

241

the titles "prophet" and "righteous one" as pertaining to Jesus himself in acknowledgment of his presence as the "herald of the messianic age," a particular focus of Matthew's Gospel.

Little Ones

An act as simple as offering a cup of cold water to "one of these little ones" (10:42) in the name of a disciple is subject to God's notice and reward. "Little ones" is understood by some scholars to mean "children of God," a term of intimacy between Jesus and his followers; others translate "little ones" as the "most insignificant." Either understanding points to the overriding truth that the disciples' power and status come from the message—and Messenger—they bear. The disciple in this sense is literally offering the world Jesus.

> **Think About It:** "Whoever welcomes you welcomes me." Does it often seem that others were more mature or more significant in the faith? Does the superiority of others prevent us from fully living out our call to discipleship in Jesus' name? Does the thought of being welcomed as Jesus should be welcomed help us overcome this obstacle?

You Will Have Your Reward

The word *reward,* though undefined, occurs three times here. *Reward* means there are consequences for our choices. Those who reject the disciples reject the One they serve. For those who receive them, promises Jesus, the reward is waiting.

Study Suggestions

A. Begin by Singing

Sing a hymn of faithful obedience such as "Lord, Speak to Me" or "O Jesus, I Have Promised." Pray together for the strength to live out God's call to discipleship and faithfulness.

B. Reflect on Sacrifice

Read Genesis 22:1-14 together. Ask members: Why would God ask for such a sacrifice and test of obedience?

Work in pairs to explore the story, noticing the long periods of silence (the three-day journey, the walk into the wilderness, the time needed to build the altar). Ask the questions in the "Think About It" paragraph, plus these: What thoughts might we imagine were going through Abraham's mind? through Isaac's? What would this sacrifice mean to Abraham? What would happen to the divine promise if Abraham were to obey? to disobey? When Abraham initially answered God's call, he proved his faithfulness; what does this new challenge reveal about the way of faith Abraham's descendants will be called to follow? What does it reveal about our faith journey as God's people today?

C. Explore Paul on Sin

Ask members to define *sin* and *freedom*. Where did these understandings develop? In this context, discuss slavery. Ask: Do our modern connotations make it difficult (even offensive) to access Paul's view of Christians as "slaves" of righteousness? Does "servant" say it better for us? Does this clarify the meaning, or change it? How do we get past our own interpretations in order to understand Paul's message?

Read aloud Romans 6:12-23, then study the commentary on pages 240–41. Ask: How does Paul understand sin? Does his concept of sin as a powerful force differ from the group's definition? What about Paul's idea of freedom? How does it differ from your understanding of personal liberty? Do we share Paul's either/or view of freedom and enslavement? If slavery is an uncomfortable image, is there another analogy for the absolute nature of sin and righteousness?

Discuss "wages" versus "gift." Ask: If death is the "payment" due the slaves of sin, how is it earned? If death can be earned, why can't eternal life? Do we treat "righteousness" as something we can earn (possibly through the avoidance of all those specific transgressions we label as "sins")? If everything depends on grace, then why shouldn't we "sin because we are not under law but under grace?"

D. Sing With the Psalmist

Read Psalm 13 together. What does the repetition of "how long?" tell you about the psalmist's state of mind? Chart the emotional movement of the psalm. On chalkboard or a piece of paper, draw a horizontal line with increments for each of the six verses. Plot the low and high points, then consider what the pattern indicates about the relationship of the "complainer" to God. What keeps the psalmist from falling into despair?

E. Focus on Discipleship

Read aloud Matthew 10:40-42, then examine the commentary on pages 241–42. Ask: What hope is offered to those who "take up the cross to follow Jesus"? How does the recognition of the "little ones" inform our understanding of our own discipleship?

Examine *reward* in light of this lection and your discussion of Paul. What is the meaning of *reward*? If righteousness cannot be earned, why does welcoming Jesus' disciples merit reward? Are the two passages understanding *reward* in the same way? What is the difference between reward earned and reward granted?

F. Close With Prayer

Drawing on their own experience and needs, ask members to compose a lament, beginning, "How long. . . ?" What answers or interventions is each waiting for? Why should God respond? Share the laments as a closing act of devotion. Pray together for the faith to trust God.

243

Lections for Sunday Between
July 3 and 9

Old Testament: Genesis 24:34-38, 42-49, 58-67

*W*ITH this lection the focus in the drama of the patriarchs shifts from Abraham to Isaac. Today's verses are the heart of a novella in which the promises of the covenant pass from Abraham to his son. They tell how Abraham's servant went back to the "old country" to find a wife for Isaac, and how God worked through this servant to bring Isaac and Rebekah together. As was often the custom in those days, Isaac married his cousin.

God Works in Daily Life

Abraham's servant clearly expected that God would guide him in choosing the right wife for Isaac. Verses 42-49, in which the servant tells Bethuel and Laban what had already happened, indicate this expectation. He prayed that God would give him a specific sign to identify the right woman. This servant (presumably the Eliezer of Genesis 15:2) is a model for disciples because: (1) he worked faithfully to carry out his master's instructions; (2) he became a conduit for God's blessing in the daily life of the family he served; and (3) he was faithful to Abraham even though Isaac received the inheritance rather than himself.

> **Think About It:** There may be only a fine distinction between faithfulness and telling God what we need. How would we see the difference? How might Abra-ham's servant be a model for our daily life?

How we expect God to work in daily life is a key issue. Eliezer asked God for guidance in very specific terms. But he also took responsibility for his mission. He did not passively turn everything over to God—doing so, taken to an extreme, could border on unfaithfulness, even making an attempt to use God for his own ends. To leave late for an appointment, then pray for a parking space in front of the door, or not to study for a test, then pray for an A, seems more manipulative than faithful.

God Blesses Faithful Followers

The story is clear—Abraham went off to a far country and became fabulously wealthy, because God blessed him. In the Genesis narratives, God's blessing meant wealth, long life, and children. Since these remote ancestors of our faith did not believe in life after death, rewards in this life were the only way to know God's blessing. Later biblical narratives will make the point that neither wealth nor poverty necessarily mean the presence or absence of God's blessing. But, in this story, Abraham's success is directly related to God's blessing.

> **Think About It:** "Abraham's success is directly related to God's blessing." Do you view material prosperity as a sign of God's blessing? How does this idea compare with Jesus' statement, "Blessed are you who are poor" (Luke 6:20)? What have been the signs of God's blessing on you?

Bethuel and Laban (24:50-51) used God language that suggested faith in God was not limited to Abraham and his descendants. Abraham's nephews also believed, probably before Abraham left on his wanderings. If so, this opens up the Genesis narratives to new understandings about the work of God. God's blessing is not limited to one person, family, or nation.

A Happy Ending!

Rebekah was willing to go with the servant and to marry a man she had never seen before. And it worked out! Isaac and Rebekah loved each other. There is more to life in God's world than just the religious dimension. God's blessings include gifts such as the love between husband and wife. God's faithfulness and steadfast love are shown in the blessings of human relationships and in the love we have for each other. In what other ways does God bless us?

Psalter: Psalm 72

This psalm reminds us that government can and should be a good thing. This prayer may have been part of the coronation ritual for new rulers; its spirit certainly echoes Solomon's coronation prayer. It calls for justice and for equity for the poor and dispossessed. The expectation is that the king will care for the poor, defend their cause, give them deliverance from the grinding oppression of poverty, and bring them hope.

The king's chief clients are the weak, the needy, those who have no helper. The implication is that, if the king does uphold the poor and needy, God will bless him and bring peace, dominion, wealth, and all benefits of royalty and power. As we celebrate Independence Day, this psalm calls us to reflect on who we are as a nation, the true purpose of government, and how well we measure up to God's expectations.

Epistle: Romans 7:15-25a

How many times we could echo Paul's words: "I do not understand my own actions!" Paul is struggling with the issue of human sin and how decent people trying to do right so often fail and end up doing the wrong thing instead.

"I Do the Very Thing I Hate"

We act contrary to our own best intentions; we try to do right but end up doing wrong. Sometimes we do so in sheer innocence. We may try to do the right thing but, because we don't have the correct information, or because of circumstances beyond our control, we wind up hurting others. At other times, we do the exact opposite of what we intend, such as being unfaithful, or trying to heal broken relationships but instead making the breach worse.

But I Have an Excuse . . .

Then Paul says that when he tries to do right and does wrong instead, it is not he who does it, but sin that lives in him. What a great excuse! This sounds almost like determinism. It is as if there is nothing good in him, and evil simply pushes him to do things. We must be careful how we tread through these verses. In contrast to this statement that sounds deterministic, there is the Christian assumption that God has given us freedom of choice. We have the option to choose the evil or the good. How, then, do we resolve this apparent contradiction between free will and what some call predestination?

> **Think About It:** Our experience tells us we have the freedom and the ability to choose. Yet, we also have Paul saying he had no choice. What is our experience? Do we have freedom to choose between good and evil? Or does sin constrain our freedom and make it impossible to choose?

The Dilemma Deepens

When we want to do good, evil is close at hand. This we all have experienced. Choice means that both good and evil are possibilities, and the two lie close together. This truth is behind the statement that there is only a fine line between great saints and great sinners.

Paul uses the term *law* to describe the inevitability of losing to temptation and sin (7:21-23). Given the general meaning of *law* to refer to the Torah or other commandments for ordering the faithful life, the term *axiom* might be clearer for us.

Thanks Be to God!

The only way out is the power of God through Jesus Christ. Christ has triumphed over sin and death, which makes it possible to resolve the dilemma into which sin has thrust us. The power of God through Christ gives us the capacity to become free moral agents and to live according to the best that God calls us to be and do.

Gospel: Matthew 11:16-19, 25-30

Jesus' story is about two groups of children. One group wants to play "weddings," a happy game. But the other won't play. So the first says, "OK, if you don't want a happy game, let's play 'funerals.' " They still won't play.

Like Children in the Marketplace

The interpretation is obvious. John the Baptist was a stern, threatening figure. People would not listen to him, because his message was too hard. Jesus came, not threatening anyone, talking about love and forgiveness, celebrating life. People rejected him because he was too soft. Jesus chided them for both attitudes. Like children in the marketplace, they did not want to play either game. Don't turn people away because you don't like the way they present their message, Jesus warned. Be more discerning.

The current national scene suggests that discernment is not one of our strong suits. It is also true that the bitter struggles in our churches over issues of biblical interpretation and how to apply the Bible to contemporary life suggest that discernment is a much-needed skill.

Discernment is the ability to see what God is doing in contemporary life. This goes beyond the simplistic response we often hear in religious rhetoric. Sometimes we identify our own position as God's will or word. Sometimes we seize on an isolated Bible passage and identify it as the ultimate expression of God's will. Discernment means being open to God's action in and through a variety of groups and understandings.

Jesus' Prayer for Discernment

Matthew 11:25-30 is also about discernment. Jesus gives thanks that God has hidden the truth from the wise and given it to infants. This suggests that discernment is not a function of intelligence, sophistication, or even education; rather, it comes from a kind of primal awareness of the reality of God's presence and action in the world.

A little girl asked to be left alone with her baby sister. Mom and Dad were reluctant but finally agreed, leaving the monitor on in the nursery. To their amazement, they heard the child say to the baby, "Tell me again what God looks like. I'm starting to forget." While that story may raise problems theologically, it points up the possibility of discernment in the very young.

Who Knows God?

Then Matthew records a statement that John's Gospel could easily have made. Who knows God? Only the Son. One implication is that we cannot know the ultimate truth about God except through Jesus Christ. Similarly, no one knows the Father except the Son—*and* those to whom the Son *chooses* to make God known.

Christian faith teaches that Jesus came to reveal God to all the world; there is a strong strain of universalism in our faith. But there is also a strain of exclusivism: Jesus chooses to reveal God only to those who believe in him and thus are receptive and understanding—that is, the community of faith.

The Invitation

"Come to me . . . and I will give you rest." What a word of hope this statement has been for so many who have been

Think About It: We often assume that to follow Jesus is either complete blessing and ease, or a life of demands too heavy to bear. Jesus is saying that the Christian life is both. Do we find that yoke easy to bear? a "burden" of joy?

tired, sick, defeated, discouraged! But this verse is also an invitation to discipleship. To take a yoke upon oneself is to bow one's head like an ox and to accept the harness that makes it possible to pull the heavy load that life and faith place upon us. We discover that it is easy to pull Jesus' yoke, however, because Jesus is always alongside us sharing in the struggle.

Study Suggestions

A. Reflect on a Patriotic Hymn

Sing or read together all stanzas of "America the Beautiful." Then ask: For what specific blessings for America does the songwriter ask? List responses on chalkboard or a sheet of paper. What would you add to or remove from this list? Why? What responsibilities come with these blessings?

B. Consider How God Works

Ask: Compared with the expectations of Abraham's servant, how do you think God acts in daily life today? Share examples from your experience. List responses. Refer to "God Works in Daily Life" in the Genesis commentary. Then discuss the "Think About It" questions.

Ask: How do you think God acts today in government and political affairs? How does "God bless America"? What does God expect of America in light of these blessings? How can we distinguish between what God has given and what we or our forebears have simply taken? List responses.

C. Consider God's Action

Review Genesis 24:34-38, 42-49, 58-67, and the commentary on pages 244–45. Ask: How did the servant expect God to act in his life? How did the servant say that God had acted in Abraham's life? How does the Genesis story say God blesses faithful followers? List these responses.

Read Psalm 72 aloud and examine the commentary. Ask: What does this psalm say about how God works in government? about what God expects of government? Again list responses.

Compare the lists from activities A, B, and C. Ask: What trends do you see in these lists? similarities? differences? Is this an emerging definition of how God works in daily life, both personal and public?

D. Consider Moral Dilemmas

Read Romans 7:15-25a. What is Paul saying about his own behavior and inclinations? Do you identify with what he is saying? Do you see Paul as a helpless figure? Is he simply making excuses? If not, what can he mean about seemingly having no control over what he does? Discuss the "Think About It" questions in the Epistle commentary on page 246.

Invite group members to describe movies, books, shows, or their own experiences that portray or involve a moral struggle. Note that wanting to do right but winding up doing wrong is a common experience. Ask: What did you find in these art forms or experiences about the dilemma of doing wrong when we intend to do right? Do we have a choice? Are we responsible for what happens? Are our actions and the consequences predetermined? How do we experience God working in our lives in these moral dilemmas?

E. Be Discerning

Read Matthew 11:16-19 and the commentary on pages 247–48. Ask: What is the point of this passage? What does it say about discerning God's plan or direction for you in general or at a particular point in your life? How is discernment a way in which God acts in your life? How can we distinguish between God's direction and our own desires or inclinations?

As an introduction to what it means to take on the yoke of Christ, ask any who are familiar with the use of a yoke for animals to share that experience. Then ask: How is wearing Jesus' yoke a comfort? a burden? In your experience, is this an appropriate image of faithful discipleship? Are there others that fit your experience better?

F. Give Thanks for God's Action

In closing, stand in a prayer circle joining hands. Give thanks for God's action in our lives and nation. Include examples that have been mentioned during the session. Also ask God to help our nation and leaders be faithful to God's expectations of justice and compassion for the poor and oppressed. Pray also for the ability to use our God-given freedom responsibly, and for the gift of discernment in our everyday decision-making.

249

Lections for Sunday Between July 10 and 16

*T*Old Testament: Genesis 25:19-34

*T*ODAY'S lection reminds us that even the most faithful people can have major family problems. Sometimes these problems come because parents love in unhealthy ways. Isaac and Rebekah were married for twenty years before they had children. They stayed faithful to God. Isaac prayed for children, and that prayer was answered. Rebekah prayed because her pregnancy was so difficult—and God told her that the twins struggling in her womb signaled the struggles of the two nations that would come from her sons.

Heredity Versus Environment

Though better understood now, the debate about the influence of heredity and environment continues. In this family, heredity was definitely part of the problem: there was something about the genetic makeup of the twins that put them at odds with each other. Their natures were completely different. Esau liked the outdoors and the thrill of hunting; Jacob liked to stay home.

Environment was also a part of the picture. Isaac and Rebekah had favorites and apparently made no secret of their preferences. Isaac loved Esau and encouraged him in his outdoor life. Rebekah loved Jacob (25:28). Those bald statements probably do not mean that Isaac and Rebekah each loved only one son; rather, they played favorites, and doing so led to trouble.

What's in a Name?

Maybe nothing, but ancient people believed that a name said something important about the nature and character of a person. *Jacob* means "he grasps by the heel"—in short form, "grabber." He came out of the womb gripping his older brother's heel and he continued to grab—at wealth, position, love—for most of his life.

The Way to a Man's Heart . . .

Another difference between the brothers was that Esau seemed to act on impulse, while Jacob looked out for the long-term payoff. When a person such as Esau, who was impatient and needed instant gratification, meets up with a schemer like Jacob, guess who usually comes up short? That happened here. Esau was hungry, and Jacob had whipped up a tasty pot of lentil soup. Esau begged for some of the soup, and Jacob "grabbed" at the opportunity. He asked Esau to sign away his inheritance in exchange for a meal.

> **Think About It:** "Jacob 'grabbed' at the opportunity. He 'struck while the iron was hot.'" But he also took advantage of his brother when he was in a weakened position. When is "grabbing" just being alert, and when does it become exploitation?
>
> In our negotiations, how can we make sure all are situated on a "level playing field"? How can we assert our legitimate rights while at the same time meeting the needs of others—who may be disadvantaged in one way or another—for equal opportunity and benefit?

In that ancient, nomadic culture, birthright was an important issue. The oldest son was entitled to the family name, a double share of the family wealth, and (in this case) the right for the covenant to pass through him. Jacob's request for his brother to trade his birthright for a little lunch was outrageous. With an exaggeration of his own, Esau claimed he was about to starve to death. We can see ourselves here: trading jibes, making wild claims that no one takes seriously. Perhaps in this light, Esau dismissed his "little" brother: "OK, fine; I swear. Now give me my soup." But Jacob wasn't kidding. Fortunately for the long term, God was also working in this equation. The Bible tells us Jacob was the one YHWH had chosen to be the bearer of the covenant.

Psalter: Psalm 119:105-112

This longest of all psalms is divided into sections, each beginning with a different letter of the Hebrew alphabet. This section is a reminder that even though life is always lived under the threat of affliction, misfortune, and death, there is still plenty of reason to sing God's praise.

The opening two lines are a wonderful statement of faith. We use them to sing about the Bible—and rightly so—but they mean much more than that. God's "word" is a revelation of God's self, of who God really is. This is a guide for life. Verse 111 is also a statement of trust and praise. The "heritage" that lasts is not material, but rather God's "statutes" (NIV). It is only the surety of God's "word" (self) that can guarantee our future.

Epistle: Romans 8:1-11

Paul has been talking about the struggle between the longing to do right and the compulsion to do wrong. Now he moves beyond that to declare that the Spirit gives us victory over the law of sin and death.

"Thine Be the Glory"

Both the great Easter hymn ("Thine be the glory, risen, conquering Son") and biblical teaching shout for joy because of Christ's triumph. Christ has won a great victory over sin, death, and the devil. In a typically convoluted sentence, Paul says that God has done what human nature and systems could never do—condemn sin. During the first 250 years or so of the church's life, this victory was a great theme in the teaching of the fathers and mothers. Writers such as Paul, Irenaeus of Lyons (died about A.D. 200) and Tertullian of Carthage (died 225) said that the *Incarnation* (Christ coming "in the flesh") set the stage for a great battle between good and evil.

Jesus, as a human being, lived the life that God intended for humans to live and became a new head for the human race. Just as Adam's disobedience and sin had tainted all human life, so Christ's obedience and perfection made all human life new. It was Jesus' life, not his death, that brought about the work of salvation. His crucifixion was important, but it was not the whole story. Jesus' whole life, from birth through resurrection, was the pivotal moment in history, the scene of the great victory over sin and death.

> **Think About It:** It was Jesus' life, more than his death, that brought about the work of salvation. Is that a new idea for you? How do you react to that statement?

For a while it seemed that sin held sway and that death was triumphant. But Good Friday was not the end of the story. There was still the third day, when Christ was raised from the dead, defeating death and trampling sin underfoot. An early fourth-century legend of the Syrian church declares that when Christ came back from the dead he brought Adam and Eve with him. This was a sign that all the power of sin and death had been overcome, since it was through Adam and Eve that sin and death had come into the world in the first place.

Join the Winning Team

Paul's admonition to the Romans is, "join the winning team." Jesus' resurrection has shown that the ultimate victor in the battle between good and evil is God. The question now is, what team will you be on, the winning or the losing one? If you choose Christ, Paul says, you are dead to sin and alive to righteousness. If you have the Spirit, then the God who raised Christ from the dead will also raise you. This is an almost irresistible invitation to believe the gospel.

252

Gospel: Matthew 13:1-9, 18-23

Jesus usually did not explain his parables; they were so obvious no one could miss the point. Hearers who did not understand were not spiritually alive enough to respond anyway. But this one he explains—to the disciples.

Sowing the Seed

Anyone who has lived on a farm or planted a garden understands the reality behind this parable. You sow the seed, creating the right conditions for it to grow. But in the long run, the result is out of your hands. You can't control rain, insects, burning heat, or other potential hazards. In first-century Palestine, farmers sowed the seed onto the plowed field and then dragged branches across the field to cover the seed, burying some seed too deep in the process. There were other reasons why the seed wouldn't sprout or mature into full heads. But in spite of all the problems, there was a harvest. Part of the seed sprouted; there was grain—not a miraculous harvest, but a good one.

In its original form, the parable was about the end result of all this work. There was a harvest, which produced a hundredfold (or sixty or thirty). The point is that God brings results. Just as God gives the harvest to those who plant, so also God gives the Kingdom to those who faithfully prepare for it.

The Interpretation of the Parable

Between the time Jesus told this parable and the time Matthew wrote his Gospel, the church began to interpret the parable allegorically. In the interpretation (verses 18-23), the emphasis is no longer on the harvest but on the soil. The different kinds of soil where the seed has landed now become symbols for different kinds of responses to the words spoken by Jesus (and the apostles?). The rocky ground represents a person who is excited when he first hears the word, but has no foundation for his faith; so his faith dies the first time trouble comes along. The path where the birds can easily find the seeds becomes the person who does not understand the word; so it is easy for evil to talk her out of belief.

For Matthew, the shift of emphasis from sowing to the soil pushes the hearer, the disciple, to take responsibility for producing fruit. The sower becomes Christ, from whom the word (seed) comes. It is Christ who is present and active in the growth of the church, but the church includes believers who have an unavoidable responsibility to be partners with Christ.

So What Do You Want Me to Do?

In preaching, one must be clear about the intended result. If someone says, "Good sermon. What do I do next?" one should always have an answer. Think about this parable and interpretation in these terms.

The parable itself says that God will triumph, the Kingdom will come.

> **Think About It:** All of us are some kind of "soil" and are expected to yield the best harvest we can. Which kind of soil are you? What is your relationship with the Sower? Do you see yourself as a partner in sowing the seed of the Kingdom?

God will bring it about. The interpretation says different people receive the word in different ways. Some will enter the Kingdom as a result. Others will lose what little faith they have. For the parable, the question, "What do I do next?" would seem to have the answer, "Continue to be faithful and trust God to complete what God has begun." For the interpretation, the answer to "What do I do next?" is, "Identify the kind of 'soil' you are, then make your 'soil' the best you can be."

Study Suggestions

A. Put the Word to Music
Sing or listen to the song "Thy Word Is a Lamp," by Amy Grant and Michael W. Smith, on her CD, *Straight Ahead* (1984), or find it in your hymnal.

B. Reflect on the Word
Read Psalm 119:105-112 (the source of the song). Note how we usually think of the Bible when we hear these words. The psalmist, however, had the Law (Torah) in mind. For the psalmist, God's "word" was a revelation of God's self. *Torah* (Law, and all its synonyms mentioned in these verses) refers not to the five books of Law but to the received and practiced oral tradition, God's cosmic law, and God's self-revelation through God's teachings. Ask: How does this reminder of what the psalmist meant by *word* change the way we think about this psalm?

C. Pick a Theme
Read the commentary on the psalm (page 251), noting that even though life is lived under threat, there is still plenty of reason to praise God. Then read Romans 8:1-11 and the commentary on page 252. Ask: Do you consider victory a key element in Christian faith? Does this word sound like an American overemphasis on winning? What does it mean to say that Christ has won a victory over sin, death, and the devil? Emphasize that what we have in the commentary is a theological statement about victory in the context of cosmic conflict.

Ask: What does victory look like in your life? (For example, being sober one more day, hanging in on a justice issue against overwhelming obstacles, keeping the faith knowing we may be dead before the year is out, or living faithfully even when we feel shut off from God.) What part does God play in these victories?

Discuss the questions in "Think About It." For many, the idea that it was Jesus' life more than his death that brought about the work of salvation is so strange as to seem almost blasphemous. Invite reactions. Point out that this approach does not discount or ignore the crucifixion and Resurrection; rather it expands the Incarnation into the seamless, saving totality of Jesus' life.

D. Tie a Theme Together

Read Genesis 25:19-34 and the commentary on pages 250–51. Ask: Where do you see victory in this story? Where is there faithfulness in small things? What is God doing here? Where do you see chances for victory slipping away? Is paying a price in the present for the sake of the future ever a real victory? Why or why not? Then read Matthew 13:1-9. Ask: How do we see victory presented in this parable? Refer to Psalm 119 (and its commentary on page 251), which praises God in spite of life's turmoil.

E. Learn About Interpretation

Read Matthew 13:18-23 and the commentary on pages 253–54. Ask: How does the emphasis change between parable and interpretation? Does this change means the interpretation was put forth by the church rather than Jesus? Why or why not? Ask: With what kind of soil do you identify? What is your relationship to the Sower? What obligation do you have to produce a harvest? How do you envision your partnership with Christ in bringing in a harvest?

F. Ask, So What?

Invite members to reflect on all the images of victory in these Scriptures. Ask: What do we do when a sermon or lesson calls us to do or to be something? Encourage those who feel so led to make or to renew a commitment to Jesus Christ, claiming the victory he brings in life.

G. Celebrate Victory

Sing "Thine Be the Glory"; then close with prayer, asking God for receptive hearts (soil), strengthened integrity (unlike Jacob), and deepened commitment to overcome evil with good (Romans).

Lections for Sunday Between July 17 and 23

T Old Testament: Genesis 28:10-19a

*T*HIS text begins with Jacob running for his life. He had continued, with his mother's help, to lie and cheat his way into the full blessing that rightfully belonged to Esau. Finally, even Esau had had enough and had sworn vengeance on his twin. So Rebekah sent Jacob back to the old country to live with his uncle Laban while things cooled off a bit (27:41-45). On the way, in the vicinity of Bethel, he finally fell exhausted into sleep.

Jacob's Dream

Jacob dreamed that a ziggurat (stepped pyramid), or a stairway, or a ramp (the Hebrew can have any of those meanings) reached from earth to heaven. Jacob saw angels going up and down the ladder. At the very least, the dream was a sign that the way between heaven and earth was open, and that the heavenly messengers could go both ways. But, the angels were not the messengers in this case—God was! God identified for Jacob their relationship in terms Jacob would understand—that is, the God of Grandfather Abraham and Father Isaac. God then made several promises to Jacob:

- the plot of land on which he was lying would belong to Jacob and his descendants (28:13);
- Jacob's many descendants would spread abroad in all directions (28:14);
- his family would be a blessing to all on earth (28:14);
- God would be with Jacob and care for him wherever he went (28:15);
- God would bring Jacob back to the land (28:15);
- God would not leave Jacob until all the promises had been fulfilled (28:15).

All the promises together made up a covenant between God and Jacob, which was primarily one of reassurance and gift. Jacob was not asked to do anything in response, though the idea of obedience and loyalty to God was probably implicit.

God Is in This Place

Jacob was changed, in some ways, by this encounter. Before, he had known God through story but not by experience. Now he had come to know that the God of whom his father had often spoken had come to him personally. God had been in this place, but he had not been aware of it. At this point, his life was not appreciably different; he went on his way much the same old Jacob, the "grabber." But his intention had always been to allow God into his life, and this would ultimately change him.

Jacob also responded to the dream in some concrete ways. Recognizing that this stopping place was indeed Beth-el, the "house of God," he set up his stone pillow as a pillar. The ordinary had become sacred. Standing stones were familiar in Israel as signs of God's presence. Other people would see it and know that God had appeared to someone there. The oil that Jacob poured over the stone would also likely discolor the stone and help others identify it as a sign of God's appearance. To be doubly sure people would recognize it, Jacob named the place "Beth-el."

Many ordinary places become "Beth-el" for us. We recognize the presence of God on the lakeshore at camp, at a tree-shaded natural shrine on a mountain, or in our own, familiar, place of worship where everything seems safe and routine. We know there is nothing sacred about the place, but it becomes a holy place for us because we met God there. It remains in our memory as the place where God became real to us, where we said in our hearts, "God is in this place!" We recognize God more often in retrospect than prospect.

Psalter: Psalm 139:1-12, 23-24

What a great statement this psalm makes about the presence of God! There is no place where we are beyond God's reach and care. We cannot hide from God, for God is present everywhere. On the one hand, this might sound oppressive—we never have any privacy where God is concerned. But on the other hand, the psalm says we are never beyond God's love and care. Wherever we are, we are in the hands of God! So we can sing this psalm as one of hope and love and God's caring for us. It's like God being with Jacob at the lowest point of his life.

Epistle: Romans 8:12-25

Paul wrote his letters by dictating them to a secretary, who then wrote out the letter on parchment from his notes and sent it off by messenger to the city where the recipients lived. As he dictated, Paul often digressed and then returned to his main thought. Even without the digression, his sentences were frequently long and complicated. In his complex way, Paul here writes of the presence of God in our lives.

Children of God

In the Roman world, wealthy citizens often adopted slaves into their family so they would have an heir to carry on the family name. This practice is probably behind the statement that we are children of God. We have received a spirit of adoption and have been set free from slavery to sin and death. We are now God's children. When we cry "Abba! Father!" it is because the Spirit gives us the gift of recognizing the presence and intimacy of this new relationship with God.

> **Think About It:** The closest equivalent we have for *Abba* is "Daddy." What in our experience prepares us to think about God in this intimate way? Are we comfortable thinking of God this way, or do we prefer to view God as more majestic and austere? Are there some persons for whom using the word *Daddy* for God might not be a sign of hope but might instead stir up anger and fear?

Abba, the word for father that Jesus taught his disciples to use, is a much more intimate word than the formal "Father." The closest equivalent we have to it is "Daddy." Simply to be able to say "Abba" is a recognition that we are God's children, that we have entered into a new relationship with the Father and with Jesus Christ, who is, in some ways, our big brother.

Eager Longing for Glory

The story of Adam and Eve in Genesis 3 suggests that, because of human sin, all of creation is out of sync. Instead of human dominion being a careful stewardship of creation, it has become a form of exploitation and misuse. Paul suggests the hope that in God's realm even the creation will be set free. What great images he piles up—creation waiting "with eager longing," like little children excitedly waiting for Christmas morning; creation "groaning in labor pains" wanting to bring forth something new and fresh.

Like creation, Paul says, we also yearn with anticipation while we wait for adoption. We have the first fruits of the Spirit, but not yet the fullness of the promise. This is yet to come, so we wait in hope. And the creation waits with us. Paul may have not been an ecologist, but he knew there was a wholeness, a oneness, about all of creation—and he dared to dream of a day when humanity would be so fully redeemed that creation could also be restored to fullness without fear we would destroy it again.

Gospel: Matthew 13:24-30, 36-43

Here is another instance where Jesus explains a parable about agriculture, but only to his disciples. This seems strange. They all lived in a rural area.

Even fishermen and tax collectors would have been aware of the realities of farming. They saw it all around them. Why would they have needed an explanation of something so familiar?

First, the Parable

The parable is straightforward. A man sowed wheat. But at night an enemy came and sowed weeds as well. These were a kind of bearded darnel, which is indistinguishable from wheat until it forms the head. Both grew, and the workers recognized there were weeds among the wheat. They wanted to go into the field and get rid of them. But the master said, "No, either you will trample the wheat, or you will pull up the wheat along with the weeds. Let it be till harvest. The wheat matures first, so we can separate the weeds when we thresh the grain, then burn them."

The meaning of the parable is also straightforward. It's not our business to decide who does and who doesn't belong in God's realm. We simply wait with patience until God brings the Kingdom, then God will do the separating. One of our great sins is wanting to take the place of God in judging who is, and is not, a worthy recipient of God's grace. The parable says this kind of judgment belongs to God. Our place is to wait patiently until God takes action.

> *Think About It:* "One of our great sins is wanting to take the place of God in judging who is, and is not, a worthy recipient of God's grace." We deny it, but it happens. Whom do we exclude from the church? Why? Are we clear on the will of God about that exclusion?

Then, the Interpretation

Matthew begins the interpretation by having Jesus go into the house with the disciples, away from the crowds. Getting to "go with them" makes us part of the "in-group" in the church. We get to hear Jesus' private teaching. This begins with a reminder that the Son of Man, a term Jesus uses for himself in the Synoptic Gospels, sows the good seed. This is not only the historical Jesus, but the exalted Son of Man who will judge the world at the end. The "seed" are the children of the Kingdom.

The key to the interpretation is the second sowing, done by the enemy. Both the parable and the interpretation say that the separation of true from false is God's business and has to wait until the time of judgment. There may have been disagreements about judgment on sinners and about church discipline in Matthew's church, just as in ours. So Matthew may have added the interpretation to make the point even clearer—we dare not take the place of God in judging others.

We sometimes try to disguise our judgmental attitudes by claiming to "hate the sin but love the sinner." But is this really possible? Can we really separate the sin from the sinner? For example, in the period before the Civil War, northern church people tried to hate slavery and still love the slave owners. It didn't work. The struggle over the issues and the people associated with them led to a breach in the nation as well as to divisions in the church.

We have the same problem in issues of judgment and discipline that divide the church today. Judgment is always a partisan issue, and we find it impossible to judge a person's actions without also judging the person. We had better take Jesus' advice, accept all persons in a spirit of love, and leave the judgment to God.

Study Suggestions

A. Share Experiences of God's Presence

Read Genesis 28:10-19a and the commentary on pages 256–57. Note that this story of Jacob is the logical outcome of his own nature. At this low point in his life, Jacob found God. Ask: Have you experienced God as present and real at a low point in your life? or known someone who has? Invite volunteers to tell their stories.

B. Reflect on Jacob's Experience

Refer to Genesis 28:10-19a. Ask: What did God promise Jacob? Explain that these promises combined to make a covenant. Ask: How did Jacob respond? Was he changed? How? In what concrete ways did Jacob respond to this experience of God? What places have been a "Beth-el" (house of God) for you? What places have become holy because you experienced God there?

C. Bask in God's Presence

Read aloud Psalm 139:1-12, 23-24. Ask: Do you recognize this psalm? What is its main message? What images help us identify this theme? Does the psalm sound like God watching over your shoulder to see what you've done wrong? or like God being present wherever you are, even in the low times? Which images in the psalm would you like to hold onto in order to remember God's presence with you?

Read Romans 8:12-25 and the commentary "Children of God." Explain the adoption metaphor; then reflect on the "Think About It" questions. (There may be persons present who have experienced a father as abusive rather than as a daddy, or as both daddy and abusive. For them, this may be a difficult discussion. They may have strong negative feelings about the image of God as father. Be sensitive to this. Such experience with a father need not negate the loving presence of God in their lives, but it may spoil for them the metaphor of God as Father.)

D. Examine New Beginnings

Read the commentary, "Eager Longing for Glory." Ask: How do you experience this image? (That is, how do you react to the idea of creation "waiting in eager expectation" [NIV] to see human redemption, because that should lead to redemption for the creation as well?) What music or art awakens in you feelings of new beginnings, fresh starts, a new world being born? Suggest that persons memorize Romans 8:19-21 and link these verses with the music or art in their minds. Then, the next time they hear that music, they will remember Paul's words about the longing of creation for freedom.

E. Deal With Judgment

Read only Matthew 13:24-30. Ask: What is the point of this parable? Bring into the discussion ideas from the commentary section, "First, the Parable."

Read Matthew 13:36-43 and "Then, the Interpretation." Invite participants to imagine themselves as the weeds. Ask: How have you been "weedy"? What attitudes or behaviors have sown discord or worked against productivity in another person's life? Then have them imagine themselves as being wheat, which is more mature than the darnel. Ask: In what ways have you seen growth in your life and faith that makes for a better harvest in God's realm?

Consider issues of judgment and the axiom to "hate the sin but love the sinner." Point to the slavery illustration. Ask: Are there situations today where we talk about hating the sin but loving the sinner? What does it mean to hate a sin? When we hate a sin, are we really able to love the sinner? Can we separate the two in real life?

F. Close With Worship

Sing "Surely the Presence of the Lord Is in This Place." Offer a prayer of thanksgiving that God is with us, even at the low points in our lives. Ask for grace to accept one another and leave judgment to our loving God.

Lections for Sunday Between July 24 and 30

Old Testament: Genesis 29:15-28

WOULDN'T you love it if you were accepted for a job, and the boss said, "name your own salary"? That's basically what Laban said to Jacob. "If you're going to work for me, there has to be some financial accounting. What do you want?" Jacob volunteered to work for seven years with no salary, provided that at the end of that time he could have Rachel as his wife. This was a bride price Laban was willing, even happy, to receive. In that culture the father of the bride collected a large sum for his daughter before she could be married.

What Goes Around, Comes Around

The wedding took place, with the bride heavily veiled according to the custom of the tribe. After a great feast, the happy couple went off to their own tent. Imagine Jacob's shock in the morning, when he discovered that his lovely bride was not Rachel, but her older sister Leah. Imagine Leah's humiliation when Jacob stormed out of the tent, demanding of Laban to know what had happened to his wife! This was not a pretty family picture.

"Oh," Laban said, "in our country, we marry off the oldest first." Was this a dig at Jacob, who had violated all the rules of the first-born when he grabbed the birthright and blessing away from Esau? Now it seems the "grabber" had been "grabbed."

> **Think About It:** "Imagine the tension in the tent. . . ." Think of times when there was tension in your tent (home). What caused it? Was any deception or manipula-tion in-volved, such as took place here? How did you feel? What did you do? What did you learn? What would you do differently if you had it to do over? How was God present and active in the situation?

262

But, true love would win out, and Laban agreed that, if Jacob would finish out the bridal week with Leah and work for another seven years, he could have Rachel at the end of the week. Imagine the tension in the tent—and the marriage bed—between Jacob and Leah. He was angry with Laban, probably also angry at Leah for her part in the pretense, and eager to wed Rachel. And all the time he had to continue to relate to Leah as part of the price for Rachel. Imagine how shamed Leah must have been—small wonder that they did not get along.

Family Values?

There was a lot wrong with this family. Laban violated the feelings of Jacob and of his daughters; in fact, it seems the wishes and feelings of the daughters were not considered at all. They were the property of their father and had to do what he told them in this situation. Laban manipulated tribal custom and the rights of the first-born to his own advantage. Perhaps the worst, to our eyes, was that they both had to co-operate, to some degree, with his scheme.

Leah had to pretend to be Rachel and go through the wedding ceremony. Rachel had at least to agree to stay hidden and keep her mouth shut. Their negative feelings toward their father would spill over later when they had to flee with Jacob—and Rachel stole Laban's household gods (31:1-21).

Interestingly, both Leah and Rachel seem to have worked out an understanding with Jacob. It was always clear that Rachel was the favorite; but legally, as the second wife, she was subordinate to her sister. Jacob seems to have treated them both well and cared for them, emotionally as well as materially. It is ironic that Rachel died in childbirth (much later) and was buried near Bethlehem, while it is Leah who was buried with Jacob in the ancestral tomb at Machpelah in modern Hebron.

Psalter: Psalm 105:1-11, 45b

This is a psalm about God's faithfulness. It lists God's gifts through the actions of the patriarchs and of Moses, who brought the people out of Egypt. The psalmist uses a series of verbs—give thanks, sing, tell, glory, rejoice, seek, remember—calling us to worship God. The call comes in the context of who God's people are—children of Abraham and Isaac. Then comes the recital of God's faithfulness. God is mindful of the covenant. God's word remains eternally faithful. The covenant with Abraham and Jacob is unending; the inheritance is sure. No wonder the people of God are filled with gratitude.

Epistle: Romans 8:26-39

How many times have you knelt to pray with a heavy heart and discovered you had no idea what to say? We are in emotional and spiritual pain, desperately need God, and don't even know how to cry for help. We're ready to pray—but what do we pray for?

Paul says that the Spirit is helping us when we don't know how to pray. We can't put our prayers into words; but the Spirit prompts with "sighs too deep for words," and God hears and understands. Since a sigh is like breath, this may be a pun on the Hebrew word for wind, breath, and spirit (*ruach*). In any event, God not only hears our prayers but also helps us utter them when we are in deep distress.

Are We Predestined?

Through the Son by the Spirit, we are enabled to love our heavenly Father. Graciously God loves us, and in this loving relationship all things work together for good (8:28-30). God actually foreknew those who would love God. What do verses 28-30 really mean? Is it really true that all things work for good for those who love God? Does that fit our human experience? If not, what could this mean?

> **Think About It:** "All things work together for good for those who love God." Then why do bad things happen to good people? What is your experience? If bad things happen to us, does this mean we aren't called according to God's purpose? What are the implications of this question?

Then why do bad things happen to good people? What is your experience? If bad things happen to us, does this mean we aren't called according to God's purpose? What are the implications of this question?

The text leaves little room to maneuver. It clearly says "predestined," which seems opposed to a belief in free will. But Paul did not have a fully worked-out system of predestination. He surely meant that it was the people of God, the church, who were predestined, not necessarily individuals. Note also that the text says "predestined to be conformed to the likeness of his Son" (verse 29, NIV). That is, God wants us to become like Jesus. God's intent is that the family of God be large. God works to call, justify, and glorify those who have been chosen.

In the Bible *predestined* does not mean that we have no choice. Paul is clear that we are free to make choices, even to reject God's love. So the word here means more like God's longing for us to follow God, or even God's ultimate will. Human freedom can thwart that will and disappoint that longing. But to those who respond to God's call, there is acceptance and celebration in the future.

The Greatest Thing Paul Wrote

There is tremendous power in Paul's affirmation in verses 31-39. What makes this so great? Look at the promises, celebrate the joy, claim the victory!

• If God is for us, who is against us (8:31)?

- Since God gave us the Son, will God withhold anything else (8:32)?
- There is no condemnation in Christ Jesus (8:33-34).
- In all calamities, we are conquerors through Christ (8:35-37).
- Nothing can separate us from the love of God (8:38-39).

Gospel: Matthew 13:31-32, 44-52

One of the delights of reading the Gospels is coming across these little gems of parables, which catch us by surprise.

Wow! That's Really Something!

There was a time when mustard-seed jewelry was popular, and people who wore a mustard seed in a pendant or charm were fond of quoting the saying, "If you have faith the size of a mustard seed, you can say to a mountain, be moved, and it will be." But this parable of the mustard seed in Matthew says nothing at all about faith; rather, it contrasts the present state of the Kingdom and its end.

At present, the realm of God is small and ordinary, just like a mustard seed, which is tiny. But its end will be like "the greatest of shrubs," a tree. The common mustard of Palestine, *Sinapis nigra*, which can grow to about twelve feet high, is cultivated for its seed. So, the tree here is not a literal tree, but a symbol of the great kingdom. The tree represents the coming rule of God, too, in Psalm 104:12, 16-17; Daniel 4:10-12; and Ezekiel 17:23 and 31:6. The point of the parable is the contrast between the tiny present state of the God's reign and its final state.

The same is true of the parable of the yeast (13:33). Yeast is most often used in Jewish tradition as a symbol for corruption. Jesus pulls a switch here and uses yeast as a symbol for God's realm. The three measures of flour would be about ten gallons, enough bread to feed 150 people. There is an extravagant difference between the small beginning and the size of the end result. Furthermore, there is an extravagant generosity in the woman (God) who gives so much yeast to the loaf. The yeast is "hidden," just as God's realm was hidden in Jesus and his disciples. The fullness of its reality would come only in the future.

What a Surprise!

The next two parables are about surprises. A man is plowing in a field and unearths a treasure (13:44). He quickly covers it up and goes and buys the field. The pearl merchant doesn't find a treasure by accident. He knows exactly what it is he is looking for. Nevertheless, he is surprised at being able to find such a wonderful pearl (13:45-46). Both men sell everything they have in order to obtain the wonderful treasure.

Jesus wants to make two points. One is the surprise and joy at finding such a rich treasure. The other is the commitment on the part of both men. They are willing to sell everything for the sake of the treasure. That's how people should be when they discover God's realm—overwhelmed by joy and willing to risk everything for the sake of the reign of God.

Dragnet—But not Joe Friday

The net is about six feet deep and several hundred feet long. It is taken out into the lake of Galilee in boats and positioned. Then the boats begin to move toward shore, bringing the net with them. The fish are trapped in the shallow water. The fishermen can then sort them out, keeping those that are good to eat and throwing the rest back into the lake (13:47-50).

> **Think About It:** God wants us to find, recognize, and live in the Kingdom; but in some ways it is still hidden. How do you recognize signs of God's reign? What would you do to obtain the treasure in the field, or the pearl?

The point of this parable is much like that of the weeds growing among the wheat, or the separation of the sheep from the goats in Matthew 25. It has to do with judgment and separation, sorting out those "fit" for the realm of God from those who are not.

Study Suggestions

A. Compare Surprises

Read Genesis 29:15-28 and Matthew 13:44-46. Ask: What surprises did you hear in each story? What was the attitude of each person *before* the surprise? *after* the surprise?

B. Follow Up on Jacob's Surprise

Invite participants to turn loose their imaginations and their knowledge of human nature when you ask the "Think About It" questions dealing with "tension in the tent." During the discussion, add insights from the Genesis commentary. Note that this was a different culture, but that we can still learn something about family relationships from the story. Ask: How would you put what this story teaches about family relationships into a proverb?

C. Find Surprises in the Parables

Read aloud Matthew 13:44-46. Ask: If there had been a news crew around when the man bought the field and dug up the treasure, what kinds of questions would they ask? How do you think the man would respond? Invite volunteers to act out this interview. Ask: Do you think the man who found the treasure and the man who bought the pearl will be different because of their treasure? If so, how? Read "What a Surprise!" on pages

265–66. Ask: What do all these parables (including 13:31-32) teach you about God's reign?

D. Think About God's Assurance
Read Romans 8:31-39. Ask: Where do we most often hear these words? (at funerals) What is there about them that gives us comfort and security at the time of death? What if we looked at them as a promise for life? What if we said to each newly baptized infant, "Here is God's promise to you," and then read these words? Would they mean something different in that setting? What would be different?

Now read aloud Psalm 105:1-11. Ask: What are the verbs in verses 1-6? What specific actions do the verbs call us to take? How do we do these in worship and in other aspects of the life of our church?

Verses 7-11 begin a long list of *why* we should do the things the verbs call us to do. Why should we give thanks, sing, and so on? What is the reason for these actions? Do the promises made long ago still apply to us? What are some present-day equivalents?

E. Consider God's Presence
Read in unison Romans 8:28-30. Ask the questions in the "Think About It" paragraph about bad things happening to good people. Then read the commentary section "Are We Predestined?" The commentary says we are *predestined*, but that word didn't mean for Paul what it means for us. Ask: What does *predestined* mean here? What is your experience? Do you experience the freedom to make your own choices? Do you have some sense of choice in your life, or does God have it all worked out? (Allow plenty of time for persons to think through these concepts. Don't rush the thinking process.)

F. Celebrate God With Us
Read aloud Romans 8:26-27 and the opening two commentary paragraphs. Emphasize that, whatever we believe about predestination, whatever struggles and problems we face (whether it is dysfunctional family values and being cheated, as in the Jacob story, or the joy of finding a treasure in the field), God is with us. Nothing can separate us from the love of God in Christ Jesus our Lord. We may not always feel that presence, but it is always with us. (For more help, check out the book *The Will of God*, by Leslie Weatherhead, a classic in which he discusses three manifestations of God's will for our lives: God's permissive will, directive will, and intentional will.)

G. Close With Prayer
Invite members to pray silently, each person thanking God for being present in his or her life. Invite those who feel led to make or reaffirm their commitment to Jesus Christ. Hum, then sing, "God Will Take Care of You."

Lections for Sunday Between July 31 and August 6

*T*Old Testament: Genesis 32:22-31

HE Old Testament passages for the last few weeks have brought Jacob's life nearly full circle. He had fled his home after stealing the blessings rightly reserved for his brother Esau. Now he was coming back home with wives, children, servants—outwardly a prosperous man, but inwardly troubled. Soon he would meet Esau.

The Setting
Genesis 32:1-21 shows a worried Jacob. He knew he had wronged his brother, so he feared for his life and that of his family. The envoys he sent out returned saying Esau was coming to meet him—with four hundred men! As a precaution, Jacob divided his convoy into two groups, with one contingent on the front lines. His wives, children, and flocks stayed back with him. If the first line were attacked, he might escape with his family. Jacob also poured his heart out to God (32:9-12), asking God's deliverance from Esau.

Jacob sent his wives and family across a tributary of the Jordan called Jabbok (modern Zerqa), about twenty miles north of the Dead Sea on the eastern side of the Jordan. He stayed on the other side of the Jabbok that night, alone. What happened to him has been interpreted three different ways; each view contains a significant meaning.

Wrestling With God
A clear identity for the being who attacked Jacob that night is not given. Verse 24 says it was "a man"; Hosea (12:3-4) says an angel. But most interpreters have understood this to be God in the form of a man. Jacob was wrestling with God; and since both possessed great strength, neither pre-

vailed. It became apparent that this adversary was no mere man. At dawn, the "man" asked to be released. Jacob refused, unless he were blessed—once again tussling, this time for a benediction. God responded by blessing and renaming him. Like Abraham and Isaac before him, Jacob finally realized that he must trust in God rather than in his own strength and wit. The experience profoundly changed him. In fact, his new name, *Israel*, meaning "one who struggles with God," represented a new identity, one which came to characterize not only him but the people that came after him.

Wrestling With Esau

Jacob may first have thought his night visitor was Esau. When they met after a twenty-year absence, he said that seeing Esau's face was like seeing the face of God (Genesis 33:10). Jacob had clashed with his brother and then with Laban. All his life he had been a grabber and a fighter, and he had not fought fairly. Jacob's contention with Esau had left him wounded and fearful; those pains surfaced as he prepared to see his brother again.

> ***Think About It:*** Jacob's past was catching up with him. Can we ever get beyond the effects of past sins and mistakes? Even though forgiven, does the residue still take its toll? How do we come to terms with our past in order to have peace in the present and hope for the future? When in your life have you struggled over past happenings—with God, with someone else, or just with yourself? How was the struggle resolved? What brought you peace—or what do you need in order to find peace?

Wrestling With Himself

Jacob was wrestling with himself as well. His past was catching up with him. He was about to face some consequences for what he had done and who he had been—a deceiver all his life. His past, his conscience, and his fears were battling within him. Some have referred to this as Jacob's "dark night of the soul."

Psalter: Psalm 17:1-7, 15

The theme of this psalm is a plea for God's intervention or help. The psalmist is confident that God will heed his prayer because he is an innocent man and has complete trust in God.

He is making a defense of himself (which reminds us of Paul's words in the Epistle lesson). He wants God to see his innocence. Whatever is happening to him or being said about him is unfair, untrue. God can see that by looking into his heart. In this he sounds like Job. He has not taken the path of violence as others have, but has kept God's laws. He is not making a proud, boastful claim to sinlessness, only a strong defense that what his accusers are saying of him is not true. He casts himself on the mercy of the court, trusting that God will vindicate him.

Epistle: Romans 9:1-5

She had been a Christian for some time when she came to talk with her pastor. In spite of all her prayers and encouragement, no one in her family would come with her to church. She wanted more than anything to see them experience the kind of love and forgiveness she had found. Her heart was broken.

In this passage we see Paul with a broken heart at the continued unbelief of his own family, Israel. His anguish is almost beyond words.

Paul's Pain

Verse 1 seems to be a reaction to some criticism Paul had received—that is, that he seemed to be uncaring of his own Jewish people. Did this criticism come from Christians or Jews or both? We don't know. One can only imagine what Paul went through soon after his conversion. Before that he had been by his own words more zealous for the law than any Pharisee. But now he had joined the very movement

> **Think About It:** Have you ever been in a situation in which lies (or partial truths) had been told about you? How did you feel? What did you do? What insights can you glean from Paul and the psalmist in dealing with this if it should happen again?

that once he had so vigorously opposed. His Jewish friends could not have held him in too high esteem after that.

Paul makes a solemn oath here, calling on Christ, his own conscience, and the Holy Spirit to bear witness to the truth of what he's about to say. He loves his people with all his heart, feels such deep sorrow for them that he would willingly lose his own salvation if it would bring them theirs (9:2-3). One could not offer such a thing for persons one despised. To the contrary, this shows the depth of his love.

Israel and Righteousness

God's love has been poured out freely. To this point, Paul had been writing about God's righteousness and the work of the Holy Spirit that enables a right relationship with God through Christ. Paul now shifted his argument to the object of God's work: Israel, the people of God. Paul's sorrow and perhaps confusion are further compounded when he thinks about all the special blessings that have been poured out on them: "sonship" (adopted as "children of the promise"); "glory" (the presence of God dwelling among them); "covenants" (with Moses and David); "the law" (teachings of Moses); "the worship" (the Temple with its rites and rituals); "the promises and the patriarchs" (the promises made to them through their ancestors, including that of a messiah). They have been a channel through which God's mercy and grace have come into the world, especially now in Christ. Jesus Christ was the crowning glory of their heritage, something many could not see or accept.

Gospel: Matthew 14:13-21

Some children were asked to name their favorite Bible story. One little boy replied, "I like the one where everybody loafs and fishes." Apparently, so did the early church because it's the only miracle story of Jesus that is found in all four Gospels (see also Mark 6:30-44; Luke 9:10-17; John 6:1-13).

Getting Away From It All . . .

. . . is not easy. Jesus had just been informed of the death of John the Baptist (see Matthew 14:12). He sought a place to escape for a while. He and his disciples headed by boat to a quiet place across the lake, variously called Tiberias or Galilee. The crowd made their way along the shore and greeted them as they arrived. So much for getting away from it all.

Great Compassion, Small Resources

Jesus, though weary, did not send the crowd away or rebuke them. Instead, he had compassion on them. So, for much of the day Jesus taught, preached, healed, and tended to their needs. But his compassion did not stop there. It was getting late in the day, and they were hungry. The disciples came and asked him to send the people away for this very reason. They were far from any town, and finding food would not be easy. Best to call it a day.

A History Repeated

The miraculous feeding that was to come is not the only one in Scripture. Jesus would have known of the experiences of Elijah (1 Kings 17:8-16) and Elisha (2 Kings 4:42-44). Elijah asked for hospitality from a widow of Zarephath in a time of famine. Widows had few resources, even in good times; she would likely starve to death. Elijah assured her she would not die; God kept her jar of meal and jug of oil stocked until the end of the famine.

Elisha, during another famine, fed one hundred persons with twenty loaves and some fresh grain. They ate and had some left. This miracle story was part of the oral tradition of Jesus and his disciples. Jesus felt the confidence of God and of his heritage, so he told them, "You give them something to eat."

More Food in the Wilderness

Put yourself in the place of the disciples. Here they were out in the wilderness. They had barely enough for themselves. How could they possibly feed five thousand men (plus women and children)? Perhaps a revered prophet like Elijah or Elisha could pull off a miracle, but for them it seemed an impossible task. In fact, in Mark one of the disciples replies, "What do you want us to do, Jesus, take two hundred denarii (over nine months' wages for a laborer) and buy them food?"

271

Nevertheless, they came up with five barley loaves and two small fish—enough for one or two people. The loaves were about the size of a small plate and the thickness of a thumb. In John's account these were offered by a boy. Imagine standing before all those hungry people with such a meager lunch!

But Little Becomes Much

We do not know exactly what happened that day. The miracle is not explained. Jesus took the food, blessed it, then had it passed out to the people. Twelve baskets of food were left over. Regardless of how this was done or where they got the baskets, the point is that the people were fed! In the hands of Jesus even the most limited of resources can be multiplied.

> **Think About It:** When have you faced an enormous task with meager resources, only to see your fish and loaves made more than adequate for the need?

Study Suggestions

A. Open With Prayer

Begin with a bidding prayer. Read each sentence below, giving participants a moment of silence after each to pray for persons, including themselves, who may be facing these concerns.

Loving God, we ask your blessing and strength for those who are:

• struggling with God or a problem . . .
• being treated unfairly . . .
• concerned about the spiritual welfare of others . . .
• facing a great task with few resources. . . .

Close with your own prayer for wisdom and guidance in this session.

B. Reconciliation—Jacob

Jacob is a case study in the pain of broken relationships—at odds with his brother, God, and himself. He was a kind of walking civil war. Read aloud Genesis 32:22-31, and explore insights concerning how God works for reconciliation in our lives. Ask: How would you paraphrase this story, especially the part about the struggle with a stranger? Who was it that Jacob was wrestling with? What does it mean that the two wrestlers were apparently evenly matched? What is the good news in this story? the hope for healing of broken relationships? Invite volunteers to tell briefly their own stories of struggle and reconciliation. Also discuss the questions in the "Think About It" paragraph.

C. Injustice—Paul and the Psalmist

Review Romans 9:1-5 and the commentary on page 270. Ask: What seems to be at the heart of Paul's anguish? When have you felt similar pain because those dear to you have rejected the gospel? What things made Paul's people special? Is being chosen for special blessing primarily a privilege or a responsibility? What are some channels of God's grace that correspond to these for us? (A Christian upbringing, a spiritual friend, grounding in Scripture, a supportive community might be mentioned.) How are we using these gifts?

Paul and the psalmist both plead their case before God. Read aloud Psalm 17:1-7, 15. Ask: What are Paul and the psalmist each asking for? Is it ever appropriate to defend yourself before God? When might we feel a need to do that? How is it most appropriate for a Christian to respond when one is lied about or one's integrity is questioned? What should we do when we hear untruths about someone else?

Paul grieves that so many of his own people have rejected the gospel. Is it anti-Semitic to feel this way or to share the gospel with Jewish friends? How can this be done respectfully? How do we treat others who reject the gospel?

D. Inadequacy—Disciples

Read Matthew 14:13-21 and the commentary on pages 271–72. Compare the story with its parallels in the other Gospels and with the miraculous feedings by Elijah and Elisha. Discuss: What was the miracle here? How do you define *miracle*? Is it a supernatural happening? a sign from God? How is God's compassion shown in this event?

Ask members to imagine themselves in the crowd that day, then list on the chalkboard or a piece of paper the various possible reactions they might have had to what took place. (For example, some may have wanted to know Jesus better, been reluctant to share, relieved to be fed, awed by the miracle, or been anxious to get home.) Ask: Would this miracle have led you to become Jesus' follower? How does God guide us when we face hard tasks with inadequate resources? What is the good news in this story for such situations?

E. Conclusion

Ask participants to respond to these statements: What I really needed to hear in today's lesson was. . . . What I need to do as a result is. . . . End by singing "Break Thou the Bread of Life" and praying the Lord's Prayer.

Lections for Sunday Between
August 7 and 13

T Old Testament: Genesis 37:1-4, 12-28

HE Old Testament passages for today and next Sunday give us the chance to look at Joseph, one of Jacob's many sons.

Sibling Rivalry

Joseph was the eleventh son of Jacob and first-born of his favorite wife, Rachel. Jacob favored the young child, even making him an expensive coat with long sleeves (also called a "coat of many colors," 37:3), which constantly reminded Joseph's brothers that he was the favorite. The difficulty of doing hard manual labor in such a coat was probably another sign to his brothers of favoritism. Jacob had apparently forgotten the ill effects of his own father's preference for Jacob's twin brother Esau.

Besides being spoiled, Joseph was also a tattletale. He would watch his brothers shepherding and report their wrongs to his father. Add to this the dreams he had (see 37:5-11) in which he saw his brothers and even the heavens bowing down to him, and you have an explosive situation. His brothers hated him and constantly hassled him.

Searching for His Brothers

At last word his brothers were tending the flock near Shechem, an ancient religious shrine built between Mounts Gerizim and Ebal. This was a several-day journey from the valley of Hebron. But Jacob sent Joseph to see how things were going. When Joseph arrived, he discovered his brothers had moved on to Dothan, a small village north of Shechem. Shepherds had to move often to find the best grazing for their sheep. So Joseph headed toward Dothan—and danger.

274

Here Comes the Dreamer

Joseph's brothers spotted him coming from a distance; no doubt the coat helped identify him. The brothers devised a plot to kill him. When Reuben, the eldest, heard of the plan, he argued that instead they throw Joseph in a nearby cistern, a (usually) bottle-shaped pit used to collect rainwater. The narrow opening at the top would have made escape difficult, but Reuben had in mind to rescue Joseph later and return him to Jacob.

The brothers agreed to the revised plan and did the deed. They stripped Joseph of his coat and dropped him in the dry cistern, evidently content to let him starve or die of thirst. While they sat at a meal, they observed a caravan of traders at a distance. The text describes them as both Arabs, descendants of Ishmael, and Midianites, en route to Egypt.

Now brother Judah revised their plan: why not sell Joseph and make a profit from the dreamer? That way they would not have to feel guilty for slaying their brother, their own flesh. So, unbeknownst to Reuben, they sold off Joseph as a slave to the traders for twenty pieces of silver. Surely in a faraway place like Egypt they would not have to deal with him any further, his blood would not be on their hands, and they would have made a profit besides.

> *Think About It:* Favoritism and jealousy are powerful and destructive. How have you experienced them in your life? How have you dealt with them? Recall an instance among your family, friends, or congregation, when envy, factionalism, or divisiveness disrupted the harmony, trust, and sense of community that had prevailed. What was the result? How was it handled? What are similarities and differences between that situation and the rancor between Joseph and his brothers? With whom do you most identify in this story: Joseph, his brothers, or Jacob? Why? Which is most responsible for the outcome? Why? How might it have been avoided and a more positive result attained?

Psalter: Psalm 105:1-6, 16-22, 45b

This psalm is a celebration of God's great deeds on behalf of Israel. It was probably written to be used at one of the great festivals in which the reciting of God's acts would be celebrated. Perhaps it was also used to teach children and others what God had done for them. It evokes responses of praise (105:1-6) and obedience (105:45b) to the God who has done all of this and who is still active among them.

Verses 1-6 call upon the people to remember the mighty acts of God and to respond with thanksgiving, praise, and singing, honoring God's holy and wonderful name. Verse 4 is the highlight, for it tells them always to seek the presence of God and continue to entrust their whole lives to God.

Verses 16-22 go well with today's Genesis reading in that they recall God's gracious acts of deliverance through Joseph. If this psalm were written during or shortly after the Exile in Babylon, Joseph's story of being freed from slavery would have had special meaning for them. Verse 45 sums it all up: in light of all God has done, obey God's laws!

Epistle: Romans 10:5-15

Paul still has in mind the plight of his own people, which he has dealt with at length in Chapter 9. Now he takes up a point made in 9:30-31: contrasting the righteousness by the law with that given by faith.

The Law and the Gospel

Law refers, of course, to the teachings of Moses, as well as to its traditional interpretations or applications. The approach of Jewish religion in Paul's day to salvation, or becoming right with God, was based on obedience to the law. It was as if each act of obedience gave one a credit with God or tipped the scales in one's favor. Righteousness could be earned. Paul quotes from several of those teachings (Leviticus 18:5 and Deuteronomy 9:4 and 30:11-14) to show the futility of this way of relating to God.

Moses indeed had said that the one who keeps the law finds life. The only problem, Paul argues, is that no one can really do this. Only one man has ever kept the law—Jesus—and his obedience has, in fact, ended that as a way to salvation (Romans 10:4). Paul quotes other passages from the law to show that the law itself was God's free gift, easily accessible to them. They could not earn it.

> **Think About It:** Why do you think the Bible tells us to remember what God has done for us in the past? Spend time reflecting on the mighty deeds of God on your behalf.

But now God has given another and greater gift—Jesus. Also, Paul says, it was not by our effort that Christ came into the world or arose from the dead. Christ is the free gift of God. God has done for us in Christ what we could never do for ourselves, not even through works of righteousness or obedience to the law.

The way to being right with God is by faith, trust, and acceptance of God's grace revealed in Jesus Christ. This is both an outward and an inward experience. It involves believing "in your heart" in Christ and that "God raised him from the dead." It also means confessing "with your lips that Jesus is Lord," the one to whom you belong and give your allegiance.

Gospel: Matthew 14:22-33

Last week's story of the feeding of the five thousand began with, "Jesus withdrew from there" (Matthew 14:13). Today's reading likewise begins with Jesus going off to pray, then reports him walking to his disciples on the water. Jesus overcame physical hunger by multiplying the loaves and fish; now he overcomes the forces of nature by mastering the sea.

On Their Own

Jesus needed time alone for prayer, so he sent the disciples on ahead across the Sea of Galilee while he sent the crowd home (14:22). This is the first time the disciples were sent out without Jesus, and things got tough fairly quickly. By evening, they found themselves in the middle of a storm, which was not uncommon on that lake.

On a Stormy Sea

Water was a symbol of chaos in Jewish tradition. It was dangerous, frightening, and held back only by the power of God (see Psalms 18:15-19; 69:1-2). The disciples were in the midst of a dark and scary chaos. It did not look good—such a great storm and such a fragile boat.

For Matthew and his readers, this was a powerful story. The church has often been portrayed as a boat, tossed to and fro in a stormy world. The first Christians had experienced the tumult of the destruction of the Temple in A.D. 70, and the storms of oppression and persecution surrounding that. The early church, too, was a small craft trying to carry out Christ's commission in a hostile world, and it seemed they made such little progress.

But Help Was on the Way

In the latest, darkest part of the night, Jesus came walking on the sea to their aid. (The NIV says it was during the fourth watch: between 3 and 6 A.M.) The miracle was the power of God that broke forth in Jesus, a power greater than the storm and chaos. In biblical thought, only God could walk on water (see Job 9:2, 8; Psalm 77:19).

Peter—representing all disciples (then and now) in his desire to keep his eyes and his faith fixed on Jesus—wanted to meet Jesus on the water. He said, "Lord, if it is you. . . ." (Recall Satan's words to Jesus in the temptation, in Matthew 4:3, 6.) Jesus had already said, "It is I." (Recall God's words to Moses in Exodus 3:13-15.) God's power was present with them in their little boat in the person of Jesus. The message is clear: Christ is present with us when the storms come and we feel we are getting nowhere in our work for Christ.

In bidding Peter to come, Jesus shared power and authority. Peter showed great faith in setting out, but his faith wavered before the storm and wind. He began to

> **Think About It:** Storms will surely come in the form of conflict, opposition, and slow progress in our Christian walk and our work as the church. Where are you and your church right now—sailing along smoothly? facing rough waters? rowing for your lives? beyond the storm and into peaceful waters?

sink and cried out for rescue. The one of "little faith" represents all disciples who experience that mix of courage and anxiety, even with the assurance of the Resurrection. We see in this a preview of what would happen again with Peter at the arrest, trial, and death of Jesus. He would waver and once again be lifted up, but this time by the One who had himself been lifted from the dead.

Study Suggestions

A. Celebrate God's Mighty Acts

Before participants arrive, post a large sheet of paper on the wall as a graffiti board. As they enter, have them write on the board one of the "mighty deeds of God" they have experienced in their lives or in the life of their church.

Read together Psalm 105. Form groups of four persons and ask each group to write its own psalm. Encourage creativity. The psalm could be set to music, including rap, or composed in the form of poetry or free verse. Have the groups present their psalms to the whole group, and later share them with the pastor or worship committee for possible use in congregational worship.

B. Sing God's Praises

Do a hymn search and sing. Distribute hymnals, and have participants choose hymns that celebrate the deeds of God. Sing or read these together, discussing the deeds each hymn celebrates. Some possibilities are "All Creatures of Our God and King," "For the Beauty of the Earth," "God of the Sparrow, God of the Whale," and "Praise to the Lord, the Almighty."

C. Joseph and His Brothers

Read Genesis 37 quickly to get a broader picture of today's Old Testament story. Then retell the story in some creative way. You might do the presentations as drama, with members taking key parts (you don't need all ten brothers); as a readers' theater; or in an expanded paraphrase, in which one person starts the story, adds "color" in his or her own words, and then passes to the next person to pick up the narrative.

Next, discuss the human motivations at work here. Why were the brothers so disgusted that they could consider killing a member of their own family? In a society of primogeniture (inheritance to the first-born son), what did it mean for one of the youngest sons to take a primary place? The first-born would likely have the most to lose. Look back in Genesis to find out which brother was the oldest. What insight does this bring to the discussion?

Consider inviting a guest with expertise in family systems or domestic violence. Use the story of Joseph to introduce the subject of how to cope with painful family conflict.

D. Paul and the Law

Review Romans 10:5-20 and the commentary on page 276. One way to present Paul's argument is to skim through a selection of the Old Testament laws to get a sense of Paul's concern. (See Leviticus 1–5 for laws on sacrifice, Leviticus 19–20 on holiness laws, or Deuteronomy 21–25 on living in community.) These were the things they must do or not do to be right with God.

Examine Paul's argument about how salvation is effected. Ask: What does Paul tell us about salvation? If salvation is based on the gifts of belief and confession, what is the place or need for laws?

E. Sensory Bible Study

Ask members to close their eyes and think of themselves as companions in the disciples' boat. Read Matthew 14:22-33 aloud, slowly. Pause during the reading to ask participants what they see, hear, feel, smell, or taste. Conclude with Jesus calming everything, including the disciples. Ask them to share situations from their lives when they felt as they do now. What is the good news in this story?

F. Prepare a Reminder

Give each person an index card. Ask everyone to reflect on today's passages and to write a personal memo about what they most needed to hear and remember. They need not share this with others, but encourage them to keep it where it will serve as a reminder. Close in a prayer circle, inviting members to offer brief prayers in response to what they experienced and learned in this session.

Lections for Sunday Between August 14 and 20

Old Testament: Genesis 45:1-15

*J*OSEPH'S life had been like a roller coaster ride. His story resumes this week with Joseph in a position of great power and prestige in Egypt, second only to Pharaoh himself.

Joseph's Time in Egypt

Clearly a lot had happened since Joseph was sold as a slave. From his misadventures in Pharaoh's prison, Joseph had risen to a place of great influence. Part of his authority as governor was to oversee the growing and storage of grain during a time of great plenty, which he knew by divine insight would be followed by a severe famine. Joseph was reunited with his brothers during the famine.

Jacob sent ten of his sons to Egypt to purchase grain. They had to petition the governor, whom they did not recognize, for this grain. But Joseph recognized them and began to taunt them. He first accused them of being spies and imprisoned them briefly (Genesis 42). Then, identifying himself as a God-fearer, he arranged to keep one brother as security while the others returned to Canaan with the grain. They were to come back with their youngest brother, Benjamin.

Jacob could not bear to part with the only remaining son of Rachel, but the famine eventually necessitated another trip. Genesis 43–44 begins the story of this reunion, in which it appeared that Benjamin would be imprisoned as well. The dismay of Judah and his brothers sent them full circle from their idea to sell Joseph into slavery. Increasingly we see the brothers' remorse and their respect for their father.

I Am Your Brother, Joseph

Today's lection begins at the point where Joseph could not contain his secret any longer. In response to Judah's impassioned plea for Benjamin, Joseph asked for privacy and revealed himself tearfully to his astonished brothers. He first asked about Jacob. His stunned brothers seemed not to understand, so Joseph proved his words by telling them what only Joseph and they knew—that they had sold him into slavery. One can only imagine what the brothers must have felt when they heard that coming from one who had the power of life and death over them.

God's Providence

Joseph reacted quickly to soothe their fear and to complete the reconciliation between them. He did not blame or scold them, nor apologize for the ways he had toyed with them. Joseph put the whole past into the perspective of the present and the purpose of God. They had done these things to Joseph with evil intentions, but God reoriented those actions for their good (45:7-9). God placed Joseph in a position to save his family, indeed, the nation of Israel, from the famine.

Think About It: "God reoriented those actions for their good." The brothers' act had a malicious intent, but God turned it to their benefit. How would they have felt? What enabled Joseph to be so gracious? Was it just his good fortune, or did God replace bitterness with benevolence in his heart? Think of a time when you did something with the intention of hurting another, but that person, instead of retaliating, reacted with kindness and good will. How did you feel? Did the positive response take the wind out of your sails? Who is responsible for seeking reconciliation—the offender or the person wronged?

The Reunion Is Complete

Then Joseph told his brothers to go back home and return to Egypt with their father, his extended family, his servants, and all his goods, flocks, and herds for the remainder of the famine. They would be given "the best of the land" (45:18)—in Goshen, in the northeast part of the Nile Delta—an area with grass for grazing their animals. The scene ended with the brothers embracing and weeping.

Psalter: Psalm 133

This psalm is one of the "songs of ascent." The Jews, scattered in exile throughout many nations, made pilgrimages up to Mount Zion to worship in the Temple during the great festivals like Passover. Often villagers, including whole families, would travel together and sing as they journeyed. A collection of their songs can be found in Psalms 120–134.

Psalm 133 sings of the joy of family unity that extends beyond biological ties. As pilgrims who journeyed with others from their village to worship at the Temple in Jerusalem with people from many different places, they felt a profound sense of unity. They were celebrating their extended family, which only God can give.

The mention of Mount Zion in Jerusalem, and of Mount Hermon about 130 miles north, famous for its dew and snow (which fed the Jordan River) may be references to the North (Israel) and the South (Judah) being reunited. In worship they experience in God's presence their true family, their true home. Indeed, what is more pleasant to see than families and whole nations at peace and harmony with one another? This psalm, the Joseph story, and Paul's argument bring together several centuries of yearning for reconciliation and unity among the children of God.

Epistle: Romans 11:1-2a, 29-32

From much of what Paul has said in the earlier chapters concerning Israel's rejection of the gospel, one would think that now they would be rejected by God. But Paul has already categorically denied that (Romans 3:3-4). Now he expands on the theme of rejection.

The Remnant

Paul draws upon the idea of the remnant (11:4-5), which we often find in prophets like Amos. Throughout Israel's history, there had always been some, a remnant, who had been faithful to God. Joseph used this thought (Genesis 45:7) when he spoke of preserving his family from famine. Because of this remnant and God's grace, Israel is still included in God's great saving work.

In the last few readings from Romans, Paul's argument has been: God has done a great and wonderful work in Jesus Christ. Through him, all who believe and confess that he is Lord will find salvation. Some reject this gift, although his people have no excuse. As God's chosen ones, they of all people should recognize the presence of the Messiah and eagerly accept him.

Think About It: We are usually without excuse for our waywardness. How do you deal with your own unfaithfulness? with being at odds with someone close? What kind of excuses do you try to make? Do you ever feel like the remnant—someone hanging onto God's promises when others fall away? If so, how do you guard against the temptations of "holier than thou" on the one hand, and loneliness and alienation from the majority on the other?

God Extends the Covenant

Israel's hard-heartedness is of the people's own doing. If, as Paul asserts, the Gentiles can understand and embrace the gospel, then surely Israel could understand. Even so, the Jews as a people are still not rejected because God's promises and nature are faithful and will be fulfilled. In addition, God is merciful and forgives disobedience. The Gentiles to whom Paul is writing should know this better than anyone.

Paul's hearers, as Gentiles, all had at one time been disobedient as they pursued their pagan deities. But now they were included among God's people. In fact, Paul says several times that it was the disobedience of Israel that led him to take the gospel to the more receptive Gentiles. Even Israel's rejection was used by God. But Paul's hope is that Israel, now disobedient like the Gentiles once were, will also come to accept the gospel.

Gospel: Matthew 15:(10-20) 21-28

In John 6:60, the disciples say to Jesus, "This teaching is difficult; who can accept it?" The teachings and actions of Jesus are sometimes hard to understand (Matthew 15:21-28).

Character and Context

The word *dogs* was commonly used by Jews to describe Gentiles. Although most references to dogs in the Old Testament are negative, Tobit 6:2 would suggest that dogs were a common part of domestic life in Jewish households. The point of the narrative is to reflect on the historical reality of Jesus' rejection by the children of Israel and his acceptance among Gentiles. Jesus had to escape to Gentile territory for safety, and it was a Gentile woman who received him with faith. Just as Paul was mystified by the rejection of Jesus, so was Jesus surprised by the depth of the woman's faith. The paradox of Christian faith is that the last are first; the most unbelieving sometimes exhibit the greatest faith.

What Was Jesus Saying?

Did Jesus share that view of Gentiles? Are we seeing an unpleasant side of his character? Matthew says the woman shouted, but Jesus "did not answer her at all" (15:23). The disciples clearly heard her.

When he did answer, what was his tone of voice? his facial expression? Often it is not just what you say but how you say it that determines your meaning. In the prior conversation with the Pharisees, Jesus seemed annoyed, angry, exasperated. Did he continue this tone? His first remark about being sent only to Israel may have been made to the disciples. It was after this that the woman "came and knelt before him" (15:25).

283

Accepting the Challenge

What's interesting is that in verses 10-20 Jesus had just declared all foods clean. It is what comes out of the heart, not what goes into the stomach, that defiles a person, he had said. Now, in this story, he was declaring all persons clean.

A Model of Faith

This woman is often held up as a model of faith. She knew she was undeserving and made no legal claims. She came to Jesus empty handed, but full of hope and faith. She did not ask for a place at the table, only for a few crumbs from it. She asked for a dog's share. Jesus pulled out a chair and made a place for her at the table. This story describes how the outcast finds a welcome.

> **Think About It:** Look into your own soul. What is your prejudice? When and how have you looked down on someone else? What does this story tell you?

Study Suggestions

A. Psalm and Prayer

Invite members to mention relationships for which they are thankful. Read together Psalm 133 as a litany or in unison. Or, if you have a musical setting in your hymnal, sing the psalm and/or the response.

B. Meet Joseph and His Brothers

A lot has happened with Joseph between Genesis 37 (last week's lection) and Genesis 45. Form three or four teams and divide Chapters 37 to 44 among them (omitting chapter 38 that does not deal with Joseph). Ask each team to skim through its section and report briefly on the main points of the story.

Now turn to Genesis 45:1-15 and the commentary, for the completion of the reunion. Ask: What issues were important at the beginning of the story (Joseph's favored treatment, his dreams and ability to interpret them, the role different brothers played in the plot, Joseph's rise to power)? What were the twists and turns in the narrative? How did attitudes change? What obstacles had to be overcome, and how was that accomplished? How do you see the will of God unfolding throughout the story? What is the most important insight for you, and why?

C. Christians and Jews

Turn to Romans 11:1-2a, 29-32. Summarize the focus of Paul's argument that has been revealed in pieces over the past few weeks. Ask: Where does Paul's argument now take us in this passage? What is his main point? What does it mean to be without excuse? What is the intended effect on a Gentile audience of speaking about Israel this way?

Consider the potential for anti-Semitism in this passage. For many centuries there has been a strained relationship between Jews and Christians, going back to the days of Paul. He longs for his people to know and accept Christ. What portions of this passage could be used to "prove" the superiority of Christianity over Judaism? Is that Paul's intention? If not, what does he mean and what is his goal? How does Christ want us as Christians to relate to Jews?

D. Just a Few Crumbs

Set up this activity in advance by having three participants take on roles unknown to the rest of the group. Serve refreshments during the session, and have one member come late. The other two should refuse the latecomer food and a place at the table. No doubt another member (or you, if necessary), will fix a plate for the latecomer and make room. Use this little drama as a way to introduce the Gospel reading and highlight the level of inclusiveness of the church in general and your church in particular. Whom do you include? leave out? Why?

Read Matthew 15:21-28 and the commentary on pages 283–84. Be sure everyone understands the terms used and the cultural realities between Jews and Gentiles. Ask: What do you make of Jesus' initial refusal to acknowledge and help the woman? of the insulting terms and innuendoes used by Jesus and the woman? of the responses by Jesus and the woman? of the healing? Is this narrative an explanation of what happened in the church as Gentiles were welcomed?

E. Reconciliation

Summarize as a group how the readings today deal with rejection and reconciliation. Ask: What is the good news in these passages? What do they call you to do or be? Close by singing "Jesus, Lord, We Look to Thee" and praying for persons in crisis and isolation and for harmony and acceptance within the human family and Christian church.

Lections for Sunday Between August 21 and 27

T Old Testament: Exodus 1:8-2:10

HE Book of Genesis ends with the denouement of the patriarchal narrative, recording the blessings, the lineage, and the deaths of the major characters. The beginning of Exodus forwards us to a time some generations after the glorious reunion of Joseph with his family and their welcome by Pharaoh to choice land in Egypt.

From Freedom to Slavery

Many scholars believe that the Israelites were welcomed to Egypt during the reign of the Hyksos, a foreign dynasty sympathetic to Semitic people. With the rise of the nineteenth dynasty, native Egyptians under Seti I (ca. 1305–1290 B.C.) and Rameses II (1290–1224 B.C.), the fortunes of Semitic people in Egypt took a turn for the worse. The Israelites were pressed into slavery.

Enslavement addressed two problems. If the populous, free Hebrews sided with Egypt's enemies in war, it could mean disaster for Egypt's rulers. In addition, the Hebrew slaves were pressed into service building fortifications and new cities, such as Pithom and Rameses. The site of Pithom is unknown; Rameses was in the Nile delta and would become the capital. Life as a slave was brutal and oppressive, but the Hebrew population continued to increase. This was seen as evidence of God's favor.

More Drastic Measures

Pharaoh resorted to two more extreme measures. The Hebrew midwives (also including Egyptian women serving as midwives to the Hebrews) were ordered to kill infant Hebrew boys at birth. In a courageous act of civil disobedience, two named midwives refused to obey. Their explanation is a

not-so-subtle insult to the Egyptians: the Hebrew women are so healthy,
unlike Egyptian females, that they give birth before the midwives could get there.

Pharaoh's next decree involved all of Egypt in genocide. He ordered any and all of his people to cast all male, Hebrew infants into the Nile. He did this to get rid of potential male enemies and as offerings to the gods of Egypt or to the Nile itself (which was seen as a benevolent god).

More Heroic Women

As a preview of more to come, God thwarted Pharaoh's plans. Amram and Jochebed (see Exodus 6:20) of the tribe of Levi had a son and hid him as long as they could, about three months. Jochebed prepared a basket from river reeds, made it seaworthy with bitumen and pitch, and put her baby in it to float down the river under the watchful eye of her daughter Miriam (see Numbers 26:59), possibly about twelve years old.

> **Think About It:** "A courageous act of civil disobedience." Whether Shiphrah and Puah were Hebrew or Egyptian, as women associated with a slave people they had extremely low status. Yet they defied the mighty pharaoh and saved a generation of baby boys, including Moses who would later become a great liberator. Recall others who engaged in civil disobedience—Thoreau who refused to pay unjust taxes; the underground railroad that spirited slaves northward to freedom; Gandhi in India; the Norwegians who sheltered their Jewish neighbors; Martin Luther King, Jr., and the American civil rights movement. Would you have the courage to follow your conscience and refuse to observe unjust laws to serve God's justice and save lives?

Pharaoh's daughter spotted the child and rescued him. We see Miriam immediately at her side with the helpful suggestion of a nurse. At the daughter's request, Miriam returned with Jochebed, who was paid to care for her own son until he grew older and was weaned. Pharaoh's daughter adopted him and named him Moses, which in Egyptian means "beget a child," and in Hebrew, "one who draws out"—either because she drew him out of the Nile or because God used him to draw out the people from slavery. Moses went from certain death to being the grandson of the king.

Psalter: Psalm 124

This psalm is the fifth in the collection of pilgrim songs. It is a companion to Psalm 123, which is a prayer asking for God's help in a desperate situation. Now Psalm 124 sings of how God has indeed helped them. In fact, God's wondrous help in time of need is the theme of both this and Psalm 121. It was also an appropriate song to sing as pilgrims traveled, for many dangers—thieves, wild animals, bad weather, disease—lurked around them as they made their way to Jerusalem to worship.

287

The psalm falls into three sections. In verses 1-5, verse 1 is repeated in verse 2, which was the way these songs were sung. The leader would sing a verse, then the others would repeat it. These verses reminded them that they would never have made it this far without God's presence and help. Perhaps they had the Babylonian Exile especially in mind. That could well have been the end of them as a people. Instead, God helped them and brought them back home.

In verses 6-7, God's deliverance is praised. Like those who escaped wild beasts, or birds released from a trap, God has set them free. The final section, verse 8, sums up—the Creator God delivers from every snare.

Epistle: Romans 12:1-8

Using sacrificial language, Paul calls upon his readers to present their bodies, their whole selves, to God. Animals were sacrificed in Israel's past and even in the days of Paul, as they were in other religions. But, Paul says, this is not what God wants.

Present Yourselves to God

God desires not dead but "living sacrifices." This means that all we have and are belongs to God and is to be used in God's service. Why? For God's "mercies," God's countless blessings, the greatest of which is God's grace through Christ. This is our reasonable response to all God has done. This is true worship, which is more than just participating in rituals and rites. Rather, we are called to worship and serve God every day and everywhere we are. Ours is to be a faithfulness and loyalty that the world does not alter. What is changed is our personhood, transformed by the Holy Spirit into the image of Christ.

Present Your Gifts to Each Other

In verses 1-2, Paul calls us to understand who we are and what we owe to God. Now, in verses 3-8, he turns his attention to what we owe one another. There is no room for highmindedness, thinking too highly of oneself. The goal is to discern the will of God, which is all that is good, acceptable, and perfect—not our own selfish will.

> **Think About It:** Our help is in the name of God. What does this mean to us who think God helps those who help themselves? Where do you most need God's help? What may be preventing you from asking?

Nevertheless, to be a productive member of the body, neither should we think of ourselves as too lowly. Using the analogy of the well-functioning body, Paul describes a unity, an integrity to each part of the body that does its part. This includes discovering and using one's gifts in the life and work of the church. Such gifts come from God and are rightly used to honor God and serve our neighbor. Such gifts are prophecy ("forthtelling"—proclaiming—rather than foretelling the future), practical ministry (deeds of loving and giving), teaching (explaining the gospel), exhortation (encouraging and inspiring), and others. The proper use of these gifts is to build up the body of Christ and to discern and do the will of God.

Gospel: Matthew 16:13-20

Jesus had been preaching, teaching, and healing for some time. But did anyone really understand who he was and why he had come? He took his disciples aside to see how well his most intimate followers understood.

The setting for this conversation was Caesarea Philippi on the southwest slope of Mount Hermon, about thirty miles northeast of the Sea of Galilee. It was a city of great political and religious significance, especially to Rome, for a great temple to the god Pan had been built there. Perhaps in the shadow of that temple, at a place of great worldly power and leadership, the disciples would confess their belief in Jesus.

What Are Others Saying?

Occasionally, it seems that Jesus' conversations with his disciples consisted of a series of *non sequitors*. The first question was "Who do people say that the Son of Man is?" The disciples offered several candidates for that title— John the Baptizer, Elijah, or other deceased prophets. Jesus asked the second question, "Who do you say that I am?" Peter's response was, "You are the Messiah." Some scholars suggest that the answer Jesus was actually seeking was, "Jesus, you are the Son of Man." The possibility this might be the case is clear from the conversation that follows. When Jesus said that he would die and be raised from the dead (16:21), Peter sharply disagreed. He said, "This must never happen to you" (16:22). In Peter's thought, the Messiah was one who would live forever and never suffer death (Isaiah 9:7); so, if Jesus were the Messiah, how was it possible that he could die? In contrast, the Son of Man was a figure from heaven who was raised from the dead and came to earth to establish God's righteous rule.

Who Is the Messiah?

Over time, Peter's confession (16:16) has become the central element remembered from this passage. In the church, the title "Son of Man" largely fell into disuse. The beliefs associated with the figure of the Son of Man came to adhere to the title *Messiah*. For Christians, the Messiah was no longer understood as the one who lived forever but the one who died and was then raised to stand at the right hand of the Father where he waits to return on the clouds of heaven with all the holy angels (Matthew 24:30). The mighty acts of salvation God brought about in the death and resurrection of Jesus created a new understanding of the term *Messiah*.

On This Rock

Jesus blessed Peter for his insight and confession, given to him not by "flesh and blood . . . , but by my Father in heaven" (16:17). In addition to this blessing, Jesus granted great privilege and responsibility to Peter and through him, to the whole church. Peter and all who make the same confession become stones in the foundation of the church (see 1 Peter 2:4-8).

Jesus enjoyed a play on words here, addressing Peter (*Petros*) as the rock (*petra*) or foundation on which he would build the church. This building would be so powerful that not even the storms of evil could destroy it.

The Keys of the Kingdom

Peter would also hold the keys to God's realm and have power to "bind and loose." Some characterizations of heaven depict Peter as the "pearly gatekeeper," who says yea or nay to potential entrants. But the "keeper of the keys" refers to the authoritative teaching office of the church, not decisions about who enters heaven. The language of binding and loosing supports this image, since it is rabbinic terminology for authoritative teaching and interpretation of Torah, which sets boundaries for what is permitted and not permitted in the life of holiness.

> **Think About It:** The church has authority to teach what is acceptable and unacceptable in living out the teachings of Jesus the Christ. Do you accept and acknowledge this authority? How does this relate to the Protestant emphasis on the individual's right to interpret the Bible for oneself?

First Peter, then the church as a whole, inherits the responsibility to teach in the name of Christ. He and the church are charged with making decisions about how that teaching applies to and is lived out in daily life.

Study Suggestions

A. Celebrate God's Help

Lead the group in reading Psalms 123 and 124 aloud, either as a litany or in unison. Invite participants to share personal experiences of deliverance by God. Then ask for names of persons who need God's help, and pray for them silently.

B. Oppression

The birth narrative of Moses is filled with drama and heroism. Read Exodus 1:8–2:10, and ask members to identify how the characters interacted to save Moses from death as an infant. Note who is named in the

Bible text and who is not. Who are the heroes? What twists occur in the story?

Review the commentary on pages 286–87. What details make the story more alive? What level of power must the pharaoh have had if he could compel Hebrews to kill Hebrews and ordinary citizens to kill babies. Ask: What social conditions allow such use of power to exist and continue? What are some modern parallels to the pharaoh's genocidal behavior? to the midwives' civil disobedience? What can Christians do about such persecution?

Moses will figure prominently in the sessions for the next several weeks. Brainstorm and list everything participants know about Moses and his life. Post the list, and revise it week by week as new insights are discovered.

C. Living Sacrifices
Read Romans 12:1-8 in which Paul makes the case for a new way of life. Try to imagine what the original way of life must have been from which he is calling them to change. Ask: What are the parallels to your own life?

Now read the commentary on pages 288–89, and ask: How does thinking either more or less of yourself than you ought to undermine the gifts God has given you? How do we discern what gifts we have? How are they best used? Ask each member: What do you consider your gift? Then encourage the group to name each other's gifts.

D. You Are . . .
Ask group members to pretend they are being interviewed on television. The interviewer has asked, "Who is Jesus to you anyway?" What do they say? What words, images, phrases come to mind to describe Jesus?

Read aloud Matthew 16:13-20 and the commentary on pages 289–90. Just for fun, invite persons to mention their favorite cartoon or joke about Peter at the pearly gates. Then ask what it means to hold the "keys to the kingdom" and to "bind and loose." Ask: How do you understand the authority of the church to determine what is taught and allowed in accordance with the teaching of Jesus? How does this relate to freedom of thought and interpretation?

E. Summarize
The passages today deal with authority and commitment. Invite members to identify how these themes appear in each of the readings. One way to describe the radical commitment required of Christians is in the phrase "24/7"—twenty-four hours a day, seven days a week.

F. Pray
Close with a hymn like "Fairest Lord Jesus" or "My Jesus, I Love Thee," followed by prayers of praise and commitment to Jesus Christ.

Lections for Sunday Between August 28 and September 3

Old Testament: Exodus 3:1-15

MOSES was now an adult and in trouble. In the last reading, he had been saved from death as an infant; now he has killed a man. Exodus 2:11-25 fast forwards us through Moses' flight to and early life in Midian.

Moses in Midian

The land of Midian is just east of the Gulf of Aqaba, which is part of the Red Sea. Midian was one of Abraham's sons by Keturah, whom he took as a wife some time after Sarah died (Genesis 25:1-6). The Midianites were nomadic, making their living by raising sheep and goats. Moses had met and married Zipporah and now tended the flocks of his father-in-law, Jethro. Other sources identify Jethro as Reuel (Exodus 2:18) or Hobab (Judges 4:11). Jethro was a priest, a religious leader among his people, and probably a worshiper of YHWH. Perhaps he provided vital guidance in leading Moses back to his spiritual roots. Maybe he even suggested that Moses take his flocks near the holy mountain.

Moses and the Burning Bush

Moses led the flock "beyond the wilderness" to "Horeb, the mountain of God," also called Sinai. We do not know its exact location. The traditional site is in the southern part of the Sinai peninsula and is called Jebel Musa (Mountain of Moses). Moses saw what seemed to be a fiery bush that was not consumed. This was God's way of getting his attention. But what he saw was not as important as who spoke to him.

The voice called to Moses, and he answered, not knowing who spoke. Moses was told to come no closer and to remove his sandals as a sign of reverence and respect, as Muslims do even today when entering a mosque.

292

The Voice Revealed

"I AM" spoke to Moses as "the God of your father, the God of Abraham, the God of Isaac, and the God of Jacob" (3:6). To Moses' forebears YHWH had been revealed and had made a covenant. Having seen the misery of the Israelites, God announced plans to deliver them from their taskmasters. God's messenger would be Moses, who would return to Egypt in the name and authority of the God of their ancestors. YHWH was going to fulfill the covenant. Moses was reconnected to his spiritual roots.

Moses' Commissioning

Moses felt inadequate for the task and offered several excuses for why he could not do this (see also Exodus 3:16–4:17). But God met each excuse. In fact, this deliverance could already be considered a done deal (3:12). Moses would one day bring the people back to this very mountain to receive the law and be bound in covenant to this same YHWH.

And how would Moses explain who sent him? God gave the cryptic answer, "I AM WHO I AM." We sometimes Anglicize these four Hebrew letters, YHWH, spelling and pronouncing them as "Yahweh," which can mean "I am what I am" or "I will be what I will be." But this could be an affront to our Jewish friends, who believe the name of God should remain unpronounced. In any case, the God who met Moses was the One who had the power to do what Moses was called to declare to Pharaoh: free the Hebrew slaves.

> **Think About It:** The letters YHWH ("I AM WHAT I AM") emphasize the mystery and austerity of a distant and powerful God. The name *Abba, or* ("Daddy"), which we encountered several weeks ago in Romans 8, emphasizes an intimate, loving God. Both are aspects of the God we worship. At what times are you addressed by YHWH? When do you feel close to Abba? What other images of God are meaningful to you?

Psalter: Psalm 105:1-6, 23-26, 45c

(Refer to the readings for the Sunday between August 7 and 13, where portions of this psalm are also discussed.) Today's verses remind the congregation of the enslavement of the Israelites in "the land of Ham" (verse 27). Ham was one of Noah's sons, traditionally viewed as the father of the nations of northern Africa, Canaan, Arabia, and Mesopotamia (Genesis 10:6).

The reference to God's blessings through Jacob, Moses, and Aaron, connect us to the Exodus reading today. The people could not but look back with gratitude to the courageous and very human leaders God provided just when they needed them. This gave hope that God would continue to provide for and protect them.

Epistle: Romans 12:9-21

Paul continues his commentary on the new life in Christ by offering a series of moral guidelines and attitudes for everyday living:

Ten Rules for Christian Life

- Love sincerely with a love that is real, without hypocrisy or selfish motives. Hate evil and love good; work against evil and for good (12:9).

- Be affectionate: love one another as brothers and sisters in God's family and show honor. Be happier to give honor and credit to others than to receive them (12:10).

- Be zealous, enthused about your faith; and don't give in to lethargy. Serve God; use every opportunity to render service (12:11).

- "Rejoice in hope." Have a positive attitude; remember God is in control. Suffer in patience; meet troubles with the confidence that Christ is with you. Pray always; stay in close communion with God (12:12).

- Share with those in need; become hooked on giving, not getting. Show hospitality; always keep your home open to persons in need (12:13).

- Pray for and bless those who hurt you—a reminder of the words of Jesus to meet persecution with prayer and not retaliation, for this is the example Christ set (12:14).

- Feel one another's joy and pain; be so close to one another that you share one another's ups and downs (12:15).

- Live in harmony with one another; always work for peaceful relationships. Avoid pride, for that brings discord. Be friends to everyone, even the lowliest person, for this is the example Christ sets. Be modest; don't claim to be smarter than you are (12:16).

- Be fair and just, setting a good example for all to see. Live at peace with all people, as far as it is in your power to do so. Never take revenge; justice belongs to God (12:17-19).

- Respond to your enemies with kindness and practical concern (12:20-21).

Words of Wisdom

Paul made only one direct reference to the specific teachings of Jesus, although his writings are consistent with the message of the Gospels. In this fairly self-explanatory and terse list of advice, two points deserve further mention:

> ***Think About It:*** Reflect on the virtues Paul lists (page 294). Which ones did you especially need to hear? Which ones do you feel describe your actions and attitudes?

- The comments from verses 17 through 21 point to the final authority of God in matters of justice. If one really does bless those who curse and persecute, perhaps these further comments are moot. But human nature being what it is, Paul reminds his readers that there is no virtue or satisfaction in revenge or retribution.

- This brings Paul to another important point: heaping burning coals. In ancient Egyptian culture, a bucket of hot coals would be brought to the forehead of a penitent to symbolize a purified and repentant mind. Paul alludes to this practice to indicate that genuine love moves us toward repentance and forgiveness, not vengeance and punishment.

Gospel: Matthew 16:1-28

This passage marks a turning point in Jesus' life. Peter had just confessed that he was Christ, the Messiah. Peter, and subsequently the church, had been given authority to proclaim the teachings of Jesus and to interpret them for the good of the whole community.

A Sad Prediction

Now the tone turned somber. Immediately Jesus explained what kind of a messiah he would be—a suffering one. Verse 21 is the first of four such predictions (see also 17:22-23; 20:17-19; 26:2). What a mood swing! One moment the disciples were thinking of power and the coming of God's reign, and the next they heard that Jesus was going to Jerusalem to be arrested, tried, and crucified! Matthew gives no reason here why Jesus must die. But later, in 20:28, it is explained as part of the divine plan: the Son of Man had come to be "a ransom for many." From this point on Jesus would be helping the disciples understand and prepare for this.

Peter's Response and a Rebuke

Peter once again spoke for them all, saying they did not want to hear that kind of talk. This was not the kind of messiah they had in mind. They wanted a Son of David, not a Son of Man; a warrior, not a wounded healer; a leader to overthrow the Romans, not a Prince of Peace.

This was exactly the kind of power-driven messiah that Satan had tempted Jesus to become at the beginning of his ministry. And this is why Jesus said to Peter, "Get behind me, Satan!" In the words of Peter, Jesus heard that not-so-subtle call to be what everyone else wanted him to be—a military messiah rather than the suffering servant God called him to be.

The Cost of Discipleship

Moreover, not only would Jesus suffer; anyone who followed him should expect the same. That must have dismayed them. Yet, if Jesus were to be a servant, even to the point of giving up his life, how could they expect a different role for themselves? In a day of easy religion that promises to solve all our problems, these words speak clearly to us: "If you are to follow me, deny yourself and take up a cross." As someone has said, if we are to be true disciples of Jesus, we had better look good on wood!

Victory Assured

In time God would make it clear that this was not a defeat but a great victory. The Son of Man would be vindicated, as would his faithful followers. Those who would lose (give) their lives—physical, spiritual, or both—for Christ's sake would find (gain) them. Without a life in him, Jesus told them, there really was no life.

Matthew then speaks of the coming of the Son of Man—Christ's triumphant return to fully usher in God's reign. This will be an occasion of vindication and reward for the faithful: "He will repay everyone for what has been done" (16:27). Some will still be alive to see these things. What things? Some say this refers to the Transfiguration, which would occur right after this. Others think he means the Resurrection, still others Pentecost. Some say the reference is to the return of Christ, although the problem with this is that it did not happen in their lifetime.

> **Think About It:** Jesus said he would suffer and die on the cross, and his followers must be willing to take up their own cross. Was it necessary for Jesus to die as part of God's plan? What does it mean for you to take up your cross? What is the challenge of discipleship for you right now?

Study Suggestions

A. Begin With Praise

Sing a hymn of praise, such as "Praise to the Lord, the Almighty" or "Joyful, Joyful, We Adore Thee." Then read together Psalm 105:1-6, 23-26, 45c. Ask: What does it mean to praise the Lord? How do we do that? For what would you like to praise God from this past week? Then lead a prayer of praise and thanksgiving for the things they have mentioned.

B. Moses, Meet God

Locate Midian on a Bible map to see how far it is from Egypt and where it is in relation to Palestine. How far did Moses travel? Skim through Exodus 2:11-25 to recall why Moses was on the run. Invite participants to imagine how the many twists of Moses' life may have affected him—from being raised as royalty, being among but above his own kin, killing someone, fleeing for his life, becoming a shepherd (a lowly occupation), then receiving God's call in such an unexpected and spectacular way. Add these learnings to the list started last week.

Read Exodus 3:1-15 and the commentary on pages 292–93. Ask who has seen one of the epic Bible movies that showed Moses at the burning bush and what impression it made. Ask: If a movie were made of your encounters with God, what would be your "burning bush"? (Point out that valid encounters come in many forms and need not be so dramatic.) What excuses did Moses offer to avoid God's call? Have you tried to excuse yourself from God's claims on you? What would be the most compelling self-description God could offer you? Also discuss the questions in the "Think about It" paragraph.

C. Christian Virtues

Read Romans 12:9-21 and the commentary on these words of advice from Paul. Divide into pairs, assigning each twosome either to search the hymnal for hymns that expand on one or more of the themes (and sing a few if they wish) or create a poster to illustrate one or more of the themes. After they have shared their work, invite the group to identify which of these words of advice are the easiest and which the hardest for them to keep. How can you help each other to observe these guidelines for Christian living?

D. Count the Cost

Read aloud Matthew 16:21-28. Try to imagine the emotional turmoil the disciples must have experienced. They have found the Messiah (Hallelujah!), but he says he will suffer and die fairly soon. (Please, God, no!) And if they are serious disciples, this may be their future as well. (Who, me?)

Read the commentary and ask: Why did Jesus liken Peter to Satan? Even with the benefit of two thousand years of hindsight, do you think you would have done any differently than Peter?

Ask: What does it mean to take up your cross? What does it mean to deny ourselves? What does it cost to follow Jesus? Do we sometimes misunderstand Jesus or try to recast him and his teachings more to our own liking?

E. Close With Prayer

Ask members what insights from the session were most important and why. Then close with prayer for courage to be faithful disciples.

Lections for Sunday Between
September 4 and 10

Old Testament: Exodus 12:1-14

*J*EWS, Christians, and Muslims ground their faith in the acts of God in history. Furthermore, for both of us, worship is essential—it helps define who we are. Worship, however, means more than singing a few songs, saying a prayer, and hearing a sermon. Worship means we re-enter and re-create the memories that make us who we are. It means we are willing to submit ourselves to the power of that memory, to set aside our rationalism and skepticism, and to become part of the people who have lived by that memory for generations. The acts of worship must allow children to participate in a meaningful way and help them understand what the celebration means and why it calls us to action.

Do This in Remembrance . . .

This lection from Exodus is about the Passover, both as the original event and as the model for celebration in the future. In order to be saved from the final plague, the community is to follow specific procedures. There has to be a certain kind of food—roasted lamb, bitter herbs, unleavened bread. There has to be a certain kind of blood—from the lamb sacrificed for the feast. Among the poor, where a lamb is a significant part of a family's capital, the lamb can be shared. The key is that every person in the faith community has access to a lamb, to the symbols for the feast, and to the memory.

The Memory Means . . .

Not only are there specific directions for the food but also for how the meal is to be eaten. The people must be dressed and shod, with staff in hand—ready to "hit the road" at any minute. The drama about the meal re-enacts the memory that leaving Egypt is a dangerous business; people are tense, edgy, and afraid. Will they actually be allowed to go? What awaits them beyond the door of the house where they are safe from death? Will God really save them?

Verses 12-13 connect the blood with the Exodus. The angel of death would "pass over" the houses marked by blood. The blood of the lamb had become a symbol that publicly marked those who were protected by God from the swath of death that passed through Egypt. (This helps explain why the early Jewish

> **Think About It:** "The drama . . . re-enacts the memory." In the Christian tradition, what formative events in our history help to form our identity? What celebrations keep the memory of our faith alive? How do we prepare for them? What physical elements are required? Which are most meaningful to you? How do the elements evoke memories of the event?

Christians, steeped in this kind of symbol and memory, would speak of Jesus' saving power as "the blood of the lamb.")

Judgment Upon All

Verse 12 says that YHWH would also judge the gods of Egypt. That was new. In all the other plagues, judgment fell on Pharaoh, the oppressor. Now the story acknowledged the gods of Egypt, though it regarded them as powerless. Behind Pharaoh's power and acts of oppression was a theological foundation—a god who sanctioned violence and oppres-

> **Think About it:** "A god who sanctioned violence." Did YHWH also sanction violence and oppression? What was the difference between YHWH and the gods of Egypt? Do you think our God sanctions violence? Why or why not?

sion and who had to be judged along with the people who actually practiced oppression. There is always a tight connection, even if it is unspoken, between theology and *real politik.*

Psalter: Psalm 149

This is a song about God's rule in the lives of people, one of five hymns of praise that end the Psalter. It was written around the time of the Exile (587–529 B.C.) and indicates a shift in thinking for Judah. Before the Exile, Judah held to a "royal theology," which said that the descendants of David who ruled Judah were responsible for bringing about God's rule in the world. This psalm has moved beyond that idea. There is no son of David on the throne. The destruction of Jerusalem and the Exile have ended that dynasty and the hopes that were invested in it. Now, the psalmist says, *all* God's people are responsible for bringing about God's rule. The *people,* not the king, are called to establish justice.

What is the role of vengeance in this psalm? Can vengeance belong to God's rule? It sounds like getting even, at least to us. But in the psalms, vengeance almost always serves the cause of justice. God's people can't just get even for the sake of revenge. Their actions must serve the cause of justice for the poor and oppressed and are the sole basis for the use of force.

Verses 6-9 invite God's people to join God at work in the world. That work is justice and righteousness. To work with God will invite opposition, which may explain the military imagery.

Epistle: Romans 13:8-14

The context of this lection is the question of obligations to the state—issues like paying taxes, doing military service, and respecting officials. Paul says essentially not to get in a position where you owe anything to anyone. Get rid of all those obligations the old-fashioned way: pay them! Pay your taxes, show respect where it is important. But there is one debt we can never discharge—the obligation to love. When we have taken care of all other obligations toward our neighbors, we still owe them love.

Love Fulfills the Law

Verses 8b-10 remind us that the commandments about relationships with one's neighbor are fulfilled in love. If we truly love our neighbor, we will not murder, steal, commit adultery, covet, lie, or dishonor our parents—or anyone else. Neighbors come in all shapes and relationships.

> **Think About It:** Love is the ultimate authority. What obligates us? How well do we love our neighbor? In concrete terms, what does loving a neighbor look like?

Paul reminds us that love is not something we grit our teeth and push ourselves to accomplish, such as being great friends with an obnoxious colleague. Trying harder doesn't make the grade here. Love is something we receive and pass on. Love is a gift of God's grace, poured out on us in Christ. It is the sure power and presence of the Spirit at work in our lives.

Be Prepared

A crisis was coming—the *parousia*, the second coming of Christ. When Paul wrote this letter, the church still clung to the hope that Christ would return at any minute. That is why he could say that salvation was nearer at hand than when he had first believed. Because Christ's return was so near, there was a sense of urgency about how Christians related to their neighbors.

Christians belong to a new order, one related to the day that shows signs of breaking. There is an old saying that "the reign of God has dawned. It is not yet full noon, but the sun is rising." In the light of that new day, Paul says, we are called to live as citizens of heaven, not as persons with special

300

privileges, but with special responsibilities for spreading God's love through all the world.

Gospel: Matthew 18:15-20

These verses are a part of what has been called the "sermon on the church," a section dealing with how the Christian community conducts its life. It is based on Jesus' teachings but reflects the needs of Matthew's church and their guidelines for congregational life. This passage asks how the church deals with unrepentant sinners who are disrupting the life of the church. We don't know anything about the background of the sin or the sinner, nor how the life of the church was being disrupted. We do know that Matthew was clear on how the church should handle the situation. There were three steps.

The Process of Discipline

• Step one (verse 15). Have a private conversation. The injured party must initiate it. The offer of grace and forgiveness must come from the one who is wronged. Conversation must be private to avoid embarrassment. The person may not even know he or she has offended. (Based on steps two and three, however, we can guess the person did know and was not repentant.)

• Step two (verse 16). If that doesn't work, take a couple of members along as witnesses and repeat the conversation. Both sinner and injured party need a fair hearing and a reliable report on what was said. This step reflects a long-standing Jewish practice of reconciliation in the synagogue. Matthew was written for a Jewish-Christian community where this practice would have been familiar.

• Step three (verse 17). If the sinner remains unrepentant, take the issue to the entire congregation. Then, if their pleas are ignored, the sinner is expelled. This is a rare glimpse into the discipline of Matthew's congregation and a look at some serious tough love. The *community as a whole* is concerned with the ethical behavior of the *individual*. So the community takes action in a spirit of love, without which the action is only punitive with no redemptive value.

Support and Accountability

First, the community lovingly talks to the sinner and asks for change. If the person refuses, the community has no choice but to take action to maintain the church's holiness. It is also necessary to shock the sinner into realizing the seriousness of his or her action and to becoming open to repentance and restoration.

> **Think About It:** How do we deal with sin in the church? Do we confront sinful action boldly and lovingly? Or do we try to ignore it? Why?

We may have trouble understanding this procedure. For us, sin is an individual matter. *It's not the community's business,* we may say; *it's between the individual and God.* But, Matthew reminds us, it *is* the community's business. What is at stake is the integrity of both the gospel and the church. If the community shuts its eyes to sinful behavior, the witness of the entire body is affected. Indeed, this kind of action has God's approval. Jesus granted authority to the church to forgive and retain sins in Chapter 16; in this passage, we see how the authority was regularized for institutional practice.

Penance

In the early church, penance was a serious matter. Penitents made public confession in the worship service and were forced to leave before the celebration of the Lord's Supper. This had to be painful and embarrassing for both them and the congregation. But out of the pain and shame of both individual and community came restoration, healing, and a deeper sense of community.

> **Think About It:** "It is the community's business." What does it mean for the church today to take responsibility for "forgiving or retaining" sins? How do we become accountable to one another?

Study Suggestions

A. Move From Event to Worship

Read Exodus 12:1-14 and the first paragraph of the commentary (see page 298). Ask: How is Israel to keep alive the memory of God's saving act in the Exodus and the Passover? What do we Christians do in the way of worship/celebration to celebrate the memory of God's acts? Do the traditions still keep alive the memory, or do we have the traditions without the memory? What physical elements help us keep the memory of God's acts alive? What is there about our worship that would cause children to ask, "Why do we do this? Why is this different from other days?"

Ask: What have we learned about how God builds community? List the responses.

B. Reflect on Debts

Read aloud Romans 13:8-14 and the commentary on page 300. Ask: How are the commandments fulfilled in love? How does the way we deal with obnoxious neighbors either fulfill or not fulfill the commandments? What does it mean that love is the ultimate authority? To what new order do Christians belong?

Add responses to these questions to the list begun in Activity A.

C. Make the Past Present

Read Psalm 149 and the commentary on pages 299–300. Ask: How does the psalm invite God's people to join God in working for justice in the world? What does our congregation do to help bring about justice in the community and world? (Distinguish acts of mercy, such as feeding persons who are hungry, visiting the sick, and conducting services in prison, from acts of justice, like examining how our economy creates and tolerates hunger, working for a system of national health care, and protesting police brutality.)

Add these responses to the list of how God builds community.

D. Explore Sin and Forgiveness

Read Matthew 18:15-20 and the commentary on page 301–302. Ask: What steps does Matthew recommend we follow when someone in the church sins and is not repentant? What stake does the community have in the behavior of an individual? We tend to think of sin as individualistic— between a person and God. What could be at stake for our community in issues of sin and forgiveness? Think of an instance when the behavior of an individual caused dissension or embarrassment to the congregation. Was Matthew's procedure followed? Might it have been useful?

Remind the group that Matthew's procedure was meant for dealing with sinners who were unrepentant. The problem we face most often is that sinners are too ashamed even to come to church. How do we reach out to them and restore them to the fellowship of the church? What steps could we take? Add responses to the list of ways God builds community.

E. Do a Roleplay

Select a situation in which an individual has committed a wrong that has offended church members—like being arrested for drunk driving, having an affair, acting without board approval, or teaching something of which others disapprove. Divide into two groups, one to prepare and present a roleplay in which this person is dealt with in the typical way your church handles conflicts, the other to confront the person following Matthew's procedure. Discuss: Which procedure was more effective? Why? How might our church improve the way we handle such situations?

F. Celebrate Community

Review the list the class developed during the session. Ask: What can we work on to help build community in our congregation? Close by singing "Where Charity and Love Prevail"; then read Psalm 149 in unison.

Lections for Sunday Between September 11 and 17

T Old Testament: Exodus 14:19-31

THE story of the crossing of the *Yam Suph* (the Sea of Reeds) is filled with nice dramatic touches. Note (verses 19-20) that the angel of God went before and behind, like divine Secret Service agents protecting the President in a crowd. The cloud also surrounded Israel like a protective screen. God's guardianship of God's people is extravagant!

Moses and YHWH drove back the water and created a dry path on which Israel could walk. Not only did the water get pushed out of the way, but the seabed dried up so Israel could walk on it. And notice—when the Egyptians reached the seabed, the chariot wheels bogged down in the mud. In some ways, this action suggests the separation of the dry land from the sea in the Creation account. God was providing another gift of creation, of life for God's people.

Why were the Egyptians destroyed? The escaping Hebrew slaves were on foot. The arrogant Egyptians followed in heavy war chariots. They were too proud to go on foot, and their pride led to their own destruction. This part of the story includes the confession on the part of the Egyptians that YHWH, who was fighting for Israel, was more powerful than they and their gods. YHWH was glorified.

Epilogue

This marks the end of the Exodus story. From here we move into the wilderness. But before we leave the sea, we look once more at the waters that so recently had been divided by the power of YHWH. Everything had returned to normal, except for all the dead Egyptians, dead horses, and broken chariots floating in the water. The statement, "Not one of them remained" (14:28), echoes the comment on the plagues. When God removed the scourge, none of it remained.

Israel saw all that destruction and realized that they were safe. And they *feared* YHWH. *Fear* here probably carries some connotation of "being afraid of," but it also means they reverenced and worshiped YHWH. They now knew that God could—and would—do for them what they could never do for themselves. They were free at last! Egypt could not do anything more to them. They believed YHWH's promises. They also believed in Moses. For the first time, they put their doubts aside and trusted Moses' leadership.

> **Think About It:** "They were free at last!" The burden of slavery had been lifted! Under divine guidance Moses had led them out of bondage. This story has been the inspiration for many liberation movements throughout history. It shows God on the side of the oppressed, overturning the mighty, actively working in history for the cause of freedom. Do you believe God works in history? If so, on whose side? Who are some leaders who have worked with God to liberate people from bondage? How does God continue to lead the oppressed to freedom?

So What Does It Mean?

When we reflect on this story, "How?" is the wrong question to ask. A better question is "Why?" Why did this happen? To that question the answer is clear. It happened to show the liberating power of YHWH and to call Israel to faith. The power of YHWH was clear; God "gained glory" over Egypt, that is, over the forces that oppressed and threatened God's people. The struggle was about power—the power of Pharaoh's injustice against the power of God. Glory belonged to the victor. Victory is an important theme in Scripture, and here we see it for one of the first times. The story is also about faith, about trusting the power of God in the face of one's enemies.

Psalter: Exodus 15:1b-11, 20-21

This lection includes the song of Miriam (15:20-21) and part of the song of Moses. Both are very old. The oldest Israelite poem in Scripture is the song of Miriam. It may have been a spontaneous composition at the time of the crossing of *Yam Suph*. The core theme, stated in the first line of both songs, is the victory of God who threw horse and rider into the sea. God has overcome the power of oppression. With the story comes dancing, which became a key part of the liturgy in Israel. The song of Miriam is the ultimate expression of Israel's faith. YHWH had triumphed!

We may have problems with the song's military images, but we need to remember such images are also a part of our own tradition. The "Battle Hymn of the Republic," for example, is a song of praise couched completely in military imagery.

Epistle: Romans 14:1-12

Who were the persons who were weak in faith? In the Roman church, they may have been persons seeking righteousness apart from the gift of God's grace. Or, persons who ate only vegetables may have been members of a sectarian group, such as the Essenes (the people of the Dead Sea Scrolls) or another ascetic Christian group. Or, as vegetarians, they may have been concerned about "eating meat offered to idols." In the ancient world, pagan temples were also the city butcher shops. Meat not used in sacrifices to the gods was sold to the public. Some Christians had scruples about eating this meat, because it likely had been offered to an idol.

Dealing With Scruples

In any case, Paul is speaking here about the practical implications of Christian love. The situations described put love to the test within the Christian community. What does the church do with these scruples about eating? This is a serious question for the people involved. The ground for tolerance is grace. God has welcomed these persons; they are baptized Christians. And we are called to welcome such as well. None of us can pass judgment on another—and persons with scruples will be able to stand because of Christ's presence in their lives. Verse 5 raises the same issue in connection with determining the day for sabbath or for fasting.

The key is in verses 5-9: We are all different. We worship in different ways, respond to Christ differently, and follow different lifestyles. But each of us is convinced that what we do fits our relationship with Christ. No one thinks he or she is deliberately violating that relationship. We all belong to Christ.

> **Think About It:** We all have scruples of some kind. How do we accept people who have different standards? who have a different understanding of what it means to be in relationship to Christ? who may judge us as less faithful than they?

The Temptation to Judge

Therefore, Paul asks (verses 10-12), how can we possibly judge one another? The temptation of the strong and free (who eat meat, for example, because they know pagan gods aren't real) is to look down on those with scruples. The temptation of the weak, who have scruples and do not feel as free, is to judge those who take liberties. Paul says that we all belong to Christ. We are accountable to him, not to each other. We must accept and trust each other.

Gospel: Matthew 18:21-35

Today's Gospel lection follows the previous teaching in Matthew on church discipline. Verses 21-22 show us how to be accountable without becoming mean or vindictive. Only a congregation that forgives seventy-seven times (that is, as often as necessary) can maintain accountability.

> *Think About It:* Accountability is derived from forgiveness. Isn't that contradictory? How is accountability linked to forgiveness? Without forgiveness, how is it possible to be accountable?

A Lesson in Forgiveness

The story shows Peter thinking he was being magnanimous. "Should I forgive as much as seven times, Lord?" Peter's willingness to forgive seven times would cancel out Lamech's threat of sevenfold vengeance in Genesis 4:24. Imagine Peter's surprise when Jesus told him he had hardly begun to forgive. The point of Jesus' comment and the story that follows is not the numbers, but that whoever keeps score hasn't forgiven at all. Christian forgiveness goes far beyond counting.

Only someone who has been greatly forgiven understands how important this story is. The first servant, a minor official to the king, was really in trouble. Either he had mismanaged what the king had entrusted to him, or he had not fulfilled a contract to raise taxes from subject nations. Now he owed an unrealistic amount of money.

That's a LOT of Money!

The talent was the largest monetary unit in the first century, equal to the wages of a manual laborer for fifteen years. Ten thousand was the largest number at the time. So the combination is the largest possible sum that could be owed—an inconceivable amount. To put that in perspective, the tax revenue for all Herod the Great's considerable territories was nine hundred talents a year. And Herod was incredibly wealthy. How could one ever pay a sum that was infinitely larger?

Clearly, the debt was unpayable; the man's situation was helpless. Jew or Gentile at that time could be imprisoned for debt, but Jews could not be tortured. Even working a lifetime as a free man would not avail. All this poor official could do was beg for mercy. To his great amazement, the king was magnanimous. The servant received mercy; his debt was forgiven.

Not So Much, by Comparison

The debt the servant's subordinate owed him was insignificant by comparison. There was an almost infinite contrast between the two. If this debt were collected, the first servant would have 1/600,000th of what he owed! Still it was an honest debt. It was a pretty good sum, but it could be repaid. This second servant did just what the first had done—he asked for mercy, but not for the debt to be forgiven. He was perfectly willing to pay it. All he asked for was a little patience, until he could get the money together.

The first servant was *not* forgiving. He had his fellow servant put in prison (thus eliminating any hope of payment). His action was so reprehensible that

307

his fellow servants reported him to the king. In a fit of righteous wrath, the king unloosed his anger on the unforgiving servant. Not only did he reinstate that huge debt, he ordered the man tortured until the debt was repaid (though there would be no chance that it could be). That meant a lifetime of torture.

> **Think About It:** Can we lose God's forgiveness if we don't forgive in turn? Is God's forgiveness conditional?

What is the point? The sure evidence we know we are made righteous by the grace of God rather than our own effort is our willingness to forgive persons who have wronged us. If we fail to forgive others, we lose God's forgiveness.

Study Suggestions

A. Power, Faith, and Victory

Begin by reading Exodus 14:19-31 and the commentary on pages 304–305. Ask: What is happening here? List responses on chalkboard or a sheet of paper in rough chronological order. Ask: What did God do in this story? What did Moses do? Did they need each other? (Moses needed God, and the story suggests that God chose to need Moses.) What are some amazing details in this story?

Remind the group that God parted the sea and caused it to come crashing back on the Egyptians. As the commentary points out, the crucial question is not *how*, but *why* God did this. What does this say about God's power and purpose? about the destruction of some people for the salvation of others? about how and to what end God works in history?

Ask: What have we learned here about faith and works? List responses on the chalkboard or paper.

B. A Song to the Lord

Read Exodus 15:1b-11, 20-21. This couplet (20-21) is the oldest Hebrew poetry in existence. Ask: What do you think about how the Israelites celebrated this triumph of God? Does the song seem like honorific praise? gloating? something else? Is there any comparable situation in the world where we could sing a similar song? How would we know the victory was God's? Does God take sides? Who are the vanquished? the victors? What was the price of victory?

C. Explore Some Practical Issues

Read Romans 14:1-12 and the commentary on page 306. Ask: What was the situation here? What was going on in the church that put love to the test? What do these issues have in common? (They were setting up some persons as different from the majority.) Who are those "weak in faith"?

308

Ask: Whom do we single out as different? What tests love in our relationships with those people? What is our attitude toward those with different religious practices than ours?

Read again verses 5b-9. Ask: In all our differences in the church, what do we have in common? (We belong to Christ.) What are the practical implications of belonging to Christ? (We dare not judge one another.) Discuss the temptations of the "strong" and the "weak" to judge. Do these generalizations seem accurate? What is the effect of carrying these judgments to some conclusion, in terms of behavior toward the other?

Ask participants to sit quietly and think about how we see judging and despising in the life of our church.

D. Seventy Times Seven

Read Matthew 18:21-22 and the commentary on pages 306–308. Discuss the questions in the first "Think About It" paragraph. Then ask: Are the numbers important for forgiveness? Can you imagine keeping score to nearly five hundred times? What do the numbers really signify? What makes it difficult to forgive?

Now read Matthew 18:23-35. Unpack the details: the valuation of the debts, the extent of the king's wrath, the possibilities for punishment and repayment of the debts. Ask: With whom do we identify in this story? Why? Why was the king so angry? Do we forfeit God's forgiveness if we don't forgive? Can we forgive like God does? Invite members to share their experiences with forgiveness.

Ask: What have we learned here about faith and works? Add responses to the list.

E. Celebrate Us and God

Reflect on the list of responses about faith and works. How do they enrich your relationship with God? Read Exodus 15:20-21 aloud together. Then sing "Come, Ye Faithful, Raise the Strain." Close with prayer asking God for help in forgiving, not judging one another.

Lections for Sunday Between
September 18 and 24

Old Testament: Exodus 16:2-15

*B*UT what have you done for me this week? This question is not new; the Hebrews under Moses' leadership asked the same thing. Just a few weeks after rejoicing over their escape from Egypt and singing Moses' (and God's) praises, the Israelites were fearfully complaining of their discomfort in the wilderness.

You're Going to Kill Us!

The wilderness was a place of hunger and death. In the Sinai peninsula food and water were in short supply. Egypt, on the other hand, was a place where there had been bread and meat. Israel had already forgotten the hardships of slavery and remembered only that there had been enough food to eat. They had paid a high price for it (their freedom), but their physical needs had been met. In this story, God once again provided. Israel would learn to rely on YHWH for food, so they would not fall back into slavery.

In verses 4-12, YHWH answered the complaint directly: there would be bread from heaven. When the Israelites first saw the flakes on the ground, they asked, "What is it?" (They called it *man hu,* or manna.) The provision of quail satisfied their yearning for meat. YHWH provided the food, but there was a price, even there. The people must trust YHWH for their food. They were not to gather any more than they could eat in one day. There would always be more tomorrow. This was literally a "give us this day our daily bread" situation. Israel could gather double on the sixth day, so there would be food for the sabbath without working. This was the only time that the food could be kept overnight and not spoil.

Here's the Point

The speeches in verses 6-15 make three points. First, God had *heard* Israel's complaint and, more, had answered it directly. Second, all the speeches were made so that Israel would *know* it was YHWH who had heard and rescued them. Finally, amid all the complaining about food, Yahweh's *glory* was known in the wilderness. The wilderness was an empty place, with barren rock, bad lands, and here and there an oasis. But it was also filled with the presence of God.

The glory of YHWH was manifested to Israel both in the cloud (mystery) and the provision of food (practicality). This revelation helped them begin to deal with reality. They now began to turn away from their romanticized memory of Egypt. It *was* a place of slavery. They could now see the wilderness as a place where they could meet and be led by God. Theirs was not a romantic, God-in-nature experience of the wilderness, but rather a realistic God-in-everyday-events idea of the wilderness.

Think About It: "The glory of YHWH was manifested in both mystery and practicality." The voice from the cloud was awesome. The food on the table met a basic need. One they demanded; the other astounded them. How and when do we experience God's glory?

The Gift of Bread and Sabbath

Egypt had been a place where Israel ate as a reward for labor and productivity. But in the wilderness, God simply gave the manna. There was nothing exploitative about food in the way it had been in Egypt. Bread was simply a gift of grace. In the wilderness, Israel also celebrated the sabbath. This, too, was different from Egypt. There the demands of productivity and the social reality of trying to provide food in a slave labor camp had meant working seven days a week. Now the sabbath was a gift of liberation. The people no longer had to live under the oppression of productivity. And neither do we.

Psalter: Psalm 105:1-6, 37-45

This is a great hymn that retells the story of Israel's history. It may have been a teaching song. Verses 1-6 are an invitation to praise. YHWH, for Israel, was always a God who acted and got things done. That is the reason for praise. "Glory in his holy name" (105:3) almost means "brag about God." The word *name* always meant more than a label—it revealed the basic nature of the person or thing named. So the phrase means, "Glory in who God is, that is the holy One." To seek the presence of God is to trust God completely with all aspects of one's life.

This psalm was probably written during the Exile, and the theme of "bringing out" (verses 37-45) was extremely important for that period. The people saw their return from exile as being a "second Exodus." The hymn ends with a great reminder that God's gracious gifts call for a faithful response.

Epistle: Philippians 1:21-30

Paul had a special relationship with the church at Philippi. They were the first converts in his ministry in Europe. There is a warm, personal tone in this letter that we don't feel in Corinthians or Romans. In today's lection, Paul writes to his dear friends from prison, probably in Rome.

Living and Dying in Christ

He begins by talking about his upcoming trial (1:19-23). He thinks he will be acquitted, but warns that he might not be. Either way it will be well with him. If he dies, his life will be fulfilled in Christ. Death and life are the same, since either way he is with Christ. But death will bring him the more intimate relationship with Christ he has been seeking. In fact, if he has to choose, he is not sure whether he will take life or death.

> **Think About It:** "I'm not sure whether I would take life or death." Is our faith such that living eternally with Christ or continuing to live in this life would be a hard choice?

Paul wants to go and be with Christ, but he also wants to stay and see the fruit of his work (1:23-24). Verse 25 probably indicates what Paul *really* feels. Although he is tired of life and wants to get away, he believes he will survive the trial and make another visit to Philippi. If he were free, this is the first thing he would do. This, in fact, is another clue about Paul's relationship with this church. He probably would not be overly excited about hurrying back to Corinth, for example, where the congregation was continually giving him problems (1 Corinthians 1:10-11).

Stand Firm and Strive

Then comes the exhortation to faithful living. Regardless of what happens to him, Paul wants them to live "in a manner worthy of the gospel" (Philippians 1:27). Whether he is freed to come visit them or not, he expects them to be unified, undaunted by hostile forces, and ready to endure affliction if need be, in order that the cause of Christ may go forward.

Struggling for the Sake of Christ

Finally (verses 29-30), Paul tells his friends that suffering for the sake of Christ is a high privilege. The reference is to Paul's own trials and to whatever the church might be facing. We know that one hundred years later the Philippian church and its friend, Bishop Polycarp, were faithful in time of persecution. But there is no indication of organized persecution of the church at the time this letter was written. The reference may be to social pressures and attacks faced by individuals because they were Christians.

Gospel: Matthew 20:1-16

Here's another story about productivity and the work force. Recognize that it reflects the economic and social realities of the time. Early every morning, day laborers gathered in the village square hoping to be hired. They literally lived from day to day; if they were not hired, they could not buy food for their families for that day. Read the story in that light, and think about the increasing desperation of those who had not been hired as the day wore on.

Split Sympathies

These economic and social realities may divide our sympathies. First, we feel sorry for those who weren't hired until late, when the pressure was on because they didn't want to have to face their hungry children with no food. But the pressure was on the landowner as well. He needed to get the crop in while it was at peak readiness for harvest. So he kept hiring more people, hoping to be done by nightfall. Perhaps those hired late in the afternoon were not very good workers. We don't know.

Finally, our sympathy is with those who were hired first. They worked all day—and for the same wages as those who worked only an hour! What's fair about that? This may be just the reaction from his hearers that Jesus wanted. By most standards, our greatest sympathy is reserved for the ones who worked the hardest. They got a raw deal.

A Deal Is a Deal

But who said life was fair? Those first workers had a contract: they would get a day's wage for a day's work. Those hired later came on the owner's word that he would do right by them. But the owner didn't say what *right* was. No doubt those hired later hoped for enough to buy bread for their children, perhaps a wage based on hours worked. It's too bad about hungry children, but business is business.

When those hired last got a full day's pay, those hired first began to dream about a bonus. After all, they had worked honestly all day in the heat and deserved some consideration and special treatment, too. That's fair—equal pay for equal work, but also unequal pay for unequal work. Sound familiar? "I worked longer and harder. I'm more productive. I deserve more." Isn't that a common social and economic reality today too?

The parable challenges conventional values of fairness and justice and forces us to consider grace. The workers hired first were looking for justice, and that is what they received. They had a contract and were paid accordingly. But they were unhappy about those who did not have a contract and were paid by grace. Probably those early workers believed in grace, just as we do. They just didn't want it applied to someone else.

> **Think About It:** What social and economic realities shape our thinking about work? Do we spend time at work thinking about work? Do we spend time at work thinking about fairness and what another worker got? Are workers today treated justly? What about corporate mergers, strikes, plant closings and downsizing? What does the gospel say to our work situation?

One fascinating aspect of this story is how the landowner responded to the complaints about justice and fairness. Look at verses 13-16. First, the landowner says, "I *was* just; I paid you what we agreed." The decision to pay everyone equally was a deliberate choice on the part of the landowner; he knew what he was doing. Verse 15 is striking: "Can't I do what I want with what belongs to me? Do you (the all-day laborers) begrudge my generosity?

Well, yes, they did, because they didn't receive any generosity. They received justice, not grace. Grace cannot be bargained for; it is always "amazing." It is also amazing because we dare not presume that we will receive it.

Study Suggestions

A. What's Amazing?

Sing one stanza of "Amazing Grace." Ask: Is *grace* a word we often use in everyday speech? Why or why not? What is grace? (*Grace* may be defined as "God's unmerited love.") What is the difference in meaning between the words *graceful, gracious*, and *grace*? What's amazing about grace? The amazing nature of God's grace is the overall theme for this session.

B. What God Has Done Lately

Read Exodus 16:2-15 and the commentary on pages 310–11. Ask: Why is Israel unhappy in this story? Whom did they blame for their predicament? In verses 6-15, who makes the speeches? What is each speech about? What is the result of the speeches?

What was the importance of sabbath for Israel? (It was both a time of rest and a time to give thanks.) How was the importance of the sabbath lifted up in this story? Is the idea of sabbath still important today? Why or why not?

What does this story about quails and manna and sabbath have to do with grace? What's amazing about this grace?

C. Explore Grace in Human Life

Read Philippians 1:21-30 and the commentary on pages 312–13. Note Paul's upcoming trial and his relationship with the church at Philippi. Ask: For Paul, what is the difference between living and dying? What, for him, were the benefits of living? of dying? Which did he prefer? What would be our thoughts if faced with this choice?

What does Paul expect the Philippians to do about grace in daily life? The commentary talks about faithful living in the face of division, opposition, and possible suffering. Ask: Is faithful living possible on willpower alone? Can one ever live "in a manner worthy of the gospel"? What makes this kind of life possible? Is faithfulness a gift or an achievement? How does God's grace figure in a righteous life?

D. Grace and Productivity

Ask: How are things at work? Is everyone doing his or her part? Do workers receive equal pay for equal work? Are they treated fairly? Is productivity a value or just a buzzword for getting people to do more for less?

Read aloud the first paragraph in the commentary on page 313, then Matthew 20:1-16. Now review the rest of the commentary. Ask: In this story about economic reality, what was the contract the owner made with the workers hired first? What did he say to those hired later in the day? Should they have hired on under those conditions? With whom do you identify in this situation?

The owner of the vineyard had a different priority than the persons he hired. His priority was to maximize the harvest, and he acted accordingly. Does Jesus want us to see that, in the kingdom of God, God may have a different set of priorities than we do? Might God's priority be grace that redeems as many souls as possible?

E. Brag About God

Read Psalm 105:1-6. Point out that verse 3 almost means "brag about God." So, it's "brag time." Invite members to tell their own stories of what God has done in their lives and what this has meant to them. After each story, have the members respond, "Glory in God's holy name" (verse 3).

F. Celebrate Grace

Sing several stanzas of "Amazing Grace." Close with a prayer of thanksgiving for God's grace.

Lections for Sunday Between September 25 and October 1

Old Testament: Exodus 17:1-7

NOTHING had changed. The people had been fed, and they had been traveling through the wilderness, as God had commanded. But they still complained incessantly, this time about water. This was no small problem. There were a lot of people with flocks and herds, and the water supplies in the Sinai were very limited.

First Verse of the Song

"Give us something to drink," the people said. Their complaint was about water, but it was also about Moses being incompetent. Why did he get them out there where he couldn't take care of them?

Actually, he probably could. Moses was an old desert hand and knew how to find water in the rocks. Water moves along the surface of impermeable layers. When it reaches the outcropping, as in the side of a canyon, it drips out. Minerals from the water are deposited and eventually seal up the hole from which the water drips. But you can always see where the hole was, and a sharp blow from a staff will open the hole again and bring water. In fact, Moses would soon provide water in this way and would get in big trouble with God over it (see also Numbers 20:2-13).

Moses countered that they were testing God. He equated his leadership with that of YHWH—not an unreasonable equation, given the situation—but he did not comment on the water.

Second Verse, Just Like the First

Just like the children's song, it was "a little bit louder and a little bit worse." This time, the people accused Moses of causing their deaths. If it had not been for him and his silly exodus, they'd be safe in Egypt, where there was always water. This was a major escalation in the rhetoric.

Third Verse

This was not Moses' first, nor his last, moment of frustration. He had thought all God was calling him to do was to go back to Egypt (where he was wanted for murder) and get Pharaoh to give up a valuable economic resource. Now he had to deal with the commotion over food and water. So, he did a little complaining of his own to God: "What do I do now? They're ready to stone me. What are you going to do about it?" His immediate concern was not for water for the people but for his own safety.

Fourth Verse

However, YHWH was also in the conversation, so it would become a source of life not death. YHWH ignored Moses' concern for safety and addressed the water problem. YHWH was committed to seeing the process through. God told Moses three things: (1) to take the elders with him as a witness to what God was doing; (2) that God would be standing before him, that is, present in tough places even before he got there, to hold him up; and (3) to take the symbol of authority, his staff, and use it to provide as God directed.

Moses could have obtained water from the rock himself, but that was not necessary. YHWH could wrest water from rock, and thereby, life from death. The ending of the story says the encounter had been about lack of faith. They even named the places "Test" and "Quarrel," because the people tested Moses and YHWH. So the story is also a critique of the kind of religion that judges God on the basis of how well God satisfies our wants.

> **Think About It:** Do we "judge God on the basis of how well God satisfies our wants"? Do our prayers consist mostly of asking for things? Do we lose heart when these are not answered as we want? What else do we pray about? How does God respond?

Psalter: Psalm 78:1-4, 12-16

This is another teaching song. It tells the story of Israel and their God so that the people will be inspired to hope and obedience. Our part of the psalm refers again to the exodus. There are reminders of God's mighty deeds in the escape from Egypt and of the celebration of freedom. Implicit is the question: How can you *not* be faithful to a God like this? But knowledge about God does not guarantee faithfulness. Personal commitment must accompany knowledge.

Epistle: Philippians 2:1-13

This lection begins with admonitions about how to live a Christian life, then moves into a great hymn about Christ's incarnation, servanthood, and exaltation.

Living the Christian Life

Philippians 1 ended with an exhortation to stand fast and work together for the sake of the gospel. In light of that appeal, Paul says we (1) can count on support in Christ; (2) have a sense of Christ's love, to give us strength; (3) have communion with the Spirit; (4) know Christ understands and sympathizes with human weakness, for he himself was human; and therefore (5) should please him by working together in unity, mutual love, and common purpose.

> **Think About It:** What situations in our congregation call for working together smoothly? Is there unity or friction in those situations? What could be done to change discord to harmony?

We don't know what situation in the Philippian church called for this response. We do know that many situations in our churches—building campaigns, mission projects, crises—call for us to work together harmoniously.

To Be a Christian

What does it mean to be a Christian? Here Paul says all Christians, however different, desire to know and serve God. We sometimes think that emphasizing our differences is the way to serve God. Paul implies that our common wish to know and serve God overcomes those differences. That's the point of working together. In fact, Paul says, humility (placing a proper value on ourselves) and caring about the needs and interests of others can go a long way toward creating harmony.

To make his point, Paul cites the example of Christ. Verses 5-11 are one of the earliest Christian hymns, written ten or fifteen years after Jesus' resurrection and already familiar at the time of Paul's writing about A.D. 56.

The Humility of Christ

J. B. Phillips paraphrases the hymn this way: "[Christ], who had always been God by nature, did not cling to his privileges as God's equal, but stripped himself of every advantage by consenting to be a slave by nature and being born a [hu]man. . . . And, plainly seen as a human being, he humbled himself by living a life of utter obedience, to the point of death . . . the death of a common criminal. That is why God has now lifted him to the heights, and has given him the name beyond all names, so that at the name of Jesus "every knee shall bow," whether in heaven or earth or under the earth. And that is why "every tongue shall confess" that "Jesus Christ is Lord, to the glory of God the Father" (*The New Testament in Modern English*, Revised Edition, translated by J B. Phillips; New York: The Macmillan Company; 1972; pp. 412–13. Used by permission).

318

The Going Forth and the Return

Later theologians would call this "the going forth and the return"—Christ coming from the Father and returning to the Father. Remember that humility has to do with placing a proper value on ourselves and others. Paul wants the church to follow Christ's model of humility, the model of cooperative love between Father and Son. The Father and Christ worked together in Christ's going forth into the world and his return. Paul is saying: In love, send each other forth to work for God in the world; then welcome each other back into the community of faith.

Gospel: Matthew 21:23-32

Conversations in which the religious authorities try to trap Jesus are such a delight. These officials think they're going to confuse and trick this carpenter-prophet. But Jesus always seems to top them.

A Question and a Trap

The conversation in today's lection is both a trap and a discussion of the main issue—who has the authority to speak in God's name? The discussion began here: Where did Jesus get his authority? By what right was he teaching in the Temple? Jesus answered with his own question: Where did John get his authority? If they would answer that, he would answer their question.

Then the priests' strategy caved in. No matter what they might say, it would offend someone. If they said John's authority was from God, they would have to deal with the next question—"Then why didn't you listen to him?" But, if they said he was not a prophet, they would turn the people against them, because the people were sure John was a prophet. Public opinion might be fickle,

> **Think About It:** "We don't know" is a legitimate religious response. Think of situations in which the response, "We don't know," might be the best one possible. Does faith require knowledge or certainty? Now think of some places in which it is a cop-out. Why do we sometimes fear to be straightforward?

but it was also powerful. Better to appear ignorant than to get in trouble. So they answered, "We don't know." This is many times a legitimate, even desirable, response, given the arrogant human tendency to claim a monopoly on truth. But here the answer was a dodge. "If you can't say," Jesus answered, "I won't say either." Then he apparently changed the subject.

The Two Sons

It appears that the parable and the previous conversation are not connected. Jesus presented the case of the two sons with the introduction, "What do you think?" One son refused to do what his father asked but later

319

changed his mind and did it. The other sweetly agreed to do what the father asked but never got around to it. Which one did what the father wanted? The answer was obvious. Words don't count for nearly as much as deeds.

Trapped Again!

Again, the priests and elders were on the horns of a dilemma. They knew that Jesus was telling the story about them. But if they protested, Jesus had only to say, "I'm sorry. I think you misunderstood. I was only telling a story to these children about how they should act."

The last comment (21:31b-32), which may come from Matthew, says that the sinners would enter God's realm before the religious authorities, because they believed John's preaching. Tax collectors and prostitutes were both despised groups in Jesus' society. Tax collectors were hated agents of an oppressive foreign government, who were amassing private fortunes at the people's expense. They were considered so untrustworthy that they could not even testify in a court of law. Prostitutes were the prime example of immorality. The religious authorities, especially, looked down on these groups and ostracized them from the community of faith. Yet, said Jesus, because of their faith these are the people God accepts first.

Jesus then brought the trap full circle and closed it tight on his adversaries. He did not appeal to his own teaching, but to that of John, whose authority had already been established in the discussion. John's power (like his own?) was in the results of his ministry. People who believed him—even those beyond salvation, as defined by the religious authorities—were acknowledging the rule of God.

Study Suggestions

A. Ask How Persons Prepare

Ask: What would you do differently if you knew that God would come into your life today? How would you get ready? After several have responded, say that today's session is about God coming into human life.

B. Sing a Song of Quarrels

Read aloud Exodus 17:1-7 and the commentary on pages 316–17. Form three groups, one to look at each of the first three "verses" of the Israelites' complaints. Answer these questions for each set of complaints: Who is griping? What about? How do the stakes get higher?

Have a contest among the groups to see who can represent their case most fervently. Encourage participants to get into their role. After "Moses" has his turn, look again at the Scripture and discuss: How is "verse 3" different? Then have everyone look at the fourth verse. What happens when God enters the picture? What three things does God tell Moses to do? Why? What is the significance of each? Does God fail us? (Only if we judge God on the basis of having our wants satisfied or forget what God has done because we want something more now.)

C. Discover God Coming in Christ

Read in unison Philippians 2:5-11, then consult the commentary on pages 317–19. Ask participants to outline the hymn. What is the "theological plot"? Record the outline on chalkboard or a sheet of paper. Ask: What does this theological plot say to you about God's "going forth and returning"? *Incarnation* (in the flesh) signifies God coming into the world. What does it mean that God became like us?

D. What God's Coming Means

Read aloud Philippians 2:1-4. Ask: What can we count on from God as we try to live a Christian life? (See the commentary on pages 317–18.) Paul is forceful here about working and living in harmony. What are some typical church situations where people do not work in harmony? (Deciding on a new building, choosing colors for new decorations, taking on a mission project, choosing worship and music styles.) What are some ways we as a congregation work together with a common purpose? some situations where we need more harmony?

A major source of discord is that people are different. Ask: What are some differences in the church that could destroy our ability to work in harmony? If all of us, no matter how different, have a common desire to know and serve God, is that enough to let us work in harmony? Why or why not?

E. Decide Who Has the Authority

Read Matthew 21:23-32. Ask: What is the plot here? What strategy did the chief priests and elders use to avoid the dilemma of Jesus' question? When we see leaders thinking and talking this way, how do we react?

Remind the group that "I don't know" can be a legitimate answer to a religious question. Brainstorm three lists (with NO initial discussion). List first those beliefs and religious issues about which you have absolute certainty. Second, list those issues about which there is little or no certainty. Then list those issues on which failing to make a decision or have a belief is a cop-out. AFTER making the lists, discuss your level of agreement on the various assertions, based on what Scripture tells us. How much agreement and harmony do you have? What does this mean? In matters of faith, or when God comes into our lives, are we responsive, or do we rationalize ways to avoid being faithful?

F. Celebrate God's Coming in Christ

Read Psalm 78:1-4, 12-16 in unison. Ask: What does this say about how God comes to humanity? Sing in closing, "All Praise to Thee, for Thou, O King Divine."

Lections for Sunday Between
October 2 and 8

Old Testament: Exodus 20:1-4, 7-9, 12-20

*T*HE centrality of today's Old Testament lection to the identity and self-understanding of God's people—Jewish and Christian—cannot be overstated. The Ten Commandments (decalogue) in fact transcend their historical and theological context, providing a moral framework for much of Western civilization. The giving of the law to Moses at Sinai also marks a pivotal moment in God's unfolding story of salvation for the Israelites.

The commandments provide clear, succinct, fundamental principles for the life of the community, where one's relationship to God is inextricably linked to one's relationship to neighbor. The common thread of relationship-with-God/relationship-with-neighbor can, in fact, be traced through each of this week's lections.

Then God Spoke. . . .

There are two general types of law in the first five books of the Hebrew Bible: case law and absolute (or apodictic) law. Case law is conditional and detailed, citing the legal consequences for specific actions. It is developed gradually to provide guidance for concrete life dilemmas as they emerge. Absolute law, on the other hand, is unconditional and overarching. Usually stated in short, to-the-point utterances, absolute law leaves little room for external interpretation of the demands of the covenant. Many scholars believe that the original decalogue ("ten words") did not contain explanatory comments (such as verses 5, 6, 9-11). These additions are thought to be the work of later writers who expanded the utterances as they were handed down, in an attempt to offer greater clarity.

At the heart of the law is YHWH (the four Hebrew letters used, but not uttered, by Jews to point to their God, which we, somewhat insensitively, pronounce "Yahweh"). This was the "God, who brought you out of the land of Egypt, out of the house of slavery" (Exodus 20:1). It was this God who initiated, who delivered, who was now meeting the wandering people at his holy mountain, in the midst of their desert journey, and calling them to enter into covenant. This covenant would bind them to a high moral standard, but also promise divine guidance and protection.

The form of this preamble or prologue to the Mosaic covenant (verse 1) closely resembles that of the suzerainty treaty, a unilateral understanding between parties of unequal power and standing. The suzerain, often a king, would initiate a covenant with a vassal, which demanded obedience while offering security to the weaker partner. Such treaties, known as covenants, were common among the Hittites in the second millennium B.C. But instead of an earthly king, Israel would have YHWH as their only sovereign.

Thou Shall Not . . .

With the exceptions of the fourth and fifth commandments, the Decalogue is stated as a series of prohibitions, often seen as negatives. The intention, however, was to stress by contrast with what is prohibited, that which was good and acceptable in the life of the community. Incredible freedom was implicit in the relationship of the individual to YHWH as well as to the community, as defined by the commandments.

The injunctions provided a

Think About It: Aside from the absolutes of the law, the individual is free to live in response to God's love. This is close to Martin Luther's summary of Christian ethics, uttered centuries later: "Love God, and do as you please." Do we need more guidance than this? How might this understanding of law and love free us to experience a deeper relationship with God and neighbor?

structure by which the community could respond to God's love. Jesus would later summarize the commandments in two positive phrases: "You shall love the Lord your God with all your heart, and with all your soul, and with all your mind, and with all your strength" and "You shall love your neighbor as yourself" (Mark 12:28-31).

Psalter: Psalm 19

Today's psalm consists of two distinct sections. Verses 1-6 glorify God through the expression of creation itself, and verses 7-14 expound the wonder of the commandments as God's greatest creative act. The heavens "tell" God's glory, the firmament "proclaims," the day "pours forth speech," and the night "declares" (19:1-2). The glory of creation points to the glory of the Creator, whose expression is the law.

The "sun" is personified as a bridegroom, an athlete, and a runner. The imagery again points to the Creator. The appropriate response is awe, praise, and obedience. God's glory is also revealed through the "law," expressed as "decrees," "precepts," "commandment," "fear of the Lord," and "ordinances." Far from the negative connotations associated with prohibitions, the law is life-affirming. Through it, the soul is revived, the heart rejoices. But the law, like the wonder of creation, is only valuable as it points beyond itself to the Giver of the law.

The psalmist understands that knowing the law is insufficient. While the commandments provide all that is required for living out the covenant relationship, the presence of God is still needed: "But who can detect their errors?" (19:12). The psalm ends in petition to YHWH for what the psalmist cannot accomplish on his own: "Clear me from hidden faults." It is not the commandments that are praised, but the love of God that provides the law for the good of the human creation.

Epistle: Philippians 3:4b-14

The theme of life in God's presence and within the community is continued in today's Epistle lection. As Paul writes of his own "straining forward" in response to Christ, so he encourages the Philippian community to live in a way that upholds the gospel.

In verse 2, Paul warns of the "dogs" and "evil workers . . . who mutilate the flesh" (Philippians 3:2), those who insist upon the requirement of circumcision for Gentile converts. In his response, he claims his own heritage as a member of the community of Israel. He reminds the Philippian Christians of his own "confidence in the flesh"—his circumcision as a descendant of the tribe of Benjamin. This suggests to some scholars that the Jewish Christians against whom Paul debated were themselves converts first to the Jewish religion and then to Christianity. Paul asserts that he is "more" confident as one born into the Jewish community. His confidence goes beyond just his birth—in terms of adherence to the law, Paul was a Pharisee. He persecuted Christians with zeal. He was "blameless" under the law (3:4b-6).

> **Think About It:** Think about your standing in the community and the church. Has your experience of Christ rendered any of your former accomplishments as loss? Has knowing Christ transformed your values?

In light of Christ, however, all these must be counted as "loss," not as entitlement. The worth of Christ far outweighs the former glories of his standing within the Jewish community. These are mere "rubbish." (Some scholars suggest that a more literal translation would be the more emphatic *dung*.)

In Christ

To know Christ, to be in Christ, is what Paul is seeking. Righteousness is not living blamelessly under the law. Paul is seeking a righteousness that is not his own doing, but "one that comes through faith in Christ" (3:9). He strains toward the goal of participation in the "power of his resurrection." He presses on, because Christ "has made me his own" (3:12). Some scholars suggest that this translation belies the urgency and forcefulness of the Greek; Christ, in Paul's understanding, "overtakes" or "seizes" the believer in an outpouring of grace. The only response is to continue striving toward the prize.

Gospel: Matthew 21:33-46

Today's Gospel lection, the parable of the vineyard, appears also in Mark 12:1-12 and Luke 20:9-19. Highlighted in this retelling is the necessity of producing "fruit" befitting the realm of God, a theme found throughout Matthew (3:8-10; 7:15-20). Such fruit is the result of complete obedience to God as lived out in the community of faith.

The Vineyard

The image of the vineyard would be immediately recognizable to Jesus' audience. They would connect the story with the vineyard of Israel depicted in Isaiah 5, a vineyard destroyed because it would only produce wild grapes. Those listening would understand the planter of the vineyard to be God and would recognize their own place in the story to be the "vines." The practice of tenant farming (akin to sharecropping) was common in the first century. The slaves sent by the planter at the harvest would be identified with the prophets sent by God to the people of Israel.

Following the beating, killing, and stoning of his messengers, the landowner sent his son to collect his share of the harvest. The son was seized, thrown out of the vineyard, and killed by the tenants, like Matthew's account of Jesus' crucifixion outside the city. As in the preceding parable, Jesus allowed his hearers to condemn themselves by their answer to his question: "What will [the owner] do to those tenants?" They stated the obvious conclusion: "He will put those wretches to a miserable death, and lease the vineyard to other tenants who will give him the produce at the harvest time" (Matthew 21:40-41). Matthew's account allows the listeners to implicate themselves in its conclusion; in Mark and Luke, Jesus answers his own question.

The Rejected Stone

The full impact of Jesus' message (and the self-condemnation of the hearers) became clear as he quoted Psalm 118:22-23. The vineyard was now the reign of God. If the original tenants did not produce the fruits of the kingdom, the vineyard would be taken from them and turned over to those who would be obedient to the will of God and whose lives would bear fruit. The story points to the inclusion of the Gentiles in the gospel message; adherence to the law could not guarantee a place in God's realm. The chief priests and

Pharisees, realizing that Jesus was talking about them, refrained from arresting him at the time, only because they feared the reaction of the crowds who saw him as a prophet of God.

> **Think About It:** The changed life, the life made new in Christ, is evidenced by the "fruits" produced. The disciple is called to a life of self-examination and faithfulness. Think about our discipleship and witness; do we see evidence of the fruits of God's rule in our life?

The Cornerstone

The image of the cornerstone, rejected by the builders, pronounces a message of vindication; God's purpose cannot be thwarted. The very community to which the Messiah had been promised had rejected Jesus. The image of the cornerstone (God) as a stumbling block is borrowed from Isaiah 8:13-15. For the faithful, God is a refuge, a sure foundation.

For the faithless, God—and later Jesus—becomes a stumbling block, a "snare." The rejected stone "will crush anyone on whom it falls" (Matthew 21:44). God's reign cannot be built on a foundation without the cornerstone of Christ. A new community, built on the foundation of Jesus Christ, would consist of all who faithfully respond to God's call. The message of vindication is the message of Easter.

Adherence to the law, privileged status as religious insiders, and reliance on "cheap grace" do not guarantee tenantship (membership) in the realm of God. The Kingdom will be given to those who "produce the fruits of the kingdom" (21:43).

Study Suggestions

A. Open With Devotions

Read Psalm 19 together in unison or responsively. Reflect together on how God's commandments (word) can revive one's soul. Pray for guidance and insight in the discussion to follow.

B. Examine the Commandments

Without looking at the Bible, work together as a group or in pairs to list the ten commandments, striving for the correct order. When did you first learn these "ten words"? How has your understanding and appreciation of them changed since then? To what extent do they still provide daily guidance for your life? Do the commandments strike you as predominantly negative or positive statements?

Now look at Exodus 20 and check the list you made. Did you remember the commandments accurately? Is there any room for interpretation in the commandments? Are they used as case law or always as absolutes? In which of these ways do you usually take them? For what moral dilemmas do they provide insufficient guidance? (Examples might include abortion, euthanasia, capital punishment, and "white lies.")

Using the commentary on page 323, discuss the commandments as prohibitions. How might they be stated as "You shall" instead of "You shall not"? How are the commandments restrictive? How are they freeing? What do they tell us about God? about the relationship between God and people? about the relationship between neighbor and neighbor? If Jesus could summarize them as "love God; love your neighbor," why didn't God say it that way in the first place? In light of this discussion, how might we respond to some outside the community of faith who claim that "religion is dogmatic," or "I don't want someone telling me what I can or cannot do"? Why do some insist that the Ten Commandments be posted in courts of law? and others object?

C. Explore "Loss" and "Gain"

Read Philippians 3:4b-14 and the commentary on pages 324–25. Working together, develop a before-and-after description of Paul's life in relation to his conversion experience. What did he give up in order to follow Christ? How did his value system change? How did his understanding of righteousness change? What did it mean for Paul to be "in Christ"? What does it mean for us? What does it mean to say that Christ has "taken hold" of or "seized" our lives? How is this "taking hold" a manifestation of grace? Does it pre-empt our freedom?

D. Study the Parable

Read Matthew 21:33-46 and the commentary on pages 325–26. How might we understand the "fruits of the kingdom"? How are these fruits made manifest in the relationship of a person to God? in the relationship of neighbor to neighbor? in the life of the community? For Paul, righteousness cannot be earned through one's accomplishment or adherence to the law. What, then, is the relationship between grace and the mandate to "produce fruit"? between faith and works? Is our motivation to "be good" primarily to please God or out of gratitude to God? How might a faithful life be described?

E. Summarize Faith Relationships

All the Scriptures today point to following the will of God. How would you summarize the main points of each lection? the theme(s) common to them all? If we take seriously all that they say, what claim will that make on our life and faith? What level of commitment are we ready to make?

F. Close with Singing and Prayer

Sing a hymn celebrating the faithful life, such as "Wonderful Words of Life" or "Take My Life and Let It Be Consecrated." Pray that your lives as individuals, and as a community of faith, may produce fruits befitting the rule of God.

Lections for Sunday Between October 9 and 15

Old Testamemt: Exodus 32:1-14

*H*OW quickly they had forgotten! Almost immediately upon receiving the law the people of Israel turned their backs on the same God who had delivered them from slavery and bound them in a covenant relationship. All because Moses had been on the mountain too long! In their impatience and forgetfulness, they turned to Aaron to create gods they could see, in direct violation of the first two commandments: "You shall have no other gods before me," and "You shall not make for yourself an idol."

Moses had returned to the mountain (and the presence of God) to receive further instruction. Chapters 21–31 record a variety of laws concerning the conduct of worship and other matters relating to the community's life. Without Moses, the mediator of the covenant, the people became restless (as they would continue to do throughout their sojourn in the wilderness). Abandoning him for dead, they also abandoned the requirements of the covenant without the slightest hesitation. Even Moses' own brother, Aaron, who had on occasion accompanied him to the mountain, offered no protest when asked to facilitate their idolatry.

He collected their golden earrings (another sign of the influence of for-

Think About It: "They have been quick to turn aside from the way that I [God] commanded them." Today's disciples are just as susceptible to the lure of the "golden calf." What idols are we tempted to follow after? (Money, possessions, success, comfort, and security might be mentioned.) From which commandments (or teachings of Jesus) are we "quick to turn aside"? (Turning the other cheek, forgiving without limit, taking up the cross, and others discussed in recent weeks could be recalled.) How do we re-center ourselves in the covenant?

eign idols, Genesis 35:4), melted them down, and fashioned a calf, a symbol of power and fertility common to religions of that era and region. The people proclaimed: "These are your gods, O Israel" (Exodus 32:4), crediting the calf god with their delivery from bondage in Egypt. Aaron, however, erected an altar and announced a "festival to the LORD," indicating that the image was, in his estimation, a pedestal of YHWH. The feast included sacrifices before the calf, eating, drinking, and reveling, which possibly involved dancing and some sexual activity.

Your People

God alerted Moses to the situation, ordering him to return to "your people, whom you brought up out of the land of Egypt" (Exodus 32:7). As the people had abandoned the covenant, so YHWH was now prepared to abandon them: "Now let me alone, so that my wrath may burn hot against them and I may consume them." The people had so incensed their God that YHWH was now prepared to reject them and instead "make a great nation" of Moses, re-establishing the covenant through his descendants alone.

Moses, however, intervened on behalf of the rebellious people. These are "your people," he reminded God, "whom you brought out of the land of Egypt" (32:11). He also reminded YHWH of the promise made so long ago to Abraham: "Turn from your fierce wrath; change your mind" (32:12). Besides, he argued, what would the Egyptians say? And YHWH was persuaded. (Genesis 6:5-6 and Amos 7:3, 6 record other examples of this divine flexibility.) The people's actions deserved condemnation, but once again God's grace prevailed.

> **Think About It:** "Change your mind," said Moses to God. Can God be persuaded to change? Or is God the one thing in life that can be counted on never to change? Can we conceive of any loving person, human or divine, who would not budge in response to a plea from a loved one? Can we affirm both that "God is love" and that "God never changes"?

Psalter: Psalm 106:1-6, 19-23

Today's psalm remembers Israel's faithlessness—and forgetfulness—epitomized by the casting of the golden calf at Horeb. Beginning with a call to praise, and then recounting God's great Exodus work of liberation, the psalm moves to confession and ends with a petition for God's help. "Blessed are they who maintain justice, / who constantly do what is right" (106:3, NIV). Israel, in the psalmist's view, has created its own unhappiness through its rebellion.

The confession covers a multitude of sins: "Both we and our ancestors have sinned" (106:6). The verses omitted from this lection chronicle the

Israelites' rebellion from the time of their deliverance. But "they exchanged the glory of God / for the image of an ox. . . . / They forgot God" (106:20-21).

The real sin is in failing to remember the God who had brought them to freedom. And Moses' role as mediator is also remembered and revered. The people deserved wrath, but Moses intervened on their behalf and God spared them.

Epistle: Philippians 4:1-9

This final chapter of Philippians reiterates many of the Epistle's themes. Paul exhorts his brothers and sisters in Christ to "stand firm in the Lord." Despite his imprisonment and separation from his beloved church, he expresses his joy and calls them to "rejoice."

Be of the Same Mind

The issue of dissension among church members is one theme. Paul urges two Philippian women, Euodia and Syntyche, to overcome their differences and "agree with each other in the Lord" (Philippians 4:2, NIV). An unnamed "loyal companion" (possibly an individual, possibly the whole church) is asked to assist the women, who have worked side by side with the apostle. The nature of their quarrel is never revealed, but a division among the leadership warranted Paul's attention. Paul's epistle would have been read aloud to the community as it gathered for worship. His concern for the women and the healing of their rift was urgent enough to bring before the body, because they were all to participate in the healing process. Paul pleads for unity within the community of believers.

> **Think About It:** "Do not worry about anything, but . . . by prayer and supplication with thanksgiving let your requests be made known to God" (Philippians 4:6). Paul, as had Jesus, instructs the disciples not to worry. For many, however, this is one of the hardest teachings to take to heart. What things tend to worry us? What would help us relax and let the peace of God "guard our hearts and our minds in Christ Jesus"?

Again I Will Say, Rejoice

The Philippian Christians are called to rejoice, to let their "gentleness" (joy and forbearance) be known. The cause for rejoicing: the nearness of God. Paul may not be present, but God is always at hand. For Paul this is both a present reality and a future promise. The presence of God negates the need to worry (again, addressing the present as well as the future); God, their peace, is in control.

Finally, Paul offers himself as an example of Christian steadfastness in faith. The list of virtues he presents is unique to this letter, although the use of such a list is common in Paul's writings. (See Romans 1:20-32,

1 Corinthians 6:9-10, and Galatians 5:19-21, as well as in the Jewish wisdom tradition.) Paul has highlighted the distinction, and often the conflict, between the church and the culture surrounding it. These particular virtues, however, were espoused by Greek moralists and ethicists. By including these traits, he implicitly emphasizes again that a person not born into the Jewish faith can still live according to the covenant's requirements.

Gospel: Matthew 22:1-14

Rebellion and forgetfulness: the sins that threatened to bring God's wrath upon the Hebrew people at Horeb were still at issue in the time of Jesus. Matthew's account of the parable of the wedding banquet, like last week's parable of the vineyard, illustrates the consequences faced by the rebellious, ungrateful, invited guests when they rejected the king's invitation to a feast of celebration. Unlike the incident of the golden calf, however, the king's wrath was executed against those who refused the invitation. Their place at the banquet—in the realm of God—would be given to those who would respond to the call with authentic discipleship.

The Honor of Your Presence . . .

A similar parable is told by Luke (14:16-24), but with a decidedly happier outcome. The invited guests in Luke's account all offered acceptable excuses (according to the law), along with their regrets, to the founder of the feast. The house owner (angry, but not enraged) responded by extending the invitation to the "poor, the crippled, the blind, and the lame." The house was filled, but the invited guests would find no place. Luke's rendering exemplifies his inclusion of the outcast and dispossessed in the all-embracing good news of Jesus Christ. Matthew's account is more allegorical, emphasizing the Jewish rejection of Jesus as the Messiah and the opening of God's realm to the Gentiles. The brutality of Matthew's version is as startling for us as it undoubtedly was for its original audience.

But They Would Not Come

In Matthew's allegory, the king is God. The wedding feast as a metaphor for the Kingdom appears again in Matthew 25:10 and Revelation 19:7-8. The invitation had been issued to the chosen people. Not only did they reject the invitation, they "seized, mistreated, and killed" the messengers—the preachers of the gospel of Jesus Christ. The king's vengeance may

Think About It: "But they made light of it and went away, one to his farm, another to his business" (22:5). Has anything (such as busy-ness, self-centeredness, or need for attention or security) prevented us from responding fully to God's invitation? How can we find more time for the business of the reign of God?

331

represent the destruction of Jerusalem by Rome in A.D. 70—as prophesied in Isaiah 5:3, 24-25. The rejection by the Jewish leaders of the invitation results in the subsequent inclusion of the Gentiles in the messianic realm. The "good and bad" (Matthew 22:10) respond, filling the hall.

Proper Attire Required

At verse 11 we notice several shifts. The persona of the king changes from God to Jesus. The feast itself becomes the scene of final judgment. The king's rejection of the last-minute guest seems particularly harsh and arbitrary; a man pulled from the street to take the place of an invited guest would hardly have time to make himself presentable for a feast. The "slaves" of the earlier verses are replaced by "attendants" (22:13), which, in the Greek, may mean angels.

With the banquet as metaphor for the Final Judgment, however, the king is understandably outraged. In this scenario, the guest had failed to do what was expected and required and thus was unable to respond. The "proper attire" for Matthew has been stated throughout his Gospel: to do the will of God (7:21) and to produce "the fruits of the kingdom" (21:43). The invitation to share in God's reign goes out to all. Many will want to be included on the guest list; many will respond; but only those who prepare themselves for the feast by genuinely seeking and doing the will of God are invited to remain.

Study Suggestions

A. Open With Devotion

Sing a hymn of praise, such as "Let All the World in Every Corner Sing" or "Glorious Things of Thee Are Spoken." Reflect together on God's acts of salvation in human history.

B. Examine Idols

Read Exodus 32:1-14 together, assigning the roles of narrator, Moses, and God. How would you have expected the characters (including Aaron and the people of Israel) to react? Do any parts of the story surprise you? What does this encounter reveal about human nature? about Moses? about God? about justice and grace?

Why did the people need to create an idol? Why was it easier to pay homage to a golden statue than to live out the requirements of the covenant as expressed in the commandments? What are some of the "golden calves" calling us to turn away from God (materialism, personal wealth, technology, medical science, sex, power, and prestige)? Do we tend to attribute our successes to these false idols instead of giving glory to God? How can we support one another in our efforts to turn from these to lives of covenant faithfulness?

C. Explore the Epistle

Read Philippians 4:1-9 and the accompanying material on pages 330–31. What would happen today if a rift between two church members was addressed from the pulpit—naming names? What did it mean for the Philippian Christians to "stand firm in the Lord"? What does it mean for us? How can Christians who disagree about moral and social issues still "be of the same mind in the Lord"?

Two of Paul's most basic instructions are to "rejoice" and "not to worry about anything." Do you find these instructions easy to follow? If not, what makes them hard for you? Paul says prayer will take care of worry. Do you agree? Share your experiences with both worry and prayer.

Ask members to close their eyes as you read aloud verse 7 several times— if possible each time from a different version. Ask: How do you picture God's peace "guarding" your heart and mind? How can these images help us relax and let go of worry?

D. Study the Parable

Form two groups; instruct one to read Matthew 22:1-14, the other Luke 14:16-24. Ask each group to tell the story from its account. Highlight the differences in two columns on chalkboard or a sheet of paper. Ask: How can we explain the vengeance in Matthew's account? (refer to the commentary on pages 331–32.) Is this image of God troubling? How are we to prepare ourselves to enter the realm of God? What does it mean to be "properly dressed" for the occasion?

Spend some time with the consequences in this parable—of those who brutalized the messengers, of those who chose not to come, and of the man pulled in unexpectedly from the street. What do these drastic consequences say about the seriousness with which God's invitation is offered and accepted?

E. Integrate the Lections

Forgetfulness and rebellion (along with their consequences) were stumbling blocks for God's people of both Old and New Testaments. Trace these themes through these lections. Ask: What happens when people forget their right relationship to God? Looking back over the lections, ask for volunteers to tell where they see themselves. With which, if any, of today's characters do they identify? What helps does God offer us for "standing firm" in the faith? How can we guard against forgetfulness? against complacency?

F. Close in Prayer

Form a prayer circle, read Psalm 106:1-6, 19-23 together or responsively as a prayer of confession and a proclamation of grace. Then invite sentence prayers voicing the learnings and commitments gained in this session.

Lections for Sunday Between October 16 and 22

Old Testament: Exodus 33:12-23

TODAY'S Old Testament lection continues the story of Moses following his return from the presence of YHWH on Sinai. Omitted from the lectionary readings in this cycle are the dramatic events recorded in the concluding verses of Chapter 32. Moses returned to the camp to find the people running wild (32:25). Enraged by the scene of reveling before the golden calf, he smashed the stone tablets upon which the divine commandments had been written—a most fitting metaphor for the breaking of the covenant and the relationship between YHWH and the people.

Moses burned the calf and ground it to a powder, which, mixed with water, he forced the Israelites to drink. Calling for those "who [are] on the Lord's side" (32:26) to come forward, he instructed the sons of Levi who would respond, to take up the sword and kill "your brother, your friend, and your neighbor" (32:27). At his command "about three thousand" of the people died. Then, in a somewhat ironic turn, Moses went again to God to seek forgiveness for the people. The chapter ends with YHWH visiting a plague upon the people.

I Will Not Go Up Among You

Chapter 33 begins with God instructing Moses and the people to "go." They were to continue on their journey to the land of promise; from now on, however, an angel would go before them—not YHWH. God knew that the rebelliousness of the people would result in their destruction along the way. The verses directly preceding this lection set the stage for Moses' ongoing role as mediator between YHWH and the people. He set up the tent of meeting outside the camp where the pillar of cloud—the presence of God—

descended, and where "the LORD used to speak to Moses face to face, as one speaks to a friend" (33:11).

Show Me Your Ways

Moses intervened on the people's behalf. "Show me your ways," he asked, seeking to understand God's refusal to accompany the people further. Again Moses reminded God that "this nation is your people" (33:13). The incident with the golden calf had shown that this nation was not set apart by its own righteousness or moral fortitude. The distinction between the Hebrews and all the other peoples rested solely in God's continued presence among them. Once more, Moses' argument proved persuasive; "I will do the very thing that you have asked" (33:17), said YHWH.

Several interesting parallels now emerge. "Show me your ways" precedes "Show me your glory" (33:18). Moses' plea now was for a sign of confirmation from God. The sign was the proclamation of the divine name. Echoing the initial encounter between Moses and YHWH in the third chapter of Exodus, the very name of God was a revelation of God's nature: "I will be gracious to whom I will be gracious, and will show mercy on whom I will show mercy" (33:19).

> **Think About it:** "This nation was not set apart by its own righteousness." Can any nation claim to have earned God's special favor through its own virtue? What happens to a people when they start thinking of themselves as better than others? "The distinction . . . rested solely in God's continued presence among them." What insures God's continued presence with a people? Is God absent from any people? How do we know when God is present with us? What can we learn as a nation from Israel's experience with the golden calf and God's response to that idolatry?

> **Think About It:** "I will be gracious . . ." (33:19). More than an attribute, mercy is part of God's very being. How does this truth inform our relationship with God? How might it inform our relationship with others?

Psalter: Psalm 99

Psalm 99 is a fitting companion to today's Old Testament lection, highlighting God's sovereignty, justice, and mercy, as well as remembering those who acted as mediators between God and Israel (Moses and Aaron in relation to the Exodus narratives). Characteristic of a hymn of praise, Psalm 99 begins with a call to praise, followed by a recitation of God's mighty acts in history. "He spoke to them in a pillar of cloud; . . . / you were a forgiving God to them, / but an avenger of their wrongdoings" (99:7-8).

Moses and Aaron gave voice to the cries of the enslaved Hebrews in Egypt.

YHWH, the "lover of justice" (99:4), heard their cries and "executed justice," freeing the people and giving the commandments as a medium of liberation. YHWH will respond when the people call. Justice is rendered with mercy as well as accountability—with tough love.

God's sovereignty extends to all creation. "Holy is he" is a refrain throughout the psalm, indicating both the cosmic scope of YHWH's dominion and the absolute power of YHWH's will. God's justice will prevail. The psalm ends as it begins, with a call to praise and humility before the One who "sits enthroned upon the cherubim" (99:1).

Epistle: 1 Thessalonians 1:1-10

Paul's First Letter to the Thessalonians, his earliest letter, is the earliest writing in the New Testament. It is intensely personal, giving an intimate portrait of Paul as an evangelist with heartfelt affection for this church. As the Thessalonians had been moved by Paul's faith, so was he moved by their response to the gospel. When Christ is shared, both bearer and receiver of the message are profoundly changed.

Paul founded the church in Thessalonica, capital of the Roman province of Macedonia, after leaving Philippi. The letter is addressed to the Gentile believers (converted from pagan faiths), although the Acts account of the Thessalonian ministry is centered in Paul's interaction with the synagogue community. One of the letter's primary concerns is Paul's thanksgiving for and encouragement of the Thessalonians, who held firmly to their faith in spite of persecution and adversity. The Gentile Christians faced ongoing pressure, and often threat of physical violence (see Acts 17:5-9), to return to the beliefs and values of the prevailing culture.

> **Think About It:** "You turned to God . . . to serve a living and true God" (1 Thessalonians 1:9). The power of the gospel profoundly changed the lives of these Christians. When they accepted Christ with joy, others were influenced by their example. What impact does our faith have on those around us? Do others see evidence of a living, joyous faith in us?

In Power

Paul never refers to himself as an evangelist, preferring the designation "apostle." The root of our term *evangelist*, however, comes from the same core as *evangélion*, which means "gospel." Not a common term among Greeks or Jews, the good news for Paul was more than a recounting of the story of Jesus. The gospel message itself had power, as was evidenced by manifestations of the Spirit among those who accepted it. Paul uses the term *gospel* more than any other New Testament writer.

The Thessalonians were moved by the example of the evangelists' faith—

336

not just their words—and became their imitators. In turn, they became examples of faith for the believers in Achaia and Macedonia and "in every place your faith in God has become known" (1:8). The power of the gospel was also evidenced by the joy with which the Thessalonians received it—joy in the hope that Christ would come again.

Gospel: Matthew 22:15-22

Today's Gospel lection sets a familiar scene: the Pharisees conspiring to trap Jesus by asking him a trick question. He responded, as was his habit, by turning the question back to them. His subsequent comment, though, is the best-known verse in this passage: "Give therefore to the emperor the things that are the emperor's" (Matthew 22:21). Taken out of context, this pronouncement of Jesus is often cited in debates over the relationship of church and state. At the heart of the lection, however, lies the truth that ultimately our allegiance belongs to God.

Strange Bedfellows

Jesus was approached by the students of the Pharisees together with a group of Herodians. Only the possibility of entrapping Jesus could bring two such divergent sects together. The Herodians, a priestly class, achieved their power and influence through cooperation with the Roman authorities. By contrast, the Pharisees—strident in their devotion to Mosaic law—regarded such collusion as treason. Stronger than the suspicion and hatred these opposing groups held for each other was their mutual desire to discredit Jesus.

The Plan Unfolds

The exchange began with false flattery: "We know that you are sincere, and teach the way of God" (22:16). They posed a yes-or-no question that could not be answered without offending one group or the other. For some of the Pharisees, even touching a coin depicting the emperor's image was offensive; to pay a tax to the occupying government, an act of utter treason. When the tax (approximately a day's wage for a laborer) was instituted nearly twenty-five years earlier in A.D. 6, some instigated an armed insurrection.

A "yes" to the question, "Is it lawful to pay taxes to the emperor," would have set Jesus against the law of Moses in the eyes of the Pharisees. To answer "no" would be an act of treason against Rome, enabling the Herodians to level an accusation against Jesus with the ruling officials. A yes-or-no answer would link Jesus either with the Zealots or with the Roman sympathizers, alienating him from the crowds. "But Jesus [was] aware of their malice" (22:18).

Whose Title?

Jesus answered with another question. Calling for a coin, he asked, "Whose head is this, and whose title?" (Between A.D. 14 and 37, a portrait of Tiberius would have appeared on the coin together with an inscription affirming his divinity.) To "give" to the emperor (verse 21) carried a different connotation than the "pay" of verse 17 (some translations render both verbs as "pay"). A more complete translation might be to "give back what is due," to both the emperor and God.

The coin bore the image of the emperor, but the Jewish believer—Herodian or Pharisee—bore the image of God. There was no competition. A tax might be paid to Caesar, but allegiance belonged to God alone. God's "due" was the complete devotion of the believer. Those listening would have to decide for themselves where their ultimate loyalty lay. But note that Jesus had to ask for a coin from the crowd; he

> **Think About It:** "Give . . . to God the things that are God's" (22:21). Believers bear the image of the Divine; believers belong wholly to God. Does this awareness influence the decisions you make in the political and social realms?

himself did not carry the image of the emperor. Their hypocrisy revealed, the Herodians and the Pharisees went away, amazed at his words.

The question of the authority of church versus state is not clearly resolved in this encounter. Requirements, such as taxation, imposed by the state, are not the main issue. The believer's total allegiance belongs to God. All other obligations are subordinate to this supreme loyalty.

Study Suggestions

A. Open With Singing

Sing a hymn celebrating God's sovereignty, such as "The God of Abraham Praise" or "El Shaddai." Ask members to reflect silently on personal experiences of God's mercy in their lives.

B. Explore Mercy

Review the commentary account of the sequence of events between the casting of the golden calf on pages 328–29 and today's Old Testament lection. How would you characterize the relationship between Moses and God? Point out that these events represent the ongoing struggle of the Hebrew people to move from the worship of many gods to loyalty to YHWH alone and from being a loose collection of slaves to a distinctive people with an identity and standards of their own.

C. Examine Evangelism

Read 1 Thessalonians 1:1-10 and the accompanying material on pages

336–37. What was it about Paul's evangelism that touched the Thessalonian believers? Note the importance of intercessory prayer (verses 2-3), preaching with power and conviction (verse 5), setting an example (verses 6-8), and turning "to God from idols" (verse 9). Ask: What are contemporary parallels to these elements in evangelism? What else must be involved in effective evangelism today?

D. Discuss Allegiance

Read Matthew 22:15-22 and the commentary on pages 337–38. Stage a debate over the question of taxation raised to Jesus, assigning half the class the role of Herodians, the other half the role of Pharisees. Discuss the validity of each argument from a faith perspective. Why did Jesus recognize this controversy as hypocrisy instead of an authentic desire to do what was right? What is the real faith issue here for Jesus?

E. Trace Common Themes

God's absolute sovereignty and the call for a faithful response are recurring themes in today's lections. Form four teams, assign each team a lection, and ask them to trace these themes through their passage. Ask: How is God's sovereignty emphasized in your passage? What kind of faithful response is called for? How would your life change if you were to take seriously the message of your lection? Have each group report its responses, write them on chalkboard or piece of poster paper, and identify commonalities in the reports.

F. Close With Devotion

Read Psalm 99 in unison as a hymn of praise, then ask members to compose brief psalms of praise, and share them with the group as a closing prayer

Lections for Sunday Between October 23 and 29

T Old Testament: Deuteronomy 34:1-12

*T*ODAY'S Old Testament lection brings to a conclusion the Torah, the first five books of the Hebrew Bible, as well as the life of Moses, the greatest of Israel's prophets. Given only a glimpse of the land he would not be allowed to enter, Moses is silent throughout the passage and throughout this final encounter with God. His presence, however, was powerful even in death. As Joshua took up the role of leader and the people prepared to enter Canaan, the memory of Moses would continue with them.

You Shall Not Cross Over

Why was this great and faithful leader refused entrance to the land of promise? The answer lies in Meribah. The name of the place itself (meaning "find fault") was given by Moses to one of the springs of Kadesh as a witness to the people's lack of faith (Numbers 20:1-13). It was at Meribah that God had brought forth water from a rock in answer to the Israelites' unending complaints against Moses. Forgetting that God had delivered them from slavery, the people again and again taunted their leader: "Why have you brought us up out of Egypt, to bring us to this wretched place?" (20:5).

> **Think About It:** "God was somehow displeased with Moses' response." What was it Moses did that displeased God? Compare the accounts in Numbers 20:2-13 and Exodus 17:1-7, noting discrepancies. Moses prayed, asserted his authority, followed God's instructions, quelled a near-riot, brought forth water, and provided drink. What was wrong with this? Could it be that he was actually punished for the sins of the people rather than his own (in that respect, a forerunner of Christ)?

It was precisely at Meribah that Moses' own faith was judged by God. God instructed Moses to strike the rock with his staff in the presence of the people; he did so, and water appeared in abundance. But God was somehow displeased with Moses' response. Interpreting his actions as a lack of faith (or proper acknowledgment of divine action), YHWH declared that neither Moses nor Aaron would be permitted to bring the people into the Promised Land: "Because you did not trust in me, to show my holiness before the eyes of the Israelites, therefore you shall not bring this assembly into the land that I have given them" (Numbers 20:12; see also Deuteronomy 32:48-52).

But I Have Let You See It

Verse 4 of today's passage reminds Moses that he would not be allowed to enter the land, but God's judgment was once again tempered with grace. In their final mountaintop meeting, YHWH "showed him the whole land" (Deuteronomy 34:1), then described for Moses the location each tribe would inhabit. And Moses died in peace (34:5), with no hint of bitterness or resentment at not being able to complete the journey.

The passage ends with Joshua assuming leadership after the thirty-day mourning period. Moses, however, was not to be forgotten. Joshua was "full of the spirit of wisdom, because Moses had laid his hands on him" (34:9). Moses' life is heralded in the concluding verses. He was "unequaled;" Moses knew God "face to face" (34:10-11). In his humanness, Moses fell short of God's command. He is remembered, however, as a model of faithful service—as one loved deeply by God, whose justice was always executed with compassion and mercy.

> **Think About It:** "But you shall not cross over there" (34:4). In contrast to the Israelites, Moses seemed to accept the consequences of his "sin" without turning away from God. Do we respond to the consequences of our failings with renewed faith and commitment, or by placing the blame on God?

Psalter: Psalm 90:1-6, 13-17

Today's psalm is connected to the passage from Deuteronomy by virtue of its source, "A Prayer of Moses, the man of God," as well as by its acknowledgment of the transitory nature of human life and the human desire to be remembered. Throughout the psalm, the limits of human existence are set against the infinity of God's realm. The psalm's two sections exemplify two distinct grammatical moods: the indicative (verses 1-6), which reflects on the finitude of human life, and the optative (verses 13-17), which petitions God in a series of commands.

The first section illustrates the contrast between the human and the divine. The Lord (in this case addressed as universal Sovereign, not in the personal

YHWH) has been the "dwelling place," the true home of humankind through all generations. Beyond God's historic relationship to Israel, God's realm encompasses the whole of human existence. The reality of human death is dramatically stated, "Turn back, you mortals" (Psalm 90:3), . . . turn back "to dust."

The optative mood uses this same phrase in a daring command to God, "Turn, O LORD!" (90:13). The psalmist is not, however, entreating God to extend the scope of human life, but to exercise power in specific ways in the life of the community: "satisfy us," "make us glad," "let your work be manifest to your servants" (90:13-16). Trusting in God as humanity's eternal home, the psalmist may in confidence call upon God for the compassion and joy that transcend the limitations of earthly life.

Epistle: 1 Thessalonians 2:1-8

A striking difference between Paul's First Letter to the Thessalonians and his later Epistles is the absence of the characteristic assertion of his authenticity as an apostle. In his evangelistic efforts among the Gentile believers of Thessalonica, however, he emphasized the personal relationship he and his colleagues had developed with the new Christians—a relationship that, in essence, defines what it means to be an apostle of Jesus Christ.

We Were Gentle Among You

The intimacy of that relationship is highlighted again in this chapter. "But we were gentle among you, like a nurse tenderly caring for her own children" (1 Thessalonians 2:7). The impact of their faith and commitment had had a profound effect on Paul and his companions, encouraging them to share themselves along with the gospel, "because you have become very dear to us" (2:8). The warmth and sincerity of their reception among the new believers is contrasted with their mistreatment in Philippi (2:2), where Paul was imprisoned in flagrant violation of his Roman citizenship (see Acts 16:19-40).

The Nature of Apostleship

The remainder of today's lection reveals Paul's understanding of the nature of apostleship by stressing its most important aspects, aspects he had exemplified in the Thessalonians' midst. "We had courage" (2:2), "our appeal does not spring from deceit or impure motives or trickery" (2:3), "we speak, not to please mortals, but to please God who tests our hearts" (2:4). Courage and integrity are hallmarks of apostleship, as is the apostle's vulnerability before the congregation. Some scholars suggest that a more accurate translation of verse 7 would be "we were infants among you," stressing his complete vulnerability to rejection and persecution. These attributes were not achievements of the apostles, but were bestowed for their ministry by God.

In pointing out these attributes of apostleship Paul also addresses the accusations of his detractors, who had charged him with heresy and immorality (including gross misrepresentation of the "kiss of peace"). By asserting "God is our witness" (2:5), Paul dismisses those who accuse him of serving his own interests.

Gospel: Matthew 22:34-46

Once again, the Pharisees devised a trap for Jesus. He had just finished a similar encounter with the Sadducees concerning marriage in the resurrection (Matthew 22:23-33). Citing the requirements of the law, the Sadducees, who did not believe in resurrection, described a widow who had in turn married each of her husband's six brothers. Jesus responded by quoting from Exodus, thereby silencing them.

The Pharisees then decided upon the ultimate question: "Which commandment in the law is the greatest?" (Matthew 22:36). The lawyer, knowing that there were 613 separate commandments, was sure that this question would be Jesus' downfall. His answer, however, again silenced his opposition, and also gave those willing to listen insight into the nature of his messiahship.

The Great Commandment

The Pharisees' question, though designed to trick Jesus (the word *test* is a variation on the word *tempt* used in the encounter with Satan), exposed the very core of what it means to live as a person of faith. The question is as pertinent today as it was in the time of Jesus (and, for that matter, the time of Moses). This time Jesus did not turn the question back to his opponents; he responded instead by quoting the Shema (literally meaning "hear") from Deuteronomy 6:5: "You shall love the Lord your God with all your heart, and with all your soul, and with all your mind." In essence, this "greatest and first commandment" is a positive restatement of the first commandment. Devotion had to be total and complete. Love for God could not be half-hearted. The crowd would have known this verse by heart. Jesus' answer eliminated any question or debate.

The second commandment was "like it." Love for God led naturally to love for neighbor. Complete devotion to God could not be abstract. It had to be expressed concretely in relationships with others. The second remains, however, the second. Love for neighbor must be based in the love of God. Love for God is the touchstone of all of human experience. By linking these commandments together, Jesus takes the believer beyond a list of do's and don'ts into a living relationship with the God who is at the heart of the law.

Whose Son?

Having answered the Pharisees' question, Jesus posed one of his own: "What do you think of the Messiah? Whose son is he?" (22:42). Their answer was more a reflection of their legalism than their faith: "The son of David." The Pharisees could only understand the Messiah in terms of their tradition (and, thus, the law). "David" is the obvious, and correct, answer, but not the complete answer, although Matthew traces Jesus' lineage back before David to Abraham. Luke goes one better in establishing Jesus' heritage beyond both David and Abraham to "son of Adam, son of God" (Luke 3:38).

> **Think About It:** "On these two commandments hang all the law and the prophets" (Matthew 22:40). What does it mean to love God wholly? Could loving God with all our heart, soul, and mind help us to love others—and ourself—more completely?

Using the tactics of his opponents, Jesus confronted the Pharisees with words they would have attributed to David himself: "The Lord said to my Lord . . . " (22:44; Psalm 110:1). David knew that the coming Messiah was greater than any anointed king. Neither David nor the law could define the Messiah. The Messiah's reign of love could not be contained by human attempts to overcome it, just as the Pharisees, Sadducees, and scribes could not contain Jesus through their trickery. They dared ask no more questions from that day onward.

Study Suggestions

A. Open With Devotion

Sing a hymn celebrating God's eternal sovereignty, such as "God of the Sparrow, God of the Whale." Reflect together on God's steadfast love.

B. Review Moses' Life

Begin by reviewing the highlights of Moses' story (from the previous weeks' lessons and individual knowledge). List these on a sheet of paper. Then read Numbers 20:1-13 and the material on pages 340–41 in order to set today's passage in context of the events at Meribah. Discuss feelings about God's judgment against Moses, and the "Think About It" questions related to this event. Read Deuteronomy 34:1-12 together.

With regard to Moses as a leader, ask: How would you characterize his leadership? Why is he viewed as the greatest of Israel's prophets? What aspects of his leadership would you want to emulate? Which would not fit our time and situation well? Then discuss Moses' relationship to God, in terms of these questions: How would you characterize this relationship? What can we learn from it to help develop our spiritual lives? Discuss the findings together. In what ways is Moses a model of faith for Christians? What is his legacy?

C. Characterize Apostleship

Read aloud 1 Thessalonians 2:1-8 and review the commentary on pages 342–43. Using Paul's description of his behavior among the Thessalonians, develop a job description for an apostle of Jesus. What are the expectations of an apostle? the characteristics? Then ask: How do the characteristics of the apostle compare to the characteristics of Moses developed in activity B? Were there only twelve apostles or are all Christians called to be apostles? Are the expectations and characteristics listed attainable for today's Christians? Name examples from recent history who would qualify.

Reflect about the vulnerability of apostleship. What risks are inherent in the ministry of an apostle? Is it possible to share Christ without sharing and risking yourself? without truly caring for the person or community to whom you are witnessing?

D. The Greatest Commandment

Ask participants to write from memory the greatest commandment and the second. Compare answers. Ask when they first learned these teachings of Jesus. Suggest that these verses be committed to memory as an act of personal devotion. Read Matthew 22:34-46 together and study the commentary on pages 343–44. What makes this encounter different from the other times the Pharisees tried to trick Jesus? Why was this a turning point in Jesus' ministry?

Form three groups and give each a large sheet of paper and markers. Ask one group to characterize loving God with heart, soul, and mind, the second to characterize loving neighbor, and the third to characterize loving self. Have groups suggest as many concrete expressions as possible, then choose one to depict in a drawing. After the groups have shared their work, ask: How do these characterizations compare to those of leader and apostle discussed earlier? Which is easiest: to love God, neighbor, or self? Which is most difficult? Why? How are the three related? Why must complete devotion to God come first? Do we actually put love for God above love for others (even our family)? What prevents us from living out the greatest and second commandments?

Return to the same three groups. Ask each to develop a list of the changes that might take place if they each wholeheartedly loved God, neighbor, and self. Have them be as specific as possible. What situations in the world, community, family, and self might be transformed?

E. Close in Prayer

Standing in a circle, read aloud the above list of changes one by one, with the group responding, "Empower us to make this change in our lives, O God," after each. Close by reading Psalm 90:1-6 in unison as an affirmation of God's steadfast love and sovereignty.

Lections for Sunday Between October 30 and November 5

Old Testament: Joshua 3:7-17

*T*HE death of Moses, which brought to a close the Torah, was not the end of the story for the people of Israel. Under the leadership of Joshua, appointed by God to succeed the great prophet, they would claim the promise made so long ago to their ancestor Abraham. They would enter the land flowing with milk and honey. Their forty-year nomadic sojourn in the desert was coming to an end; their new life was soon to begin.

The Book of Joshua begins the second major division of the Hebrew Bible. Known as the Prophets, this section is made up of two subsections, the Former Prophets (from Joshua through Second Kings) and the Latter Prophets (from Isaiah through Malachi, excluding Daniel). Joshua, the first of the Former Prophets, is considered prophecy, as opposed to history, because of the influence of the great prophets of the eighth and seventh centuries B.C. in interpreting this period of Israel's history. The books of the Prophets, therefore are not factual records of historical events, but rather a theological interpretation of these events from particular perspectives.

The Book of Joshua, therefore, describes events that took place 1250–1200 B.C., interpreted from a prophetic viewpoint emphasizing that it was YHWH's intent that Israel receive the Promised Land, but that to keep it they must faithfully observe God's covenant requirements. This is made clear at the outset (1:1-9). The book begins with YHWH summoning Joshua to lead the people into the land. The condition for attaining the land was that Israel must "act in accordance with all the law" of Moses (verses 7-9).

"By This You Shall Know. . . ."

Today's lection begins with God's assertion that Joshua is Moses' appointed

346

successor. YHWH would perform a sign in the people's midst, so that they would know that "I will be with you [Joshua] as I was with Moses" (3:7). The sign itself was a recognizable one; God would hold back the waters of the Jordan, allowing the Israelites—and more important the ark bearing the Torah—to cross on dry land. This action would authenticate Joshua's leadership in the eyes of the people. The text is careful to point out that this crossing was to take place during the spring harvest, which follows the season of heavy rains.

> **Think About It:** "The waters flowing from above stood still . . ." (3:16). God's delivery of the Israelites into the Promised Land reminded them of their release from Egyptian bondage by passing through the Sea of Reeds. What events in your life do you understand as signs of God's guidance, providence, or protection?

The Israelites were not simply crossing a river. They were crossing a river ravaged by floodwaters. Twice the waters are described as standing in a "single heap" (3:13, 16), signifying their intensity. It is only by God's hand that the people were able to pass through on solid ground.

Coming Home

Verse 10 lists the pre-Israelite population of Canaan. Located in the politically strategic passage between Egypt and Mesopotamia, Canaan was divided primarily into autonomous city-states. YHWH, the "living God," would "without fail" drive out the inhabitants of the land before Israel (3:10). Their years in the wilderness, which disciplined them in their life before YHWH, had also prepared them for the rigors of battle.

But first they had to enter the land. The people crossed over the Jordan River preceded by the priests (the only persons allowed to touch the ark), who stood on the dry riverbed as they entered the land. God's people and God's law had crossed a boundary into a new stage of their history.

Psalter: Psalm 107:1-7, 33-37

Psalm 107 is a characteristic song of thanksgiving, recognizing and responding to a particular action of God on behalf of the psalmist, perhaps a pilgrim traveling to Jerusalem. The psalmist has experienced God's steadfast love firsthand in concrete redemptive situations. God has redeemed the people "from trouble" (Psalm 107:2) and "gathered" them from east and west. *Gathered* is often used in reference to the scattered people. These images would bring to mind both the Exodus and the Exile—more specifically, the end of the people's exile from the land of Canaan.

Some scholars believe that verses 33-43, which praise God's bounty, were probably not original to the psalm. They affirm, however, that it is only by God's hand that prosperity and blessing come to the people. God alone brings forth life.

Epistle: 1 Thessalonians 2:9-13

Today's Epistle lesson continues Paul's remembrance of his earlier visit to the church he established in Thessalonica. Like the preceding passages, this section offers encouragement to the Thessalonian believers and highlights Paul's close and abiding relationship with the young church. Paul also asserts once more the purity of his motives and behavior in the context of this relationship.

"You Remember Our Labor"

While in Thessalonica, Paul did not rely on the charity of his fellow believers for support. He and his companions worked at his trade in order to provide for their physical needs. In that way, no claim could be made that he burdened the members of the church as he shared the gospel with them. This claim also dispelled the attacks of Paul's critics, who often accused him of preaching for personal gain.

The *Didache*, called the "Teaching of the Twelve Apostles" and considered the first book of Christian order or discipline, warned against false prophets who took advantage of the hospitality of first-century church communities: "But if he be minded to settle among you and be a craftsman, let him work and eat" (*Didache* 12:2). Paul reminds the Thessalonians that he had paid his own way among them.

God's Word, Not Paul's

As Paul recounts the blamelessness of his conduct, he does so in the context of the close and loving relationship he has established with the community; "As you know, we dealt with each one of you like a father with his children" (1 Thessalonians 2:11). Beyond the intimacy of his relationship to the Thessalonian believers, however, is the precedence of the message over the messenger.

Think About It: We plead that you "lead a life worthy of God, who calls you into his own kingdom and glory" (2:12). Paul reminds the followers of Christ that their day-to-day dealings in the community are as much a part of their witness as the gospel message they proclaim. Think about how we conduct our life and business. Do those with whom we work and interact see evidence of our faith?

The Thessalonians are commended because they have received the gospel as God's word. There was no confusion concerning the source of the message. The Thessalonians received Paul warmly, but they did not receive the message as merely the word of Paul. Thus, God's word "is at work in you who believe" (2:13, NIV).

Many scholars believe verses 14-16 are a later addition to the Epistle by someone other than Paul, because of their anti-Jewish sentiment, which contradicts the spirit of Chapters 9–11 of Paul's letter to the Romans, and because of its uncharacteristic structure, exemplified in part by a second thanksgiving. If it is original to Paul, however, it must be seen as a specific reaction to a specific series of actions by specific individuals and not as a judgment against the Jews as a whole.

Gospel: Matthew 23:1-12

In preceding weeks' passages, Jesus had encountered the Pharisees, Sadducees, scribes, and Herodians—all intent upon tricking him into a public violation of the law. In each of these contests, Jesus had emerged the victor. While this episode begins with a denunciation of the practices of the scribes and Pharisees, the focus had shifted. The crowd surrounding Jesus no longer consisted of those seeking to foil his message and ministry; they had given up their efforts. Jesus was now speaking a word of warning directly to his followers—then and now. The message is as clear and poignant today as it was then: If you want to be a disciple—an effective witness to the gospel— you must practice what you preach.

"Do Whatever They Teach You"

As with today's Epistle lection, care must be taken that the message is not understood as a condemnation of the Jews. Jesus, as a Jew, was exhorting his own community after the example of the Old Testament prophets who called their own people to accountability. The scribes and Pharisees "sit on Moses' seat" (Matthew 23:2); by teaching the Mosaic law, their words conveyed (at least to a degree) the truth of God. Indeed, the law was God's gracious gift to Israel, a manifestation of God's great love. This was certainly the understanding of Matthew, who saw Jesus as the fulfillment of the law. The fault of the scribes and Pharisees was not in their teaching, but in their hypocrisy. Jesus used them as a reverse example of faithfulness.

"Do Not Do as They Do"

The Pharisaic interpretation of the law included countless rules and procedures that were impossible to follow in their entirety. They turned the law into a "heavy burden" and laid it "on the shoulders of others" (23:4). Bogged down in legalistic minutiae, the scribes and Pharisees had lost sight of the God whose love and compassion were given expression in the law. Jesus also cautioned against their ostentatious displays of piety. In accordance with the mandate to keep the commandments "as a sign on your hand, . . . an emblem on your forehead" (Deuteronomy 6:8, 11:18; Exodus 13:9), leather pouches containing verses of Scripture (phylacteries) were worn on the arm and forehead. Those of the Pharisees were especially large. Another reminder of the commandments were the fringes at the corners of the outer garment (Numbers 15:38; Deuteronomy 22:12); the Pharisees sported the longest fringes in town.

Do Not Exalt Yourself

Jesus' final example of their hypocrisy dealt with power issues in the faith community. The scribes and Pharisees saw themselves as morally and socially superior to others. By virtue of their standing in the synagogue, they felt entitled to places and titles of honor. Titles of honor, however, were to be reserved for God; what earthly rabbi or leader could rival God? By exalting themselves, the scribes and Pharisees—as well as disciples—would only bring themselves down by their own self-righteous claims. "All who exalt themselves will be humbled, and all who humble themselves will be exalted" (Matthew 23:12).

> *Think About It:* "But do not do as they do, for they do not practice what they teach" (23:3). Have you ever found yourself saying, "Do as I say, but not as I do"? Think about our discipleship. Are our actions consistent with the message we proclaim as Christians?

The abuses of power, the displays of false piety, and the lure of prestige, which ensnared the scribes and Pharisees, are just as real—and dangerous—for all Christian disciples. Only in servanthood and humility before God is true faithfulness expressed. Our actions must be consistent with the gospel message that we confess.

Study Suggestions

A. Open With Singing

Sing a hymn of practicing what you preach, such as "Lord, I Want to Be a Christian," or "Take My Life, and Let It Be Consecrated." Pray together that our witness, in words and actions, may present a consistent picture of discipleship.

B. Enter the Promised Land

Read Joshua 3:7-17 and the material on pages 346–47. Explain the interpretive viewpoint of the Former Prophets from which the book is written. Ask: What sets Joshua apart as a leader? What sets the Israelites apart from the people already inhabiting Canaan?

Ask group members to skim Exodus 14:15-27. How are the stories similar? How are they different? How is God's presence experienced in each? Why would God choose a repeat miracle to bring the people into Canaan? Why does the ark both precede them into the Jordan and follow them onto the banks of their new home? What is the word of God that precedes and follows you? What impact does this have on your life?

C. Examine Witness

Read 1 Thessalonians 2:9-13 and the commentary on pages 348–49. Ask: Why does Paul spend so much time asserting his own purity of motive among the Thessalonian believers? Why is the integrity of the messenger a vital component of Christian witness? Can one's witness be believed (and believable) if one's lifestyle seems incompatible? Give examples from your experience of times when a person's witness was undermined by his or her behavior.

Read Acts 18:1-3 together. Ask: How might Paul's faith have been revealed in his work as a tentmaker? Ask members to name several occupations, including their own. Divide into pairs; assign one of the listed occupations to each pair, asking them to brainstorm ways that persons in this field could witness to their faith in the workplace. Then ask them to brainstorm a second list of behaviors that could diminish their witness. Bring the groups together to discuss their findings. How can we become more effective messengers of the gospel in secular life? One helpful set of categories for witness in the workplace are ministries of words (sharing our faith), ethics (living our faith in relation to moral issues), justice (changing systems), and service (helping others).

Does today's Epistle lection imply that "tent-making" evangelism is "more blameless" than full-time, professional ministry? Discuss: What happens when the messenger is given (or takes) credit for the message? Name some examples of gospel messengers who became larger than the message. How can we support one another in leading lives "worthy of God" and in keeping our focus on the gospel itself? Assess both our faithfulness and our effectiveness in our ministry of word, ethics, justice, and service. In which of these areas do we need the most growth and help? Why?

D. Explore Jesus' Teaching

Read Matthew 23:1-12 and the material on pages 349–50. Ask: How is the message "practice what you teach" similar to Paul's understanding of the relationship between the messenger and the message? Why did Jesus teach this lesson by using the negative example of the scribes and Pharisees?

Assign one of the following passages to each of three groups: Matthew 23:4; 23:5-7; 23:8-10. Ask each to discuss the way in which the scribes and Pharisees failed to "practice what they teach," then identify some modern parallels. How are legalism, pietistic boasting, and an inflated sense of power and prestige expressed in the church today? Have groups share these discussions with the entire class. Then ask: How can these pitfalls undermine true faithfulness? How can they be avoided? What do we consciously do to ensure that our witness is without blemish? How can we help one another do this?

E. Close With Devotion

Read Psalm 107:1-7, 33-37 responsively. Invite members to share personal experiences of God's steadfast love and redemption. Offer a closing prayer of thanksgiving for God's presence and guidance in this session.

351

Lections for All Saints (November 1, or may be used on first Sunday in November)

First Lesson: Revelation 7:9-17

*A*LL Saints Day is the time in the church year when we remember those who have died in the Lord—both noted Christians down through history and the faithful in our own congregations and families. This week's readings throw light on this tradition from several perspectives.

The Book of Revelation can be a great source of hope and encouragement to people who are oppressed, fearful, or downhearted. But it also can be misinterpreted by those who use it literally to foretell the future or to condemn their enemies. The book's puzzling language and strange symbolism make it easily misunderstood. We need to realize that it was written to address a specific time and situation—the cruel persecution and martyrdom of Christians around A.D. 95. under the Roman emperor Domitian, who required all his subjects to worship him as a god. It belongs to a type of Jewish literature of that time (200 B.C.–A.D. 100) known as apocalyptic, which contained mysterious visions and a focus on the end times and last judgment.

It is clear from Revelation 1:1, 3 that the writer expected his words to come to pass at once, not in the future. Christians under severe persecution needed encouragement to hold steady and to hope that the end of current suffering and the advent of a new world were at hand. Like other Jewish writings of that period (such as the Book of Daniel), the writer predicted the end of the world as the only solution to present suffering and as hope for future reward. The author, traditionally thought to be John the apostle, writing in exile from the island of Patmos, called all believers to be willing to die rather than venerate a mere man. He assured them that Christ was soon to come, to judge God's enemies and to welcome the faithful into the reward of eternal happiness.

The Saints Before the Throne

The purpose of this week's passage is to encourage Christians to stand firm in the face of hardship. The scene is heaven; and a huge company, coming from all nations, is gathered at the throne awaiting the final enactment of God's plan. Dressed in the white robes of martyrs and waving palm branches to express gratitude for victory, they remind us of Jesus' triumphal entry (Revelation 7:9; see John 12:13). The seer hears them shout praises for God's coming victory (Revelation 7:10), surrounded by ranks of heavenly beings who bow in homage before God and respond to the multitude's song with a glorious tribute of their own (7:11-12).

> **Think About It:** "To encourage Christians to stand firm in the face of hardship." What gives us strength to stand firm? When we face rejection, disappointment, obstacles, ridicule, or loss because of our faith, where do we turn for encouragement to carry on? Is the hope or promise of eternal reward a primary factor? Or is it the support or example of others, our relationship with God, a commitment to Christ, our call to discipleship, a concern for the needs of others, or some other reason that keeps us going?

A senior angel asks who they are, then answers that they are those who remained faithful through the ordeal of persecution. Their robes have been washed clean by the shed blood of Christ (7:13-14). Their loyalty to the death has been rewarded by being welcomed into the presence of God, who will protect them from any further harm or suffering, whether it be from hunger or thirst or the elements. Christ will be their shepherd and will offer them the cleansing waters of eternal life. The tears of suffering are wiped away by the tender touch of a loving God—forever (7:15-17).

What a comforting, hopeful word for hard-pressed Christians to hear.

Psalter: Psalm 34:1-10, 22

The praise of God by the faithful, which we encountered in Revelation, is the core in this psalm of gratitude by one whom God has rescued from difficulty. He is so thankful he can't stop praising God (verse 1). He does not brag about his own achievement; he gives the credit to God and thereby exemplifies humility for others (verse 2). All are invited to join him in his adoration of God and affirmation of God's gracious name or nature (verse 3).

Then he gives his testimony (verses 4-7). He was in trouble; he prayed for help; God heard and came to his aid. Those who trust God will not be disappointed; they will smile with gladness because God's angels (messengers) care for them. So, he says, put your trust in God and God's goodness will not let you down (verse 8). Bow in awe before God and you will lack for nothing (verse 9). Even young lions, noted for their hunting prowess, may go hungry; but if you trust, God will always provide (verse 10). If you seek God you will be saved (verse 22).

This is a song of one of the saints of God. Like those gathered round the throne in Revelation, the psalmist trusted God, remained faithful through trials, was blessed with deliverance, and humbly praised the redeemer.

Epistle: 1 John 3:1-3

First John traditionally has been attributed to the apostle John, who had gone to Ephesus after the fall of Jerusalem in A.D. 70. and become the leader of the churches in Asia Minor. Now up in years, he writes to them as a fatherly pastor and caring friend, emphasizing the central themes of the Christian faith in opposition to the teachings of Gnosticism—eternal life, God's great love, and loving one another, but primarily Jesus Christ the foundation of all.

Accepted as Children of God

In today's verses John extols God's amazing love that claims us as his children. Others may reject us because they have also rejected God. But this is not important; it is God's acceptance that really counts (verse 1). There is more glory ahead, though we don't know what it will be. We can be sure, though, that when we enter fully into God's presence we will be transformed and take on a godly identity (verse 2). Motivated by this expectation, we prepare ourselves by seeking to be cleansed of sin, think godly thoughts, live dedicated lives, and become as much like God as possible (verse 3).

> **Think About It:** "How great is the love the Father has lavished on us, that we should be called children of God" (3:1, NIV)! Being saints is not something we earn; it is God's gift. Do we think of ourselves as children of God? How does this affect the way we live? Does it cause us to think of others as children of God, too? Is being a child of God the same as being a saint?

Like Revelation, this passage anticipates a glorious future when all the saints will be with God, will be transformed into God's likeness, and will find joy in praising God. Does looking forward to heaven bring us comfort and gladness? Does it encourage us to get ready by purifying ourselves? In a sense, life after death is living in the presence of God. Like being in a bright light, it will be heaven for those who have prepared themselves by getting used to the light, but hell for those who have been living in the darkness and hence are burned and blinded when suddenly thrust into it without being ready.

Gospel: Matthew 5:1-12

The biblical term *saint* does not mean an especially holy or devout person; it simply refers to a believer, a Christian, a church member, a disciple. The saints are the faithful, those who have been redeemed and brought by Christ into relationship with God. Tradition, however, has assigned a second meaning—a martyr, a holy person whose devoted life has been marked by special service or sacrifice that the church has recognized with canonization (sainthood). Those who really live by the Beatitudes would fall into this category, though Jesus meant these sayings to apply to everyone. We are all called to be saints, so we all are expected to live the life described in these memorable verses.

We are to be humble, to be subject to the Rule of God. When we subordinate our will to God's we won't demand personal prerogatives or expect special favors, but, amazingly, will be surprised by special blessings (verse 3).

We are to be sorry about all the suffering in the world, to show concern and compassion. When we thus take into our hearts the pain of others, we will discover that God feels that pain, too. It is comforting to know that we are sharing with God the burdens of all humanity (verse 4).

We are to be accepting of things that come our way, not complaining or dodging or blaming, but always looking for the opportunities, lessons, or challenges God is offering us in every circumstance. When we have this kind of positive attitude we will be blessed with the realization that all our needs are being met (verse 5).

We are to have a heart eager to know and do all that is good. And what we seek we will find. To think good thoughts, do good deeds, and expect good results will be a self-fulfilling prophecy (verse 6).

We are to care, to forgive, to serve. When we do, others will treat us this way too, and we will be blessed (verse 7).

We are to have pure motives, not trying to deceive, take advantage, pretend, or manipulate. We are to be persons of integrity. When we treat others with honesty and respect, we affirm the image of God in them, and God is revealed to us in the relationship (verse 8).

We are to work for harmony, justice, and understanding in all situations. We are to practice no violence or domination, but to represent God's shalom among all people and all creation. When we do, others will recognize that God is in us (verse 9).

355

When we live this way others will feel threatened and judged by our lifestyle. They will lash out at us, try to trip us up, take advantage of us, stomp out the reminders of their own shortcomings. This will be painful, even dangerous. But in our hearts we will know that this is the way to live; this is God's way; this is the way lived by many "saints" before us; this is the way it will be in heaven; this is the way to work with God to bring his reign "on earth as it is in heaven" (verses 10-12).

> **Think About It:** "This is the way to live; this is God's way." Whom do you know whose behavior and choices are guided simply by what is right and not by the benefit to be gained, by the opinions of others, or by the rules to be followed? What factors influence our behavior and choices? Are pure motives really possible? Is this way of life a prescription for all the "saints" (all Christians) or only for those who are especially "saintly"?

Study Suggestions

A. Honoring the Saints

Explain that the biblical term *saints* refers to all Christians. Invite participants to name faithful people in the Bible and in church history whom they would consider saints, and write their names on the chalkboard or a sheet of paper. Add the names of past and present saints in your congregation and families who have left a deep impression. Include pastors and laity, rich and poor, parents and grandparents. State why you consider them saints, and write the qualities of "sainthood" alongside their names. Then stand in silence to honor these who have faithfully served Christ and meant so much to the church at large or to your group. Sing "For All the Saints." Read an All Saints Day prayer from your hymnal or worship book, or offer spontaneous prayers of gratitude for their faithful witness.

B. The Identity of Saints

Distribute paper and pencils. Ask group members to complete the sentence, "I am . . ." five times, writing a different word or phrase each time describing who they understand themselves to be. Either invite each in turn to share their responses, or ask each to call out just one. Write all responses on the chalkboard or a sheet of paper. Note the categories of responses—roles (parent, farmer, nurse), responsibilities (homemaker, bread-winner, gardener), characteristics (patient, stubborn, cautious), situational (busy, grieving, optimistic), and faith qualities (dedicated, prayerful, forgiving). Point out that it is from these very ordinary qualities that the stuff of saints is made.

Read aloud 1 John 3:1-3, then repeat verse 1. Stress that for John our identity as children of God is central to all the qualities mentioned. Did any list

356

"child of God"? Would they now? Point out that "sainthood" is neither a deserved birthright nor an achieved characteristic, but a gift of God through Christ.

C. The Faith of Saints
Read Psalm 34:1-10, 22, and the commentary on pages 353–54. Explain that this is the song of a saint who has put his or her faith in God in time of trouble and now is singing God's praises for deliverance. From the list of saints mentioned earlier, name some who could have sung this psalm. Are there any present for whom it comes close to home? Invite members to share their experience of faith.

D. The Life of Saints
Ask for two volunteers to read alternatively—one the Beatitudes one by one, the other the interpretation from the commentary on page 355. Pause after each to discuss: Is this what Jesus meant? How might we state it differently? Did the saints we have named live this way? How would our lives change were we to live this way? Is this possible or practical for saints like us, or only for "saintly" saints? (In this discussion, draw as well on the commentary on the Gospel lection for the fourth Sunday after the Epiphany [see pages 79–80], which also treats the Beatitudes.)

E. The Joy of Saints
Explain the background of the Book of Revelation from the commentary on pages 352–53, then read 7:9-17. Discuss: Is this literal or symbolic language? If literal, what is your expectation of how it will be realized? If symbolic, what does it represent? (Possible answers: the majesty of God, the reward for faithfulness, the joys of heaven.) Why would this give hope and encouragement to those enduring persecution? What do you think heaven (and hell) might be like? Share the above analogy of entering bright sunlight whether prepared or not, and invite reactions. Discuss: If heaven is a reward for faithful living, what is the meaning of salvation by grace?

F. The Challenge of Saints
Read or sing "I Sing a Song of the Saints of God," and challenge members to make the last line, "And I mean to be one too," their prayer for the week.

Lections for Sunday Between November 6 and 12

P Old Testament: Joshua 24:1-3a, 14-25

REVIOUSLY, we studied how God arranged for a crossing of the Jordan River that would allow the Hebrews to relive their parents' deliverance at the *Yam Suph*. The purpose was to renew their confidence in YHWH's "going before them" to deliver what YHWH had promised, namely possession of the land, just before the conquest of Canaan. This week's reading jumps ahead to the days prior to Joshua's death, after the conquest had been completed and the Israelites had settled in the land of God's promise.

It must be noted that the account in Judges differs markedly from that of Joshua. In Joshua, the tribes invaded as a united force and completed the conquest and extermination of the Canaanites in just five years (14:10), after which they parceled out the land to the tribes and controlled the entire territory. The picture in Judges, however, is of a gradual infiltration of poorly armed nomadic tribes, settling in widely separated areas, intermarrying with the settled farming population, and carrying out ongoing guerrilla warfare with the kings and armies of city states. Thus, the Israelites slowly gained control over a period of two centuries, until they finally established a kingdom under Saul, David, and Solomon. Most scholars believe the Judges version more accurately depicts the history of the period.

God's Benefits Call for Response

Today's lection reports how Joshua reminded the people of all YHWH had done for them, beginning with Abraham. While Paul would remember Abraham chiefly for his faith, most Jewish authors remembered his rejection of idolatry and his decision to serve the invisible God. In verses 3b-13,

Joshua continues his recital of YHWH's beneficence from the Hebrews' release from slavery in Egypt through their settlement in Canaan.

On the basis of these saving acts, Joshua called the people to make a proper return of gratitude to YHWH, which would require showing exclusive loyalty to the God who had so blessed them by offering the service commanded in the covenant. His appeal echoed the language that began the recital of God's deliverance, namely the mention of the "other gods" served by Israel's ancestors "beyond the River," the Euphrates. These gods were of no help to their worshipers, while YHWH had shown his people beneficent care coupled with power and fidelity.

Committed to Faithful Service

The people acknowledged God's protection and provisions, promising to stand with Joshua and his house in loyal service to God. Verses 19-20, which show YHWH as quite vindictive, are probably a later addition from a time after Israel had proven its inability to keep its oath. They represent Joshua as challenging—indeed, provoking—his hearers so they will be more committed and honor-bound to live out their oath. Sadly, their history is full of instances where Joshua was right, and this prediction of their punishment for infidelity (24:20) was all too true.

Fidelity to the covenant would become their means of proving themselves honorable. This oath has had an abiding impact on its Jewish readers throughout the centuries. A first-century text, for example, describes the willingness of Jews to be tortured to death rather than transgress the Torah, since that would violate the oath of their ancestors and shame them (4 Maccabees 5:29).

> **Think About It:** Joshua calls us to decide who is God in our lives and not to waver in our service. When have we placed some other idol (value) before our service to God? How has God proven more faithful than other "gods" to which we devote our time and energy? How does God empower us to trust God and set aside our idols?

Psalter: Psalm 78:1-7

This psalm laments the Israelites' failure to live out the high resolve displayed in Joshua 24, particularly the disasters that overtook the ten northern tribes. The fatal flaws were distrust in God, even after God had given so many clear signs of trustworthiness (78:21-22), and forgetfulness of God's power and past help (78:42-43)—mindfulness of which could have provided the remedy for distrust.

This week's lection focuses on God's command to God's people to teach their children about God's goodness, works of kindness and mercy, and the obligations of the recipients of God's favor (78:4-7). Deuteronomy especially emphasizes the command to families in the Shema to teach their children about God and what kind of life God wants the people to live (6:4-9, 20-25). Pious Jews recited these passages daily at morning and evening prayer. Twice within this "creed," and hence four times each day, they would remind themselves of the charge to repeat the commandments to their children. Children brought up in such a home would not depart from God's ways, even when faced by extreme tests.

Fourth Maccabees 8–18 tells the story of seven brothers who chose loyalty to God over a king's best promises and worst torments, a firmness ascribed to training in the home (18:6-19). The psalm reminds us of our responsibility for the religious and moral education of the children God entrusts to us.

Epistle: 1 Thessalonians 4:13-18

Martyrdom was not widespread in the first century; but Christians frequently faced insult, slander, hostility, prejudice, and even physical assault because of their association with the name of Jesus. This hostility arose because of the Christians' explicit dissociation from the worship of the Roman gods and emperor. This was a duty considered essential for good citizens, who by their display of gratitude in worship secured the favor and gifts necessary for the continued well-being of the city. Paul spends the greater part of this letter helping the Christians make sense of the rejection they have encountered from their neighbors. Then he turns briefly to the question of what happens when a Christian dies, a question probably passed on to him from the believers through Timothy (see 3:6).

Covering All the Bases

The Thessalonian church had lost some members, most likely to natural causes. If they had been martyred, we would expect to find Paul assuring them of God's vindication of the faithful through resurrection, of God's rewarding them for their faithfulness. Seeing fellow believers die raised an uncomfortable question: If we die before Jesus returns, do we miss the promised rewards? Do we lose both in this life (because of the losses and trials one has to endure) and for eternity (see 1 Corinthians 15:19)?

> **Think About It:** How real is the hope of resurrection to you? In what ways has this promise affected your experiences of grief? When has it given you courage to choose faithfulness to God's call or will, even when that meant some temporal loss for you?

Paul must integrate death—the extreme experience of disintegration—into the Christian hope. He affirms that God's faithfulness and generosity transcend death; and that in Jesus' resurrection we have the guarantee of our own. Whether we live or die, we are still in God's saving hands (Romans

360

14:8). Loyalty to God remains the single most essential value for life, since this is the path to receiving God's favor beyond death.

Gospel: Matthew 25:1-13

In Matthew 24, as in Mark 13, Jesus discloses the signs that must precede the end. The material in Matthew 25, however, is not found in Mark. Matthew 25:14-30 has a parallel in Luke, but Matthew 25:1-13 and 25:31-46 do not. These three passages underscore the point made in Matthew 24:36-51: no one knows the timing of Jesus' return except God, and therefore we must constantly live in readiness for that return. Indeed, most of the "signs of the end" given in Matthew 24:1-29 had already been fulfilled by A.D. 70, the time of the destruction of Jerusalem, so that Jesus' return might come at any time.

The Wedding

This lection, the parable of the ten wedding attendants, shows a familiar scene from Palestinian wedding practices. The groom would go from his house to the house of the bride's father and finalize the wedding contract. At the bride's home, the groom greeted the family, exchanged gifts, and had refreshments (perhaps the cause for the delay in the story). He then returned with his bride to his own dwelling where the nuptial festivities would continue. The responsibility of the bridesmaids was to welcome the groom and his company to the household. Comparing the coming of God's reign with a wedding has strong roots in the Old Testament and remains a prominent metaphor in the New Testament (see Matthew 22:1-14; 2 Corinthians 11:2-3; Revelation 19:21-22).

Party Poopers

We may not much like the wise attendants at first. Jesus had said, "Give to everyone who begs from you" (Matthew 5:42); but the "wise" refused to share their oil. Their concern, however, was not necessarily selfish. They wanted to ensure that some lamps would be burning when the bridegroom came, rather than have the whole procession utterly spoiled by spreading out the oil too far.

By their lack of foresight and preparation, and by their poor use of the delay, the foolish attendants had actually dishonored the groom. They were not able to do their part to honor the day with their presence and their lamps, and so they ended up absent for the reception and excluded from the party.

Seize the Delay

One problem with the parable is that, while the moral of the story is to "keep awake" (25:13), both wise and foolish attendants slept as they awaited the bridegroom's coming. The point of the story, of course, is to be found prepared for the master's return, not to be caught off guard. The parable tells us how to respond to the Lord's "delay."

The foolish bridesmaids, like the wicked servant (24:48), had allowed the passing of time to rob them of their readiness to meet the coming one. Their oil was used up, yet they slept rather than use the delay to replenish their supply.

Live Today

The parable admonishes us so to live each day as to brighten the Lord's coming. We are to add to the celebration rather than the grief of that day. It also cautions us to be committed for the long haul, to live for Christ's return. No matter how long he may tarry, we are warned not to fall back into a lifestyle that shows apathy or negligence with regard to the things that will honor Christ at the time of his appearing. We are granted the opportunity to adorn ourselves for the celebration. Jesus says: Make the most for the reign of God of every day the bridegroom tarries!

> **Think About It:** Living a life daily attuned to God is like having the oil at hand to light the bridegroom's way. What act of kindness, justice, or reconciliation would we regret not accomplishing should Christ return today? How are our lives helping the world to welcome Christ?

Study Suggestions

A. Sing a Hymn

Begin by singing together "Come, Let Us Use the Grace Divine" or "Jesus Calls Us, O'er the Tumult" Then offer a brief prayer asking God for guidance and insight during today's study session.

B. Make It Personal

Read Joshua 24:1-3a, 14-25, and review the commentary on pages 358–59. In pairs, have members identify things other than God they have relied on in the past for self-worth, help, or security. (Such things as money, education, parents, friends, employment, insurance, recognition, and advancement could be mentioned.) After they have talked a few minutes, have them call out these things and write them on chalkboard or a sheet of paper. Then ask: Do we view these things (idols) as displacing God in our lives? Have they? Need they? When do such things come from God and when do they get in the way of God? How would our lives be affected if we consciously tried to put God ahead of these things?

Still in pairs, share memories of God's faithfulness breaking into our life. (Examples might include help in solving a problem, an unexpected gift when times were tight, the strength to hang in when facing tough going, finding a new friend or companion, or grace to cope with grief or loss. Then, as a group, build up a collective memory of the works of God on your behalf.

The Joshua lection challenges us to respond to this faithful God with our loyalty and service. Bring the group together and ask: Remembering the faithfulness and mercies of God, will you make or renew your commitment to serve God and follow Jesus faithfully, not heeding the voices of other gods served by our society? Use Joshua 24:24 as a group response.

C. Declare It to Your Children

Read Psalm 78:1-7 antiphonally; then examine the commentary on pages 359–60. Ask: How have we brought Scripture, prayer, and discipleship training into the lives of children? How do we talk about God with our children and help them experience God? Connect this discussion with the stories members have told about God's faithfulness. Ask: Have we told these stories to our children or to the youth of the church? Brainstorm ways of accomplishing the urgings of Psalm 78:1-7 with children and youth at home and in the church.

D. Staring Down Death

Ask someone to read aloud 1 Thessalonians 4:13-18. Set the passage in context using the commentary information on pages 360–61. Ask: Why was assurance about resurrection important to these early Christians? Share with one another the degree to which the hope of resurrection or eternal life is important. How has this hope affected the way we experience the loss of a family member or dear friend, or face a serious illness?

E. Are You Ready?

Read Matthew 25:1-13 and the commentary on pages 361–62. Ask: With whom do we identify—the wise or the foolish attendants? If the bridegroom were to return (or, if Christ were to confront us), would we be ready to greet him properly and joyously? Would there be unfinished business—reconciliation not sought, habits not overcome, growth not achieved, acts of mercy not performed, people God has placed on our hearts still unreached? How are we using the bridegroom's delay day by day?

F. Pray and Reflect

Ask members to share any inner stirrings, confessions, or prayer concerns that have arisen in this discussion, then pray together about these. Before saying "Amen," invite participants to reflect in silence on how their lives would be different if they took seriously the teachings of today's Scriptures. Conclude by singing "O Jesus, I Have Promised" or "I Would Be True."

Lections for Sunday Between November 13 and 19

Old Testament: Judges 4:1-7

*T*HIS reading highlights a theme that runs from Deuteronomy 1 through Second Kings (and Second Maccabees)—Deuteronomy's theology of history. Articulated most clearly in Deuteronomy 28–32, the message is that obedience to God's law leads to political power and economic well-being, while disobedience leads to oppression, misfortune, and misery.

Trouble in the Land

In Judges 4, Israel's sin resulted in God allowing Jabin, a Canaanite king of Hazor, to gain the upper hand over them through a brutal general named Sisera, who lived in Harosheth-ha-goiim (Harosheth of the Gentiles). The fact that these Gentile strongholds in the midst of land assigned to Zebulon and Naphtali could dominate the northern tribes of Israel shows that the "conquest" had been far from decisive. Not until the reigns of kings David and Solomon would Israelite control be extended decisively across the region.

> **Think About it:** "The 'conquest' had been far from decisive." Some today claim that this land belongs to modern Israel because God promised it to them and they occupied it long ago. What do the facts that the conquest was incomplete and short-lived, that it was accomplished through theft and bloodshed, and that God's promise was contingent on Israel's keeping the covenant, have to say to this claim? Does God reward violence and injustice? What would be a just solution to the current "trouble in the land"?

Help Is on the Way

Still true to the Deuteronomic pattern, the Israelites cried out for help, and

God heard them. Help came, and it came through women. The story opens with Deborah, the prophetess, engaged in administering justice. Deborah heard God's word and ordered Barak in the name of YHWH to lead the tribes into battle against Sisera. Barak refused to go unless Deborah accompanied him. But the hero of the story, and of the more ancient poetic version in Judges 5, was not Barak but Jael, a non-Israelite woman.

After his army was defeated, Sisera fled on foot to Jael's tent, expecting to find refuge since his king and her clan were allies. But Jael dared to violate the sacred code of hospitality and drove a

Think About It: "Help came . . . through women." In a patriarchal society like ancient Israel, this was news. God used two persons whom most thought had little to offer to accomplish what men had been unable to do. Deborah and Jael are just two of many women in the Bible who were used by God in significant ways, thereby affirming that God values, needs, and uses all of God's children. Also, this points up that God's help can come through unexpected channels. When has a word or timely help from God come to you from a surprising source, someone whom you might not have thought worth listening to?

tent peg through his head. Her wiles and courage were remembered as providing the turning point in Israel's dealings with Jabin, who was soon after defeated.

Psalter: Psalm 123

This is a psalm of ascents, most likely sung in processions up to Jerusalem. It is well suited to the Judges reading, representing the kind of cry to God that frequently went up from Israel. Are the servants looking to the hand of the master or mistress for an end to punishment? Or for the provision of food or other favors (see Psalm 145:15-16)? Either way, the psalm articulates the truth of our relationship to God (a truth more evident to those in distress, but no less true for the happy and content). We depend totally on God and can cry out in times of need and heartache, confident that God will hear and respond.

Epistle: 1 Thessalonians 5:1-11

The early Christians' neighbors were pressing them to return to a more respectable lifestyle. Paul counters that pressure by underscoring the incredible advantages the believers now had over their neighbors and the ways in which their eyes had been opened to God and their world. They could no more return to the bosom of a pagan society than a butterfly can return to the cocoon.

Insider Knowledge

Paul's language aims intentionally at reinforcing the boundary between believers and those urging them to conform to society's standards. The believers were as different from nonbelievers as day is from night, light from darkness, wakefulness from sleeping, sobriety from drunkenness—unbelievers faring badly in each comparison.

Paul presents their neighbors as sleeping under the delusion of "peace and security." This is quite possibly an ironic reference to the "Roman peace," gratitude for which motivated the worship of the emperors, and the preservation of which was the aim of public Greco-Roman worship. In reality, however, being in league with those gods was not the source of security but of grave danger. The people were in a drunken stupor, unaware that God was about to "tear open the heavens and come down" (Isaiah 64:1).

Paul's goal throughout the letter was not to arouse contempt for the non-Christian, who was still the object of love, respect, and good deeds (see 1 Thessalonians 3:12; 4:11-12; 5:15), but rather to divorce believers from concern about their neighbors' approval and disapproval. This passage advances that goal in an important way. Any contempt or suspicion held by unbelievers toward Christians on the basis of their commitment to follow Jesus arose from ignorance of the big picture of what God was doing in the world and what God looked for in human beings. Christians should not, therefore, hide their commitment or withdraw from doing God's will on account of sensitivity to insults or hostility. Rather, Paul was encouraging them to continue to live in line with the larger perspective of the gospel. They could have confidence that the day of the Lord would see them vindicated in the sight of those who now despised and insulted them for their choices and values.

> **Think About It:** In what ways does our faith in God and confidence in the ultimate outcome of history shed light on our day as we establish priorities, choose tasks, and encounter people? In what ways are we tempted to close our eyes and live from the more limited perspective of the world?

Putting Knowledge into Practice

The Christian has advance warning of the coming judgment and thus has opportunity to prepare. But this privilege is meaningless without follow-through. There is the danger even in the bright light of Christ that one may close one's eyes and fall asleep—that is, go back to living the kind of life that does not honor God in each choice, act, and relationship.

The Thessalonians *could* fall back into seeing women as instruments of sexual pleasure rather than as "heirs of the gracious gift of life" (1 Peter 3:7), harboring unchaste thoughts and relationships (1 Thessalonians 4:1-7). They *could* set their hopes again on winning respect and securing wealth in place of single-minded devotion to God. God had, however, given them the possibility of living in line with their best destiny—the reflection of the holiness of God (4:3, 7). Keeping their eyes open to the light of the coming judgment could make their lives a "light" in a dark place (5:5). God had provided them with the "armor" they needed to win the contest of the soul, but they had to put it on and encourage one another in the thick of the struggle (5:8-11).

Gospel: Matthew 25:14-30

This is the third of three parables (see 24:45-51 and 25:1-13) focusing on how to respond to the master's absence, the time between the Ascension and the Second Coming.

A Hard Master

Here we find the master of a house entrusting his property to his servants before going on a journey of unspecified duration and purpose. Information lacking in Matthew's form of this parable (which is provided in Luke's version, in 19:11-27) is that the master gives no explicit instructions concerning the property before he leaves.

The servants gave some evidence of knowing, however, that when the master entrusted his property to them, he entrusted them with the profitable use of that money so the master's estate would continue to grow. This is especially clear in the excuse offered by the third servant, who was aware that his master looked for a harvest where he had not sown. His knowledge of the master's expectations made his failure to produce an increase more of an act of disobedience than of fear, as he claimed.

The Talent

The fact that the Greek name for a measurement of weight (*talentum*) coincides with an English word for skill or ability (*talent*) is rather unfortunate, since it tends to have a limiting effect on the application of the parable—use your talents well! We should rather take it as all-encompassing: we should use whatever God has given us—our skills, yes, but also our property, money, position, influence, wits, whatever—to produce increase for God. Moreover, we are entrusted with perhaps the most precious possession during the absence, namely the family of God, the church. This is the "estate of the master" that we are called to augment with our all.

That Jesus chose this unit of weight—the talent—is also significant. The master did not entrust his servants with just his spare change but with an immense

> **Think About It:** Jesus has entrusted us with his property, the church. Are we more interested in keeping undesirables away from his estate or in bringing them into it. How do our energy and industry in looking after our own household compare with what we invest in growing God's household?

treasure. Annual tribute from one country to another (national debt, if you will) was measured in talents. This was an enormous responsibility to lay upon the servants, but with it came the opportunity for two out of the three to prove their reliability and diligence.

To Obey Is to Dare

Despite some questions (Did the servants *know* they were expected to engage in trading rather than simply to protect the wealth? Was the third servant's estimation of the master, and hence his fear, justified?), the point of the parable remains clear. Those who threw themselves into the risky business of increasing the master's estate received approval, advancement, and a share in the "joy" of the master. (At this point the ultimate horizon of the judgment begins to intrude upon the story.) The one who acted conservatively, hiding away what had been entrusted to him, received harsh censure, demotion, and exclusion from the master's presence (the "outer darkness" is an eschatological—end time—image).

A Time of Reckoning

Salt is given to bring taste; light is given to illumine the darkness; and Christians are given property, skills, and position—along with the master's trust—to proclaim God's reign. One aspect of the parable that we cannot downplay, for all our emphasis on salvation by faith, is the focus on the accounting at the master's return and the subsequent destiny of the servants. With resources comes responsibility, and with responsibility comes accountability.

Study Suggestions

A. Begin With Prayer

Open by reading Psalm 123 responsively, prefacing the reading with the commentary on page 365. Ask members to talk about what they wish would change in their lives for the better. What shadows darken their days? Ask each person to write these concerns in the form of a cry to God for mercy (using verse 3 of the psalm as a model). Pray the psalm together again, this time having participants read verses 1 and 2 together, with each in turn adding his or her own verse 3.

B. God's Female Faces

Read Judges 4:1-7, setting it in context theologically (the Deuteronomy pattern) as well as sequentially (the remainder of Chapter 4). After reviewing the commentary and the "Think About It" paragraphs on pages 364–65, ask: What issues are raised by this story? In what ways did Israel believe God was at work in this situation? What questions are raised about the Deuteronomic theology by our understandings of the nature of God as revealed in Jesus?

Now ask group members to recall times when God spoke to them through a woman or brought them help through a woman or other unexpected source. Ask: What hinders us from seeing women as agents of God, as ones who carry forward God's vision and direct God's people? What other marginalized persons do we likewise sometimes see as unlikely sources of God's wisdom and guidance?

C. The Light of Day

Read 1 Thessalonians 5:1-11 and the commentary about it on pages 365–67. Ask: Why would the early Christians be tempted to return to their old ways of living? What strategies does Paul use to remove the temptation?

Invite the group to think about the images of "light" and "darkness." Ask: What meanings or feelings do these images evoke? What truths of God do you turn to for light, for a vision of life's meaning and purpose? Now ask members to reflect in silence on what is still "dark" within them. What aspects of their being, longing, and doing do not reflect Christ's love and holiness but instead the world's strife and selfishness? Invite the class members to renounce the works of darkness using words from the baptismal liturgy.

D. Serving the Master's Interests

Assign parts (narrator, master, first servant, second servant, and third servant) to volunteers for a reading of Matthew 25:14-30. Ask group members to talk about their impressions of the parable. What do they hear as its main point? Review the commentary on pages 367–68 as follow-up to this discussion.

Help participants survey the extent of God's estate entrusted to us. Ask them to consider the many people we meet in the course of a week, whom God might touch through us. Brainstorm ways to use our homes and possessions to serve God's purposes. Think together about ways members can use their professions, public offices, expertise, and gifts to advance God's interests. Have them spend some time in silence, asking God to show them other ways they can use what God has entrusted to them in service to others during the coming week.

E. Close With Song and Prayer

Sing "A Charge to Keep I Have." Ask the group to share feelings about stanzas 3 and 4—the "strict account," the warning against betraying God's trust. Or, sing "Lord, You Give the Great Commission," and ask members to share something God has laid on their hearts to do to build up God's people. Close by praying for God to give each member the opportunity and strength to fulfill what God is calling her or him to do.

Lections for Reign of Christ, Sunday Between November 20 and 26

I Old Testament: Ezekiel 34:11-16, 20-24

IN the church year, this last Sunday before Advent is called the Festival of Christ the King (Reign of Christ). The four lections deal with key dimensions of Christ's reign—his concern for justice (Ezekiel), his dominion over all (Ephesians), his steadfast love and faithfulness (Psalms), and his final judgment based on who does or does not care for "the least of these" (Matthew).

Ezekiel was a prophet of the Exile. Part of the first deportation of the Judean elite in 598 B.C., he delivered the message of God near Babylon. Today's lection forms part of God's answer to the news of Ezekiel 33:21—Jerusalem had fallen. This chapter is a turning point for the book, which now turns to promises of restoration, including plans for a restored temple.

God's Shepherds

This lection captures the three major themes of this oracle (message from God), which appears to have grown out of reflection on Jeremiah 23:1-6. The first part (Ezekiel 34:1-16) addresses Israel's "shepherds," a common image for kings in the ancient Near East. YHWH indicts these kings for neglecting their responsibilities to care for the weak and injured, using their power instead for satisfying their selfish interests. Because of this, God had brought an end to the Davidic dynasty.

God's Sheep

This week's reading begins with God's remedy for the ills suffered by God's people, the "sheep" whom the "shepherd" had neglected and abused. God would search for them and gather them together from all the lands throughout which they had been scattered. God would bring them back to the land of God's promise and establish them there in safety.

370

It was not enough, however, to point fingers at the rulers—a practice that too often substitutes for soul-searching and taking responsibility for local or personal wrongdoing. The second theme (34:17-22) indicts the stronger and more aggressive "sheep," who had taken the best for themselves by shoving aside the weak. God identifies with the victims, God's "sheep." The exploiters had alienated themselves from God by victimizing and exploiting the weak.

One Shepherd Over All

The third theme, begun in 34:23-24 but continuing through verse 31, concerns God's bringing to this flock the fulfillment of all God's promises. No duration or degree of human iniquity was sufficient to cause God to give up on God's promises (see Jeremiah 33:17-26).

The fulfillment of this prophecy would begin with the restoration of the Davidic line of kings, particularly a king whose heart would be after God, like David's, and not after self-interest. In this future time, God would bring peace, which is described as the freedom from fear, from want, and from violence. Such peace would come only with justice and the abolition of exploitation. The quality of servanthood, so lacking in the shepherds indicted by Ezekiel, is anticipated in the Messiah, who would come to serve "the least of these" (Matthew 25:39).

> **Think About It:** God will destroy the "fat and the strong" and feed the weak and injured "with justice." God would take the side of the poor and exploited against the rich and powerful. The Bible consistently depicts God as taking up the cause of those unable to defend themselves. Liberation theologians call this God's "preferential option for the poor," which is the basis for calling Christians to join in the struggle of the dispossessed for justice and equality. Does God really take sides? Do we sometimes cheer for the underdog? Or, has the law of the survival of the fittest affected the way we look at the weak and indigent? Which principle guides our social, political, and business dealings with other people?

Psalter: Psalm 100

This familiar psalm is a hymn giving praise to God and listing the reasons for such praise. Its motive is to give thanks for God's character and favors. The first reason for praise focuses on God's creative involvement in our lives ("he made us," 100:3). This might refer to the gift of life itself, as in our formation. It has also been suggested that the psalmist is drawing attention to the fact that God has made the congregation a "people" (as in "he constituted us"). As Ephesians points out, if we are in any way good or righteous, advancing in discipleship, this, too is the work of God in us (as in "he made us what we are").

The other motives for praising God are God's tending of and claim on God's people (100:3) and God's character (100:5), namely God's "goodness" (kindness, generosity), constant love, and reliability. These characteristics are apparent both in both the promises of Ezekiel and Ephesians. The only appropriate response to such beneficence is thanks and honor from joyful hearts and voices.

Epistle: Ephesians 1:15-23

Ephesians appears to have been written and dispatched (through Tychicus and Onesimus) along with letters to the Colossians and to Philemon. While the last two letters addressed a specific situation, Ephesians was written as a general, edifying letter intended for circulation among the different churches in Asia Minor (some manuscripts leave out "in Ephesus" in 1:1). It sought to raise the hearers' awareness of God's design for the church (the "mystery," verse 9) and God's immense generosity toward believers (Chapters 1–3), which would then become the basis for living out the vision for Christian discipleship (Chapters 4–6).

The Scope of God's Design

All the thanksgiving sections of the letter give thanks to God for the achievements of the churches being addressed. Any progress they had made, any virtue they had displayed, was evidence of God's gifts and power at work in their midst. He also told the hearers that he had been asking God to give them yet another gift: a deep, rich, heart-knowledge of the hope they had in Christ, the breadth of God's cosmic design, and the power of God to make it all happen.

Reminding the believers of what God had done for them and would yet grant them (their "hope," verse 18) set God's favor at the heart of their sense of time (past, present, and future). If the hearers would adopt this way of looking at their lives, they would be motivated to make the expression of gratitude to God their primary agenda. This response would include giving God the "praise" and thanksgiving underscored in the letter's opening (1:6, 12, 14), but also honoring God through the good use of God's gifts, the imitation of God's love, and avoidance of what God hates (hence Chapters 4–6).

A Grand Scheme

The letter combines this with a second perspective—now not our inheritance in God (1:11) but God's inheritance in the world (1:18-19). The writer's rhapsodic words about the calling together of Jew and Gentile into the one church expanded Ezekiel's vision of God's gathering the scattered together and making a people for God's own possession. He prayed that each Christian, including Gentiles, would gain a sense of the grand scheme that God was working out in the world and a positive appreciation for the growth of God's people, the church.

Christ, exalted above every rival and aggressor, is the demonstration of God's power at work. Stronger than death, God's power had brought Christ to his appointed destiny, just as it would bring those who are "in Christ" to theirs.

Gospel: Matthew 25:31-46

This parable of the Last Judgment emphasizes the necessity of being prepared when the Son of Man comes. This passage makes up for any vagueness in the moral exhortations of the three parables that precede it.

Who's Who in the Drama

Interpreting the passage depends largely on whom one understands to be included in "all the nations" and who constitutes the "least of Jesus' sisters and brothers." According to one reading, the Gentile nations will be judged on the basis of how they treat the Jews (Jesus' ethnic kin) in their midst. Other Jewish texts (such as Second Baruch) do articulate such a vision, but the identifications are more explicit.

A second reading identifies the "least" with Christian missionaries: giving them food, drink, and shelter and tending them in prison is a sign of acceptance of their message. Thus, the vision becomes a symbol for justification by faith. A third reading suggests that all people will be held accountable on the basis of how they respond to the needs of the poor in their midst, with whom Jesus identifies.

> **Think About It:** Acts of kindness offered (or not) to "the least of these" are in fact offered (or not) to Jesus himself. How have we been attentive to the needs of Jesus' family? How have we shut our ears to their cries for help?

All three readings, however, neglect Matthew's use of family language and especially the term "little ones" throughout the Gospel. Jesus' family are those who do God's will (Matthew 12:46-50), and the "little ones" are the weak or, from a worldly point of view, unimportant members of the Christian community (18:6-7, 10-14). While the term *nations* distinguishes Gentiles from Jews, the phrase *all the nations* is universal in scope, including both Jewish and Gentile peoples.

This vision is first a word of encouragement to those Christians facing need or hostility: all will be held accountable for their response to these believers. Second, it offers a word of warning to all (including Christians), that care for these "least ones" will be the single most important criterion for admission to God's realm.

Caring for the Least

The scandal of the last day is that we are not judged on the basis of decisions about Jesus' lordship, but on the basis of living under that lordship by caring for, protecting, and sheltering the weak, indigent, marginalized, and persecuted members of the family of God. It is a surprise to both the sheep and the goats that such service was actually service offered to Christ, but hearers are left in little doubt concerning what will be required of them.

Returning the Favor

The last public teaching of Jesus has some important connections with the first of Jesus' teachings in this gospel. In Matthew 6:25-33, Jesus told of God's generosity in providing for our needs, focusing especially on food and clothing. Here, we see our opportunity to make a good return to God for these gifts. In the person of the needy or persecuted sister or brother, we can return the favor to God.

Neglect of such opportunities, moreover, would be understood as a display of ingratitude toward the Giver. In Matthew 7:21-23, some of those who call Jesus "Lord," who have done flashy works in Jesus' name, will be excluded at the judgment because they have not done "the will of my Father in heaven." There, Jesus told them, "I never knew you." Here we read perhaps how we come to be known by Jesus. We associate with him and join ourselves to him in the person of the "least" of his family across the world.

Study Suggestions

A. Entering God's Courts

Open by singing "All People That on Earth Do Dwell," a metrical setting of Psalm 100. Invite the group to reflect on how God's love and faithfulness have touched them and their families this week and to give thanks to God for these blessings.

B. Examining the Flock

Drawing on the commentary on pages 370–71, highlight the three themes emphasized in Ezekiel 34:11-16, 17-22, and 20-24. Form into threes to discuss: Whom do the "sheep" represent? What will be the consequence of their actions? With which sheep do you identify? When have we been sleek sheep, seeking to take the best portion for ourselves and butting others out of our way? When have we experienced hurt or disappointment resulting from bearing the brunt of a sleek sheep's aggression?

Invite group members to take these concerns to God in prayer, offering confession and receiving forgiveness for riding over the interests of others, and naming hurts.

C. Looking Out for Number One

For reading Matthew 25:31-46, ask one member to be the narrator and another the king, dividing the rest of the group into "those at the right" and "those at the left." Then review the commentary on pages 373–74, and discuss which of the three readings seems the most authentic and why. Ask: With which group do you most identify (the sheep, the goats, or the least)? Why?

D. Capturing God's Vision

Read aloud Ephesians 1:15-23, setting the context with the commentary on pages 372–73. Ask: What is suggested here about what God is doing around the globe by bringing people from every nation and language into God's family? Where do we see God at work locally, nationally, and internationally toward realizing the cosmic design depicted here? What obscures from our view what God is doing? How can we discern God's work in ordinary events? What is our place in this grand design? How can we contribute to it?

E. Receiving God's Power

The Ephesians lection seeks to open us up to the resources of God's power. The same God who raised Christ from the grave to the highest places also helps those who are in Christ. Form small groups and share: Where in our life do we need God's power for redemption and building up? Is there a particular temptation, trial, or anxiety that weighs on us? Pray for these needs in the small groups.

F. Drawing the Lections Together

Main themes running throughout the lections include dimensions of the reign of Christ, solidarity and cooperation among the global Christian family, the tension between the "preferential option for the poor" and the "survival of the fittest" mentality, and concern for the needs of the invisible, indigent, shut-in, and powerless. Ask: How have these Scriptures spoken to us about these themes? How do you feel led to respond? Are there particular individuals or groups, locally or globally, that our group can commit to serve in some specific way?

G. Singing a Hymn of Dedication

As an act of dedication to service, sing "Cuando El Pobre (When the Poor Ones)" or "The Voice of God Is Calling." Mention one by one the human needs that have come up during the discussion, with the group responding after each with the refrain, "We pray for the least of these, O Christ."